D0458906

Healing the Heart Of the World

Harnessing the Power of Intention to Change Your Life and Your Planet

edited by

DAWSON CHURCH, PH.D.

associate editors

Geralyn Gendreau

Randy Peyser

www.HealingTheHeartOfTheWorld.com

Elite Books
Santa Rosa, CA 95403
www.EliteBooksOnline.com

Library of Congress Cataloging-in-Publication Data:

Healing the heart of the world : harnessing the power of intention to change your life and your planet / edited by Dawson Church, Geralyn Gendreau, Randy Peyser. —1st ed.

p. cm.

Includes bibliographical references.

ISBN 0-9720028-5-3

1. Intentionalism. 2. Human ecology. 3. Sustainable development. 4. Health. I. Church, Dawson, 1956- II. Gendreau, Geralyn. III. Peyser, Randy.

BF619.5.H43 2005

304.2 — dc22

2005030047

All chapters © 2005 by the authors and/or Elite Books, except where noted.

Chapter 2 is from *How Did I Get Here?* by Barbara de Angelis, ©2005 by the author and reprinted with permission of St. Martin's Press, LLC.

Chapter 15 is reprinted with permission of Simon & Schuster Adult Publishing Group from *Naomi's Breakthrough Guide: 20 Choices to Transform Your Life,* © 2004 by Naomi Judd.

Chaper 25 is reprinted from *Living In Process,* by Anne Wilson Schaef, ©1998 by Anne Wilson Schaef used by permission of Balentine Books, a division of Random House, Inc.

Chaper 32 appears simultaneously in *Shift,* the journal of the Institute of Noetic Sciences, and is used with permission of author and publisher, © 2005 Bruce Lipton.

Chaper 26 appeared initially in the *Leifer Report,* and is used with permission of author and publisher, © 2005 Joan Borysenko.

Chapter 35 is excerpted from *From Science to God* by Peter Russell ©2004, and is reprinted with permission of New World Library, www.newworldlibrary.com.

Some material in Chapter 31 is reprinted with permission of HarperCollins Publishers from *Love and Survival* ©1998 Dean Ornish.

Chapter 36 "The Great Work" from *Blessing, the Art and the Practice* ©2001 David Spangler. Used by permission of Riverhead Books, an imprint of Penguin Group (USA) Inc.

Chaper 37 is adapted from a speech given by Prince Charles on July 10, 1995, and is used with permission of Clarence House, © 2005 Clarence House.

Chapter 40 "The Birth of Love" from *Going Home: Jesus and Buddha as Brothers* ©1999 Thich Nhat Hanh. Used by permission of Riverhead Books, an imprint of Penguin Group (USA) Inc.

All rights reserved. No part of this publication may be reproduced, stored in a retrieval system, or transmitted in any form or by any means, electronic, mechanical, photocopy, recording or otherwise, without prior written permission from Author's Publishing/Elite Books, with the exception of short excerpts used with acknowledgement of publisher and author.

Cover design by Victoria Valentine
Typesetting by Nan Sea Love
Copyediting by Melissa Mower
Typeset in Mona Lisa and Book Antiqua
Printed in USA
First Edition

10 9 8 7 6 5 4 3 2 1

CONTENTS

Section Four: Engaging With Nature

Section Five: Empowered Outer Action

Section Six: The Emerging Scientific Revolution

Section Seven: Passionate Spirituality

Geralyn Gendreau:

Introduction

The collection of ideas you have in your hands grew out of a passionate conversation between a modern day mystic and a spiritually astute Ph.D. science buff about the essential paradox of our time. The question, "Will humanity respond to the global crisis brought on by our habits and behavior and radically change our ways before it's too late?" has kept both of us enthralled throughout our adult lives. Together, we breathed a sigh of relief once our last anthology, *Healing Our Planet, Healing Our Selves* was complete and on its way to book shelves across the country. But on our very next in breath, we discovered that the conversation would not be shelved.

One particular chapter in that collection, an essay by Andrew Harvey called *Mystical Activism* (reprinted here as Chapter Thirty-Nine) kept snagging our attention. We talked about doing another anthology by that title, and I spoke to Marilyn Schlitz at the Institute of Noetic Sciences about my dream of creating a conference on the subject — only to discover two months later that Rabbi Michael Lerner had picked up the ball and was sprinting down the field of all possibilities toward that very goal. The Spiritual Activism Conference, sponsored by *Tikkun* magazine in the summer of 2005, had an unexpected turnout of over a thousand people, confirming our sense of urgency about a conversation that is clearly on many people's minds. But the term *mystical activism* left some flummoxed, despite mystics having just

Geralyn Gendreau, M.S. is a yoga lifestyle trainer, martial dance artist, and professional muse. The embodiment of coherent emotion and devotional ecstasy, she is best known for her stage recitations of poetry from two great mystics—Rumi and Hafiz. She is the author of *When I Became God's Lover,* a collection of stories, poems and essays on the sacred erotic. Both on stage and with clients, she works to ground the light of pure genius to sculpt a more balanced world. She is currently editing an anthology called *The Marriage of Sex and Spirit* (Elite, 2006), and is a contributing editor to several other anthologies (www.TheNewVoices.com). Find her on the web at www.themagdalenesect.com.

been given a gold star by scientists in the quasi-documentary, *What the Bleep Do We Know?*

The vital question that led to the metaphor "heart of the world" was this: Would we continue to turn this beautiful blue green planet into a battlefield if, in our heart of hearts, we could see the way clear to turn it into a field of dreams?

Since "see the way clear" is the operative here, those of us with the ability to perceive and articulate the new way are faced with an awesome responsibility. We are the pioneers who have blazed a new trail and changed our basic assumptions and presuppositions about existence. The authors in this book give myriad examples of how humanity is hacking through the jungle of misconception and denial to a new freedom. Between George Leonard discussing social aikido and macro trends, Jean Shinoda Bolen calling upon women to light the sacred fire, Neale Donald Walsch giving us a snapshot of the mind of God, Fred Mitouer helping us name and tame our dragons, and Jodi Serota tuning us in to the foundational frequency of love—what you have here is a gorgeous, fascinating mandala.

-§-
Humanity is hacking through the jungle of misconception and denial to a new freedom.
-§-

Recently, I had one of those paradoxical, mixed-bag, agony and ecstasy experiences at the Burning Man Festival in the Nevada desert. It being my first time going to "The Burn," I'd been duly warned of the basic modus operandi in Black Rock City: radical self-reliance. A lifelong friend who kept inviting me to join the party year after year made it absolutely clear to me on more than one occasion that Burning Man is dangerous. In fact, I was already well aware of this, as another dear friend was fatally injured on the desert playa in 2003 and never came home. Only after I did make it home, half-dead myself from lack of sleep, did I read the "official" guidelines some forty thousand festival-goers are handed upon arrival. In that document, radical self-reliance is third on the list of Black Rock City conventions. Radical inclusion is first.

Like the all-night party animals going wild on the playa in the absence of any external authority, humanity is working through an adolescent rebellion, as Anodea Judith documents in her brilliant analysis of our status as a species. Adolescents playing with real guns is dangerous; humankind must deal with its current developmental crisis or perish. As teenagers, we can afford—for a time—to be oblivious to the consequences of our choices and actions, but self-responsibility is required for a successful transition into young adulthood. We simply cannot rely on our same-old behaviors and understandings of how things work to build the future.

As Deepak Chopra pointed out at the Global Mind Change Forum recently, "We are coming to a time when the Information Age will make everything we knew in the old paradigm totally irrelevant." Recall the scene in *What the Bleep Do We Know?* wherein Spanish galleons remained invisible to the native eye until one among the natives carefully watched the pattern in the waves. Speaking as a wave-watcher to other new-paradigm-builders, the time has come to align our heart of hearts and look toward the horizon with unblinkered eyes.

Chopra points out we have "modern capacities, and ancient tribal habits." An important part of our work is to counterbalance the ancient ways—turned delusional in the nuclear age—with more insightful and sustainable ways of being like those advanced by this book. If our current leaders could come in from the fringes and take the seat of power, people of conscience now on the fringe can take heart, knowing that they are aligned with the next turn of time's inexorable wheel.

On the fringe I inhabit, the offspring of theology and ideology are, at this very moment, evolving a rarified form of sight. This emergent form of intelligence is a distinct faculty that allows us to sense the unseen bonds that sustain every integer of matter in the universe. That penultimate expression of consciousness we call "enlightenment" may very well be the next step in our collective evolution. My friends and I have been calling this new, or latent, or evolving sense *kaleido* from the Greek root meaning "with a beautiful form."

Humanity is pregnant and about to reach full term. A new kind of human, as well as a beautiful new brave and brilliant world is being born. For the newly emerging human, our world is no more round than it was flat. When seen through kaleido, the Earth looks far more like a flowering seed of life than a globe. And when the veil across the battlefield is finally lifted, we may well see a field a dreams welcoming us home. For creation, it turns out, is a constantly arising holographic organism of consciousness. Birthed by the big bang, the universe hums and spirals its way through an intricate labyrinth that is our existence. All of life is a constant turning in on itself in the very process of birthing more of itself into being. As Rumi says, in the Coleman Barks translation: "Whatever circles comes from the center." And everything circles. Reality is an intricate play of mirror images. Everything we do to others plays back in reverse order, both sooner and later.

-§-
"The Information Age will make everything we knew in the old paradigm totally irrelevant."
—Deepak Chopra
-§-

I learned this most pointedly in 1987 when I broke my neck in the surf at Point Reyes. My cervical spine had just been crushed by a head-on impact with a very large wave, sending a bone-crunching sound through my body-mind that triggered a remarkably calm thought: *so that's how it ends.* Sprung loose from the cross of time and space, I moved into a dimension wherein the ripple-out effect of my every act could be tangibly felt. A common thread in many near-death experiences, this reckoning is a passage that the personal self—quite simply—does not survive. I always remember this, and cringe at what is in store for the tyrants of the world.

-§-

People of conscience now on the fringe can take heart, knowing that they are aligned with the next turn of time's inexorable wheel.

-§-

Dragged out of the surf completely paralyzed, I gazed at my hand resting on the sand near my face. In that moment of recognition—*oh my God, I'm paralyzed*—I experienced a very strange sensation, as if my known reality had just been ripped to shreds. My first thought was, "I'd rather be dead."

From a state of mind and being I can only describe as extreme, I saw before me three distinct images. In the first, my three brothers stood beneath the baby star pine near my father's grave—they were looking at my casket. In the second image, I was sitting in a wheelchair. A red plaid blanket covered my legs. In the third, a woman with long, golden hair was dancing on stage, spinning in a dervish-like trance. Needless to say, I picked option number three. Today, that vision has become my reality.

I consider my near-death experience a basic lesson in the nature of the quantum field. According to quantum physics, at any given moment, a myriad of potential futures exist. As Marya Mann, Ph.D., explains, "At a subatomic level, matter does not exist with certainty at definite places, but rather shows *tendencies to exist.* Called probability waves, these potentialities move at light-speed, and when enough of them intersect, a new particle is formed. This is known as the Quantum Wave Function, or *quiff.* As agents of free will, we select how and in what direction we want to move and act…focus with conscious intention on particular probability waves gives chosen potentials a set of barbells, builds their strength, and constellates particles to bring forth an actuality."

My near-death experience led me to believe that potential futures align along three specific universal trajectories. These trajectories have been expressed in thermodynamics, systems theory, the Upanishads, and poetry. They are: 1) entropy, i.e.: going out of existence as in the second law of thermodynamics, 2) homeostatis, or maintaining the *status quo,* and 3) the anti-entropic evolutionary spiral I think of as the upward pull of Heaven's portal. The Upanishads delineate the *gunas* — three manifestations of the Aum vibration that reverberates throughout the universe as creation, preservation, and destruction. Rumi said: "It is always sad and terrible before that cross-over move that makes nine levels of ascension ordinary ground."

As a result of my near-death experience, the aperture of my inner eye opened, helping me — over time — grow into an understanding of our innate capacity to both see and seed the future. This only became clear after a number of unlikely potentialities came to pass after feeding them with intentional focus and passion, as Barbara De Angelis emphasizes in her chapter.

These days, I adopt unlikely potentialities the way some people adopt pets. At the risk of sounding foolish, I'd like to introduce you to my new pet favorite — I named this one "Mitosis."

If we are to believe the admonition, "as above, so below," logic would hold the reverse is also true. In the same way that cells divide when they are ready, I believe human consciousness is in the process of separating and evolving, or devolving as the case may be, into two distinct organisms. One will spiral up and ascend, and one will go out of existence along the entropic spiral.

As for fundamentalists who cheer the destruction of the environment in the name of the Bible while expecting to be Rapture-d out of here just in the nick of time, they may well be the key to our success. Good-hearted, well-meaning people for the most part, they are people who have simply been led astray. I think of them as sheep herded by wolves in sheep's clothing. As Bertrand Russell said, "Man is a credulous animal and must believe *something.* In the absence of good grounds for belief, he will be satisfied with bad ones." If author Timothy LaHaye can weave together a narrative and sell millions of end-times novels to scientifically naïve Christians, surely those who wish to sustain the Earth with all the high-tech cinematic tools at their disposal can capture that energy and redirect the herd.

-§-
Creation, it turns out, is a constantly arising holographic organism of consciousness.
-§-

The kaleido capacity reveals at least one, and often two, parallel worlds, co-existing alongside the generally agreed upon consensus-reality. That may sound strange, but imagine how unthinkable a round world seemed to the people who lived a mere five hundred years ago. In the round world, the balance in the games of good and evil are tipped in favor of evil, and the dragons of fear and greed rule human thought. A pair of much friendlier dragons governs the streams of human thought in the flowering seed of life that is the new world—their names are Grace and Beauty. In this parallel world, we are well on the way to what Jean Houston calls Jump Time. The new Renaissance has already begun.

When we weave together a more coherent story, one that resonates with love for the heart of the whole world, most members of the human family will readily turn like a thirsty herd, and walk toward the well. The tender human heart has become dry and parched in the feeble hands of a dying old man called "patriarchy." How can we possibly resist circling around a spring that bubbles with new life? The soul-drenching practices and ideas expressed in this collection herald change in every aspect of society, as sure as the flip of reality in an Escher painting.

As a young woman, I often took respite from life in Los Angeles by traveling to Sequoia National Park, where my favorite hike led through the ancient redwoods of Giant Forest to the feet of the Sherman Tree. Something about standing at the feet of this enormous, towering living being always restored my sanity. But the Sherman Tree is not the largest organism on Earth—as I had been led to believe. The largest living organism is a distant relative of the tiny mushrooms growing next to the giant sequoia. Perhaps, like *Armillaria*—the species of honey mushroom that spreads invisibly, interlocked below the surface, for miles—the human species, too, has a subterranean identity. The vast looming mushroom that makes its home in the forest lives primarily underground, out of sight to the human eye. From the multidimensional outlook that kaleido provides, we can see and seed a time when humans live together as one peaceful family.

-§-
"Man is a credulous animal and must believe something. In the absence of good grounds for belief, he will be satisfied with bad ones."
—Bertrand Russell
-§-

Evolution has the human species in a pressure cooker designed to pop the lid on a more balanced world. Consciousness is waking up at a marvelous rate, and the recognition that we are co-creators with God—and thus the "Christed ones"—is hitting people everywhere right smack between their unblinkered eyes. Once we are thus struck, our kaleido capacity allows us to *see it feelingly* just like the blind man, Gloucester, in Shakespeare's *King Lear*. From this perspective, we see nature, the quantum field, and the human heart conspiring with great glee in the name of the greater good. Lynn Twist, a contributor to our forthcoming anthology *Einstein's Business*, tells the story of visiting a tribe in Africa that faced with extinction as their existing well gradually dried up. But when the leaders finally agreed to let the women dig a well (traditionally men's work) in a location of their choosing, abundant water was discovered.

Will the outcome for the human race be a slow and agonizing death by thirst as the old cultural wellsprings die up, or will we break the hypnosis of our ancient violent consensus and dip our bucket into the abundant streams of renewal that are represented in this book? Do we choose Armageddon, or rebirth? That depends on you and me. In Black Rock City, where post-modern, Information Age wizards are busting out of their adolescent britches at a sleep-depriving decibels twenty-four/seven, the consensus holds that art-

-§-

The new Renaissance
has already begun.

-§-

ists, musicians, and a new tribe of free spirits are "the chosen ones" who will usher in a new world. I'll stake my burning life on that potential future, and as Jean Shinoda Bolen suggests, light a sacred fire and call in the goddess of love and beauty to co-create a new Renaissance.

PART ONE

Hearts On Fire

Caroline Myss:

Invisible Acts of Power

To be of service is a spiritual and a biological imperative. Being part of a community is a psychic necessity. It's an emotional necessity. When I hear someone say, "I want to be a hermit," I think of Thoreau. He was no more a hermit than somebody who lives near a modern city. Though he wrote his books in solitude, he came into town on occasion and socialized with his friends at a tavern.

It's abnormal to want to be disconnected. It's abnormal to not want the help that is normal. If someone in front of you drops something, you don't have to think, "Do I pick it up, or don't I?" You simply rush to the call. You have to work hard in order to become frozen.

There is a maturation process to a person's capacity to give, and to be of service. If that maturation process is woven into one's self-esteem, it has a direct impact on the maturation of one's intuition, and the ability to be intuitive.

There is a deep-seated misconception that being intuitive is a gift. It's not. There is no such thing as a gift for intuition. I have finally realized that courage is the true gift, and intuition is sharpened as a result. Either you develop the ability to respond physically to what you are hearing, feeling, and sensing on the inside—or you don't. Responding to others takes guts. What determines whether or not you have those guts is self-esteem. It is a strong sense of self. It is a willingness and ability to take charge of yourself.

Caroline Myss, Ph.D., is dedicated to creating educational programs in the field of human consciousness, spirituality and mysticism, health, energy medicine, and advancing the science of medical intuition. She has an international reputation as a renowned medical intuitive, and with C. Norman Shealy, M.D., Ph.D., co-founded the American Board of Scientific Medical Intuition, which offers professional accreditation in this emerging field. Her book *Anatomy of the Spirit* (Three Rivers, 1997), was a *New York Times* best seller; her sixth book is *Invisible Acts of Power* (Free Press, 2004). Her personal passion is the mystical history of America. Full information is at www.Myss.com.

What determines the point at which a person develops this courage? It comes about when you finally get a grip on yourself and say, "I can handle survival. I don't need my survival to be guaranteed in order for me to listen to my spiritual guidance." That is the surrender point. That's the point at which a person finally engages his or her highest potential.

Most people who come to my workshops are pursuing their own "spiritual" lives. Yet I wonder, are they really pursuing spirituality, or are they pursuing intuitive abilities, subtly disguised as spirituality? They may say they want guidance to figure out how to survive in their career. I ask myself, "What deeper goal are they seeking?"

There is always a deeper goal. You can't develop intuition solely for your own ends. You may think you're developing your intuition to find your higher calling at work. But if you're intuitive, you're going to wind up being more sensitive and aware of others. You're going to become a healer. You can't pursue your own good, and say goodbye to helping other people. You can't say, "I'm just going to be intuitive for myself. When I look at someone else, I really don't want to do an accurate intuitive reading. I really don't want to risk sensing that they might need support. I really don't want to sense that they are really hurting because of something I said to them. I really don't want to face that, so I'll use my intuitive abilities just for my own benefit." People limit their own development continually in this way. Some are frightened, some are cautious, some are bitter, some are negative. They really don't want to be intuitively clear about people they have an interest in controlling. Most people want intuitive clarity about their own future and their own life. Then they want to put up a barrier when it comes to intuitive clarity about others. But intuition doesn't work that way. It gives you insight into both.

-§-
You have to work hard in order to become frozen.
-§-

An invisible act of power is to say, "I am going to put my energy behind you in support of you, and not in front of you obstructing you." Crossing that bridge of service leads to your own highest potential. It takes honesty and self-esteem. Real generosity, a real intuitive act of power—invisible work—is to get to the point where you can say, "I have got to be clear across the board—not just for me."

Everybody notices a homeless person, even if they pretend not to. They may turn away, and engage in conversation with a friend, just to avoid seeing the homeless person. Yet they are still extremely aware that there's a homeless person on the block. They may not want to respond, or feel the vulnerability of that homeless person.

You don't need a lot of self-esteem. A little bit goes a long way; suddenly you are generous enough to give up the need to control other people. You don't need to become 100% empowered. A 51% to 49% ratio will do the trick. Just get to the point where you're conscious enough to hold yourself accountable for your own feelings. Just admit that you're jealous, or embarrassed, or that you could betray a friend. Just get a little bit honest with your shadow. The moment you arrive there, you can really start dealing with your life.

You can't live your life if all you focus on is how other people's shadows have hurt you, you poor thing. You've got to get to the point where you look at the weapon that you've hidden in your own dark space. When you get to that point you can start looking at the healing of your self-esteem. As soon as that self-esteem is in place in a little bit of a way, you don't pretend you don't see that homeless person. You acknowledge that, "I see that person and I'm choosing to ignore that person." You don't turn away and engage in conversation with a friend, in order to convince the friend that you didn't see the homeless person. You don't worry that if you didn't do this, your friend might think you're a terrible person because you're walking by; you're hoping that they think, "She didn't see the homeless person because she's talking to me." At the same time you're hoping the homeless person doesn't say anything to the two of you, and become impossible to ignore, because you don't want to part with a dollar. That's a lot of psychic drama, all because you don't want to admit that, intuitively, you feel the energy of that homeless person; you go to all this trouble to avoid taking action on your intuitive hit. You've just received an intuitive hit, and not acted on it. That's low self-esteem. If your intuition gave you the perfect instructions for your own physical healing, are you then going to say, "I can't do it. What will the neighbors think?"

§

You can't develop intuition solely for your own ends.

-§-

I collected the stories of dozens of people for my book *Invisible Acts of Power*. One was of a man who was on his way to kill himself. He was trying to make his last decision: "Should I use pills, or a razor?" As he stood at a crosswalk waiting to cross the street, a woman stopped for him. He waited for her to accelerate, but she didn't. She looked at him and smiled. Their eyes linked. She didn't say anything. He locked into her; he couldn't take his eyes off her. All she did was smile, but it wasn't an ordinary smile. She flushed him full of grace. It washed over him. He wrote, "She brought me back to life with that smile." Was it the smile? No, it was grace. She channeled grace to him.

Another person wrote, "You know what brought me back to life? Someone held the door open for me. And I'll tell you why that seemed so important: I couldn't take one more person slamming a door in my face." What determines who channels grace and who doesn't? What does it take? The management of power is archetypal and symbolic and spiritual. And if you knew that opening a door was an act of life or death, symbolically, you wouldn't go near it. It's better you don't know. Down here it's all illusion, and you don't know what you're doing. As I read these stories, I realized, "Oh my God, there isn't a thing we touch—there is nothing at all—that is not connected to someone else."

You might be worried about the state of the world, at the twenty thousand children dying each day in poor countries. Yet think of the problems of our own culture: People lying twenty thousand times a month. Which is the greater tragedy? In our culture, our poverty of spirit is horrible. Most of us are far more focused on managing other people's dishonesty than in developing our own wisdom.

In our culture, lying is regarded as dialog. When you think of poverty in Western civilization, which chakra's poverty do you want to contemplate? Poverty of judgment? Poverty of wisdom? Poverty of forgiveness? You don't have to go to another country to deal with poverty. Just pick a level of poverty close to home.

In 1975 I attended my very first lecture on consciousness. I was in my early twenties, and it was the first time I'd seen someone from the East. The teacher said, "The best gift you can give anyone in this life is to become a fully congruent human being." The first thought I had in response was, "In a world that's starving, what kind of self-centered, selfish idea is that?' But today, I can't imagine a more compassionate thing. The finest force you can be is a fully con-

-§-
You don't need to become 100% empowered. A 51% to 49% ratio will do the trick.
-§-

gruent soul. A master is a fully congruent being. Their thought goes into form instantly because there is no distortion in them. Healing is instant. Kairos goes immediately into Chronos.

Someone asked the Dalai Lama in an interview how to deal with the Chinese who are occupying Tibet. He replied, "With compassion." If you're competitive and incongruent, that kind of spiritual work doesn't satisfy you; in fact, it doesn't make any sense. If you're congruent, it makes perfect sense. You understand that taking care of "in here" and "out there" is the same instruction. When you encounter violent energy and do not respond in kind, you absorb it, putting an end to the cycle. That takes away the power of those opposing you. If you don't respond to their provocations, then they have to change.

That's an invisible act of power, even though in the middle of it, you cannot see that power. It is unimaginable how powerful that type of approach truly is. The impact of prayer, the impact of compassion, the impact of good and kind thoughts and actions, is incalculable. The accumulation of all the good sparks that jump out of people counteract all the dark sparks. They are the reason this world is still alive.

Prayer, and these wonderful acts of service, and this light of goodness, carries immense power. Whether you're opening a door, saying one nice thing, or delivering one meal, you have saved a life. It may be a meal for you, but the recipient writes to me and says, "The man who delivered that meal saved my life. I was about to commit suicide when he came." And for you it was a casserole; you might think, "For me, it was nothing." While it may have been nothing for you, behind the scenes, angels made sure that the casserole was delivered. You might have thought that it was just an idea that just sprang into your head, when in reality it was an intuitive hit. Acting on it channeled healing power. In the moment you responded to your intuition, alchemy occurred, and you became a healer. The energy of healing poured through you. An invisible act of power of a cosmic quality occurred around and through you, because you accepted the instruction, and you stepped into the authority of a healer. That's an invisible act that's happening around and through you because you listened to this inner voice, that you've been spending so much time developing. The casserole may look like nothing more than a casserole, yet it carries a vibration of heart and intention.

-§-
The management of power is archetypal and symbolic and spiritual.
-§-

When you have healthy self-esteem, you stop worrying what anyone else will say or think about what you're doing. You glide with life, going where you're called. Your intuition leads you effortlessly into acts of service. You channel grace. Even just closing your eyes and thinking about a problem, you channel grace.

BARBARA DE ANGELIS:

Finding Your Way
Back to Passion

We do not have to die to enter the kingdom of Heaven.
In fact, we have to be fully alive.
—Thich Nhat Hanh

There is a power in our heart far greater than anything we can imagine. This power is our passion—the life force that pulsates within us, bringing energy, vitality and meaning to everything it touches. When that passion flows into our relationship, it brings intimacy and deep connection. When that passion flows into our work, it brings creativity and vision. When that passion flows into our quest for Truth, it brings wisdom. When that passion flows into our spiritual journey, it brings awakening.

No matter how battered we are by love or life, no matter what we endure, we never really lose our passion. Perhaps we leave it for a while, but it never leaves us.

When what you held dear has been lost or taken from you, you still have your passion.

When love seems to have abandoned you, and your heart and your body ache for union, you still have your passion.

When you are disappointed and disillusioned, you still have your passion.

Barbara De Angelis, Ph.D., is one of the most influential teachers of our time in the field of personal and spiritual growth. For twenty-five years, she has reached millions of people with her positive messages about love, happiness and meaning. She is the author of fourteen books, published in twenty languages, including the *New York Times* best sellers *Real Moments* (Delacorte, 1994), *Secrets About Men Every Woman Should Know* (Delacorte, 1990), and *How Did I Get Here?* (St. Martins, 2005). She has hosted her own TV shows on CNN, CBS and PBS, as well as an award-winning infomercial, *Making Love Work.* You can find her on the web at www.BarbaraDeAngelis.com. Photo by Charles Bush.

When you are balancing precariously between the past and the future in an uncertain and shifting present, you still have your passion.

When you are weary of traveling a new and unmarked road to a destination that has not yet come into clear view, you still have your passion.

Just as a fire whose flames have died down hides its heat in the glowing coals, so your passion still smolders within you, waiting for the moment when you will call on it to rise again and burn brightly. It is from this fire of passion that all of your new beginnings will emerge.

As you travel life's difficult roads and meet unexpected challenges, it is your passion that becomes your saving grace. It keeps you going forward even when you feel like giving up. It keeps you searching for love even when you are afraid you will never find it. It keeps you awake. It keeps you truly alive.

If you have read this far, if you have been digging deep, if you have been inviting truth into your awareness, then you have already been reclaiming your passion. Can you feel it waking up inside of you?

Right Here, Right Now, There Is Passion

The aim of life is to live, and to live means to be aware,
joyously, drunkenly, serenely, divinely aware.
—Henry Miller

Today is the day to be fully alive. Today is the day to reach out and embrace the joys available in each moment. Today is the day for passion.

Passion is not something we are only supposed to experience on a romantic vacation or while visiting an exciting destination. It is not something to be rationed out in reasonable doses or saved for special occasions. It is not only available to people with unlimited funds and free time.

Passion is not found in escaping from
our usual life in a search for
some high-charged experience.
We rediscover our passion when we
open ourselves fully to every
experience, and learn to see the
world with passionate eyes.

How do we do this? It is simpler than we realize.

We learn to be aware, to pay attention to the ordinary, everyday miracles that are all around us: the sound of tree branches dancing in the wind; the delicacy of a cloud; the tender kiss from a young child; the enthusiastic greeting of your animal companions when you arrive home; the sweet juiciness of a piece of ripe fruit; the soothing hot water of your bath or shower; the songs birds sing as they wake up the dawn.

We take these and so many other natural gifts for granted. In the midst of our overscheduled and stressful days, we often fail even to notice, let alone rejoice, in the abundance of the marvelous and the amazing that surrounds us.

Imagine for a moment that the night sky was always devoid of all light — no moon, no stars, no planets, no galaxies — utterly black. Then imagine that suddenly one evening a veil was lifted and all of these shining, celestial bodies were made visible. All over the world, the people of the Earth would stare weeping up into the heavens, certain that the Divine had finally revealed itself.

Are the stars any less awe-inspiring because we can see them every night? Is the love of our mate, our children, our best friend any less precious because we assume they will be there the next day, and the next? Are our body and our brain any less magical because they continue to function the way we expect them to? Is our existence any less miraculous because we are blessed with so many days of it in a lifetime?

Living a passionate and awakened life means

looking at the stars each night as if it were your

first time and as if it were your

last time. It means embracing your

loved ones as if this were the only

embrace you will ever be granted.

It means living each day with reverence

and wonder as if it were the only

day you will be given to live.

• • •

Last year, one of my dear friends had emergency triple bypass surgery on his heart. Samuel is only sixty years old and always thought he was in excellent health, so his heart failure came as a total shock and, needless to say, a very dramatic wake-up call.

Samuel has a very successful career as an actor. Like many of us, he gets caught up in the pressures and demands of his work. Before his illness, he never seemed to take time to relax or even enjoy the full and prosperous life he'd created for himself. Now all of that has changed.

When I told Samuel I was writing this book, I asked him to describe what he learned from his brush with death, and to articulate how his life is different. He described it this way:

> Now, I consciously evaluate my life on a daily basis, judging it by how the day was, and not what new movie I was cast in, or how my investments are doing, or what awards I've been nominated for. I keep asking myself, *"Would I want this to be my last day?"* This keeps me focused on what is important—my relationship with my wife, my kids, enjoying very simple pleasures. I am so acutely aware of how limited our time on Earth is, my time, and how at any moment it could all be over. Knowing that, I don't want to miss anything.

Samuel is more alive now than he ever was before his life threatening heart failure, not because he is in better physical health, but because he has committed himself to living each day with awareness and gratitude. He has stopped postponing his joy and started actively searching for things to be passionate about. For the first time in his life he is at peace.

The Courage to Live Passionately

I've been absolutely terrified every moment of my life—
and I've never let it keep me from doing a single thing
I wanted to do.
—Georgia O'Keeffe

It takes courage to live passionately. The choice to live with passion is the choice to open yourself fully to each moment and to each situation. You give everything. You hold nothing back.

Living with passion means sometimes living on the edge of our comfort zone. We are awake. We are alive. We are feeling— everything. We meet the circumstances and challenges of our life boldly. *It's not that we don't feel doubt or fear—it's that we learn to make our passion for growth and truth stronger than our fear.*

This kind of courage isn't the same as physical bravery. It is *emotional courage.* Emotional courage allows you to participate 100% in whatever you are doing and wherever you are going. It allows you to see beyond that which is the way of your dreams, your desires, your destiny, and to go forward with enthusiasm. You aren't saving some of your passion for a time in the future when you will be absolutely certain about how things will turn out. You are offering all of who you are to life right now.

Mark Twain wrote:

"Twenty years from now you will be more disappointed by the things you didn't do than by the ones you did do."

Emotional courage helps you venture out of your safe harbors into open and exciting seas, to do the things you want to do so you do not end your life with regret.

Opening up to passion means becoming open to the mysterious, the unexpected, the subtle, and allowing that which is out of the ordinary to reveal itself. This means being willing to let go of control, and adventure into new pathways of feeling, of perception, of experience, pathways that will lead you to more joy and wonder than you knew was possible.

• • •

One certain way to kill your experience of passion is to care too much about what others think. This will cut you off from your intuitive wisdom. *The more careful, calculated, and analytical we are, the more difficult it will be to be passionate about anything.*

The only person's opinion that is going to matter to you at the end of this lifetime is yours. To reclaim your passion, you must push past your fear of what others think of you and do what makes you think well of yourself.

Someone recently sent me this beautiful poem by writer and teacher Dawna Markova, who when faced with a life-threatening illness retreated to a cabin in the mountains where she contemplated how she could reclaim her true passion. She writes:

I will not die an unlived life

I will not live in fear

of falling or catching fire,

I choose to inhabit my days,

to allow my living to open me,

to make me less afraid,

more accessible,

to loosen my heart

until it becomes a wing,

a torch, a promise

I choose to risk my significance;

to live so that which came to me as a

seed goes to the next blossom

and that which came to me as a blossom,

goes on as fruit.

Reclaiming our passion means choosing to fully inhabit our days, living our lives so that no moment goes unlived, no delight goes unnoticed, no sweetness goes untasted. Right now, all around you, there are a thousand things for you to be passionate about.

Living a Turned-on Life

There is a land of the living and a land of the dead,
and the bridge is love,
the only survival, the only meaning.
—Thornton Wilder

When we wake up from the sleep of numbness and denial and reconnect with our own inner passion, then, and only then, can we infuse that passion into our emotional and sexual life.

To reawaken the erotic intimacy in a relationship, we
must first rediscover and reignite our own secret fire.
Then our passion will not be dependent
upon being stimulated from the outside.
Rather it will emerge from our own
consciousness, our own vibrant
aliveness, our own willingness
to feel fully and deeply.

Often people ask me: "How can I put the passion back into my relationship?" This is how I respond:

Are you passionate about your everyday life?

Are you passionate about your work?

Are you passionate about yourself?

Are you passionate about loving your partner deeply?

Are you passionate about being alive?

If you cannot answer each of these questions with an emphatic "yes," then there is no way you can put the passion back into your relationship. The passion has to be alive in you before you can experience it in something else."

When you are not turned on inside yourself,

your partner will have a difficult time doing it for you.

If you are the one who has been the ghost lover in a relationship, if you are the one who has been turned off and shut down, you must first embody yourself again in love and passion. Then, and only then, can you offer that new self humbly to your beloved, hoping she or he will receive it. You will need to be patient as your partner learns to trust that you have indeed come back from the emotional dead. With luck, you can resurrect your relationship and create the magical connection in body, mind, and soul for which you have always longed.

Sometimes it does not work out this way. You find your way back to your own passion only to arrive and discover that your efforts are too late. Your partner has grown weary of waiting for you to feel again and has closed the door to his or her heart. Instead of facing what you hoped would be a wonderful new beginning, you face a painful good-bye. "What horrible timing," you proclaim in despair. "Finally, when I am ready to love again, my mate no longer wants me."

If this is the case for you, remember: things are not what they appear to be. What looks like a dead end will soon reveal itself to be a doorway.

Your awakened heart, your rediscovered passion will not be wasted. They are being saved for someone else whose name and face you do not know yet, but who is praying to find you. When this person does, he or she will be grateful for all of the courageous work you did to melt the ice around your heart. He will honor you for every hard-earned moment of revelation and growth. And he will joyfully drink every drop of love you have been saving up.

The course of love is mysterious and unfathomable. Some intimate relationships endure for a lifetime. And sometimes we are destined only to share our journey with a mate for a while and then we separate, either by choice or by fate.

No matter what the outcome of our connection
with another person,
when love enters our lives,
it never leaves without transforming us to the
very depth of our being.
We may lose the relationship, but we never lose the love.

Look for the Daffodil

Every now and again take a good look at something
not made with hands —
a mountain, a star, the turn of a stream.
There will come to you wisdom and patience
and solace and, above all,
the assurance that you are not alone in the world.

—Sidney Lovett

On a frigid February day several years ago, I was in upstate New York, staring out the window at more than two feet of snow covering the ground. This was definitely *not* California — it was an uncivilized nine degrees outside, twelve below zero with the wind chill. *"How did I get here?"* I said to myself, more out of amazement than a sincere inquiry. Because, of course, I knew the answer: the true love of a remarkable man. What else could prompt me to regularly leave the warmth, the ocean, and the delight of Santa Barbara for weeks at a time? Still, it is not always easy to be so far from home, especially when it is brutally cold and I hadn't seen the sun in what seemed like decades.

I bundled up in my enormous coat, thick scarf and heavy boots to make a trip to the supermarket, hoping to finish my shopping before the next blizzard arrived. My car slipped and slid along the icy roads, and by the time I arrived, my hands were stiff from gripping the wheel so tightly. As I waddled as quickly as possible through the parking lot into the store, I caught a glimpse of myself in a mirror — I looked like a walking sleeping bag! I noticed to my amazement that many of the other customers — obviously native upstaters — were just wearing light jackets, in spite of the frigid temperatures, I smiled apologetically as I passed them in my arctic attire, as if to say: "Have pity on me: I wasn't born here!"

As I wheeled my cart toward the produce section, I spotted a display of live plants and fresh flowers across the store, "JUST IN TIME

FOR SPRING," the sign optimistically read. My California soul, thirsty for green, took over and I found myself practically racing toward the foliage. Then I noticed it, there in the middle of the aisle—a potted yellow daffodil just beginning to bloom.

My first reaction when I saw the daffodil was a bittersweet rush of sadness. It reminded me of home in California, where everything is always in bloom, and where my garden was overflowing with a colorful variety of lovely flowers. Even though I chose to be here and not there, I still missed it terribly. Suddenly I knew that I must buy this little daffodil as a defiant act against the interminable bitterness of winter. It would be my piece of sunshine against the backdrop of gray. It would be my own little secret garden.

When I arrived back at the house, I placed the potted daffodil on my desk where I do my writing. Outside the window, I could see the snow once again beginning to fall, until soon there was nothing but white. Another storm had arrived. But my daffodil and I were safely inside.

I cared for my daffodil tenderly, and it rewarded me by blossoming in golden abundance. Each day I delighted in its refusal to acknowledge winter, and its persistence in blooming despite the icy, sunless times. Its tender yellow petals glistened with the promise of regeneration. When it seemed the world had come to a frozen standstill, my daffodil's bold burst of color sang out with triumph and passion: "Spring is coming!"

Something is always blooming in cold, dark times. Even in the midst of challenge and difficulty, we must look for signs of beauty and delight. Even in the midst of turmoil, there are miracles. Even in the midst of desolation, there are moments of passion.

Look for the daffodil.

Measuring Your Life in Love and Miracles

When it's over, I want to say:
all my life I was a bride married to amazement.
I was the bridegroom taking the world into my arms.
—Mary Oliver

This year a dear friend of mine passed away from leukemia at the untimely age of fifty-two. Kathy was everything that is good about this world. She was brave, wise, loving, and passionate. Kathy did not want to die. She underwent two excruciating bone marrow transplants, fighting for every extra day of life she could grab.

It was impossible for me to imagine that someone who possessed as much energy and vitality as Kathy could be worn down by cancer, but in the end, even she realized it was time for her to go. When her spirit left her battered body, Kathy was in a state of peace and grace, knowing that she had died with as much courage, consciousness, and dignity as she had lived.

When Kathy's family asked me to perform her memorial service, I felt humbled and honored. I prayed that I would find the right words to give some comfort to her mother, her siblings, her friends, and especially her son and only child, Gregory, who was just about to graduate from college. Kathy had been a single mother and had done a remarkable job raising Greg to be a sensitive young man with a beautiful heart. The two of them had always been very close, and I knew that losing his mother when he was still so young was going to be difficult for Greg to bear.

Before everyone arrived for the service, I went into the chapel to spend some time alone meditating, praying, and preparing myself for whatever wanted to come through me when I spoke. There in the front of the room was Kathy's body laid out in the open coffin. I was surprised at how strangely distant I felt seeing it. *"That is no longer Kathy,"* I thought to myself. Kathy's spirit had ascended to another realm, leaving her old body behind, a cast-off shell that had once housed her soul, and no more.

In that moment, I was struck once again with a truth I have always known and try each day to remember: **We are here on this Earth for such a short while.** I have always been amazed when I witness people living as if they do not understand this—squandering time, hiding from love, getting caught up in things that do not matter, and never attending to what does.

Kathy understood. She had been completely and radiantly alive. She had always thrown herself into everything she did as if she had no time to spare, and it turned out, sadly for those of us who will miss her, that she was right. In her dying, as in her living, Kathy gave the people she loved a priceless gift – *the reminder to live and love with joy, determination and passion, so that at the end of our days, we will have no regrets.*

I think about Kathy every day. I started out as her teacher and mentor, but in the end, she became my teacher and my inspiration. I know she would be pleased that I am writing about her so that even in death, she can help make a difference. Her goodness continues to touch and open hearts, even from the unseen places beyond this physical world.

• • •

FINDING YOUR WAY BACK TO PASSION Barbara De Angelis

A joyful heart is the inevitable result of a heart burning with love.
—Mother Teresa

How do we measure a life? In dollars earned? In awards won? In how many material things we possessed? In how perfectly we did everything? In what other people thought of us? In how old we lived to be? In his remarkable Broadway musical *Rent*, the late Jonathan Larson, who tragically passed away just weeks before his show opened, suggests that we measure in love.

When I measure my life in love, I find myself rich beyond imagining. I have loved deeply. I have loved often. I have loved passionately. Somehow I have emerged from my own recent challenges and awakenings able to feel even more, give even more, love even more.

We do not need to be in a relationship to love. We do not need to have money to love. We do not need to have conquered our fears to love. We do not need to know where the road is taking us to love. All we need to do to love is find the passion and sweetness in the center of our heart. All we need to do to love is to feel the love that is already burning inside us, a fire whose spark cannot be extinguished. All we need to do to love is...just love.

• • •

There are only two ways to live your life. One is as though nothing is a miracle. The other is as though everything is a miracle.
—Albert Einstein

Recently I was walking my dogs in one of our favorite Santa Barbara parks. It was a glorious afternoon with warm temperatures and a cloudless azure sky. Ahead of us down the path, I noticed a strange-looking man sitting on a bench. He was oddly dressed and had an air about him that told me he was a few degrees shy of normal.

As we got closer, I saw that this fellow was trying to speak to everyone who passed, although they were all ignoring him. He pointed a finger up into the air and emphatically repeated a phrase that I couldn't quite hear. "Maybe he's drunk or disturbed," I thought to myself, wondering if I should avoid walking in his direction.

Just then one of my dogs began pulling me directly toward the bench where the man sat. When he noticed me approaching, he smiled tenderly, and with wide eyes full of wonder and with passionate reverence in his voice, he pointed to the sky and announced:

"The sun is awake! The sun is awake! The sun is awake!" It took me a moment to comprehend what the man was saying, and why he was

so excited by it. Then I got it: *The sun is awake. Once again, it has showed up to bless us with light and warmth. The darkness has vanished. Another day of life is here. What a miracle!*

I looked into the man's eyes and nodded: "Yes," I said to him gently, "you are right—the sun *is* awake!"

His face broke out into a wide grin. He had delivered his message, and I'd received it into the very depth of my being. What could be more cause for celebration than the fact that the sun is, indeed, awake? Why wasn't I getting up each day and, upon looking out of my window and seeing the Earth bathed with light, rejoicing in the sun's faithful and benevolent presence? What could be more of a miracle?

Perhaps some would say this man was developmentally challenged. I prefer to think of him as a special being with an innocent heart, capable of seeing things most of us don't normally see, of feeling things most of us can't normally feel. Maybe he was an angelic messenger sent to remind anyone who would listen of the truth we often forget. Maybe he was sent just for me. All I know is that ever since that remarkable encounter in the park, not a morning goes by when I do not rise from my bed and smile as I greet the day, thinking with gratitude: "The sun is awake!"

• • •

What is this precious love and laughter
Budding in our hearts?
It is the glorious sound
Of a soul waking up!
—Hafiz (tr. Daniel Ladinsky)

What is not a miracle? This body that houses our spirit? This consciousness that tells us "I exist"? These eyes that perceive an unending parade of wonders? This heart that feels love, longing, aching, everything? This life, this ecstatic, maddening life? It is, all of it, utterly miraculous.

In the end, it is the celebration of this miracle of our own self that will fill our hearts with the most independent and lasting joy, and the most unabashed passion. Like the unlikely prophet I met in the park, we announce our delightful discovery.

"I am alive! I am alive! I am alive!"

ALLAN HARDMAN:

The Perfect Dream

Until all humans understand that they are dreaming reality, and that each person's dream is the truth for them but for no one else, only then will there be peace in the hearts of all humans, and the broken heart of the world can heal.

Do you remember a drawing in your school biology textbook of a tree and an eyeball? It illustrates that when you look at a tree, you are not really seeing the tree. It shows how light is reflected off the tree, passes through the lens of your eye, and stimulates the rods and cones in the back of your eye. The rods and cones transform the light waves into neural impulses that travel into your brain and reproduce an image of the tree in your brain. Because of how the lens of your eye works, it actually projects the image of the tree upside down on the back of your eye. Your mind inverts the image.

Fascinating, isn't it? You are not really seeing what is out there in the world; you are looking at an inverted image made from reflected light and neurological impulses projected into your mind. You are looking at a little Virtual Reality that exists only in your mind.

It is fascinating to me that the virtual reality we see in our minds is not an accurate representation of our physical world in at least three major ways. First, we *add* information that is not really "out there." Second, we *miss* most of the available information about our physical universe because of the limitations of our senses, and

Allan Hardman is a gifted spiritual counselor and Toltec Master personally trained by Miguel Ruiz, author of *The Four Agreements* (Amber-Allen, 1997). He is a born teacher, whose piercing insight and compassionate humor create a loving environment that supports growth on the path to Personal Freedom. Allan is an expert in emotional healing, and healthy communication in relationships of all kinds. He hosts an online apprentice community at Joydancer.com—a thriving Internet resource for spiritual seekers. Allan teaches in Sonoma County, California, and leads "Journeys of the Spirit" to Peru and Mexico. His extensive website of writings and journeys is at www.joydancer.com.

third, we *distort* the information coming from our senses as it travels through our minds.

We Add Information To the Light

I am going to use the word "light" here to represent all of the information that our senses perceive, including visual light, sound, taste, smell, and touch.

Much of what we believe we perceive through our senses is actually added by our minds. Colors, sounds, tastes, smells, and other sensory information we imagine we perceive do not actually exist in Creation; we have learned to interpret the nerve impulses created by sense organs and call them "green" or "loud" or "sour" or "fragrant." Most of us agree about these interpretations so we do not stop to question them. The reality is, there are no colors until we "see" them with our mind. There are no sounds or tastes or smells until our mind creates them in its virtual reality.

We Miss Information In the Light

We also *miss* most of what is happening in our physical universe because of the limitations of our senses. The wave lengths of visible light, for example, are a tiny sliver of the entire electromagnetic spectrum. If you were building a scale model of the entire spectrum,

-§-
Much of what we believe we perceive through our senses is actually added by our minds.
-§-

and made the width of the band perceptible to humans equal to the width of a hair, then the entire spectrum would stretch one quarter the distance to the nearest star! We perceive just a tiny sliver, and miss all the rest of the information in the full spectrum. What would your world look like if you could see the light given off by variations in temperature in the infrared spectrum? Or if you could perceive the waves carrying television programming or cell phone communications through the air?

Imagine what the world looks, smells, and sounds like to a snake in the grass, a bat tracking a mosquito with its sonar, a worm tunneling through the garden soil, or an eagle soaring on an updraft. The quality and scope of the images collected and processed by their brains create a world in their minds that we would not recognize at all.

What then, is the real world? The worm's? The eagle's? Yours?

We Distort the Information In the Light

There is a third very important reality about how we perceive. In the teachings of the ancient Toltecs of Mexico brought to us by my mentor, Miguel Ruiz (author of *The Four Agreements* and other books) we learn that we also *distort* the limited and enhanced information collected by our senses, *before* we create the images of "reality" in our minds.

As the light, sound, and other perceptions are collected by our physical senses, they must travel through our *channels of perception* before they reach that place where they project the virtual reality in our minds. These channels of perception are filled with what the Toltecs call "stored light." It consists of all of the experiences, memories, beliefs, and opinions collected throughout a lifetime. As the incoming sensory information passes through these channels, it picks up pieces of this stored light that are similar in quality, so that by the time it creates the virtual reality in the mind, it is very different from what the senses actually brought in from the outside world.

Let's look at the source of the information stored in your mind's channels of perception. Where does it come from? Very early in your life, you began collecting and storing knowledge about what is good and what is bad; what is right, and who is wrong. You stored emotional memories and fears from your childhood. Your parents, siblings, relatives, teachers, religious leaders, peers, magazines, and TV, all downloaded information into your mind about the world, how it should be, and how you should be in it. You listened and stored opinions about sex, drugs, and rock and roll—not to mention politics, love, work, money, marriage, God, anger, and your body. That process has continued all of your life, supplemented by lovers, mates, bosses, talk show hosts, and beer commercials. All that knowledge is stored in your channels of perception, and distorts the reality perceived by your senses.

Here is an illustration of how the emotional programming works: A young woman grew up with a father who was always sarcastic and angry with her, and punished her harshly. The father wore a large bushy mustache. The images of the mustache, along with the painful emotional memories of her father's abuse, were stored in the young woman's channels of perception. As an adult, whenever she met a man with a large mustache, she felt a disquieting fear that she could not explain. When she learned that the reality of these men was being distorted by the memories and images stored in her mind's channels of perception she was able to understand her fear—and eventually

free herself from it by clearing those old images and beliefs from those channels.

Your eyes, ears, and other physical senses collect data ("Light") from the outside world that is both enhanced by the mind and limited by your sense organs. This light then travels through channels of perception in your mind that are filled with stored light: old experiences, beliefs, opinions, and emotional memories. The stored information is added to the light the senses have collected and distort it. That distorted light is projected into your mind, to create your personal virtual reality.

The best way to describe this little virtual reality in the human mind is to say that it is a dream. We are all dreaming. The dreamed reality is unique and personal to each person—and does not exist anywhere in the outside world.

Imagine that five people go to a party. The first is someone who knows and loves you from your childhood. This person meets a stranger at the party, strikes up a conversation, and tells him about her longtime friend, you. The next person who arrives at the party is your mother, and she meets the same stranger. Your mother tells him all about her wonderful (or incomprehensible) child. The stories are completely different, and the stranger believes he has heard about two different people. Imagine then that someone who is angry with you arrives, meets the stranger, and tells him the angry story about you. The fourth person to arrive at the party is an ex-lover of yours (you know the one) who has a big story of his or her own to share with the stranger. Finally, you arrive at the party. You meet the stranger, and share your story about yourself. The stranger believes he has heard about five different people! He has heard five different dreams of you, each true for the teller.

Which story describes the real you? *Is* there a real you? What then is reality?

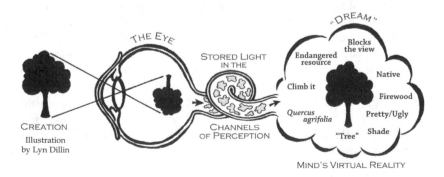

THE EYE

STORED LIGHT IN THE

"DREAM"

Blocks the view

Endangered resource

Climb it

Native

Firewood

Quercus agrifolia

Pretty/Ugly

CREATION
Illustration
by Lyn Dillin

CHANNELS OF PERCEPTION

"Tree"

Shade

MIND'S VIRTUAL REALITY

The Freedom of Awareness

There is tremendous freedom in the awareness that you are dreaming. If you recognize that your dreamed reality is unique to you and you alone, you can be free of all conflict. You will no longer need to defend your point of view, nor convince anyone that they are wrong about theirs. You will honor your beliefs and opinions as absolutely true, but true for you only. You will respect the beliefs of every other person, knowing that how they dream is the perfect expression of who they are and from whence they have come.

-§-

There is tremendous freedom in the awareness that you are dreaming.

-§-

This freedom is not easily won. The old dream is strong. It knows who is right and who is wrong, what is good and what is bad. You learned it long ago. It is embedded deeply in the recesses of your mind, and shared by most of your culture. The various versions and nuances (often conflicting) are enforced and enhanced by every subculture to which you belong—consciously or unconsciously.

People are rarely interested in hearing that their opinions and beliefs are not "true" outside of their own minds. Imagine you are a member of a progressive ecology-based political party, and you are invited to speak at a Young Republicans rally in the Midwest. What would they think of your description of the political problems in this country? How would they receive your solutions for change and your ideas about progress? Probably not very well. Why? Because they already know what is true, and they would know you are wrong. The same difficulty would exist if they came and spoke at your progressive party rally—you would know *they* were wrong. Without awareness, everyone believes that their dream of reality is the *true* reality.

When planes flew into the Twin Towers in New York City in 2001, the media in the U.S. was filled with stories and images of the terror, anger, pain, and disbelief that swept through this country. Did you also see the photos of people dancing in the streets, shooting guns into the air in celebration and joy? Celebrating made perfect sense to them. They were in a different part of the world, a different culture, and in a different dream about the U.S.

If an infant human pops into the world on the Palestinian side of the street, he is going to be taught a dream that believes the Israelis are a threat and deserve to be harmed. If that infant happens to enter the world on the Israeli side of the street, he learns that the Palestinians are the enemy. Their learned dreams of what is true are so real to them both, they are willing to kill and be killed in defense of them. They will die to defend a virtual reality constructed of distorted

information that has been programmed into their minds that has nothing to do with what is really "out there."

The Tutsis and Hutus in African Rwanda lived together in peace for centuries. They shared a common language, customs, genetics, and religion. After WWI, their Belgian colonizers decided that the minority Tutsis were a superior "race," and issued ethnic identity cards to separate them from the Hutus. The Tutsis learned to dream their superiority, and became harsh masters of the Hutus. When the limit of Hutu tolerance was reached in 1994, the Hutus slaughtered a million Tutsis and moderate Hutus in a one-hundred-day rampage.

-§-
Believing that our personal dream is the truth creates conflict and separation.
-§-

Chaos and death were the result of an outside dream, enforced on peaceful people, and believed by them.

Our lives are filled with examples of how believing that our personal dream is the truth creates conflict and separation. A mother alienates her teenage daughter in a fight about the family rules. A husband and wife grow distant from arguing over who is right about the best way to manage money. Your inner voices argue about which outfit to wear, the mistakes you make, and the best course of action in your business. Religious organizations split over interpretations of doctrine. Saints are venerated and sinners are persecuted. Sides are chosen and conflict follows. Right and wrong circle each other, looking for weakness, proving points, creating winners and losers. The opinions, fears, and dogmas learned and believed create conflict, war, divorce, hurt, anger, hatred, and death.

The Path to Freedom

If you believe that the personal dream in your mind is a true representation of what is "out there," it will cause you endless conflict and suffering. You will believe that you are right about what you see and know, and others are wrong. You will create conflict through your need to convince others and defend yourself. You will be afraid of being wrong.

There is a simple price for freedom from the conflict and difficulties that I have described above: Understand that you are dreaming, and give up your need to be right.

The price is simple, but it is not easy. Your entire identity is created by, and depends on, what you believe is right. When you *know* you are right about politics and wars, global warming and the rain forest, teenage morality, the best spiritual path and the right diet, you feel safe. It is as though you have created a little island of safety in the midst of the chaos and turmoil of a confusing and unpredictable world. The price of freedom is to leave that island of safety, to face the unknown, and to understand that you do not know, and perhaps will never know, what is true and real in this universe. You can only dream your dream of it — and every other person can only dream their dream of it.

By leaving your island of safety, you offer yourself the opportunity for real personal freedom. You will discover that the fears, opinions and beliefs programmed into your mind are mostly lies that you were required to believe as a child. You are no longer the vulnerable child who had to conform or perish. As an adult you have resources and wisdom that can support and guide you into a new relationship with life, and all of creation.

You can change how you dream. If you have been distorting the incoming light with the beliefs and opinions stored in your channels of perception, you can clean those channels. You can find and delete the beliefs based in fear and limitation. You can choose new beliefs that make you happy. If your mind was programmed once, you can program it again — your way. We can instead learn to dream a new dream of love and acceptance for ourselves, our mates, our parents, our children, for every religious, political and cultural expression, and all of creation.

After all, if you are dreaming, why choose a nightmare?

Start with your own mind. Listen to the voices arguing to be right, making other parts of you wrong. Do not believe them! Begin by knowing that you are a perfect expression of Life in this universe — the same life that animates every being and event and all space in creation. Life is in the trees, the oceans, the exploding novas far out in space, the air molecules, and Life is in your mind and body. There is no place or time that Life ends and something else (like you) begins. You are Life. See creation through the eyes of Life. See the perfection. See the mysterious unfolding of something so big and so infinitely small that it is incomprehensible to the human mind. Determine to clean out the old distorting light so that you can perceive the beauty and mystery of life with clarity. Risk the unknown.

-§-
Understand that you are dreaming, and give up your need to be right.
-§-

I want to offer you a process you can use to examine and clean old programming and distortions from your channels of perception. Approach this exercise as though you are a curious computer programmer, tracking down the faulty parts of a program that cause the

printouts of your life to be distorted. Find the glitches that cause you to suffer, and rewrite a program that makes you happy. Do not judge what you find. Simple enough?

Make three vertical columns on a piece of paper. Label the one on the left "The Event," and the one on the right "My Reaction." With the center column blank, notice that there is no direct connection between an event in Creation and your reaction to it. What connects them is how you dream the event. Now label the center column "My Dream" or "My Story."

If something makes you angry, depressed, hurt, sad, jealous, frustrated, scared, annoyed, or afraid, write that emotional reaction in the "My Reaction" column. Now put the event that "caused" the reaction in the "Event" column. Maybe someone was late to meet you, a pet died, you dented a fender, lost a love, or your child disobeyed *and* spilled the milk again. Perhaps you read about a war or natural disaster, lost a job or were ignored for a promotion, felt disrespected by a co-worker, or suffered another paper cut.

Use your chart to demonstrate to yourself that your emotional reactions to the events in your life result from how you dream them, *not* from the events themselves. As the curious programmer, see if you can find the old programs in your dream that create any reaction you do not want. If you change any story in that program, it has to change the reaction. Same event, new reaction. It may take some practice, and it won't always happen in the heat of the moment, but I guarantee that if you work with this, you can change your programming, your dream, and your reactions to creation.

The fears, opinions, and beliefs programmed into your mind are mostly lies that you were required to believe as a child.

It is important to note that Creation itself has no emotional content. The universe itself does not know good and bad, right and wrong, or beautiful and ugly. All judgment, categorizing, and the resulting emotional content is added by the human mind. What we add is different for each individual, each religion, each gender, and each culture or nationality. It is all a dream.

Here is an example: Imagine you are driving on the freeway, and an aggressive driver cuts in front of you, narrowly missing your car. Perhaps you react with fear and anger, you yell at him, flash your lights, maybe even tailgate him to teach him a lesson. Did the event cause your reaction? What stories are you telling yourself about this event? How are you dreaming it? "Crazy damn people, somebody should get them off the road. I could have been killed! Where are the cops when you need them?" If you decide that you would prefer to not react with fear and anger, you can change the story. Since you know you are dreaming, pick a story that makes you feel good.

How about dreaming that the driver is a man rushing his wife to the hospital? She is laying in the back seat, about to have a baby. He is desperate. He cuts you off. Same event, new story, new reaction: "Wow, be careful, and good luck! I will get out of your way. God bless the mom and baby!" Do you see that your reactions come from your dreaming mind, from the habits and programming from the past—*not* the event? And do you see that you have the power to reprogram your mind and give yourself choices about your emotional reactions? And if you have a choice, won't you choose to be happy and at peace with the world?

> -§-
> Find the glitches that cause you to suffer, and rewrite a program that makes you happy.
> -§-

Now try the process I described to explore your emotional reactions to wars, teenagers, inconsiderate neighbors, an enemy, terrorists, a boss, your mate or lover, the weather, abortion, the death penalty, global warming, species extinction, or anyone or anything that upsets you in any way. Especially, use this process with yourself. Clear the old programming that causes you to be upset or angry with yourself. Explore how you are distorting yourself, and how your distortions and stories make you feel. You *can* free yourself from your old dream of yourself, and all of creation. It is worth the effort.

The Gift of Freedom

There is an exciting freedom available to you in your new dream. You will dream acceptance of what is, the way it is, without resistance, anger, hurt, or fear. You will be free to choose a new dream of acceptance and love for your body, mind, and spirit.

In this freedom is complete peace. Your inner voices will no longer make you wrong for how you act, talk, eat, dress, sing, dance, think, or feel. Nor will you make others wrong for their politics, habits, beliefs, or actions. You experience an inner peace that no person or event can take away from you.

You will know that everyone else is dreaming, and nothing they say or do has anything to do with you. If they are angry at you, judging you, or in awe of you, it will be clear to you that they are describing a virtual reality of you in their own mind. You will know not to believe them! You will know that they are dreaming just like you, and it is not personal. You are free to be you.

CHAPTER THREE

In your new dream the acceptance you feel for yourself extends to every person, creature, politician, war, natural disaster, love lost and love found, and all of Creation. You see and know the perfection.

In this clarity and freedom a great love for life radiates out from you, touching all of Creation. Your life becomes effortless, and the abundance of Life is offered to you in response to your love. Your heart is always open to give and to receive.

A Plan For Peace

As this understanding spreads throughout the evolving human consciousness, more and more people are taking responsibility for their personal dream, and the distortions that create it. In time, perennial enemies will awaken from their nightmares to discover that the reason they perceive their neighbors as an enemy is because they are distorting them with old beliefs programmed into their minds by someone else.

-§-
Everyone else is dreaming, and nothing they say or do has anything to do with you.
-§-

Imagine what will happen in this world when the Israelis and the Palestinians, the Irish Protestants and Catholics, the Hutus and Tutsis, the factions of Iraq, and fundamentalists of all kinds, realize that the only reason they are in conflict is the result of how they are dreaming themselves and each other — and their dream is not real.

This is my peace plan for the world; for the Middle East, for the North, South, East and Westernmost parts of this Earth. This is my peace plan for couples in relationship, for parents with teenagers, for all races and religions, and for governments and their soldiers. And this is my plan for peace in the mind of each individual in the world: *Know you are dreaming.*

Know you are dreaming and change your dream. With a new dream, we create a new world.

Jeanne House & Dawson Church:

Signals of the Soul

The crash was heard twenty-three miles away. A small grey Honda sedan, traveling too fast on a slick express lane, and ignoring a Dangerous Curve sign, had nudged the guardrail. The driver lost control, and skidded across the slower lanes. A huge yellow double-length moving truck swerved to avoid the Honda and jackknifed into the oncoming lanes of traffic. As it flipped, it forced three other semi tractor-trailers traveling in the opposite direction out of their lanes. One flipped, taking out a whole line of cars. The other two collided, forming an impassable barrier. The air was filled with the sounds of smashing metal, squealing tires, and blaring horns. Before the carnage was over, forty-seven vehicles, from a giant refrigerated truck, to a classic Morgan sports car, had been wrecked in the pile-up. Frozen chickens, racks of luggage, boxes, and bags of groceries, littered all six lanes of the expressway. Some vehicles were flung as far as three hundred yards from the epicenter of the crash, spilling their human cargo as they pivoted. It was the worst automotive disaster the city had ever experienced.

After the last crash died away, an eerie silence descended over the expressway. The dust settled, and dazed survivors began to stag-

Jeanne House, M.A., has headed up the sales and marketing efforts of two book distributors, Summit Beacon International and Associated Publishing Group, as well as holding prior positions with NBC-TV and Miami University. She has a postgraduate degree in Consciousness Studies, and is completing a second M.A. in Transformational Psychology. She has a passion for collaborating with people who are working on the evolution of planetary consciousness, and is currently the Marketing and Sales Director at Elite Books.

Dawson Church, Ph.D., has edited or authored over 200 books. He is a co-founder of Aslan Publishing, a former CEO of Atrium Publisher's Group, and current publisher of Elite Books. During a long publishing career he has worked with many best selling authors, as well as developing the careers of unknowns. He is passionately committed to social causes, especially ending social injustice. He teaches publishing classes, and assists authors who are self-publishing through www.AuthorsPublishing.com.

ger from the wreckage. Bodies lay everywhere. A fuel tank exploded; several small fires began to fill the air with smoke.

In the distance the whine of ambulance siren came steadily closer. Police cars rushed to the site of the accident, first one, then three, then ten. A huge emergency crew descended upon the scene. The Dangerous Curve sign stood high above the wreckage, a mute testimony to the truth of its message, futilely warning the luckless bodies below, and mocking the survivors.

-§-
When you listen to the signals of your soul, the entire shape of your life can shift in a single moment.
-§-

As the small army of medics, firefighters, and emergency personnel converged on the scene, a very strange thing happened. They raced past the burning wreckage of the vehicles, and the knots of puzzled survivors. Sirens wailing, they clustered around the danger sign. Policemen, firefighters and medics swarmed up the pole, focusing all their attention on the warning signal. The survivors, battered and bleeding, numbly watched the whole armada of assistance drive by, ignoring their needs, and congregate around the signal.

Does this seem too absurd a picture to be worth entertaining? It's no joke, for millions of people do this same thing, every day, but in their internal worlds. You have probably done something like this in the last few days, and if you don't catch yourself, you might well consign yourself to the misery of inner pileups for years to come.

All the distressing problems in your life are no more than signals. Any and all time you spend fussing with them is wasted. It's simply a distraction from where the signal is directing you: to listen to the voice of your own soul. When you take your attention off the wrecks, and listen to the signals of your soul, acting from the wisdom deep within you, the entire shape of your life can shift in a single moment. But while your attention is entangled in these pileups, while your emotions are engaged in the disharmonies around you, you are simply not available to the vital work that your soul longs to do through you.

It means disengaging from the wreckage, and tuning in to the subtle signals of heart and soul instead. It means noticing where you are directing your energy, and making a conscious choice to send it in a direction that will bless the world, rather than contributing to the chaos of the world.

Each of us has fears, distortions, and inbred patterns vibrating full force. When we come together with other people and their vibrating patterns, our patterns interact with theirs, like one ripple pattern in a pond interacting with another to create a third set of waves. The energy of these interactions can interfere with the clear mirror we require in order to produce good decisions and right actions. Only if we choose to see past these patterns, and recognize that they are not real, do not require our attention, are not worthy of our concern, and are not causes for action, can we keep our creative field clear. We recognize that they are simply signals. Their energy motivates us to return to our center.

So treat those feelings of anxiety, conflict, need, desperation, fear, and lack, simply as *signals*. They are *not real*. They are simply flags going up and saying, "Hey! It is time to come back to source." By treating the car wrecks of our lives as flags, not as problems we need to fix, we can make true creative use even of distortions and upsets. This way, even our seeming tragedies bring us right back to our inner source—and from that place everything we need is supplied.

This doesn't mean denying our patterns or problems. The more aware we are, the more we benefit from them, because we receive a stronger signal. Being aware of our destructive patterns, and then withdrawing our energies from them, coming instead into congruence with the radiance of our own soul, we will find that 99% of our worries are groundless, and 99% of our problems work themselves out effortlessly. If we experience any feeling of effort or struggle, we simply note it as a sign that we have moved out of our center.

-§-
Tragedies bring us right back to our inner source—and from that place everything we need is supplied.
-§-

If we find ourselves in apparent conflict with someone, the solution is to always come back to center. Don't dwell in the place of struggle. Conflicts may seem real, powerful, even life-threatening—yet most of them are based simply on fantasies and hallucinations, with no genuine power whatsoever. We can treat them purely as signals and signposts to remind us to come back to center.

Struggles command our attention; they are trying to hook us into old ways of being that we are familiar with, even though that old consciousness may have terrible results. That is why we feel so much distress. Yet the anguish of the tragic pileups in our lives is simply a device used by a compassionate universe to point our attention back toward the calm, abundant, fully empowered heart of love. Within each of us there is a place of security, of harmony, of joy, of purpose, of vitality, of passion, and of engagement. Deep down in our secret convictions we know that this place exists. We intuitively and absolutely know that this place is possible. It resides in our hearts.

Imagine fully embracing that pure joy within—hour by hour, minute by minute, second by second. We need to learn to make this feeling our *default setting.* Many of us are addicted to stress. We seem to think that we are not accomplishing anything of value if we are not feeling the rush of the hours, the strain of the activities. We associate the stressful state with accomplishment, and with getting things done. Organically, our nervous and hormonal systems are so used to *stress consciousness,* and our bodies to being embedded in the neurochemistry of that state, that this has become our default setting. As a culture, we are unfamiliar with the notion that we can manifest simply by *being and flowing.* Most of us have no experience to use as a basis for believing that hands-off, stress-free being, and in-the-moment, flowing consciousness can be more creative than the most frantic of driven, Type A states of being.

-§-

99% of our worries are groundless, and 99% of our problems work themselves out effortlessly.

-§-

By refocusing ourselves into flow, we are cultivating both a *consciousness* and a *practice.* The practice springs forth from the consciousness. Coming to consciousness allows us break the stress cycle. We need to do this many times each day in order to repattern ourselves; there is a seductive power of stress. We have patterns of pressure that are familiar to us. We live in them easily. It is hard for us to pull loose from these patterns.

The secret is this: Don't even try. A few simple exercises can bring us back to harmony:

1. Find a place of flow and harmony within.

2. Set the intention to live our day from the highest place of purpose.

3. Notice the direction that possesses the most efficient channel for forward movement. Don't charge ahead with our plans until we do.

4. Flow with the creative energy, easily and effortlessly. As you examine your projects, notice items that feel blocked. Bless them with grace — and put them on hold.

5. Set aside the blocked items on your list and go back to them at another time, if they feel unblocked then. Let go of work places and projects that are stuck, and easily flow through your work and day.

6. Look at your To Do list and notice which words, people, and projects flash and sparkle in your eyes. Put your maximum energy there. Once that project is complete, repeat the process. Find the next sparkling, joyous task. One task will lead into the next, eventually forming an organic whole.

7. Check areas of impeded energy flow within your body. Notice where you feel them, and then release them. Check in scores of times a day, even hundreds of times per day, and notice where your body is tense—then release that tension. If you are sitting, get up and walk around in order to break the pattern of stuck energy.

8. Raise your metabolic rate. Take five minutes every hour for vigorous physical activity. Exercise is useful to keep our body in a heightened state of metabolic function: walking, jumping jacks, or anything that will shift you into the present. You may not think you have time; yet it is a fact that you will accomplish far more in fifty-five minutes of activity that follows five minutes of exercise than you will accomplish in sixty sedentary minutes.

9. Say a prayer. Formulate whatever words have impact upon your particular mind. It might be one of these:

I go through my day easily and effortlessly.

I have no struggle, no worry, no anguish.

I easily inhabit the world of time without pressure; I have all the time I need.

There is always time to do the things that need to be done.

My work is filled with joy and flow.

10. Practice, practice, practice.

We pay a great deal of money to those who peer into the future, whether they're economic forecasters, or gypsy fortune tellers. Yet it is a great deal more demanding to see the *present* than it is to see the *future*. Slowing down allows you to see what is right in front of you. While we might have questions about the big picture, we don't need to put in a great deal of energy trying to figure the future out. Our great task is to handle the micro level of living well in each moment—and surrender the macro level to a higher will.

-§-

Conflicts may seem real, powerful, even life-threatening—yet most of them are based simply on fantasies and hallucinations, with no genuine power whatsoever.

-§-

If we allow ourselves to get carried along with the universal current of creation, we will contribute to the making of a universal masterpiece, a tapestry of spiritual and physical beauty. Your life and all of your experiences are mere tests of the strength of the love within you. Love and sacredness is the nature of your soul. When many souls flow in the stream of love, they weave a tapestry full of artistry, joy and abundance in the world.

CHAPTER FOUR

If we view our work as simply a mechanism for our souls to express, and a ministry of love and wisdom, we can experience work as a sacred opportunity to express our highest gifts of ingenuity, power, passion, and joy. We can work with a sense of celebration every day. Our work becomes a celebratory spiritual assignment, a channel to express the divine. Our aim is to make our outer world completely congruent with our soul's inner world. Such a life is a walking prayer. By allowing love to flow through us unimpeded, we live love. Living in love is not a romantic escape, but a daily heart-congruence with life.

-§-
Stress has become
our default setting.
-§-

A sure way to live in love is to give thanks. We can each give thanks at any time. We can give thanks especially during crises. The ray of thankfulness connects us immediately back to our souls, and ultimately to the heart of love. When we are faced with challenging situations, we can always give thanks that we are right where we are. Thankfulness is the alchemical mystery that transforms the dross of life into the gold of love.

This may seem simple, even elementary, yet it is a practice that few people have mastered. There is no one thing more effective in pulling us straight back into the heart of love than giving thanks. We can monitor our consciousness daily, and reflect on whether we are in a state of thankfulness or not. Even if we feel anger, stress, or any other form of discomfort; if we give thanks, everything changes. This does not mean that everything happening around us is okay. It simply means that we choose to bless ourselves with the response most likely to turn the whole situation into a blessing. Even if the people around us are locked in illusion, by giving thanks to the heart of love, suddenly we are in that heart, no matter how bad the external circumstance.

Only love is real, only love endures. In a million years from now, when everything we know will have vanished, love will still be there. So to the extent that our being is drawn into, and participates in love, we will be there. We need to seek the heart of love in each other and see everyone through the eyes of love, even if they are in distress. Living in love is about being in love with life and its source. Remember that all struggle and stress are merely *signals* guiding us from the periphery of life, back to center.

A signal is just a signal.

A signal is not a place for us to reside in. So if our plans don't work out, just sit in love, without feeling that we have to leave love and go into that struggle. Because the moment we leave Love, we have stepped out of the solace, we have stepped out of encompass-ment, we have stepped out of the embrace of being conscious in the moment. Our difficult experiences teach us that we are meant to live in the heart of love.

We can train ourselves to look at all areas through the eyes of love, and not to tie into the distress of our world. Merely send bless-ings to our conflicts, consciously living from a place of serenity, will allow us to become rooted into the only thing that endures, which is love.

Instead of focusing on our inner car wrecks, we can choose to enter the stream of love. We can bounce joyfully on the grid of energy that love provides us. We can merge with the glistening clear light that billows from heaven, rather than getting stuck in the muck of our consciousness. All streams of love are tethered to the heart of God; as our identity shifts to love, it escapes the limits of time and space and shifts into the bliss, grace, beauty and radiance of the infinite heart. It endures, even when the worlds of anger, fear, doubt, envy, and greed dissolve, taking with them all consciousness that has rooted itself there.

Your mind may tell you many lies; you may have many false assumptions about yourself and the world embedded in your subcon-scious. Your mind may have been conditioned from an early age with thousands of messages of being worthless, of being small, of being weak, of being unable, of the world being much larger than you.

This may have been true when you were two years old. But it is not true now. You are much larger than you think. You not only have a grown and capable physical body; you have subtle bodies, and those subtle bodies are capable of accessing all of history and all of the intelligence in the cosmos.

One of the biggest lies that your mind may tell you is that you are tiny and ineffective and cannot change the world. *You are changing the world every day.* You are changing the world with every thought you harbor. You are changing the world with every word you speak. You are changing the world by whether you allow your thoughts to dwell on negativity, stress, strife, problems, challenges—all the worst of what's around you, the worst of yourself and the worst of others—or whether your mind is a crystal gem through which the light of heaven may shine.

-§-

It is a great deal more demanding to see the *present* than it is to see the *future.*

-§-

You may, gently and lovingly, each day, lead your mind back to the inner truth of your heart. Your heart is a repository of light and joy, power and peace, passion and compassion. From this

infinite space, you can think new thoughts, enact new actions, and speak new words. At each moment, you can choose to center yourself in that great strong magnificent Truth of you, rather than all the small truths.

The small truth may be that you are sick today, or have PMS, or a cold, or feel feeble and weak. The Great Truth is that you are infinitely capable of doing good, thinking and saying kind words, and acting in loving and gentle ways. Truth with a small "t" may be that you live in a Third World slum on two dollars a day. Small truth may be that you are a billionaire, living in a compound with security guards inaccessible to frank interactions with your fellow human beings.

Yet each of those people—and everyone in between them—is capable of coming from that heart center, and of radiating universal love, and the universal joy of that soul that lives within them.

Truth with a small "t" might mean that you have a difficult job, a difficult child, a difficult spouse, or parent. Truth with a large "T" is that you are enormously larger than all of these limitations that you see yourself being bound by. Big Truth, expressed in even the smallest of actions, finds a way to create Big Results in your life. The Great Lie is that you don't have the power or the money or the health or the creativity or the imagination or age or the youth or the beauty or the strength or the wisdom to do the work of the universe.

-§-
You are changing
the world with every
thought you harbor.
-§-

The Great Truth is that *you do.*

As you gently but firmly detach your attention from the signals of strife and conflict in your own mind and in the world, and place your attention instead on listening to the signals of the soul, you will find that Great Truth waiting for you. As you act on it just once, you will become better and better at discerning—and expressing—your soul signals.

At first, you may only hear the most obvious and loud signals. With practice and discernment, you will begin to hear the subtlest whispers of the soul. The still, small voice within will nudge you quietly and often. Imagine a world where everyone is as adept to listening to—and speaking from—their soul, as they now are at listening to and speaking from their small self, the limiting self. Heaven is that close.

Transformation is just one thought away. Transformation is the next thought you have…and the next thought…and the next thought…and the next thought. Join now with all other forms of life on Earth to transform the world one moment, one thought, one kind word, one magnanimous deed, at a time. Then you will find that, without struggle, enormous global change follows!

JODI SEROTA:

The Frequency Of Love

In the realm of spiritual understanding and the vast field of personal growth and transformation, ancient forms help us bridge the internal with the external worlds. These empowering, primordial patterns inherent in nature and intrinsic to our consciousness can catalyze awareness of what we are as love. Love is more than just a feeling. Love is an actual frequency resonance, an all-inclusive frequency that binds all of us to ourselves, to each other, to God, and to everything that exists. Love has no conditions and brings us into our unified consciousness.

The labyrinth has been used around the world for many centuries as a tool for personal growth and spiritual understanding. Used in prayer, ritual and initiation, this ancient mystical tool can assist us in raising our consciousness and experiencing deep levels of healing. As both a powerful metaphor for our lives, and as an actual experience when we walk a labyrinth, this beautiful symbol allows us to embody a fuller sense of our innate wholeness and come home to what we truly are as love.

Often, when people see a labyrinth for the first time, they immediately think of it as a maze. But a labyrinth is very different from a maze. A labyrinth is unicursal; it offers one route to the center and back out again. There are no blocked areas or dead-ends. A maze requires the use of logic to figure out and solve the puzzle in order to get through the pattern. The design of a labyrinth is such that, at

Jodi Serota is a life-changing metaphysical educator, channel, vibrational healer, and professional artist. Her in-depth intuitive abilities and her remarkable sound healing powers are used to create initiations and activations which instantly make major shifts in consciousness and healing. She holds individual sessions, teaches classes and creates multimedia concerts and events for personal growth, transformation consciousness-raising, and the creative process. She is also the founder of META Center New York—META is an acronym for Multidimensional Education and Transformational Arts. Information about her work can be found at www.jodiserota.com.

any given point on the path, the center is visible. Having this visual reference point of the center allows us to be gently led through the labyrinth's circuitry to the center. The center of the labyrinth—often a flower with six-petals—automatically draws us to it. The center is the place where we know ourselves in relation to the greater whole and understand that our true nature is divine love.

Arriving at the center of the labyrinth symbolizes finding the "center" of our being where we are one with God and all of existence. Similarly, in our walk through the twists and turns of life, no matter where we are, we always have the option to come back to our center and return to love. Having a sense of our center, and a direct experience of the self as love, is a vital reference point. As in the labyrinth, no matter where we are on the path we can always find our center because there are no walls. Where we get lost is in our perceptions—which are veils that may feel like walls until the light of love reveals the truth.

Everything that exists vibrates as sound, color, and light. In my work, I use the audible vibration of sound, the visual vibration of color, and electromagnetic vibration of all of it as light. Love is unique in itself as a frequency—absolute, unwavering, all-embracing. It resonates wholeness and therefore we experience ourselves as divine truth.

During a labyrinth walk, the left and right hemispheres of the brain are balanced, leading to a perfect state for accessing intuition and creativity. Walking into the labyrinth is a going inward that stimulates and activates the right side of the brain. This is generally thought of as the more feminine, intuitive side of our being. The walk out is a carrying forward into life of the jewels of intuitive knowing that come from the feminine, with an intention to act on what we have discovered. This engages the masculine aspect of our essential nature. The walk is facilitated by a perfect combination of breath and movement. Walking the labyrinth also gives access to the universal energy field of the artistic pattern expressed through the labyrinth's sacred geometry.

-§-

Where we get lost is in our perceptions— which are veils that may feel like walls until the light of love reveals the truth.

-§-

Everything is related to everything and the geometry of a spiral such as the labyrinth makes this both visually and kinesthetically clear. As you walk a labyrinth, the spiral pattern is soothing because it is familiar to our consciousness all the way down to a cellular level. If you look at a fingerprint, you will see a spiral formation; likewise, the colon, the brain, and the inner ear. The spiraling form of the DNA double helix is in each and every one of our cells. Throughout nature, for example, in a nautilus shell or a pinecone, a specific universal proportion, known as the golden mean or Fibonacci spiral, is expressed.

In my work as a metaphysician and vibrational healer, I use a labyrinth that is similar in design to the one at the Chartres Cathedral in France. Built around 1,200 A.D., the Chartres labyrinth is laid directly into the floor of the cathedral. The lore around this ancient cathedral holds that the labyrinth was laid into the floor with such precise proportions that if the entire cathedral were folded in on itself, the flower pattern at the top of the cathedral would line up exactly with the one in the floor. From a metaphysical perspective, this architectural feat can be seen as an expression of our relationship with God; "as above, so below." What we are at the very core is nothing less than pure divine love.

-§-

What we are at the very core is nothing less than pure divine love.

-§-

The Chartres labyrinth has eleven circuits. Eleven is considered a master number in numerology. Walking the labyrinth through eleven circuits is a ritual for attaining mastery. My labyrinth is painted on a thirty-six-foot diameter canvas. When I had it made, I specifically chose the Chartres pattern and asked the artist to make it with twelve sides, in the geometric form called a dodecagon. This brings in another aspect from sacred geometry. The number twelve represents wholeness, and the twelve-sided dodecagon helps us gain a sense of ourselves as many sided, and grow in the feeling that we are complete.

The symbolic importance of the number twelve as an expression of completeness can be seen in the many ways twelves appear. For instance: we have twelve strands of DNA, twelve months in a year, twelve zodiac signs, and twelve tribes of Israel. Interesting to note, the number thirteen is considered representative of the Christ Consciousness, or the energy of pure love: twelve apostles plus the Christed one equals a total of thirteen.

When we walk the labyrinth, we experience the eleven circuits. Those, plus the center, equals twelve. When we add ourselves to the equation, it equals thirteen, bringing us into resonance with wholeness and divine love. This refined unifying resonance is available to all who intentionally tune into it. The labyrinth—which often has a cross at the center—can facilitate a recognition and embodiment of what Christ the man stood for. From the spiritual rather than the religious perspective, Christ was a man who walked on the planet as ourselves, but who did so with a profound self-realization that allowed him to express qualities of God. This means that he was able to embody, emanate, and express divine action and unconditional love.

From a metaphysical perspective, the vibration of love dissolves anything with conditions. This dissolving of conditions allows us to embody wholeness. Often, what gets in the way of our direct experience of love and wholeness—which is always present in the core of us—are the illusory patterns that keep us feeling separate. These patterns are like dirt on a window, producing an obstructed view. This limits our ability to live freely and openly. We then get a signal from our core that the time is ripe for healing. To move in the direction of healing, we need to experience the pattern from all sides—dark and light, painful and joyous. Coming into full awareness of the pattern and truly grasping it—without denial—is an important part of the healing process. Like walking the full course of a labyrinth, it pulls us into the center of our being. Here, we reside and abide in the all-inclusive frequency of love which naturally and easily dissolves the pattern—often, for good.

-§-

It is only in our perception that we are broken, and yet that perception keeps us from seeing the center.

-§-

Sarah, a long-term client of mine, arrived for a session emotionally distraught and confused. She had recently left her boyfriend Ed, with whom she'd been living for eight years. Although she'd always assumed that she and Ed would eventually get married, over time, she lost faith in that dream. While attending a business conference, she was introduced to George and they instantly shared a lively rapport. George quietly pursued her over a number of weeks, and his flirtatious attention stirred up feelings in Sarah. She had been frustrated about not having a full marriage commitment from Ed, and began to think that George might be a better match for her. Thinking the new relationship would fulfill certain needs that were not addressed in the relationship with Ed, she moved out of their downtown apartment and took a place of her own.

But when it became obvious that George was also unwilling to fully commit to a relationship, Sarah could not let go. She had a deep fear of abandonment and loss. Despite having realized that the relationship with George was causing more confusion in her life than ease, she refused to release the attachment and held on to him emotionally. She continued to stand by George, out of a fear of loss, at great expense to her heart. George took advantage of her neediness and spent time with Sarah when it suited him. After we did some deep introspective work to get to the root of her frustration and pain, Sarah realized that her previous relationship had been far more fulfilling.

Moving into another relationship did not solve a more basic problem, and in fact, revealed the underlying pattern she had not seen before. In both situations, with Ed and George, Sarah wasn't totally satisfied. In both circumstances, she failed to address what was incomplete within herself, and instead looked externally to find the answer to the problem—in the man. Once she began to recognize her pattern and take responsibility for her part, she could celebrate having attracted the exact situations that would help her learn about herself. From that perspective, she was able to appreciate, value, and heal her original relationship. Eventually, she and Ed re-established their life together.

Only when Sarah understood the entire pattern was she able to move through it to the other side. The labyrinth of life took her through the twists and turns of the situation, drawing her toward her own center where she could finally release her misleading attachment. The desperate need to have someone outside herself to make her feel whole, lovable, and deserving no longer held her back from simply being love. Once having connected to the source of love inside her, she was able to make clear decisions that served her whole being. Whenever we come to the ultimate realization of an experience like this and finally understand a pattern of behavior, we are naturally prevented from repeating it.

Important lessons can be taken from the labyrinth whether we choose to walk it or simply contemplate the metaphor. Humanity has reached a point where we must move from survival to living. Experience is demanding that we cease identifying with illusions rather than the truth. To go on just functioning is no longer possible with all the rapid change in the world. We must live fully now. This is one of the requirements to move into new levels of consciousness—we must consistently be more present and begin to have full conscious compassion for ourselves, for each other, and for the greater whole. When we remember, or discover,

-§-

Rarely is the overt symptom what needs most to be addressed.

-§-

that we are whole and complete as opposed to broken and needing to be fixed, we begin to grow in new ways. A shift in perception is crucial, because it is only in our perception that we are broken, and yet that perception keeps us from seeing the center. Perceptual errors such as this put us in the maze of the mind. When we reconceive who we are and recognize the center of our being as love, everything changes.

We all want to heal the imbalances we see around us in the world. An imperative first step is that we look within and examine what needs to be refined in our own innate structure. Humans have a deep need for a sense of purpose or mission. We all feel the longing to feel connected, both within ourselves and to each other. The heartfelt concern

expressed by so many about healing our planet and all the inhabitants of the Earth evidence our true nature. It is part of our innate structure to have compassion for the greater whole. Instinctively, we know that we are all connected, even if our culture does not reflect that just yet. The term *healing* implies transmuting or changing anything that is in a state of dis-ease back into a state of at-easement. In other words, being brought back to the original pure intention—the divine configuration or blueprint—of the underlying structure of consciousness.

Without a personal experience of ourselves at this level, we have difficulty feeling completely connected to anything, either in the physical or the unseen realm. This need to feel connected at a basic level is what brings many people to healers for assistance. Rarely is the overt symptom what needs most to be addressed. Rather, people want to actually feel unity consciousness, which naturally leads to having a focus on what works for the well-being of the whole.

-§-
We as inhabitants of the planet have been, in a sense, existing by candlelight until recently; now we've hooked up to a grid that brings a huge wattage of energy that reveals everything we are.
-§-

Walking through our lives, as in the labyrinth, we sometimes feel like we're going around and around. At different points on the path, we feel like we're going further from the center, but actually we're closer. The twist and turns of our lives can make us feel that we have to stop, take inventory, and redirect ourselves to make sure we're going in the direction of choice. This is going on at a meta level right now. The human race is collectively stopping to take a look at where we are going.

From a metaphysical perspective, we are in a time right now on Earth, when a huge quickening of the frequency or intensity of the energy is occurring, accelerating everything and everyone. For individuals, this higher frequency is moving us from a more dense level of understanding to a higher level of knowing. As if we are living under a high voltage spotlight, this accelerated frequency is serving to illuminate all those aspects we have not wanted to face. It's as though we as inhabitants of the planet have been, in a sense, existing by candlelight until recently; now we've hooked up to a grid that brings a huge wattage of energy that reveals everything we are. This translates on a personal level in a fuller understanding of who we are, and in claiming our own personal truths.

We all want to be recognized, to know who we really are. However, if an exposure to truth happens too quickly, we can feel torn open, vulnerable, and exposed, rather than simply recognized. We need time to integrate changes. We need to experience a transmutation process, whereas in the past we dealt with transformation. An ocean wave may knock you over, but you have time to get your feet back on the ground before there's another wave. When another wave comes, you're prepared for it—that's transformation. What's happening with our current level of rapid acceleration is more difficult. It's as if the waves are coming too close together for us to really feel where we stand.

Imagine now that the waves are pure light, beaming down, with no space at all between them. This luminous vibration activates our own light within, to produce enlightenment. The universe is spotlighting our own innate brilliance, and full radiance of being. Being in the spotlight allows us to more completely recognize ourselves. This results in a greater remembrance and embodiment of our wholeness and self-worth.

Clearing our inner conflicts, and embodying personal wholeness and truth, creates a strong, stable foundation. By first addressing the origins of our own personal physical ailments, emotional pain, mental confusion and spiritual traumas, we can have a deep, long-term impact on the world.

Also, by being illuminated in this way, we get to see what part of us we've kept in the dark—even to ourselves. As our dark side is revealed in the light of new awareness, we begin to recognize which of our perceptions are true and which are false. We are all on this planet to re-member or re-group all the parts of ourselves that have disconnected or detached because of disappointing or painful circumstances. We need to re-examine what is important to us in order to know our internal desires, so that we can reinstate our own inward connection. Our heartfelt enthusiasms—what we feel passionate about—are what direct us forward. When expressed, they give us a feeling of great pleasure, but we must stay present within in order to feel anything.

-§-

If an exposure to truth happens too quickly, we can feel torn open, vulnerable and exposed, rather than simply recognized.

-§-

John, a tall, intelligent, well-built, young man, walked into my office looking pale and panicked. Based on his stature, John seemed quite capable of handling just about anything. But just below the surface, I could sense that he was petrified. His boss, thinking him the perfect candidate for a job, requested that he give a verbal presentation to the entire company. It was a compliment to be selected, but he had an overwhelming phobia of public speaking and had no idea why. From the moment his boss made the request, an ongoing sense of doom made him feel sick to his stomach.

We began to do healing work by looking back into his history to see the origin of this fear. John had grown up in an erratic and dangerous household and had to always be on guard. He experienced physical, emotional, and sexual abuse throughout childhood, and, as a result, became very intuitive, always needing to know what to look out for to protect himself. His abuser often told him to stay quiet, directing him not to speak, and threatened further abuse if John told anyone what had happened. To manage the continuous fear and devastation he lived in for years, he moved aside from himself in order to not be fully present to feel the pain of what was happening.

When fear takes hold of us, we often use the phrase, "I'm beside myself." At the level of the energetic body, this is quite literal. The energetic body actually moves to the side when we are not able to trust that we are safe in a situation. This is what happened with John. He continued in survival mode from that point on, always on guard. Having spent most of his life as an observer rather than a participant, he continued to feel numb.

So many of us have been taught about love by parents, caretakers, and teachers who themselves experienced only conditional love. The impression of love was passed on as a façade of the true vibration and experience of real love. Conditions create an illusion of love. We have not been taught the authenticity of pure love and genuine compassion. Most of us have no reliable reference point for truly loving or being loved.

-§-

By first addressing the origins of our own personal physical ailments, emotional pain, mental confusion, and spiritual traumas, we can have a deep, long-term impact on the world.

-§-

When we rid ourselves of our internal conflicts, or at least lower the volume on them, we can begin to understand ourselves as part of a more expansive orchestration known as God. Then we can begin to truly vibrate that truth through our consciousness, connecting with that vibration in everything, even during the bleakest of times. When New York was attacked on September 11, 2001, the response by The Dalai Lama exemplified the purest knowing of the meaning of love in its most unconditional form. His Holiness issued a statement that day which said:

"If we could love even those who have attacked us, and seek to understand why have they done so, what then would be our response? Yet if we meet negativity with negativity, rage with rage, attack with attack, what then will be the outcome? Today the human soul asks the question: What can I do to preserve the beauty and the wonder of our world and to eliminate the anger and hatred—and the disparity that inevitably causes it—in that part of the world which I touch? If you wish to experience peace, provide peace for another. If you wish to know that you are safe, cause [others] to know that they are safe. If you wish to better understand seemingly incomprehensible things, help another to better understand. If you wish to heal your own sadness or anger, seek to heal the sadness or anger of another. Those others are waiting for you now. They are looking to you for guidance, for help, for courage, for strength, for understanding, and for assurance at this hour. Most of all, they are looking to you for love. My religion is very simple. My religion is kindness."

It's helpful to see ourselves as beacons of light assisting each other in co-creation. As we each allow ourselves to be individual lighthouses — expanding outwardly and emanating from within — we merge together and form an even greater illumination. We must, in a sense, stay plugged into ourselves and shine our full God-love presence outward, and then we can collectively radiate the absolute consciousness of love. Only then, will we begin to collectively pulsate as one heart beating as the life force of love, truly connected, as shining gems with all our facets gleaming outwardly in a unified expression of harmony, tranquility, joy, and peace. We are love, and that's the all-inclusive frequency that connects us all.

-§-

Most of us have no reliable reference point for truly loving or being loved.

-§-

Fred Luskin:

Escaping Your Tragic Stories

W hen I began my work in forgiveness research at Stanford University, I had a very hard time getting anybody interested. We couldn't even get the local newspaper, the *Palo Alto Weekly*, to write a story about what we were doing. We approached the editor and he wasn't interested. So we went to the assistant editor, and then the assistant to the assistant editor. No one was interested. They eventually tossed us off to a new intern and said, "How would you like to write this story on forgiveness?" When she came to us, she had a blank look on her face as if to say, *Why study forgiveness?* Imagine then, what a thrill it was to receive a phone call from the CNN television network not long ago, asking me to talk about forgiveness—for a full two minutes!

For the most part, the message on CNN, twenty-four-seven, is all about the horror of "we don't give a damn about each other." That's what the news is: a chronicle of the enormous violence, hostility, lack of care that this world offers too many people. There is violence everywhere. It's not a quality that humans invented; it is part of nature. We see this expressed in Hinduism as Brahman, Vishnu, and Shiva—the Creator, the Sustainer, and the Destroyer. These are endless cycles. But our bodies do have immune systems; they can adapt. We have learned the same thing in our research at the Stanford Forgiveness Project: forgiveness can be learned.

Frederic Luskin, Ph.D., is the co-founder and director of the Stanford University Forgiveness Project. He has a doctorate in counseling psychology, and is a clinical science research associate at Stanford University School of Medicine. He is the author of *Forgive for Good* (HarperSanFrancisco, 2002), and co-author of *Stress Free for Good* (HarperSanFrancisco, 2005). His research shows that forgiveness is a learned skill. He works with many groups in conflict, such as those in Northern Ireland. He has also worked with individuals struggling with divorce, abuse, and the murder of loved ones. He travels and speaks widely about this work.

Prior to the current surge of interest in scientific research on the subject, the importance of practicing forgiveness was extolled in both religious and psychological traditions. Our research has now confirmed the virtues of forgiveness in the promotion of psychological and physical health, as well as in improving relationships. Forgiveness has been shown to reduce anger, hurt, depression, and stress—while leading to greater feelings of optimism, hope, compassion, and even self-confidence. But most important—and this is the crucial message coming out of our research—people can be taught to forgive, just as they can be taught to play the piano.

The bottom line in the work I've done—and we have eight research projects that prove this now—is that forgiveness works. We've been able to prove two things: one, forgiveness is good for your physical and emotional health, and, two, it can be taught and practiced, and learned. My book, *Forgive for Good*, spells out specifically how to forgive.

There is something quite profound to be learned about forgiveness in the message of Jesus's life. On Palm Sunday, Jesus rode into Jereusalum and was well received. Then, within a week, he'd been killed. The enormity of that challenge is striking to me, especially when I see the tremendous difficulty everybody I know has handling their minor challenges. I had a pulled muscle in my leg not long ago, and that alone was enough to get me cursing. Look how upset people get while driving when the traffic stinks. I'm not using this example to make any of us feel bad, because we're not supposed to be Jesus. But his message—and his example—is to handle whatever is thrown at us with grace and dignity. No matter what the provocation—and crucifixion seems like a rather intense provocation—handle it with grace and dignity and kindness.

-§-
People can be taught to forgive, just as they can be taught to play the piano.
-§-

This is a stiff challenge. I can get over a pulled muscle, but I don't think many of us get over crucifixion. The reason that Jesus's message has resonated for so long is that Jesus responded to the worst that people could throw at him without expressing hate. Our challenge is to respond to whatever people throw at us. The message is clear: whatever is thrown at you, handle it with grace.

Not having the ability to do that is what got me into the forgiveness project in the first place. Many years ago, I suffered incredibly at being rejected and abandoned by a very close friend. What he did was not the impetus, however; how badly I handled the situation was. He did what people commonly do, and I reacted the way people commonly react—terribly. I made everybody's life worse with my hysterical overreaction. My discomfort and my hostility in handling a normal life event started the whole Stanford University Forgiveness Project.

What I now understand about forgiveness is that it wipes away the reasons for us to be unkind. That is both the purpose and the goal of forgiveness, and why it is one of the cornerstone spiritual practices. Almost all of us use what has happened to us — whether getting stuck in traffic or having suffered abuse as a child — as an excuse to be less kind. Forgiveness plucks that excuse away and says, "Now, it's not that this or that happened, it's that you no longer have any crutch to hold onto for your unkindness." That's the purpose of forgiveness. It's not to reconcile with people who have hurt you, and it's not necessarily to heal physical wounds — although it will because forgiveness has a healing quality as well. But I believe its purpose is to nourish the whole. And it nourishes the whole both by example and by reducing our readily available excuses for unkindness.

-§-
Forgiveness wipes away the reasons for us to be unkind.
-§-

When I discovered that forgiveness could dampen and tame my hysterical overreaction, I began to look more objectively at the world. I saw that people act out in selfish, unkind, and dishonest ways and that sometimes I'm the basis. How to deal with that? We always have a whole range of options. For myself, I found that the difference with one of those options — forgiveness — reduced my distress. And, it offered a chance to reclaim the relationship. Not everyone needs to become as miserable as I did with what I call my "Grinch heart" before they start to make changes. Those with a better-functioning heart feel compelled to offer kindness without the motivation of pain.

An objective world, separate from how we perceive it, does not exist. Therefore, if we perceive the world with more kindness, there is more kindness in the world. This is very hard to apply in social dynamics, especially when there is hostility and violence and threat. This is the situation we see in so many areas of the world. Finding ways to transcend that is a huge challenge to human beings because all the social support in most groups is aimed at finding an enemy.

Let me give an example from our work with people in Northern Ireland. We were working with people who had members of their immediate families murdered. We were working with people on both sides of the conflict. My partner on the project was a Presbyterian minister with many contacts in Northern Ireland. One afternoon, he drew a square on the board, and put the word *murder* in the square. Pointing out from the square he drew two arrows — one pointing to the word *community* and one pointing to the word *individual*. What makes the challenge of forgiveness so gruesome, he explained, is that if a person forgives or releases resentment toward the murderer, their own community sees them as a traitor. In situations where there is ongoing violence, as in Northern Ireland, there is a very powerful tension between individual healing and the group energy that collects around having an enemy.

The central tension lies in being aligned, with your group, against someone who harms you as an individual. If you release that burden through forgiveness, allowing yourself to be less grievously wounded, you are violating the shared alliance of the group. To stop being an angry person, or stop hating, means violating the norms of the group and perhaps of your family of origin. To become kind and offer forgiveness violates the norms of the bigger culture. If you become more generous of spirit, you risk losing the relationships that formed who you think you are. This constant tension—and the enormous support for unkindness and hatred that is provided at the tribal level—is a huge hurdle to forgiveness.

This is an entirely frontier area. The solution—learning how to provide some modest kindness in response to unkindness—is what we are attempting to forge in the junkyard of human emotion. We take people who have been grievously wounded and see in what ways can they accept a new model, or another way of handling the pain. Of course, we have to work at the political level as we did in the Northern Ireland. Without some kind of established political communication—a Peace Process—it is very hard for most people to even think about relinquishing their defensiveness because the defensiveness is warranted. People on the other side do indeed want to kill them. That is a very tough place, much different than an individual who asks, "Can I get over the loss of my son?" You may be able to get over a personal tragedy that happened in the past; it's much more difficult when the environment requires that you stay on guard.

-§-
In each moment, we can choose not to say an unkind thing. You can choose to stop.
-§-

The freeways in the San Francisco Bay Area where I live and work can be very crowded. If you're in a hurry, you're not going to have a good time on the highway. You can be stuck behind four thousand other people all trying to get to work at the same time. That's your forgiveness moment.

Do you come into the office and give everyone around you a hard time because you had a difficult commute? How much of your discomfort do you dump on others, and what excuses do you use for dumping it? You might say, "Of course I'm in a bad mood. I was stuck in traffic!" So now you make the people around you suffer because you were stuck in traffic. Perhaps you were abused as a child. The reason you have for passing along your suffering doesn't matter. What matters is whether or not you continue the chain by inflicting unkindness on other people. Forgiveness takes away your excuses for inflicting unkindness. It has you say, "Things happen to me, many of which hurt, many of which I wish hadn't happened. But I'm not going to hold them and use them as excuses for unkind behavior, for even a moment." We may not know how to live our entire lives, but in each moment, we can choose not to say an unkind thing. You can choose to stop. You can choose to offer patience.

-§-
How much of your discomfort do you dump on others, and what excuses do you use for dumping it?
-§-

Those moments won't come if you've given yourself permission to be a victim; a victim of anyone or anything. Victimhood gives you an excuse not to forgive, and to pass the violence along to those you interact with.

You can get into work and notice, "It's a beautiful day!" Then you've spared the world some unkindness. You haven't passed on the negative experience you had being stuck in traffic. The victim mentality gives us permission to pass it on. It's a dangerous strategy for ourselves, and for the long-term health of our planet.

This is why the planet is in the terrible state that it's in. Everybody's been hurt. Every country has somebody to hate. Every organization has some enemy. Every person has some story of victimhood to share. Everywhere there are reasons not to open our hearts.

We may not be able to heal the planet at one stroke. But we can at least make a little difference to the two or three people closest to us. That moment only comes when you stop giving yourself the slack to take out your ill feelings on them, when you take responsibility for what comes out of your mouth.

What I can give as testimony from the work I've done, and from speaking in front of thousands and thousands of people, is that people can be taught to hold less animosity toward life, toward other people, and toward themselves. I've seen the impact on people of teaching them how to forgive. Everybody's got a heart, and that heart can be touched. I have no idea whether we're gaining ground or losing it, because there's always somebody else down the block advancing more hate. Yet one-to-one, one-to-ten, and one-to-one-hundred, a difference can be made. There is an alternative to hate that can be learned. Deep spirituality is always about changing oneself. "Doing good" has always involved people who can master themselves.

We can learn to forgive with these nine steps:

CHAPTER SIX

1. Know exactly how you feel about what happened and be able to articulate what about the situation is not okay. Then, tell a trusted couple of people about your experience.

2. Make a commitment to yourself to do what you have to do to feel better. Forgiveness is for you and not for anyone else.

3. Forgiveness does not necessarily mean reconciliation with the person who upset you, or condoning their action. What you are after is finding peace. Forgiveness can be defined as "the peace and understanding that come from blaming that which has hurt you less, taking the life experience less personally, and changing your grievance story."

4. Get the right perspective on what is happening. Recognize that your primary distress is coming from the hurt feelings, thoughts, and physical upset you are suffering now, not what offended you or hurt you two minutes—or ten years—ago.

5. At the moment you feel upset, practice a simple stress management technique to soothe your body's flight-or-fight response.

-§-
Victimhood gives you an excuse not to forgive, and to pass the violence along to those you interact with.
-§-

6. Give up expecting things from other people, or your life, that they do not choose to give you. For your own health, recognize the unenforceable rules you have set up for how you or other people must behave. Remind yourself that you can hope for health, love, friendship, and prosperity—and work hard to get them.

7. Put your energy into looking for another way to get your positive goals met, other than through the experience that has hurt you. Instead of mentally replaying your hurt, seek out new ways to get what you want.

8. Remember that a life well-lived is your best revenge. Instead of focusing on your wounded feelings, and thereby giving the person who caused you pain power over you, learn to look for the love, beauty and kindness around you.

9. Amend your grievance story to remind you of the heroic choice to forgive.

Learning to forgive can help counterbalance all the violence and hatred in the world. As a skill, it helps people have a place in themselves to evaluate whether this is an appropriate moment to let go or not. Angry, violent, hostile responses are so overpracticed and so overlearned that we don't have enough ready access to other responses in those moments where a softer, letting-it-go philosophy would be appropriate. Following these nine steps can help people who may not be comfortable or well versed in forgiveness make a better choice.

JOHN GRAY:

Forgiving the Unforgivable

"**W**hen I look at the state of our world and the state of my country, I feel distressed. Yet I'm not immobilized by that distress. I recognize that distress comes from a feeling of powerlessness. Powerlessness springs from a fear of loss. When we believe that loss is unjust, we get angry.

We can get caught up in many emotions as we contemplate our world: fear, grief, sadness, anger, and distress. These are powerful emotions. They free us from having to witness the full, deep impact of the events we see on television. The way we deal with our emotions, either through denial or projection, makes our problems worse. Some people detach, saying, 'I don't want anything to do with this.' This reinforces their sense of powerlessness.

Others deal with their emotions by blaming, pointing the finger outwards. Blaming someone else may relieve your feelings. But it also reinforces your sense of powerlessness, and makes forgiveness difficult. People mistakenly think that forgiveness means releasing someone else from blame. Their reasoning goes, 'If I release someone else from blame, then the only person left to blame is me.' We can't bear that thought. So our response to emotional pain is usually to blame people or situations outside ourselves. Our defensive reaction is to say, 'This problem is someone else's fault.' This means that we are not the ones who are going to be punished. This reaction makes perfect sense in a world in which people are punished for making

John Gray, Ph.D., is the author of fifteen best selling books, including *Men Are from Mars, Women Are from Venus* (HarperCollins, 1992), the number one best selling book of the last decade. In the past ten years, over thirty million Mars and Venus books have been sold in over forty languages throughout the world. He has appeared on *Oprah, The Today Show, CBS Morning Show, Good Morning America, Larry King,* and many other shows. He has been profiled in *Newsweek, Time, Forbes, USA Today, TV Guide,* and *People.* John Gray is a certi-fied family therapist, and is the premier Better Life relationship coach on AOL. More at www.MarsVenus.com.

mistakes rather than being forgiven. For all of us who have been raised in such an environment, the only way we can see to gain relief from emotional pain is to blame.

For many years, I've wanted to understand the emotional pain and mental conditioning that leads people to commit violent crimes, so I arranged to teach my 'Healing the Heart' seminar at San Quentin, the most infamous prison in the San Francisco Bay Area. It was a very difficult experience, but it changed my life.

The day started out poorly. When I arrived at the prison, not one single inmate showed up at the meeting place. I got mad because I had come all that way, with thirty-two assistants, all ready to teach this class, and the room was empty. So I got huffy and asked the prison official helping me, 'Have you got a PA system? Let me talk to the prisoners.'

He took me to the communications center, gave me a mike, and cranked up the volume so that the sound reached the whole prison.

I said, 'I'm Dr. John Gray, and I've come to teach the Healing the Heart seminar. Thirty-two prisoners signed up to take this seminar and nobody is here. I know why you're not here—because you're scared. You're scared to come. And all the rest of you were too scared to even sign up!

'But I also understand why you're scared—because I speak the truth, and when you hear me talk, you're going to think about who you are, and that's going to make you sick because you've made a lot of people sick in your lives. You've hurt people, you've been mean to people, you've lied to people, you've cheated people.

'Some would say that you're the scum of the Earth, and you don't deserve anything better than what you're getting in this prison. That's what you've been told your whole life.

-§-
Our response to emotional pain is usually to blame the people or situations outside of ourselves.
-§-

'But the real truth, the complete truth, is not that at all. I'm here to tell you that you're not the person your parents told you you are. You're not that person who deserves to be treated like dirt in the gutter, to be washed away and forgotten. You deserve everything that anybody else deserves. And you have the chance, right now, to find who you really are, to let go of all those voices from the past of people who have treated you like you were nothing.

'But you have to face your fears. You have to look at what you've done, and then find forgiveness for yourself. That's a hard step to take. You've also got to look at what other people have done to you, and find forgiveness for them, and you have to do that first, because without that, you'll never be able to forgive yourself for your imperfections. We're all flawed, we all make mistakes, but you'll only be able to forgive yourself and breathe freely when you have forgiven those who have mistreated you.

'I can help you do that. I can help you find out who you truly are. You truly are a loving person. You have gifts in this world, and I'm here to help you find them. I'm starting in five minutes. If you're not there, you can't be in the rest of the seminar.'

Five minutes later, the room was packed.

My helper from the prison took me aside and said, 'John, you're in danger here because you just said all those things to these inmates.'

But I knew better. I was already checking the room to find my friends. When I give a talk, there are always a few people whose faces shine because they really like what I'm saying. I noticed one man in particular, the biggest guy in the room, just beaming, loving everything I was saying. A few minutes into the teaching, I said, 'Now, a lot of you guys looking at me think you can take me out. But I'm not standing here alone. I have a bodyguard. I have somebody who will take care of me. If you have any problem with me, first you have to get through this guy right here.'

-§-
People who commit the most hideous crimes have had hideous things done to them, so they go numb.
-§-

The huge man stood up, crossed his arms, and said, 'That's right. You mess with him, you're messin' with me.'

I continued, 'Okay, so we got that straight.' From that point forward, the prisoners liked me. In the end they were calling me 'the little man with the big voice.'

Later in the seminar, as I was helping people understand forgiveness and why people do what they do, I was processing with this same guy and I asked him, 'Who is it who bothers you the most, has mistreated you the most, that right now you need to forgive or that you can't forgive?'

'The guards,' he said.

'What do the guards do?' I asked. He listed what the guards did and how they mistreated him.

I inquired, 'Why do you think they treat you that way?'

I could see from his face that he'd never asked himself that question before! There was a long pause, and then he said, 'Well, because we treat them like shit! They're scared of us!'

It was a huge shift for him to be looking at the issue from the other person's perspective. Such a shift helps us find that little seed of forgiveness in our hearts, and opens our minds to understanding. We ask, 'Why did you do that?' with genuine curiosity and connection, as opposed to saying, 'Well why on Earth did you do *that!*' in a spirit of accusation and blame. As we understand, our minds open, our hearts open, and the love in our hearts begins to shine. Not only is the world a better place because we make this effort to forgive, but we grow as well.

I asked another man, 'When you look at what you did, how do you feel inside?'

He said, 'There's no feeling, man. I'm numb.' And he knew why. He told me, 'When I was a little boy, my mom was raped. I watched it, and I could not bear it. I ran and got a gun and I shot the man. But the bullet went through him and it killed my mother. So I don't feel.'

Criminal behavior results from an inability on the part of the perpetrator to feel the effect on others of what he is doing. Conversely, empathy is the capacity to understand where another person is coming from—to feel with them. When we're hurt, in order to heal, we need somebody to feel with us. That's what compassion is; that's what love is.

-§-
I cannot feel your pain until I feel and heal and remember my own pain.
-§-

Empathy transforms us. But I cannot feel your pain until I feel and heal and remember my own pain. Otherwise I push your pain away because it reminds me of my own.

We have to forgive and keep on forgiving, but that doesn't mean we have to let people walk all over us. We may need to put a criminal in prison so that he doesn't hurt anybody, and leave him there until he's healed. But to allow healing, we have to make prisons a place where inmates can be educated, where they can grow and change.

I remember one man in the seminar who had no capacity for empathy because of all of the things that had been done to him.

I said to him, 'I'm going to help you find your feelings right now. How many children do you have?'

'I have twelve children.'

'How long are you in prison for?'

'Life,' he answered.

'How do you think your children feel about you being here?'

He shrugged. 'There's nothing I can do about it!'

'How do you think they feel?' I asked again.

'There's nothing I can do about it!'

'What are their names?' He told me some names. 'How do you think little Johnny feels when his daddy's not home?'

'I can't be home! There's nothing I can do about it!' he repeated. His mind was expert at keeping him from feeling.

I said to him, 'Fine, close your eyes. Your twelve children are here in front of you right now. Just listen. You don't have to say anything, just listen. Johnny is going to talk first: 'Daddy? Where are you? Daddy, where are you? I miss you. I miss you!'

That was all it took. His body started to shake as he felt the unconscious pain that he had been pushing down his whole lifetime. Then he fainted—right on top of me. I grabbed him and eased him into a chair. When I looked up, all the prisoners in that area had stood up and were leaving. One of my assistants asked, 'What happened? I know we felt some pain there, but what's the big deal?'

The big deal was that the prisoners had so little love for themselves—and such a small or nonexistent store of love they had ever received from anyone else—that they had no cushion of empathy to help them bear the pain. It's horrible to feel emotional pain without love. We can't handle it. We take drugs, or drink, or become violent, or numb ourselves by over-exercising or overeating. If we thaw out and feel our pain alone, it's too much to bear.

Those prisoners have no love at all that they can count on in their lives. They can't bear the pain of living without love, so they inflict pain on others. It's a reaction: I'm in pain, and I can forget my pain by making you suffer.

Action movies have this structure. The bad guy is identified by his evil deeds at the beginning. The good guy spends most of the movie trying to get back at the bad guy. But the bad guy does worse things to the good guy. At the end, when the good guy finally gets the bad guy and causes him major pain, the audience cheers. 'Yippee! The bad guy is being punished. He's suffering! He's getting what he deserves!' The bad guy's deeds allow us to rationalize the treatment he receives.

But no one ever deserves to be treated that way. Never. The cruelest, most hardened criminal is just sick. Who are we to apply the death penalty? Who are we to make choices like that? Each person bears some responsibility for the crime in his or her community, because it's neglected people who commit crimes. We comfort ourselves by believing that there are bad people out there and we have nothing to do with their behavior. In reality, we have everything to do with it. All it takes for pain and violence to prevail in this world is for the people who themselves have love to do nothing. Take away the love, and you allow the forces of evil take over.

Of the one hundred and fifty prisoners who showed up for the seminar at San Quentin, only thirty-two stayed untl the end. They stayed because there were thirty-two assistants with me, people with the healing power of love in their hearts. In the presence of my trained assistants, something important happened: those guys cried for the first time in their lives.

-§-
All it takes for pain and violence to prevail in this world is for the people who themselves have love to do nothing.
-§-

When the prisoners who didn't have the benefit of an understanding and nonjudgmental assistant tried to do the exercises in pairs with each other, nothing happened. They had nothing to give each other. They were empty. If you're empty, you're happy to get filled up. By way of contrast, the assistants were full. Once you're full, you have something to share. Sharing comes from overflow. We give what we've received. That's how the world is healed.

After the seminar, the prisoners begged us to come back and work with them again. I said, 'Okay, this will be my gift to society. We'll come back whenever you want.' So the prisoners wrote letters to the governor and the newspapers asking to have us back, but the prison wouldn't consider it. I made an appointment with the warden and asked, 'Why?'

He gave some reasons, like, 'It's too expensive.'

'Okay, I'll pay,' I responded.

He said, 'No, you don't understand, we have to hire extra guards to protect you.'

I said, 'I don't want the protection, but if you have to hire more guards, I'll pay for them. My contribution.'

He still said, 'No. You're getting all this notoriety about the seminar. Many prisoners wrote letters to the newspapers afterwards, and reporters wrote articles because the prisoners liked the course so much.'

I told him, 'Okay, we won't have any articles or letters to the editor. I don't care if nobody knows. I'm just doing this to help the prisoners.'

He still refused, giving some other excuses.

Finally I asked him, 'What is it really?'

The room darkened. He said, 'Okay, you want to know the real reason? The prisoners are not here to have a good time. They're here to be punished.'

Let's relate his perspective to that of child psychology. If a child has been beaten and abused, that child will justify the abuse, saying, 'I was bad and I deserved it.' As an adult, that person believes that others who are 'bad' also deserve to be punished. Punishing others justifies and gives meaning to the abuse that that person has suffered.

Here we see the development of a belief in capital punishment. The idea is 'You should suffer if you do something bad. And if you do something really terrible, you should die.' Our life experience gives rise to our sense of justice.

In the old days, when a monk had impure thoughts, he would whip himself, believing that the physical pain would release the pain of his transgression. Parents often punish kids by inflicting pain on them, on the assumption that this will make them more cooperative, loving people. The problem with this model is that it's based on fear. If you control your children through fear, how can they feel free to talk to you when they make mistakes? Instead, they put up a wall that doesn't let your love in—or give you the opportunity to forgive them.

-§-
Our challenge is to create families where people can mistakes, where forgiveness is a part of life every day.
-§-

For people raised in families where mistakes are forgiven, not punished, the experience is different. The child learns, 'I am forgiven for my mistakes, and from those mistakes, I learn to do better.' Then, when she sees others make mistakes, she doesn't want to punish them or make them suffer. Instead, she recognizes that there is a problem, that someone is making a mistake, and she forgives that person—and lets them know what would work better.

Our challenge is to create families where people can make mistakes, where forgiveness is a part of everyday life, where people don't have to be perfect, and where they're not afraid of punishment when they make a mistake. That's forgiveness.

There may be real injustice or harm that's been done to you. Forgiveness doesn't mean saying that the act against you was okay. *It means letting go of making the other person responsible for how you feel.* When you hold onto the pain, you feel that the person who hurt you owes you. Forgiveness is releasing the debt the other person owes you—and releasing yourself.

Only a secure person can forgive. That's why powerlessness is such a block to forgiveness. If I feel powerless to get what I need, then I want you to change in order to get me what I need. But when I believe that I possess the power to create what I need in my life, then I am able to let you off the hook. If you owe me money and I feel powerless to create money, then I focus my attention on getting what you owe me, as my only source of money. If, on the other hand, I am confident of my ability to create money, then I'm not fixated on having you provide it for me.

The American spirit is one of confidence that we can accomplish great things, that we can make the best of any situation, and that we can rise above any adversity. Yet our sense of our might has been dented. The country seems to have become immobilized by the actions of a small group of terrorists. We're like a person going through life feeling very confident, till he gets punched in the stomach, and realizes that he is not as invulnerable as he believed. Our fear has allowed our political leaders to push our whole country into war. Wars are always profitable for some. Citizens of a country rarely want war—it's governments that need wars. Governments manipulate problems in order to motivate their citizens to support wars. And the meanings that citizens give to events can lead them to either become anti-war activists or indeed, in favor.

-§-
Tragedies, particularly ones that are close to home, give us the fire, the passion, to find our purpose, and to seek a fair and just world.
-§-

Tragedies, particularly ones that are close to home, give us the fire, the passion, to find our purpose and to seek a fair and just world. Tragedies can transmute that fire into purpose. We can choose to give tragedies meaning. We can make good and kind meanings out of tragic events.

For instance, if you're a parent and your son dies in Iraq, you will want to give meaning to the tragedy. You might assign it the meaning, 'He died to protect America from a threat. His death saved a thousand deaths at home.' Yet that attempt to give meaning to a child's death perpetuates an endless war on terror.

If you believe that the war itself is creating an even bigger threat to our country, then your child's death has a different meaning. It's part of a huge mistake. That personal loss may then become a catalyst to motivate you to seek an end to the war, in order to prevent other parents' children being sent into the same mistake.

The same event has then given rise to two very different meanings. That weekend in San Quentin, I began to understand why these prisoners had done what they had done, even the rapists and killers: they don't feel love. If you are a person who feels love, you will feel suffering when you cause pain to another. But when you're discon-nected from your heart, when you're connected only with your mind, you can hurt others and not feel it.

We can each choose to bring love into the world. We can choose to speak in a loving way to the people closest to home. If your kids make a big mess, and you feel like getting mad and blaming them, wait! Remember the times you've made a big mess. Think about how it feels to be punished and how it feels to be forgiven. Then, instead of getting mad and yelling, you might say, 'This is a big mess. This is a mistake. Next time we don't want to make a big mess. Let's do it differently.'"

PART TWO

Radical Healing

GABRIEL COUSENS:

The Culture of Liberation

To live as spiritual people in a material world is to sanctify everything we do. The teachings of the Kabbalah and Yoga show how to create a sacred unity out of chaos so that we reflect the universe at its highest octave. More than a philosophy, spiritual living involves daily actions that express holiness in every moment.

We express holiness in daily life by treating food as a love note from God. For example, devotional eating begins and ends with a prayer. It involves slow, conscious eating, sensing the food's energy and divine light, rather than rapid, automated eating—while driving in the car or watching TV. Conscious eating evokes a bodily feeling of the cosmic energy or bliss of the food, energy we transform from the living planet into our own beingness. Gratitude and present moment awareness are also key. Food is then experienced as a gift from the divine.

Another vehicle for holiness in daily life is making love. In alchemically merging with a mate, we allow ourselves to be lived by love. Ultimately we unite with the whole world. Consciously seated in the genitals, we move beyond organism, beyond duality, connecting all people in love. Making love demonstrates our powerful connection with all.

As a physician, holiness in daily life means to express my sense of the divine truth of a patient's essence and needs. I essentially deliver

Gabriel Cousens, M.D., is founder of the Tree of Life Rejuvenation Center in Patagonia, Arizona. Dr. Cousens is a holistic medical doctor, licensed psychiatrist, family therapist, and a licensed homeopathic physician. Dr. Cousens uses nutrition, naturopathy, Ayurveda, and homeopathy, blended with spiritual awareness. His best selling books include *Rainbow Green Live-Food Cuisine* (North Atlantic, 2003), *Spiritual Nutrition* (North Atlantic, 2005), and *Depression-Free for Life* (Morrow, 2003). Dr. Cousens is known worldwide as an empowered spiritual teacher and the leading medical authority on vegan live-food nutrition. Find more information at www.treeoflife.nu.

this truth with kindness, and I create a heart connection. For example, as a child, one patient had suffered harsh mental abuse from her father. As I was kind to her in every session, seeing her for who she is, she gradually released her view of the world as her father judging her. Instead of hiding in her home, she began driving a car and socializing with family and friends for the first time in a long while.

Kindness and heart-based spiritual medicine at times involves tough love. For example, I frankly reminded one rebellious, alcoholic patient in her twenties of the purpose of life—to wake up; not to play out teenage, ego-driven patterns. Hearing the truth conveyed with loving kindness, she transformed into a spiritual devotee. She stopped identifying with her ego and recognized the truth of who she is.

> -§-
> More than a philosophy,
> spiritual living involves
> daily actions that express
> holiness in every moment.
> -§-

I bring a sense of the sacred to medicine spontaneously through years of focused practice. I help thousands of patients bring to consciousness their unconscious attachments to ego. One challenge I face, like the Dalai Lama said when held captive in China, is having concern not for myself but for always maintaining my connection to the Divine. It is a process. At times, witnessing a patient's trauma, I remind myself of the advantage being in the West rather than alone in a cave meditating; here I continually sharpen my consciousness as I help patients transform polarities into oneness.

Practicing spiritual medicine means constantly cultivating an awareness of oneness. The gift of this approach is an opportunity, as shown in the Kabbalah, to receive in order to share. I have received tremendous light and truth through my work, which I express as service. My purpose is to help patients wake up, often stretching them beyond their perceived capacities. That is my role as a spiritual physician and teacher. I also serve as a spiritual food preparer and culinary artist to help people wake up.

In difficult cases, I remember the Kabbalistic principle of *hesed*—open-heartedness and kindness. I apply this principle when distinguishing between patients who are ready to wake up—no matter how sick they are—and those resistant to doing so, consciously or unconsciously. In short, I recognize patients prepared to receive and use what I have to offer. I do not push those who are not, but help them reach a point of readiness. I intuitively make this distinction, often in simple ways. For example, I may recommend five nutrients to one patient who then complains that the regimen is excessive. Another patient may immediately agree to incorporate twenty-five new nutrients into his diet. This clearly shows me the latter patient's intention to heal—to wake up. A patient's intention may have no correlation to their spiritual background. I see individuals with a vast spiritual background caught in strong ego defenses and others with little background completely ready to wake up.

As a spiritual physician, I also work with patients who have lost hope. I help them find hope, or what the Kabbalah calls *azamra*—to see and acknowledge their inner light. I ask them to tell me in detail about what is meaningful in their lives. One may share, "I work really well with horses. I can speak to horses too." I say, "Wow that's great!" and then we start talking about the light of God in animals, how people have that too, and what a special gift it is. So I probe for, and focus on, whatever connects patients to their omnipresent divinity.

My psychiatry background also guides the form of spiritual medicine I practice. I have developed a unique approach to waking people up from their ego-entrenched trances called the Zero Point Process. This four-day course has three phases:

1. Seeing the personality as a case of mistaken identity;

2. Examining aberrant thought forms, or *vasanas* and,

3. Locating and dissolving the source of those thoughts, *(mantrika shakti)*, using special techniques I teach. Patients learn why any identity is detrimental and begin recognizing who they are behind their egos.

The basic principles of the Zero Point Process are probably thousands of years old, but they can be traced back to Tibet. Tibetan yogis discovered through meditation how to see themselves as independent from thought forms. I began this practice in my own creative work as a psychiatrist, and have refined it for about fifteen years. The Zero Point Course basically reflects the foundations of *jnana yoga*. Jnana yoga makes it clear you are not your mind or your body; you are that which is prior to that—I Am That. A yoga or meditation practice is not required for the Zero Point Course. Some, in fact, do better without it, coming in without preconceptions. I see most course participants successfully reaching *mantrika shakti*—recognizing the thoughts with which they are identifying, dissolving those thoughts, and ceasing to generate them anymore.

-§-

We express holiness in daily life by treating food as a love note from God.

-§-

The larger context of the Zero Point Course is to introduce people to the *culture of liberation*. The culture of liberation means knowing and being the purpose of life, which is to know God and be open to the living presence of the divine in every moment. In this state, we go beyond egocentric and ethnocentric views. In other words, we release

attachments to our identities, and release our judgments of other people's identities or traditions. We embrace mystical oneness, seeing all as having something valuable to contribute. Finally, we allow ourselves to be lived by love; with its corollary—to love your neighbor as yourself, your divine Self.

The Zero Point Course symbolizes the story of Abraham. El Shaddai, the feminine aspect of God, told him, "*Lech lecha* — leave your

-§-
I remind myself of
the advantage being
in the West rather
than alone in a cave
meditating; here I
continually sharpen
my consciousness.
-§-

father's country. Leave your mother's home. Leave all you know. Go to the self." So Abraham literally left all of his traditions and went deep within, becoming the path of liberation. Through the Zero Point Course, I guide people in taking this mystical journey. They learn to let go their stories and archetypes and go to the truth. People experience the freedom of the Culture of Liberation very fast. They have a context and support for understanding how to work on themselves. I have helped approximately two thousand people—in groups of twenty to thirty at a time—since I began teaching Zero Point in 1988.

Feedback on the Zero Point Course is consistent. People immediately say it's the best course they've ever taken. The longitudinal feedback interests me most. I want to hear the results of prolonged practice of the Zero Point process—remembering you are not your body or your mind. Continued practice brings profound life changes. I invite past participants to retake the course at half price. Retaking it brings deeper insights. Evolution takes time. Many people continue to use the Tree of Life Rejuvenation Center as a primary health and spiritual support source. We have had people come to us from more than seventy-eight different countries. We provide them *sangha,* a sense of family and connection, as well as spiritual guidance. I encourage people to create local support as well. When surrounded by the group support of a sangha, they are more empowered to work on themselves.

My new book, *Spiritual Nutrition,* incorporates the Zero Point Process to support people in daily spiritual growth. It provides six foundations for the spiritual path, the first of which is nutrition. Spiritual nutrition is vegan, organic, live-food, high-mineralized, low-sugar, individualized, moderate in intake, well-hydrated with pure-living water, made with love, and includes spiritual fasting. Spiritual nutrition and fasting practices open your heart immensely. Your body armor melts.

The remaining foundations of spiritual life further open people to joining the culture of liberation—waking up to who they are and their life purpose. The second foundation is Building Prana, which is done through yoga, *pranayama* (breathing exercises), Tai Chi, Reiki, Tachyon Energy and other energy practices, and sacred dance. The third is Service and Charity, allowing us to face our attachment to things and feel connected to humanity. Its focus is on receiving in order to share. The fourth foundation is Spiritual Guidance and Inspiration. This includes guidance and inspiration from an awakened spiritual teacher and *satsang*, which is the support of a spiritual group. Spending time in nature, zero point or *jnana* yoga, sacred music and dance are also included.

The fifth foundation is Silence, involving meditation, prayer, mantra repetition, and chanting the names of God. All wisdom and understanding come out of silence. The sixth is Kundalini Awakening with *shaktipat*. Shaktipat is the descent of grace. It activates the *kundalini* to move out of its potential state, and into the cosmic, holographic, oneness of who we are. It connects us to the evolutionary octave. About 90% of people undergoing a spiritual fast experience a kundalini awakening. The group process is powerful, as forty people feel their oneness.

The rare instances of disordered kundalini unfolding may be balanced by four things:

1. Giving *shaktipat* which reorganizes the energy;

2. Building *ojas* to reverse depletion;

3. Psychospiritual counseling to gain perspective, and,

4. Doing practices that nurture and feed the kundalini in the right way.

In disordered kundalini cases where the nervous system is sensitive, moderate practice of the six foundations is helpful. For example, we may meditate for ten minutes, rather than six hours. We learn together what can be handled to increase the capacity to receive the light. The Kabbalah states that in the beginning the vessels could not hold all the light. They shattered. The six foundations are about repairing the vessels so that they can hold the light.

-§-
I probe for, and focus on, whatever connects patients to their omnipresent divinity.
-§-

We have helped a few people diagnosed as psychotic avoid hospitalization, using this program, coupled with specific nutritional support to assist their bodies in creating neurotransmitters. Our success rate with depressed patients is 90%, which is much higher than for conventional treatments. I also work with many patients who have chronic health conditions. Others real-

ized that they're functioning at less than peak potential, and simply want to get healthy. They may have the intention to awaken—or not.

More Western physicians are opening to the work I do, and to holistic health practices generally. This group is still a minority, but I am receiving more referrals, and I am engaging in more dialogue. While fostering these connections with conventional physicians is important, I focus on the many underserved patients at the cutting edge, those committed to waking up and joining the culture of liberation. Many of those I work with follow vegan, live-food diets, and are having an active awakening of their kunalini energy.

The success we experience at the Tree of Life Rejuvenation Center comes from empowering people to release resistance to living open to life. It is a common condition. In the Zero Point Course we begin by helping people acknowledge that resistance is common—and to accept it. People are naturally afraid to leap into the unknown. Once they acknowledge it, they can face it and be comfortable with it. We next involve people into a *sangha*, establishing a support system though group connections. They see they are not alone. Everyone is facing similar issues. Additionally, the Tree of Life Rejuvenation Center offers an overall context for living a spiritual life. Everyone here lives a spiritual life grounded in ancient teachings. They have access to a spiritual teacher who guides their journey into the self, and toward the truth of who they are.

-§-

Spiritual nutrition and fasting practices open your heart immensely. Your body armor melts.

-§-

Resistance to living an open life takes many forms. For example, people often come to the Tree of Life Rejuvenation Center refusing to give up comfort foods, like doughnuts, that undermine their physical or spiritual health. We acknowledge it is perfectly fine to keep eating doughnuts even though it is harmful. We accept their having doughnuts as often as desired as long as they are willing to pay the price. We remind people of the larger issue: that they came to the Tree of Life Rejuvenation Center to heal. Eventually, we dissipate the barriers they put up to avoid facing their resistance. Once we embrace resistance, and see it as normal, we begin to open to transformation.

The strongest incentive for people to integrate practices for waking up is what I call the "subtle kiss." The subtle kiss is the bliss we experience when consciously connected with the divine. As people shed their identities and attachments to ego, no matter how fleetingly, they experience this subtle kiss. This moment can be highly motivating because we are intrinsically attracted to being in a constant, eternal subtle kiss. For me, this kiss has been a driving force in my own spiritual evolution. I say, "So there is some resistance. Big deal! I like the kiss more!"

Regardless of your specific health problems, the most important priority is to heal the whole person. Even with difficult diseases, I focus treatment on the most important thing in life—to know God. I help people focus on the light and the bliss of the subtle kiss, rather than obsess about their physical states. I commonly encounter patients who have been treated by as many as twenty-five different healthcare practitioners. Yet we can still usually make a breakthrough—and it comes from placing spiritual awakening first. That's why I view myself as a physician of the soul.

My medical practice has its basis in Kabbalistic healing. Spirit comes first. Without a connection to God, people lose faith. Then they become hopeless about healing. One group I see in this category is people with eating disorders. Lacking faith and hope, they suffer from what I call a hungry soul. There is never enough food to feed the hungry soul. People who undereat may also experience an empty soul. They relate starving to being seen as beautiful or lovable. That is why with eating disorder individuals I emphasize healing the soul first, so it is no longer hungry or empty. When experiencing the kiss of the divine, food issues recede.

More broadly, my medical approach offers a model for planetary healing. I integrate homeopathic, Chinese, Ayurvedic, and naturopathic medicines with the Kabbalistic healing practices. I believe I draw on the best aspects of these medical modalities. Our programs also incorporate Yogic, Essene, and Native American practices. For those who are on the cutting edge the Tree of Life Rejuvenation Center is wonderful. For people wed to the allopathic, the Tree of Life Rejuvenation Center may stretch their horizons and take them beyond their comfort zones. We essentially offer practices and programs for waking up. We draw on ancient healing traditions that offer a much deeper understanding of the human organism and what healing is about.

-§-

All wisdom and understanding come out of silence.

-§-

We do not require people who come to have any spiritual background. We are an oasis for awakening, teaching the culture of liberation to all. The truth is that liberation takes us beyond all ego- and ethnocentric viewpoints. That's a very important message. We provide unique support systems like Zero Point, Conscious Eating and Sacred Relationship Courses, and Spiritual Fasting. Other support systems include apprenticeships in sprouting, vegan farming and live-food preparation. They are part of our Vegan Live Food Masters Program, the first in the world. Our programs and courses are unique because they are holistic. In short, we encourage people to participate in an entire lifestyle that supports spiritual awakening while they are here. It is one thing to say we are all one; it is quite another thing to live the experience of oneness, and to provide basic skills—emotional, spiritual, and ecological—that allow us to enjoy the experience every day. That is our mission.

My personal mission involves a constant commitment to being open to the unfolding of the divine within me. I aim to facilitate liberation within every being, unmasking their unique expression of the poetry of the divine. Yet, while everyone is born an original, most people die as copies. The whole point of the Zero Point Course and the way I live my life is to be an original expression of the divine and to model that for others. To know if I am staying true to my path, I look beyond what feels easy to do. I meditate, and wait for a message, as Gandhi would do. I may contemplate something for months before taking action. I need a green light. My life mission can be stated as *tikkun ha-nefesh, tikkun ha-olam,* which means healing and transformation of the self and the planet. The leading theme in my work has been world peace. I have been doing peace work, especially meditative in focus, since 1985.

-§-
We begin by helping people acknowledge that resistance is common—and to accept it.
-§-

We know that when people meditate and open their hearts to the divine, it shifts the planetary mind. Fear and terror also shift the planetary mind. Love shifts the planetary mind toward harmony and peace. One aspect of my peace work that promotes planetary harmony and peace is called Peace 21. On each equinox and solstice, we meditate for peace at 7 A.M. and 7 P.M., historically known as nodal times of the day. We know that this practice correlates with a decrease in the amount of sunspots. I believe through this meditative peace work a harmonic conversion of the planetary mind takes place.

After about two weeks of Peace 21 practice, the effect wears off. So the Peace Every Day initiative is to meditate for peace at the nodal times each day, sunrise and sunset, seeing the planet surrounded in light and connecting to the peace workers everywhere. Constant meditative input and clear intention are key to transforming the planetary mind on a daily basis.

My mission chiefly lies in teaching sevenfold peace. This practice involves peace within the body, within the mind, within your family and all families, within all communities, with all cultures, with the living mother/living planet, and with the divine. If all seven of those are in alignment, then we have world peace. It is hard work. But that's what the mystic is committed to. The mystic sees the light in all things, and practicing that light in conscious living produces sevenfold peace.

ALAN DAVIDSON:

Your Body Speaks the Truth

AUYNA PICCHU, Peru, August 1986—Wheezing, with burning legs, I stopped to catch my breath. The climb was harder than I thought. The steps rising before us, tread by the ancient Indians at least five hundred years ago, were well-worn, steep, and often tall. Ropes were stretched along this part of the incline to keep tourists from plummeting—almost straight down—to the thin strip of tropical rainforest below. Three young men hiking their way down from the peak turned the sharp bend ahead of us. I was still huffing and puffing as they passed us by. One of the boys muttered something in Spanish as they passed us. The others laughed. I made out the word *gringo,* foreigner, but missed their slur. My friend Dr. Wayne, in his kindness, spared me the translation.

We resumed our hike up the peak. The valley below, and the other mountains that surrounded it, were lost in dense clouds. It was winter and the rainy season in South America, a happy retreat from Houston's scorching heat. An eerie mist tickled my lungs as we climbed up and up the spiraling 800-foot incline. The clouds began to rise as the morning sun hit the valley. Wispy streams of white flowed past us, picking up speed as they rose, till they vaporized in the heat and humidity of the Amazon jungle air overhead. Suddenly the clouds opened below us.

On the mountain opposite us, lime-green vegetation shone. Saddled between two peaks, rising a thousand feet above the roil-

Alan Davidson, C.M.T., is the owner and director of Essential Touch Therapies in Houston, Texas. He has a bachelor's degree from University of Houston, with an emphasis on psychology, sociology, philosophy, and religion. Alan is fascinated with the intersection of bodywork, psychology, ritual, and spiritual practice. Alan is the author of the forthcoming book *Living Through Your Body.* He has taught massage, meditation, yoga, aromatherapy, and human transformation since 1990 and is a certified Nia White Belt. Alan is currently on the teaching staff at Source Vital College of Holistic Studies and NiaMoves Studio. He is on the web at www.throughyourbody.com.

ing Urumbaba river valley below, lay the jewel of South America: the ancient city of Machu Picchu. The stone temples and terraces carved by the Incas were vivid in the distance, as mysterious as they were extraordinary. There was no rope to guard the drop-off on this stretch of the climb. Wayne and I both stood stock still, mesmerized by the view below. Involuntarily, my fingers clutched the rocky wall of Hauyna Picchu, the mountain we were ascending. Dragging our eyes from the spectacular view, we returned to our climb. When we reached the top, I was breathing as though I just finished running a marathon—as much because of the altitude as from the extra pounds I carried.

Panting like a bellows, I dropped to a boulder. I longed for a cup of the coca tea—the local remedy for the altitude—that I'd tasted back in Cuzco. The clouds had completely evaporated by now. The sun was shining strongly, though the air was still cool this early in the morning. The tranquility of the mountaintop was awesome; so was the view. Machu Picchu's spectacular location was apparent. From the crown of Hauyna Picchu, I had a circular view of the surrounding mountains. Granite crests alternated between green jungle and snow-peaked summits. The river circled the base of the site, enclosing the access to the old city. Birds soared through the valley. Bromeliads grew sporadically on the sheer cliffs of the opposing mountain walls.

-§-
Ancient temples and lost civilizations invite us to live their secret mysteries into the world.
-§-

A rag-tag group of trekkers—young Austrians, Germans, Australians, and Americans—held a reverent silence as they sunned on the high boulders. These hardy trekkers had camped the night at Aquas Calientes after days hiking along the Inca Trail. Dr. Wayne and I had chosen the three-and-a-half-hour train ride instead. Aquas Calientes, named for the natural hot springs in the valley below, is the village where visitors to Machu Picchu, hikers and train tourists alike, begin the 1,500 foot climb to the ancient ruins. These trekkers hiked up the eight kilometer road, hairpinned with thirteen zigzag switchbacks, while most tourists from the trains, Dr. Wayne and I included, opted for a precarious shuttle bus ride up the mountain. We then spent the night in the delightful Machu Picchu Sanctuary Lodge, adjacent to the ruins. The best advantage to staying so close to the ruins was the near-privacy of the mornings. The first train full of tourists arrived from Cuzco about 10:30 A.M. Until then, the handful of overnight visitors had the entire complex and the narrow trail up Hauyna Picchu to themselves.

I was breathing normally after a pause, and I decided that it was a perfect moment for a meditation. I lay on my back, with my head tilting off the edge of the cliff, and filled my mind with one of Shakti Gawain's meditations. I saw my life as perfect and happy, bathed in pink light. The work of the climb, the pure air, and the awesome quiet all combined to bring me the gift of perfect peace. My breathing deepened as my mind calmed. Or was it the other way around? Did my mind calm down as my breathing deepened? Either way, I felt great. Unbeknownst to me, Dr. Wayne snapped a picture of me, thinking I looked like an offering to the ancient gods — by this stage of my life, I was hardly a virgin sacrifice! At the end of my meditation, I offered my vision, wrapped in pink light, to the Andes, which they received with quiet austerity. Climbing Hauyna Picchu was a rich moment; the first time I had experienced the power of physical effort, combined with conscious deep breathing, meditation, and transcendent calm.

Later we explored the ruins of the old city. I was still in a delicious altered state from my experience on Hauyna Picchu's higher peak. We wandered from the "Temple of the Moon" to the ceremonial center of the abandoned city, the *Intihuatana*, a granite altar ritually used to tie the sun to the Earth at each equinox.

It's easy to understand why pilgrims flock to sacred sights like Machu Picchu. As Hamlet says, "There are more things in Heaven and Earth, Horatio, than are dreamt of in your philosophy." Graceful ruins coupled with natural beauty fire our imagination. They remind us of mysteries greater than ourselves. They nudge us from our comfortable ways of being in the world. I've felt this pull to mystery at Stonehenge on Salisbury Plain, at the Taos Indian Pueblo in New Mexico, and the Buddhist temples on the islands near Hong Kong. But there's more to it than just sensing the mysteries of the world as greater than ourselves. These places provide us with a reminder that we ourselves are vaster than we know. Our pilgrimages to these sacred places spark our longing for our own greater truths; these ancient temples and lost civilizations invite us to live their secret mysteries into the world.

Nineteen years later, I cruised along Houston's Memorial Drive, noticing the lush green parks flanking both sides of the thoroughfare. The city was green for this late in the summer. The heavy rains and high humidity had wetted the usually-parched Earth. The canopies of Live Oak trees shimmered in the early sunlight. Willow and camphor trees rimmed a bayou that snaked through the park alongside me. Just past the bayou bridge on my left were the elegant stepped pyramids of the Fallen Houston Police monument. On my right was one of Henry Moore's sculptures. The spindle of smooth bronze pressing up to the sky reminded me of the Incan altar, *Intihuatan,* tying the summer sun to Texas. I exited right to Houston Avenue just as the road vaulted between our grand postmodern temples to Dionysus, the opera house and theater center.

I was almost late for the 8 A.M. yoga class I taught. Impatiently, I noted the long line of cars at the next red light; commuters filing downtown for their Monday morning's work. I figured it would take three cycles of the light for me to clear the intersection. I felt anxious about the possibility of being late. I was captive for those few minutes. Yet I knew that feeling stressed wouldn't speed the traffic lights. Instead, I could use the congestion as a chance to breathe and relax. I started my ritual: I breathed in for a count of three, and paused. I breathed out for a count of six, and paused. "Repeat as needed" were the words I would speak to my class, so I did. This rhythm, with the emphasis on the out-breath, soothed me. My mind and body, well familiar with the tempo, began to calm. The line of cars edged along as the light cycled.

-§-
I hated to be asked for money, hated to say, "no."
-§-

And then I saw her, sitting small against the backdrop of the Hobby Center for the Performing Arts looming a few blocks behind her. This intersection attracts panhandlers; usually the homeless people who live under the nearby bridges weaving into downtown. I didn't know her name. I often passed her on my way to the studio where I teach. Sometimes she held a sign asking for help. Other days she simply held out her palm, daring to look into the waiting cars for some sign of kindness. The line of cars crept along, as the light cycled again, from a brief green, then back to red.

As I rolled closer, the pillars of the overpass on my left shifted to frame her from behind. Through the cement columns I saw Houston's Municipal Courthouses, with people resigned to their day in court, streaming across the streets toward the Hall of Justice. The panhandler sat motionless. The cars ahead of me seemed to ignore her. I understood their behavior. I used to avoid panhandlers, these social outcasts, even crossing the street to avoid them if I had to. I hated to be asked for money, hated to say, "no."

Now I shifted my breathing ritual: I focused my attention in my center, the core of energy in front of my spinal column. I then deeply asked myself, "Do I want to give this woman anything today?" I listened for the answer coming from deep within me. Today I heard, "Five dollars." Without questioning, I reached for a five dollar bill in my ashtray. Some days I hear to give her fifty cents, or a piece of fruit I have with me. Some days I clearly hear, "no," and I don't give anything. I've come to trust whatever that deeply given answer is.

Rolling down my window as I stopped beside her, conscious of slowing traffic as I did, I offered her the crisply folded bill. She peered up, eyes sharp, her face swollen. I thought she'd been beaten. She stood to take my gift, and told me, "I was in a car wreck." Our eyes met and I said, "Thank you for asking." Lifting my foot off the brake, I rolled forward. She started to say something else, but as I pulled away she said, "I'll tell you tomorrow." As I drove on I felt it again, a sense of delicious and transcendent calm pouring through me. It was very close to the same expansive high I felt exploring Machu Picchu and the other sacred sites I've seen in the world. I have realized that there's something magical about asking what's true for me in the present moment, listening through my body for the answer, and sharing my truth kindly with the world. It unlocks a tangible sense of my sacred self, which then pours into my everyday world.

I call this simple process "Living Truer." I've found this method of:

- asking deeply of myself, "What's true for me,"

- listening through my body for the answer, and

- sharing my truth kindly with the world

works in all situations. It's most obvious to me with the panhandlers because of my fear of them. They're the ideal laboratory to practice my experiment in living truer.

Asking Deeply of Myself, "What's True for Me?" What a simple and profound question. For any possibility of an answer, I must cut through the tapestry of stories my mind weaves. I love the *Tao te Ching's* advice: "How do I know this is true? I look inside myself and see." Often I see panhandlers with signs claiming, "Homeless vet"; "Homeless Christian"; "Ill and hungry"; "Will work for food," or "Will work for dog food." And often I notice how freshly bathed they seem, or nicely dressed they are, with new tennis shoes that undermine their claim. My thoughts tell me that they are liars and are not worthy of my kindness. My mind's judgments about these people (and about life in general) are just unexamined thoughts, opinions, and beliefs. They are simple distortions of reality that I hold to be The Truth, when in fact they are my own personal illusions.

-§-
There's something magical about asking what's true for me in the present moment, listening through my body for the answer, and sharing my truth kindly with the world.
-§-

I am deceived by believing my story. That's the beauty of living truer. It cuts through those beliefs with the question, "What's true for me?" or in this example, "Do I want to give this woman something?" It doesn't matter what I see, or what my mind says about the circum-

stance. I simply ask deep into the heart of my sure self. I reach into a place truer than what my mind can even grasp. As Byron Katie says, "Without a story there is only love."

Listening, through My Body, for the Answer. It is one thing to ask, "What's true for me?" but rarely do we listen deeply to hear that sure voice within. Most of us tend to go through life without paying much attention to our bodies. Unless they're hurting, that is. We don't start to notice our bodies until we're running on fumes.

But the extraordinary thing our body gifts us with is the experience of the divine present moment. Our body always happens in the present moment. The entire life of our bodies — all our functions and sensations — happen in the absolute present. Just take a few minutes to sense your body. Sit comfortably, relaxing your hands in your lap. Take a deep breath and notice all the sensations of your body as you sit for these few minutes. Feel your feet touching the floor; the feeling of clothing on your skin; the weight of your thighs and hips on the chair; the subtle movement of air through your nose and throat. If you find yourself thinking, very gently come back to just the sensations of sitting. Sense the rise and fall of your chest; the movement of your belly with each breath; the movement of air against your skin. Take a deep breath and open your eyes and come back. You have just experienced the miraculous present unfolding, moment by moment.

Some people have a hard time concentrating on their bodies. They are sucked in by the thoughts going through their minds. Others report a sense of relaxation infusing their bodies. A guideline I strive for comes from Lily Tomlin and her one woman show, *The Search for Signs of Intelligent Life in the Universe,* "She listened with an intensity that most people only have while talking." Developing this sensory skill is the first step to listening through our body. Once we are comfortable with these primary sensations, we can begin to question our truest self. In my

-§-
I must cut through the tapestry of stories my mind weaves.
-§-

experience, that sure self, when questioned, always answers. It is the voice of mystery and truth flowing through the lattice of my body's consciousness. It speaks through me into the world. My challenge is to focus my attention enough to hear the answer given. Listening through our bodies is a skill that, when practiced often, becomes automatic.

Sharing the Truth Kindly With the World. Kindness is a function of evolving consciousness. The Dalai Lama simplified his life to the formula, "Kindness is my religion." Once I've asked and received an answer from my surest self, I live that truth into the world with as much kindness as I know. In the example of the homeless woman, I act on the truth I'm given. I give what I'm told: fifty cents, five dollars, a plum to eat, nothing at all—whatever my body truth guides me to give in that moment. What unlocks my sensing is to look her in the eye and say, "Thank you for asking." I thank her for reminding me to ask my body what's true for me in this moment. I thank her for the opportunity to see my truth lived in the world. I thank her for the invitation to join—no matter how briefly—with another person. Kindly living my truth into the world stirs and wakes a great mystery at the core of my human consciousness. My heart and my mind expand. I touch, for a while, the vastness that I am.

-§-

We don't start to notice our bodies until we're running on fumes.

-§-

Living truer, as a practice, is like listening through your body. When remembered often, it becomes automatic. Not automatic as in unconscious, but a ritual for life. It's in those remembered moments when delicious truth, the same truth invoked by the world's great ruins and temples, shines through me. Just like the *Intihuatana;* that column of granite the old Incas used to ritually tie the sun to the earth, this practice becomes my Rock of Gibraltar. It ties the light of my truth from the center of my being out into the world. In this way, life's great mystery flows through me, making every moment precious

Zhi Gang Sha:

Heal the Soul First

Many people suffer from chronic diseases, acute illness, and life-threatening conditions. Others struggle with addictions, depression or a general lack of well-being. Over the last few decades, the mind-body connection has become well-known and it is indeed a giant step in the right direction. It has cleared the path for many insights and advances. But *mind over matter* is not enough. Whatever conventional medicine may state, all illness and dis-ease originates from energy and spiritual blockages. *Soul over matter* is the true place where all healing, all blessing, all life transformation begins. *Heal the soul first, then the healing of mind and body will follow.*

The dimension of the soul will become very important in the next few years. Soon it will literally burst onto the scientific stage because all is energy, and all energy is soul in action. The primary role of the soul in health and healing is becoming apparent, as well as its vital contribution to longevity and rejuvenation. New domains will be scientifically mapped and taught, as the possibilities of soul healing become apparent.

We stand at the gateway to a new dimension in healing. The Soul Light Era has recently begun, where all can learn to access the power of the soul to invoke, among other higher forces, the holy Saints, Buddhas, healing angels, spiritual beings, and masters from every religious tradition. The power of the Soul Light Era creates an opening for anyone, beyond any form of spiritual belief, East or West,

Zhi Gang Sha is an M.D. from China, a traditional Chinese medicine doctor, and an extraordinary healer. The best selling author of *Power Healing*
(HarperSanFrancisco, 2003), he has been featured in a PBS television special
as one of the most powerful Qigong masters of our time. His teachings emanate
from a lineage of Buddhist and Taoist spiritual wisdom thousands of years old.
His own powerful contribution is to make these teachings simple, practical, and
accessible. Master Sha offers free remote healing every Tuesday and Thursday
evening via teleclass. The list of healing and blessing miracles reported on his
website (www.drsha.com) grows weekly.

to embark on the journey of self-healing and realization. It is accessible to even the least initiated student of modern times, to anyone who simply wants to understand and use his own healing abilities. Ultimately, every form of healing goes back to the divine: love melts all blockages. Compassion gives strength and boosts power. Light heals and blesses.

One of the fundamental revelations of the Soul Light Era will be that everyone and everything in the universe has a soul: not only human beings but mother Earth as well, each tree, each river, each flower, and all the stars and all the universes both large and small. In this sense, each cell has a soul, each organ, each system of the body — and all are responsive to the healing vibration of love. The soul loves to serve and has great healing capabilities. You can simply request the soul to heal itself. This is a deep healing secret.

-§-
The primary role of the soul in health and healing is becoming apparent, as well as its vital contribution to longevity and rejuvenation.
-§-

As an example of the power of the soul, I invite you to contact your own inner being if you want to improve your health and boost your stamina and vitality. One way to do this is to practice "Say Hello healing," one of the simplest and deepest healing techniques you will ever learn. In Say Hello healing, you simply "say hello" to the small being within you — your soul — or your Inner Child if you prefer — and allow your soul's own deep healing wisdom to enfold you, as you enfold him or her.

Here's how to do it. View your soul as a small person, as a tiny baby even, kicking away happy and strong, glowing with universal light in your lower abdomen. For a few minutes each day, go within in meditation and talk to this beautiful baby, cooing and enveloping him or her with your love and positive energies. At the same time, feel the warmth and comfort of being enveloped by your own abdomen. A miniature version of yourself, this small person nestled there includes your physical, emotional, mental, and spiritual bodies. In fact, this small person is your soul. Communicating often is a secret pathway to health, long life, and happiness known and practiced by ancient Taoists.

My training for my life's mission began when I was six years old. My parents would take me to the park on weekends; there, I saw many elders practicing martial arts. One day, I witnessed a Tai Chi grand master propel a student twenty feet with the merest touch of his hand.

"I have to learn this!" I exclaimed. I ran to the elder, begging, "Teach me, grandfather. Teach me, teach me please." The Tai Chi master looked at me for some time, and then said, "My child, you are too young." I would not take no for an answer and, after some lengthy discussion with my parents, I was allowed to begin the training that would see me named Qigong Master of the Year at the Fifth World Congress on Qigong in San Francisco in 2002. I studied acupuncture, and also, at fifteen began training in Shaolin Kung Fu kick boxing and blade practice at fifteen. I progressed over several years to become a Grand Master of Tai Chi, Qigong, I Ching divination and Feng Shui. I knew, without words, that it was vital for me to learn their powerful secrets in order to be of service in the world.

In my village, I often saw people sick and in pain from diseases or accidents. I vowed to find simple ways of helping people heal themselves, and others. By the time I was twenty-one, I had discovered that by combining the power of martial arts training with the action of acupuncture needles, I could multiply the strength of the stimulus many-fold, and achieve noticeably better results in a fraction of the time required for standard acupuncture treatments. I was later invited to teach this revolutionary technique for the World Health Organization in Beijing.

I earned a medical degree in Western medicine at Xian Jiao Tong Medical University. However, my work as an institutional physician soon revealed that Western medicine was unable to help many patients. I realized that integrating it with traditional Chinese medicine would combine the best of both systems, so I obtained certification as a doctor of traditional Chinese medicine. Word spread, and I found myself the personal physician to many of China's top government officials. At the same time, I also held street clinics to treat the poor, to help relieve their pain, and to teach them how to self-heal.

I became a disciple of Dr. Zhi Chen Guo. Dr. Guo is a veteran medical researcher. His clinic, four hours from Beijing, has hosted up to *twenty thousand* patients at a time! He has had remarkable results, especially with cancer patients. Dr. Guo has combined fifty years of clinical research with his own remarkable medical intuitive faculties in discovering a vital transfer mechanism between matter and energy at the cellular level. A quantum discovery, this transfer mechanism uses the space available in the body, the gaps between cells and between organs, to keep the body and its energy flow

-§-
I witnessed a Tai Chi grand master propel a student twenty feet with the merest touch of his hand.
-§-

healthy. Moreover, claims Dr. Guo, that space can be influenced by the intention of the mind and also by soul power, just as intentionality can change the properties of water, as shown by Dr. Masaru Emoto in another chapter of this book. Dr. Guo believes that new scientific knowledge can be approached only from left field as it were, by using the right brain to stake out the claim of age-old insight. He maintains that paradoxically, for him and for many other hard-nosed researchers on the quantum edge of medicine, one of the best ways to explore and understand such insight is to enter the realm of inspiration—scientific, cultural, and otherwise.

Under Master Guo's rigorous training, I learned the spiritual secrets that allow us to communicate with the soul world. My spiritual channels were opened, and I became a medical intuitive. I began spreading the concepts of Master Guo's Zhi Neng Medicine in the West. *Zhi Neng* means the "power and intelligence of the mind and soul." Soul Mind Body Medicine is a revolutionary new form of medicine that emphasizes the role of soul over matter. It teaches people how to heal the soul first, removing the energy blockages that produce disease and pain in the mind and body.

-§-
Space can be influenced by the intention of the mind and also by soul power.
-§-

Soul Mind Body Medicine teaches that love, forgiveness, and compassion are the keys for healing when combined with the Four Power Techniques: Soul Power, Mind Power, Sound Power, and Body Power. These Power Techniques, when used together, can prolong life, increase energy, prevent illness, and rejuvenate the body:

Body Power

Body Power is the use of special hand positions for healing. One unique Body Power technique is called One Hand Near, One Hand Far. The Near Hand points toward the sick area in the body and is held four to seven inches away from it. Generally, there will be pain or inflammation in this area because the body's energy is "high-density," or concentrated, there. The Far Hand is placed twelve to twenty inches away from the lower abdomen, where there is relatively normal, lower-density energy. Just as winter air will rush into a warm room if the window is left open, this technique moves energy from the high-density to the lower-density area. The energy will naturally flow from the sickness area to the lower abdomen, which contains the body's storehouse of healthy energy to deal with it. Wen Hao of Singapore wrote these words after using these techniques:

"I am a physicist turned healer. I first found out about Dr. Sha's work on the Web in April 2005. After I read his book *Power Healing,* I started practicing the recharging exercise for about a half-hour a day for several weeks. Subsequently, all my chronic back pains and muscle aches disappeared completely, even to this day! Even the muscles around my eyes, which usually hurt due to reading too much, have stopped hurting. With the pain gone, I now enjoy life and work more. So much result with so little effort!"

Sound Power

Sound Power is the use of mantras or special vibrational sounds to stimulate cell expansion and contraction and thus propel the body's energy to move. Sound Power includes ancient healing mantras and special number sounds in Mandarin Chinese that vibrate the individual organs and body systems. One very special healing mantra for the Soul Light Era is 3396815, *san san jiu liu ba yao wu* in Mandarin Chinese, pronounced "sahn sahn joe lew bah yow woo." This sacred healing number sequence was received by Dr. Guo. It is the key to unlocking the voice of your soul, and the voice of all souls and of the universe. Replacing your negative internal sounds with sacred vibrational sounds can have powerful healing effects in your life. Jerry Crambe, of San Francisco, used to be plagued by incapacitating negative thinking. After using these methods, he wrote:

-§-
Heal the soul first, removing the energy blockages that produce disease and pain in the mind and body.
-§-

"One of the biggest life transformations I have had was at the workshop with Master Sha in December 2004. My life has improved dramatically. My relationship with my mother has improved greatly. This has always been a difficult relationship for me but now we are able to get along and talk without arguing. My relationships at work have also improved. I don't worry as much as I used to. My level of fear has decreased. The tape of negative thoughts that use to play continuously in my head seldom plays anymore. Now when this tape does start to play, I can turn it off. I was never able to do this before. Not hearing that tape of negativity is a tremendous blessing."

Mind Power

Mind Power is the power of creative visualization or "mind over matter." The mind has creativity, intelligence, and innate capabilities to heal, which may be set to work for healing. I teach many unique, *active* meditation practices for developing inner strength and power, as well as for healing and blessing all aspects of the physical, emotional, mental, and spiritual bodies. Patricia Bennett, of Haiku, Hawaii, writes of her experience:

"All of my life I have been a very passive-aggressive person. My pattern of relationships was one where I would say 'Yes, yes, yes,' when I meant 'No, no, no.' Then I would become dissatisfied in the relationship and would either lash out in anger or passively leave the relationship. This pattern has left my life empty and unfulfilled. Since I have been practicing with Master Sha and practicing the purification techniques, I have found that my relationships are changing quite dramatically. I am able to relax and allow the relationships to flow without being too eager to please or too eager to complain. I am able to speak my mind in love and compassion, and know that whatever my truth is at that moment, it is perfect."

Soul Power

Soul Power is the power of "soul over matter." Every unit of being — from the galaxies right down to the tiniest photon, and even "empty" space itself, has an individual soul. Using Soul Power, one can request the souls of the body, organs, and cells to heal themselves. Using Soul Power, one can direct love and forgiveness to the sick organs and cells with "Say Hello healing."

I honor Western medicine, but I encourage you to experience how effective these ancient techniques can be for your health and well-being. Millions in China have used them for centuries. Thousands of people in the West have been introduced and awakened to their potential. Try them out, and you will discover their profound benefits.

Love and forgiveness are the key elements for spiritual healing. Love melts any blockage. Forgiveness cleanses obstacles to our sense of peace. This wake-up call for humanity is a necessary bridge to the realization of the primacy of the soul in all aspects of our journeys and our existence. My deepest wish is that you will all learn to create your own healing miracles. Remember that you have the power, heaven has the power, Earth has the power, and the universe has the power to heal. Combine these powers together. Balance heaven, Earth and human being. Heal your soul, mind, and body. I have the power to heal myself. You have the power to heal yourself. Together, we have the power to heal the world.

-§-
The power of the soul is accessible to even the least initiated student of modern times.
-§-

FRED MITOUER:

Taming the Dragons: The Biochemistry of Transformation

We humans love the idea of peace. Throughout civilization as we know it, we have spoken of "Peace on Earth" as a most noble and desirable aim. If, however, we intend to bring peace—and "Joy to the World"—into reality rather than merely pay lip service to the notion, we must look at a difficult truth. And that truth is this: while we find the idea of peace alluring, in practice, we find it boring. In contrast to the state of hyper-arousal that constant conflict breeds, peace is a rather ho-hum experience. Our mind and our heart may desire peace, but our bodies have become conditioned to the adrenaline spikes that war and day-to-day disharmony generate. And so we unconsciously further our sense of separation out of habit, encouraging the stasis of our non-peaceful states.

Conflict may be inevitable in our world, but it does not necessarily have to lead to armed warfare. In situations where no alternative exists, force can and ought to be used to accomplish strategic goals without devastating humanity's soul. This soul devastation, sadly, is the core issue of our day.

We are now, as a species, facing an evolutionary emergency. Necessity being the mother of invention, we *must* redefine the human condition in light of newly acquired knowledge about the biochemistry of aggression. We know that healing, conscious touch not only ameliorates aggression, but substantiates peaceful states of being. This knowledge must now be skillfully applied.

Fred Mitouer, Ph.D., is internationally known for his uniquely shamanic somatic therapy. He has been a featured presenter at The International Somatics Congresses, State of The World Forum, and International Conference on Conflict Resolution. He is the founder of Dragons' Breath Theatre and Pacific School of Massage. His writings have appeared in *Perspective, Massage Magazine, Common Ground,* and *Yoga Journal.* He and his wife, Cheryl, homestead on California's Mendocino Coast where he practices his groundbreaking Transformational Bodywork™, sculpts in iron and stone, and rides his two life-sized fire-breathing dragons. Find him at: www.bodyworkmassage.com.

As a healing touch professional, I have massaged the war out of many Vietnam vets. I shudder when I consider the psycho-emotional fallout of the current generation's returning soldiers—not to mention those involved in the clandestine theater of torture. When these people come home after active duty, they are in some gradient of post-traumatic shock, deeply in need of a healing process to help them transition from soldier to citizen. When Athenian soldiers returned from battles with Sparta, they stopped at the temples en route. There, they were bathed, lovingly touched and anointed. As a result, they left the war behind and returned to their families to play the roles of father and husband. A *personal disarmament* occurred to protect the social fabric from the energetic of violence. In contrast, returning Vietnam vets had no cultural support in making the transition and, in fact, domestic violence soared from psychological wounds left untended. We are still today coping with the national karma of our ignorance about armament and disarmament.

-§-
"Another world
is not only possible,
she is on her way.
On a quiet day, if you
listen carefully, you can
hear her breathing."
—Arundhati Roy
-§-

Soldiers returning from battle are not alone in needing to be anointed with love and allowed their transformation. Every soul who witnesses the suffering of the world thirsts for spiritual communion to make sense of grief and despair. Indeed, each of us, in our spiritual heart, searches for the temple gates so that, once inside, we can grow into *Homo sapiens pacificus*.

Years ago, I came upon this story:

There was a time, before history, when the wise elders of the original human race gathered together to discuss the fate of humanity.... Knowing the human capacity for mischief, the wise ones were wary of offering access to the keys of knowledge for they knew that many would exploit this knowledge and disrupt the divine natural order of things. All of the wise elders argued against giving human beings another chance to possess divine knowledge—their true inheritance—except one. This one spoke passionately to the assembled elders, saying that he understood their concerns given the divisive racial history of human beings, but insisted the divine order called for each human to be given a chance to return home to oneness by virtue of his own effort.

The elders then remembered that this was, indeed, one of the divine laws governing the world of duality. One elder spoke: "All right, we'll offer divine knowledge to humanity but we shall hide the wisdom where the mean and greedy humans will not find it...let's put it at the bottom of the ocean." Another elder, remembering the clever excesses of Atlantis, said, "These humans will surely find it there, let's project it out to space." After this was also dismissed, the lone wise elder stood up to speak on behalf of humanity, saying:

"We should hide divine wisdom in a place where no exploitive human being with less than divine intent will ever look. Because exploitive humans are always looking outward for more to conquer, they never look within. We shall hide divine wisdom within the inner spaces of their own bodies. That way they will be brought to wisdom through investigations of the mysteries of their own hearts, from where only good could flow."

All the elders agreed on this solution to their dilemma. And so the human body became the map for the journey home.

As a veteran bodyworker, I have spent more than thirty years moving my hands over every type of human body. What I have found, over and again, is this undeniable truth: underneath our physical and psychic armament, humans yearn to love and be loved. And from the sense of *oneness* the experience of love engenders, peace becomes established in a person's life as fear and anxiety are overcome, neutralized, or outgrown.

I realize this sounds simple and obvious, but the bottom line is this: love is the most powerful force in the universe. And yet, as we all know, "just 'cause it's simple, doesn't mean it's easy."

Rubbing up against thousands of embodied lives from my box seat perspective, I have been fortunate to watch the dance of light upon darkness. Every one of these folks whom I have had the privilege to work with and teach have verified that human beings *can* realize "amazing grace" by surrendering to the body's wisdom. I convey this good news not as some starry-eyed optimist, but as a practical realist who has gone the messy distance with many brave souls who have shattered their illusions to find what truly matters.

-§-
"Gentleness is
a divine trait.
There is nothing stronger
than gentleness.
And there is nothing more
gentle than real strength."
—Kabir
-§-

We are living in a time when old beliefs must be confronted and transformed. No longer can we indulge the "eye for an eye, tooth for a tooth" impulse without suffering the devastating backfire of our myopic righteousness. Witness, for example, the blowback from the American invasion of Iraq or Hamas's insistent acts of vio-

lent martyrdom. Compare that with Gandhi's ability to oust Great Britain from India through non-violence, or Desmond Tutu's work to bring about a peaceful end to apartheid in South Africa. Both of these men represent the emergence of a new human mythos—one in which conflict is resolved without resorting to bloodshed. Peace works!

When Michelangelo was asked why he had chosen a particular piece of marble to sculpt into one of his masterpieces, he said, "There is an angel in it and I want to free it." Similarly, we must reinvent ourselves, and our mythos, with an eye for the angel inherent within. Then, with our will as a hammer, and discernment as a chisel, we can set the angel free. The swing of the hammer and the placement of our chisel is nothing less than love. One of the most powerful sculpting experiences is loving touch.

Love, as a human instinct, is expressed through the sense of touch. Beginning with the mother-child relationship, our primary bonding experience comes through holding and touch. When loving touch is present, a sense of wholeness characterizes our lives. When bonding and nurturance are lacking, however, feelings of well-being are elusive. And if abuse occurs, in any of its many forms—and a world in conflict is, in fact, a pervasive environment of abuse—fragmentation will result and further diminish our sense of security in this world. From this core insecurity, the dualistic reality that permeates the modern world is born and sustained.

Dualistic reality, sensed in the body, is a stark contrast to the reality of *oneness*. Dualism generates the split between *I and Thou* and alienates *me and you* until it culminates in the oppositions of *us and them* that drive us toward war. The fact that mass consciousness accepts this dualistic perception and its coarser instincts as "normal" is insane. The core belief upon which this peculiar insanity is built holds that the primary command of our DNA is sheer survival.

I take another viewpoint—one that embraces the will and capacity to thrive and to express deep care in all aspects of embodied human existence. From this point of view, the evolution of the collective human heart might very well hinge on the discovery of a relatively untapped strand of our DNA. In the year 2000, the human genome was completely mapped. Incredibly, we are now able to identify genetic patterns for a plethora of psychosomatic conditions such as panic attacks, Attention Deficit Disorder, depression, memory loss, obesity and hundreds more. During the last few years, advances in stem cell research point with great promise to many breakthroughs ahead. In the next decade, it is highly probable that medical science will discover some

-§-
Human beings can realize "amazing grace" by surrendering to the body's wisdom.
-§-

novel approaches to mitigate personal aggression and social conflicts. But we don't have to wait for a magic bullet to transform the human condition. We already have the power to make the leap into the wisdom world of the ancient elders *right now.*

The open secret is this: We need healthy, loving touch because without it we become aberrations of our essential nature.

In the early 1980s, James W. Prescott, Ph.D., a developmental neuropsychologist, discovered that when the brain's pleasure circuits are on, the violence circuits are off, and vice versa. Electrical stimulation of the pleasure centers in a raging animal's brain causes the animal to calm down suddenly. Conversely, stimulating the violence centers will just as quickly end an animal's sensual pleasure and peaceful behavior. Let's underscore those last five words: *Sensual pleasure and peaceful behavior.*

-§-
We need healthy, loving touch because without it we become aberrations of our essential nature.
-§-

Imagine peaceful human beings sharing pleasure. Then imagine what it would take to motivate them to rev up for a nice little war, or at least some random violence. Now, play this in reverse. What would it take to reintegrate war-weary soldiers into civil society?

Researcher Lionel Gambill summarized the experimental data on touch and development, and noted that:

- Touch and movement are essential sensory nutrients for the developing human brain.

- Sensory deprivation early in life results in brain dysfunction or damage to the cerebellum, which plays a key role in regulating emotions and balancing the limbic structures of the brain, especially the front temporal lobes.

- The neurological dysfunction that results from Somatosensory Affectional Deprivation (SAD) in infants leads to violent and depressive behaviors including withdrawal, hyperactivity, and head-banging; and, in monkeys, chronic toe and penis sucking. These compensatory behaviors correlate with the amount of sensory deprivation early in life.

- Increased vulnerability to alcohol or drug abuse and addiction is correlative as a coping mechanism for the emotional pain of adult human beings with SAD.

Both in monkeys reared in isolation, and in highly aggressive institutionalized children, researchers have found exceptionally low levels of platelet serotonin, a condition associated with extremely violent and anti-social behaviors. Cats deprived of their sense of touch

become self-destructive. Dogs and monkeys in these conditions will bite and chew flesh from their fingers, hands, arms, or legs. These aberrant instincts in the human context develop into the mechanisms of sadomasochistic and suicidal behaviors as well as sexual violence.

The evidence is overwhelming: physically affectionate human beings are highly unlikely to be physically violent, and pleasure is highly therapeutic for the rehabilitation of aggression. The divine hardware of our brain's one hundred billion cells—with each cell linked via synapses to as many as one hundred thousand others—is bathed in the hormones and neurotransmitters that are activated in response to new experiences.

-§-
We still don't know how to raise and educate children in non-authoritarian, peaceful ways.
-§-

Deep in our limbic brains we have come to view the biochemical nature of peace in pejorative terms: less valid or less real. In peaceful states, we also let down our defenses and feel more vulnerable. Because vulnerability is perceived as a liability, rather than an asset, we maintain our defenses. We are a species heading for extinction because our life force is directed toward armament rather than the pursuit of a disarmed way of living.

Students of life know that all intimacy and spiritual growth depend upon the art of personal disarmament, of learning how to be appropriately disarmed. When we open to our vulnerabilities, we invite peacefulness, and become less charged-up on a physiological level. Our subjective experience is the sensation of flow; we feel more round than edgy. And our sense of self evolves into a more selfless state. This is where our personal peace spreads into social realms and has the potential to become truly transformational.

Humanity's great challenge is to heal forward into *oneness* so that we can live in alignment with the laws of nature. From a healed place, enlightened behaviors will naturally ensue. Most observers would say that our present world situation is too complex for a transformation that is grounded in the stark simplicity of human biological healing. But in truth, the elegant solution, I believe, lies in our capacity to exchange thinking for sensing, allowing a new, embodied understanding to cultivate a wholly different peace-loving bio-programming. To do this, we must understand how far we have strayed from our biological wisdom. And we must stop congratulating ourselves on how well we are doing in the game of survival. The law of survival is an evolutionary dead end. We need to cultivate a new human paradigm based upon the instinct to thrive. Bottom line: "Make love not war."

The need for healing has never been greater. With all the talk of family values, people have never felt more fragmented and in need of real emotional security. Traditional religion, never a great friend to the human body, has largely been co-opted by fanatical flat Earth fundamentalists. Our devotion to materialism has neither improved the quality of medical care nor made the workplace more enlightened. We still don't know how to raise and educate children in non-authoritarian, peaceful ways.

After all the so-called progress, we really have very little to show as far as advancement in levels of human happiness. Each of us who cares deeply must turn to the subject of personal healing and ask, "How can I bring about a positive change in my life? How can I find the compassion and courage to confront my personal demons, befriend their energies and re-awaken my aliveness?"

It is logical to ask, "How can the healing work I do on myself truly make a difference?" And, at first glance the odds seem formidable. But if we appreciate that the universe is not linear and static but rather multidimensional, evolutionary and dynamically interdependent, we can see that one person's true transformation has the potential to holographically leverage the metamorphosis of the human species by altering our way of perceiving. If we find this notion too far a reach, then simply contemplate the lives of Mother Theresa, Jesus Christ and Gautama Buddha as a starting point. And start we must!

The amazing opportunity of the current emergency involves transforming our perception of our very existence. We are literally poised at a threshold of perception wherein the linear and dualistic old adage, "I'll believe it when I see it," morphs into the multidimensionally unifying lens: "I'll see it when I believe it."

In the former example, we human beings peer out of our survivalist lenses into a threatening world. Adrenaline runs supreme and we do not really "see" anything that does not fit into our preconceived belief structures. Within this mental prison, we selectivity judge anyone who does not agree with us. The violence in our world arises from this basic reaction against those who don't agree with our beliefs. Just consider the fate of two noble warrior kings who sacrificed their lives for peace in relatively recent years: Anwar Sadat and Yitzhak Rabin. They were not killed fighting against one another's armies in the Sinai Desert. They were assassinated, respectively, by an Islamic fundamentalist and a fanatic orthodox Jew — both addicted to a mean old story. We can do better!

Our transformational threshold is rapidly approaching. Each of us is sensing this metamorphic moment in unique proportion to our individual perceptions and beliefs.

Fundamentalist Christians, for example, speak of the rapidly approaching End Days, where the Kingdom of Heaven intercedes to save humanity from its sinful nature just as we descend into apocalyptic collapse. The quicker the collapse, according to this thinking, the sooner God comes to *save* us. Of course, other religions have their own version of the Rapture. And Paradise awaits any true believer who sacrifices his life by killing the infidel.

-§-
The new humans of today are presently awakening amidst the chaos of a dying root race addicted to the adrenaline of fear, greed, and war.
-§-

The common thread of Fundamentalist viewpoints is the view that embodied human life is sinful, evil and wrong. Women don't come out very well in these patriarchal takes on reality. A lot of blame and shame is being tossed around, and the word *God* is often used to justify mean-spirited behavior. It's time for a new human story.

Quantum physicists speak of causal links between thought forms and their material manifestations. Social esotericists have translated the physics paradigm into the more poetic expression: "there is nothing more powerful than an idea whose time has come."

The classic example of this "powerful idea," is the widely disputed cultural mythos of the Hundredth Monkey phenomenon, as popularized by Ken Keyes Jr. What began as a personal change with one monkey—washing a sandy sweet potato before she ate it—morphed into a new social custom for ninety-nine monkeys; and then, at a metamorphic threshold, one humble hundredth monkey catalyzed a universal revolution. Or so goes the story.

In human history, we know that the Renaissance was generated by a relatively small group of people who demonstrated that there is nothing more powerful than an idea whose time has come. Jean Houston Ph.D., has named this metamorphic threshold "Jump Time."

Transformation at the level of behavioral change—whether in humans or monkeys—demonstrates how one individual can make a revolutionary difference. Most monkeys, (think *Homo sapiens pacificus*), are either among the first ninety-eight or the hundred and one to a trillion that follow. Their endeavors may not be catalytic, but in the deeper reality, it doesn't matter whether one is the star, or the one in the right place at the right time, or simply part of the chorus. What matters is that one is open to a new way of being truly alive and co-creative with the mystery that goes by ten thousand names.

Thirty thousand years ago, the new humans roamed the same plains as the Neanderthals. The new humans of today are presently awakening amidst the chaos of a dying root race addicted to the adrenaline of fear, greed, and war. This is all in the order of things.

In the brief slice of time that is our modern era, many spiritual paths have characterized the journey of awakening as long and arduous, requiring cloistered submission to a hierarchy and laborious discipline. Many potentially enlightened people have been discouraged from opening to the life of true spirit. But there is a quickening occurring with the healing work that has become the Twenty-First Century's spirituality. Healed people are, by definition, whole instead of fragmented and thus able to live with pleasure and joy, in service to others.

Once we decide to heal on a bio-psychic level, we begin a journey that embraces the peaceful resolution of conflict on all levels. As we perceive our wounds as opportunities, we find that the energetics that were tied up in confusion become fuel for our spiritual unfolding. In essence we compost our difficulties into soulful realizations and we find ourselves walking more gently on this Earth.

This pivotal time period is filled with great possibilities alongside the inevitable suffering that a dying species evokes. But suffering can lead to enlightenment, as Buddha invited us to see. For without suffering, we seldom develop our compassion. And so, it is appropriate that, as we open to our healing—from all the lack of bonding or the presence of abuse—we will touch what needs to be healed. And there we will find our shadow sides that hunger for the light, not unlike the way a photograph develops from a negative to make a positive.

I call these shadow sides our dragons, for they can be fierce and protective and scare us away. But there is a spiritual service they provide, and it is sacred—for in the law of polarity, we need to feel our weakness to find our strength, our pain to find our pleasure and joy, our fear to find our security and safety, and our loneliness to find our capacity to love. Many years ago, I took it upon myself to build two life-size dragons on my land. They have aged nicely and breathe holy fire, fueled by two propane canisters buried in the ground. Everyone who sees them is filled with awe and appreciation, for subconsciously dragons ignite the mythos of power and protect the treasures. The greatest human treasure is our divinity. Our divinity needs to be touched by human love. This is the reason we incarnated. This is our birthright and, ultimately, our destiny.

CHAPTER ELEVEN

The ancient myths throughout the world describe dragons turning into princesses at the last moment. "Perhaps all the dragons of our lives are princesses who are only waiting to see us once beautiful and brave," says poet Rainer Maria Rilke. "Perhaps everything terrible is, in its deepest being, something helpless that wants help from us."

Perhaps we humans can awaken from the consensus trance that tells us that the best way to live is to get comfortable and avoid pain at all costs. Perhaps our terrible dragons and deepest sufferings are nature's way of compelling us to investigate the mystery hidden by the ancient elders deep within the cellular matrix of the human body. And, perhaps our struggles are designed to humble us so that we cannot help but surrender to the mystery that wants us to know it for All That It Is.

VASANT LAD:

World Medicine

Revolutionary advances in modern medicine are emerging as Western practitioners begin to integrate holistic health approaches. Ayurveda, one of the most ancient healing sciences, is being recognized for its comprehensive and complementary role in bringing balance and well-being to all humanity.

Ayurveda is the science of life. And life exists together as the body, mind, and consciousness. No matter where we live, we are exposed to the five great elements *(pancha mahabhutas* in Sanskrit): Ether, Air, Fire, Water and Earth. Changes in these elements directly impact our health. Today we are facing radical environmental, economical, relational, and nutritional changes. The nature of these changes and their health consequences differ worldwide. In developing countries, pollution and educational disparities lead to epidemics. In the West, nutritional imbalances underlie obesity, diabetes, strokes, and cancer.

Although the problems in the East and West seem to differ, the root cause is the same, according to Ayurveda—imbalances among the three bodily constitutions, or *doshas—Vata, Pitta, Kapha.* Vata is the principle of movement, sensory stimuli, and motor responses. Pitta is the energy of transformation and digestion of food and regulates all biochemical changes. Kapha is the cementing and constructing material of the body. These three doshas are constantly exposed to

Dr. Vasant Lad is an Ayurvedic physician. He received a Master of Ayurvedic Science degree (M.A.Sc.) in 1980 from Tilak Ayurved Mahavidyalaya, in Pune, India, as well as studying allopathic medicine and surgery. He served as Professor of Clinical Medicine at the Pune University College of Ayurvedic Medicine for more than a decade, before bringing his wealth of classroom and practical experience to the United States, where he founded the Ayurvedic Institute in Albuquerque, New Mexico, in 1984. Dr. Lad is the author of several books and is respected throughout the world for his knowledge of Ayurveda. More at www.Ayurveda.com.

the environmental and emotional changes that determine individual physical, mental, and spiritual health.

First we should understand what healing and health is. The ancient Sanskrit writings of Ayurveda, approximately 10,000 years old, state that health, or *svastha,* is the state of balance between body, mind, and consciousness, the bodily seven tissues *(dhatus),* the elimination of wastes *(malas),* the three bodily doshas (Vata, Pitta, Kapha)—as they govern psycho-physiology—and thought, feelings, and emotions. When any of these are disturbed, the person becomes out of balance, and left long enough, disease begins. Despite the different illnesses facing persons living in the East and West, we are all basically similar. Our thoughts and feelings are the same. Our emotions are the same. And to a certain extent, our problems are the same. The problem is too much expectation in relationships, too many demands, excessive desire, and—as a result—underlying dissatisfaction. People are unhappy with who they are and what they have. These are the leading factors affecting individual health.

-§-
You can transcend the problem into bliss in a fraction of second.
-§-

The state of ill health is a moment to moment happening. Healing is moment to moment balance, bringing awareness to our thoughts, feelings and emotions and how we respond. For example, the instant we wake up in the morning, the first thought, the first feeling in the heart of every human being, is I AM, I exist. That existence is I am-ness. That I am-ness is common in all people whether they are Indian, Japanese, American, or Russian. It doesn't matter. Every person has that constant inner feeling of I am-ness. Yet when problems erupt, what happens? We identify ourselves with our thoughts and emotions. We remain stuck with the problem. That is the root cause of ill health.

So to heal, we must inquire. We must ask, "To whom is this problem happening? To whom is this sadness coming?" In that inquiry you will see, "Oh it is happening to the body, or to the mind. It is not me. I am far beyond the body and the mind. I am just awareness. I am that I AM. I am that pure awareness." Suddenly you can transcend the problem into bliss in a fraction of a second. You are separated from the problem. And you enter your peaceful existence and being.

Bring awareness to the pure self that is there in every moment, in every event, in every walk of our lives. That self must be understood. We don't understand ourselves—for the mind self, the emotional self, the time-bound self—is the false self. Yet the true self is always present. In this fast-paced world, we have forgotten our true selves, who we are, and what really we are. The true self is awareness, consciousness. The true self is liberation. You are that awareness. You are enlightened. Yet you are still stuck with your body and mind, with your conclusions and judgments, and therefore you are suffering this misery. In every walk of our lives, we must feel the true self; "Oh, this is me, I am." Feel your presence. Feel your being, your I am-ness. I am. I am that I AM.

Meditation means moment-to-moment awareness of I am-ness. We must commit to this practice. Practice beyond the one little corner of your room. Practice when your wife is yelling at you, when your husband is criticizing you — when a war is going on in your kitchen. In that moment, feel your I am-ness. You will suddenly go beyond that suffering. Suffering is what is. That is why we need spirituality in every walk of our lives, in every moment of our breath. Spirituality brings the transformation that opens the door to healing.

Such transformation is taking place everywhere. America is a country where people are highly spiritual, even amid our current problems. No one can avoid social, political and environment upheavals. People are contemplating the causes of all this suffering. In that inquiry, people are asking, "How can we help each other?" "How we can heal each other?" and, "How we can heal ourselves?" That is very important, since healing is first. When you heal yourself, then you can heal others. If you do not heal yourself, how can you heal others? That is why Ayurveda, the science of self-healing, is the foundation for transformation.

Over the last thirty years that I have practiced medicine, I see a radical transformation happening in personal and planetary health. People are expressing hope. However, we must go beyond hope, because at any moment that hope may become hopeless. Do not hope. Simply do your *dharma*, your duty — your responsibility as a human being. My responsibility as a human being is to heal myself, heal my friends, and heal my family. Hope has no place in this work, whether people like it or not. Flowers are blooming. Rivers are flowing. Winds are blowing. And the sun is rising. There is no cause for their actions. There is no hope in their action. And there is no desire out

-§-
The time-bound self — is the false self.
-§-

of which they are acting. They are simply performing their dharma. The same thing is required of us; we do our dharma as humanity. That is the powerful message of Ayurveda, which names four aims of life as the foundation of health — Dharma (our duty), *Artha* (livelihood), *Kama* (happiness or desire) and *Moksha* (liberation). Having dharma means that, the moment you are born, it is your responsibility to protect this Earth, to take care of yourself. That is why Ayurveda is the most practical medical science of life.

CHAPTER TWELVE

People in the West are seeking natural and holistic ways of healing. They want organic food, environmental cleanliness. In the developing world, overpopulation and poverty is prevalent. People fight day to day to get bread and water, especially in the cities. So for them, making the practical changes central to holistic health is not easy. But it is happening. I see it in the rural areas, including in India, where I operate my clinic. By the next decade I expect radical changes in Third World countries. Environmental pollution is a critical problem. I feel sad that in many areas of the world, people cannot breathe fresh air or drink fresh water. They cannot find healthy, organic food. It is time to focus seriously on our population and pollution problems. Ayurveda offers unique solutions to such problems.

-§-
Practice when your
wife is yelling at you,
when your husband
is criticizing you—
when a war is going
on in your kitchen.
-§-

Historically, modern medical doctors have not been open to Ayurveda—even Indian doctors. However, interest in Ayurveda is growing. I have seen this change; I am now invited to give lectures at many U.S. universities and clinics. I see the greatest advances in holistic health coming from educating lay people about Ayurveda. Twenty-five years ago I started teaching the Ayurvedic concepts of nutrition and lifestyle in the United States. After they heard me, patients went to their doctors asking new questions about what to eat and how to live in balance. They sought answers tailored to their unique constitutions (Prakruti) and for creating whole person health—body, mind, and consciousness. Doctors are discovering that patients know more than they do. Now doctors and nurses are taking Ayurvedic classes and adopting Ayurveda into their lives. It is important to train the Western medical profession in Ayurveda. This group is the leading authority in this country in the field of health and nutrition. This training is flowering, and it will bring harmony to doctor-patient relationships—and between the environment and humanity.

There is a concern that Ayurvedic remedies may have high levels of heavy metals. This must be addressed. Some Ayurvedic remedies do include specially prepared heavy metals. However, the toxic properties of heavy metals in some Ayurvedic remedies are nullified through ancient, alchemical processing methods. Research proving the toxicity of properly prepared Ayurvedic remedies has not been done. However, if doubt exists about these Ayurvedic remedies, don't use them. Ayurveda is a vast medical science. Use the foundations of Ayurvedic diet, organically grown herbs, detoxification programs (panchakarma), and rejuvenation programs (rasayana) to bring balance and well-being. It is safe and effective!

I hope to see improved integration of Ayurveda and Western medicine in the future. I think we all need education about what *integrative* means. Integration means that the two medicines are complementary, so that the terms of one system can be explained in terms of the other—with each maintaining its integrity. Integration happens at the theoretical and clinical levels. For example, in my lectures, I explain the Ayurvedic concepts of *Ojas, Tejas* and *Prana* using modern Western medical terms. Ojas governs cellular immunity. Tejas governs cellular intelligence. Prana is the flow of cellular communication. Theoretical integration also involves mutual understanding by Ayurvedic and Western doctors of—on the one hand, Ayurvedic perspectives of the five elements, seven tissues (dhatus), three doshas, and nutrition—and on the other hand, accurate models of physiology, pathology, symptomatology, and nutrition. Second, integration at a clinical level means, for instance, coalescing Western and Ayurvedic remedies. To illustrate, bodily constitution plays a major role in how patients assimilate medicine. In the case of a person with a pitta constitution taking aspirin for a fever—classically recognized as a pitta type of imbalance—taking *shatavari,* an antacid, can improve aspirin's action. I have seen shatavari help patients accept even chemotherapy. In sum, true integrative medicine involves integration at both the theoretical and clinical level.

Integrative medicine is especially is useful for disorders that—in Western terms—have no name. Take, for example, a patient experiencing low backache, constipation, body aches and bloating. Their physician might report them—after a full examination—to be quite normal. With Ayurveda, the troubling symptoms can be easily understood as a vata imbalance. Vata-pacifying remedies can be applied to relieve the symptoms and restore balance. While every symptom is not the symptom of disease, certain symptoms may be signs of doshic imbalance. The beauty of Ayurveda here in a complementary role is its ability to remedy doshic imbalances and prevent the seeds of disease from sprouting. As an Ayurvedic physician, I see the integration of the art and science of Ayurveda and Western medicine as the key to healing for all humanity.

-§-
The moment you are born, it is your responsibility to protect this Earth.
-§-

PART THREE

Cultural Earthquakes

ANODEA JUDITH:

The Next Rite of Passage for Humanity

13

The human race has reached a critical turning point. On center stage, world events focus our attention like never before. Dramas that were once local have now become global. The audience stirs, over six billion strong and still growing exponentially, peeking out from every corner of the globe. Some watch anxiously, with bated breath; others are still sleeping or barely awake, still rubbing their eyes. From living room televisions, car radios, newspapers, magazines, and the World Wide Web, countless individuals are drawn toward the unfolding collective drama, bearing witness to humanity's current rite of passage.

As we meet for coffee, for dinner, for walks, for business meetings, or romantic dates, the conversation buzzes, like an audience murmuring between acts. What will happen next? What should be done? What's wrong? Who's right? How do we find our way through? Even those who live outside the theater, far removed from the continual broadcast of Western civilization—they too are impacted by the actions taking place on center stage.

As are we all.

In the theater of the world, we are simultaneously audience and cast, playing our scenes to an instantaneous feedback system that continually shows us our reflection. But rather than the image of a single character, we are witness to a global tapestry, weaving itself

---

Anodea Judith, Ph.D., is a therapist and workshop leader who has written extensively on the use of the chakra system as a template for transformation. Her books include *Eastern Body, Western Mind* (Celestial Arts, 1996), *Wheels of Life* (Llewellyn, 1987), and numerous audio and visual works, including a spectacular DVD, *The Illuminated Chakras* (Sacred Centers, 2003). This article is excerpted from her current work in progress: *Coming of Age in the Heart*, which will be published by Elite Books in 2006. For more information and sample chapters of this exciting forthcoming book, see her website: www.SacredCenters.com. Photo by John Frick.

a new picture. Its threads, spun from archaic forces long ago, have been woven together by the myths, legends and heroic deeds of our ancestors. To weave a new picture, we must engage these forces and take them into our own hands — with maturity, understanding, and most of all — with heart. For those of us alive at this time — whether we like it or not — are undergoing *a rite of passage into the next era of civilization.*

To understand the new picture and find direction for these trying times, we must inquire into the essential questions asked by myths of all ages: *Who are we? Where do we come from? Where are we going?* It is these questions that give meaning to the drama, revealing the genius behind its many layers. Here we find crucial instructions, not only for our personal struggles, but also for the larger story of what we are becoming together — as a growing collective entity, living on a finite jewel of a planet, maturing into the parents of the future.

Who Are We?

We enter the scene in the present moment, well into the show, suspended in a cliff-hanger between the third and fourth acts. In the drama thus far, humans have become an astounding race of creatures unlike any other. Birthed from the primal womb of nature, billions of years in gestation, we have now risen out of Stone Age infancy, crawled across the land in teeming toddler-hood, and labored through five thousand years of sibling rivalry, to emerge at the present time in the tumultuous throes of adolescence. Highly powerful but still immature, we stand poised between epic creation and potential annihilation, equally capable of either.

-§-
We are undergoing a rite of passage into the next era of civilization.
-§-

Issues of power and love, war and peace, prosperity and consumption, freedom and tyranny, individual rights and community needs — all hang unresolved in our story. While none of these issues are new, it is only recently that they have global consequences, impacting our survival into the future. Though it is a time of unprecedented change, major players in this drama still read from outdated scripts that no longer serve our present needs, let alone those of the future. The curtain is rising on the next act.

As the scene opens, we find an adolescent race entering into a monumental rite of passage, undergoing an initiatory process into adulthood. Like an adolescent, we have reached adult size in our population with little room to grow further. We have gained tremendous power, yet still naively expect that Mother Nature and the powerful

Daddy at the helm will continue to take care of us, even as we struggle against their control. Our entertainment is adolescent: flashy and fast moving, focused on cars, sex, and shoot 'em up power contests.

Unlike tribal initiations at the hands of wise elders, there are no elders who have already been where we're headed—into a way of life that has never before existed. Instead, we are being initiated by the byproducts and demands of our own civilization, bringing us blinding paradox at every turn. We are witness to our own creation of heroic achievement and environmental destruction, caught between the ability to splice genes and the inability to feed the hungry. The agents of our initiation broadcast realities into our living rooms, from local snipers in our neighborhood to bombs dropped on the other side of the globe.

-§-

Major players in this drama still read from outdated scripts that no longer serve our present needs, let alone those of the future.

-§-

They appear as data on the information highways that tell us our world is in danger, and news media that keep us preoccupied with stories of mass distraction. They come from transportation systems that mingle cultures from all over the planet and threaten us with terrorism in our own backyard. They come from the possibility of nuclear disaster, environmental collapse, genetic modification, global warming, unchecked population growth, and a technology that is loading real time Technicolor into the global brain and taking it to the stars.

As forces compress humanity into an ever-smaller world, there is nowhere to escape the increasingly insistent challenge to our adolescent lifestyle. In every walk of society, we are being asked to wake up, to mature, to come of age as a species. As it is for initiates, the ultimatum is written on every wall: *transform or die.*

The old story of warring empires struggling for dominance must give way to new myth of cooperative interdependence. An era of the heart, based on integration, compassion and community is essential if we are to move into the future. This is our collective rite of passage. It takes us from opposition to synthesis, competition to cooperation, separation to integration, and most importantly: from the *love of power* to the *power of love.*

What does it mean to "come of age" as a species? How do we outgrow dependent childhood and adolescent rebellion to grow into productive maturity? How do we create the necessary transformation without elders to guide us? And how do we make sense of what we've done in the past so to better understand what we must do now? Carl Jung said that we become enlightened by making the darkness conscious. Our culture is caught in the shadow of our own blinding light. Our history is our collective unconscious. To truly come of age, we must understand the developmental dynamics of our past, in order to weave these threads into a vision fit for the future.

Where Did We Come From?

To answer this question is to examine the archetypal dynamics that ruled previous ages. Here we discover that our collective history mirrors the progression of childhood development as well as the unfolding of the levels of conscious evolution described in the yoga tradition represented by the chakra system.[1]

Stage One: The Great Mother (approximately 30,000 BCE to 7,000 BCE).

Life first emerges from the mother. Historically, we find an awakening of consciousness in the Paleolithic Stone Age (though this era could be seen as starting much earlier), an era that corresponds to the infancy of civilization. We began in symbiotic enmeshment with the forces of Mother Nature. Like the infant child who cannot move too far away from the mother and still survive, humanity was bound to the cycles of nature, unable to deviate from them and still survive. We were earthbound for our survival, following the wild game and collecting plants where they grew, living in caves and makeshift structures, traveling across the land in small tribes. Embeddedness in Nature represents the primal *thesis,* from which all life has evolved. The collective intelligence of this age was focused on *survival,* the consciousness level of the first chakra, whose element is earth.

-§-
We are caught between the ability to splice genes and the inability to feed the hungry.
-§-

Stage Two: The Mother and Son (approximately 9,000 BCE to 3,000 BCE).

This stage is marked by the development of agriculture and trade by sea. Its archetypal motif is the dynamic between the Great Mother and her young son, who is growing out of infancy, but still in a toddler phase. (In some iconography the motif of son and lover overlapped as one.) This era focused on community building, farming, and animal husbandry, with a peaceful religion still centered around the reign of the Great Mother and the cycles of Nature. This era reflects the focus on sexuality and procreation, related to the water element of chakra two. Fertility and birth were revered, which resulted in exponential population growth. This created new challenges in social coordination and necessitated the higher organization of the next era.

Stage Three: The Dynamic Masculine (3,000 BCE to the Birth of Christ).

As population expanded, land and water rights became the cause for wars and skirmishes, resulting, over time, in a militaristic society based upon hierarchical rule. This period is typified by the patriarchal domination that overthrew the Great Mother and forced higher levels of organization through the development of human power structures. It is marked by the use of fire to forge metals and make weapons, the beginnings of technology, sacred kingships, city-state politics, and territorial expansion through violence and warfare. The archetypal

-§-
The ultimatum is written on every wall: transform or die.
-§-

motif reflected here is exemplified by the maturing son who breaks away from the mother. He transforms the cultural values of the previous era into their complete opposite, *creating an antithesis to the original thesis.* Thus the power to kill held more influence over behavior than the power of birth. Heaven was holy, Earth was profane; men ruled, women were subordinate.

This age, corresponding to the third chakra element of fire, brought us power, technology, individual will, and personal freedom, along with its shadow of destruction, violence, domination, and environmental pollution. It pulled us away from our basic thesis, in order to make a new polarity, but in this pulling away, we lost vital parts of our roots.

Stage Four: The Christian Era (The Birth of Christ to the Present).

The fourth and most recent stage contrasts and balances the Mother/Son-lover motif with the archetypes of the Great Father and his daughter/wife—a wife whose status was diminished to that of a daughter. In this way the values that were antithetical to our original nature became the central values of the current era. All that was holy in the earlier phases: nature, the feminine, the body, sexuality, emotion and worship of Nature became repressed or marginalized, while "higher" values were placed on the masculine aspects of mind, spirit, control, aggression, technology, militarism, and institutionalized power. Clearly these values still hold predominance today.

The Christian era, with its tenet that "God is Love" began as a much-needed attempt to ascend to the heart, or fourth chakra, but one that failed to achieve that goal because it arose in a paradigm that was still making separation between essential aspects of our wholeness. It didn't foster equal relationships between the powers of heaven and Earth, mind and body, male and female, but instead overvalued one at the cost of the other. Rejecting half of humanity—and the reality of our physically embodied and ecologically embedded lives—cannot lead to the unification of a true paradigm of the heart. Furthermore, enforcing this great separation requires a state of internal warfare: mind at the expense of body, rules at the expense of instinct, obedience at the expense of empowerment.

When essential aspects of the psyche are repressed, their shadow becomes projected onto others. The Crusades, the Inquisition, and the often brutal dominance of indigenous cultures by Christian missionaries, disguised in moral righteousness, can hardly be seen as fostering the compassionate love of the heart. This dueling dualism wastes precious energy in struggle, whether it be between nations, races, religious beliefs, political parties, or aspects of the self.

Where Are We Going?

In all of our past mythologies humans have been in a childlike position to parental gods. This creates an infantile expectation to be taken care of, to follow rigorous parental codes without question, and to engage in collective sibling rivalry over whose god is right, the basis of many wars. While it is certainly important to retain humility in light of divine forces, we have failed until now to employ a mythology that encourages *balanced partnership between the genders and a co-creative relationship with the divine.* Represented by the Sacred Marriage, or *hierosgamos*, this new archetype, as a symbol of balance and integration, emerges as the guiding archetype for our present era. Its symbol, two intersecting triangles, is coincidentally the same symbol within the lotus of the heart chakra as drawn in the Tantric texts, signifying the integration of spirit and matter.

-§-
It is the developed world that has the capacity to save or damn our future.
-§-

Having experienced the original *thesis* grounded in the archetypal Mother, followed by its *antithesis,* experienced through the masculine Father, the time is now ripe for a new and higher synthesis. We are no longer helpless children in the ever-abundant Garden of Eden where Mother and Father supply our every wish. We are now ready to meet each other as equals, just as adolescents begin to form equal relationships between the genders. But like adolescents, we are still clumsy at relationships and too egocentric to really love. We have barely awakened our hearts.

The intersecting triangles of the heart chakra imply that it is the great integrator whose chief property is one of balance: balance between above and below, mind and body, masculine and feminine, heaven and earth. This means we must place equal spiritual value on the beauty of the earth and the power of nature as we do on a transcendent God, denying neither. Only then can we address environmental challenges that are essential for our survival. We must reclaim the rejected body as an undeniable aspect of health, equal to the powers of the mind. Only then can we live healthy and embodied lives. We must integrate the values of the feminine along with the masculine, valuing the distinct offerings of each gender. This means valuing both rational and intuitive modes of thinking, both structure and process in organization, both thinking and feeling in our experience, and both progress and sustainability in our civilization. Just like a window or a drawer becomes stuck when one side gets ahead of the other, we must first achieve this balance in order to move forward into the future.

Awakening the Global Heart

Lasting transformation cannot be generated by fear, guilt, or control, but must come from a true inspiration of the heart — literally from the act of falling in love, perhaps the most transformative experience a person can have. When we truly love something, we care for it willingly, even joyfully; such as we do for our children or mates. Can we fall back in love with our world?

In walling ourselves off from nature, as we did for the purpose of defense during the third chakra stage of sibling rivalry, we reduced the world around us to something "other," to an inanimate thing, devoid of spiritual value, a view that became crystallized during the "Enlightenment" of the eighteenth century. This created an "I-it" relationship with nature and with each other. From the slaves of distant times to the exploitation of the environment, we inspected, dissected, used and abused, without regard to the subjective experience of the other. We can worship inanimate things as idols, but this is not love. For love requires that we recognize the sacred subjectivity of the 'other.' In this way we move beneath the surface, to the interior of another being, culture, or ecosystem. It is through this depth that we mature.

-§-
Can we fall back in love with our world?
-§-

As expressed by the late systems theorist, Erich Jantsch, the *I-it* relationship is a product of rational thinking, as in documenting the scientific details of an ecosystem or a population. It is objective, full of information, but devoid of meaning, which can only be arrived at by looking at the whole. By contrast, the *I-thou* relationship is mythic, emerging not from details but from the essence. When we experience the world around us as "thou" we touch its numinous quality. Then

we can love something for its own sake rather than purely selfish interests. This kind of love seeks to preserve rather than exploit. From the *I-thou* perspective, we see our world as a living entity, and this mythos gives us new meaning and purpose. Only then can we grow into the co-creative evolution of a collective "we."[2]

In order to truly love we must heal the heart by reclaiming what has been rejected and neglected. We need to integrate the values of psyche and of society that have created division rather than unification. This integration occurs through the realm of relationship, *for the act of relating creates compassion* and awakens the heart. We are less likely to harm something to which we relate, just as we are not likely to eat the family cat, even if we otherwise eat meat from the market. As we learn about other cultures, other environments, other ways of being, awareness begets relationship and offsets harm.

This requires compassion and empathy, essential aspects of the heart chakra. Empathy develops when we acknowledge our wounds, our shadow, and reclaim the feeling function that allows us to "feel with" another. Empathy allows us to move from an *I-it* relationship, into an experience of *I-thou*, a realization of the other as equally sacred.

This is where the role of initiation comes in. Initiation breaks down the narrow-minded arrogance of adolescence and opens a larger vista. Initiation often begins with a wound or loss that strips us of our innocence and develops empathy. The events that destroyed New York's World Trade Center on September 11, 2001 can be seen as an initiatory wound for the U.S., one that opened many people's hearts to the larger matrix of suffering that exists and is even caused by the hidden shadow of U.S. foreign policies. Despite the governmental decisions to repeat the tragedy of war in Afghanistan and Iraq, there has been a deeper outcry against these wars—with larger peace marches and more public discussion—than has ever occurred in history. This outcry was not just among Americans, but occurred worldwide. Such awakening is clearly not coming from the dictates of the father at the helm, but from the growing population of individuals who are awake enough to have empathy and caring for the innocent victims of war on the other side of the globe.

Such a longing for peace reflects the Sanskrit name of the heart chakra, *Anahata*, which means, "sound that is made without any two things striking." When we have at last risen beyond the constant struggle of opposing forces, both within and without, the energies previously spent in defense, destruction, and control can then be harvested for building a more cooperative and enlightened world.

It is in crisis that we are confronted with the loss of what we have denied. It is through initiation that we are stripped of our old way of being and launched into a larger vision. From the initiatory wounds of the September 11 disaster in the U.S., to the floods, famines, and foes that ravage people's lives, humanity is faced with threats that are breaking down barriers of separation and forcing community cooperation. Our problems are too overwhelming to solve in any single aspect of society, but must be confronted with a whole systems approach, bringing all aspects of our world back into *relationship* with each other.

As the essential feedback mechanism in an evolving system, our media can enhance or inhibit the awakening of the global heart. We can feature sensationalist stories of celebrity sex-capades, and numb our senses with constant violence—or we can witness the reality of Nature and our fellow humans as they are: beautiful, exotic, precious, and seriously threatened. It has long been said that the truth will set us free, and it is the job of the media to broadcast truth into the homes and hearts of every global citizen. Unfortunately, public media is often distorted, like a funhouse mirror, giving us an inaccurate picture of our collective reality. But beneath the increase of reporting on violence, crime has declined by half, social organizations with altruistic goals have increased exponentially, and the quality of life continues to improve globally, even though many lag behind. Fortunately the World Wide Web and the instantaneous availability of information can foster networking and reorganization on a global scale, at least in the developed world. For it is the developed world that has the capacity to save or damn our future.

Even in these wee hours of the dawning, there are many of us who are awakening from slumber. We are becoming repossessed by the sacred instead of dispossessed by its lack. We are awakening to passionate dedication rather than spineless obedience. We are bringing ourselves into deeper and more informed relationships with both self and others. Our vision is weaving a new tapestry of healing and restoration.

When the global brain achieves the self-reflective consciousness that allows us to see both the light and the shadow of our world, we will awaken the passion of the global heart. With open hearts we enter the adult realm of the world community. As global citizens, we become cellular elements beating in unison with the soul of the world itself. This is the task of our initiation, but we must undergo the rite to discover the mystery.

GEORGE LEONARD:

And Everything Was Different

Peak experiences have a way of rearranging our perception in a manner that is both permanent and pervasive. An experience of this type taught me both the import and impact of blending, one of the foundational practices of aikido. It demonstrates how a change in context can completely change our experience. In this case, truly grasping the practice of *blending* made old-style confrontation obsolete in my life.

I was traveling around the country, giving speeches at major universities, after my first big book, *Education and Ecstasy,* came out in 1968. *Look* magazine, my employer at the time, had serialized the book in three straight issues. In addition to being on the cover of Look, the book was featured in full-page ads in the *New York Times.* It sold over 300,000 copies within a year. The late 'sixties was a very explosive and confrontational time in America, and the model of education I proposed in that book was revolutionary. Wherever I went, there was both interest and resistance to my ideas.

One evening, I was giving a speech at the Unitarian Church in San Francisco. I had only been studying aikido for three months at the time. Although I was not feeling well that day, I decided to go ahead with my talk anyway. After my presentation, I called for intermission before what I felt certain would be a fast and furious question and answer period. While walking through the lobby on the way to the

George Leonard, a pioneer in the field of human potential, is the author of twelve books, including *Education and Ecstasy* (North Atlantic, 1987), and *Mastery* (Dutton, 1991). During his seventeen years as senior editor for *Look* magazine, he won an unprecedented number of national awards. Leonard holds a fifth-degree black belt in aikido, and founded Leonard Energy Training (LET), a transformative practice inspired by aikido. He is a past president of the Association of Humanistic Psychology, currently serves as president of Esalen Institute, and holds several honorary doctorate degrees. His latest book is *The Way of Aikido* (Dutton, 1999). More at www.ITP-Life.com.

men's room, I saw a stocky, florid man haranguing a crowd of people around him. When he saw me he shouted, "Get over here, Leonard!"

I turned in his direction. He viciously attacked me verbally, saying, "Not only will your book destroy our schools, it will probably mean the end of Western civilization." He stood waving his arms and cursing in colorful, forceful language. I begged off his challenge, saying, "Excuse me, sir, but I'd like to get to the men's room. After intermission, I promise to recognize you first."

Upon stepping back up to the podium, I located the man sitting six rows back and said to the audience, "I promised to recognize this man first. Please sir, did you have a comment or question?"

He stood up and started letting me have it, cursing as he had in the lobby, only worse. He insisted that only bad could come of my approach to education and that terrible things would happen to our children as a result. He continued along these lines for several long minutes.

Then it was my turn. I had faced this type of confrontation countless times and was quite practiced in how to manage angry opposition. My limited aikido practice had not yet given me a firm understanding of the connection between the body and the mind. I could speak of the connection; I could speak also of the *concept* of blending, but had not yet realized or embodied it. On the contrary, rather than blending with the angry man, I gave him his hostility back. Even worse, I got the whole audience howling with laughter at his expense as the poor man sank lower and lower in his seat.

-§-
A change in context can completely change our experience.
-§-

A few days later, while in my downtown San Francisco office at *Look*, I received a special delivery letter. I opened it and read, "I am the man that you humiliated at the Unitarian Church." The letter went on to say how completely shamed and destroyed he'd been by what had happened. *Oh, my God,* I thought, *What have I done?*

I can be a slow learner, but in that moment—boom—I realized that had I made the choice to blend with him, everything would have been different. I could have taken his point of view, absorbed it, then made my point very effectively.

Two weeks later, I gave another speech, this time at the University of Colorado. The big auditorium was packed with a lively crowd. A group of graduate students sitting toward the back of the crowd were making wisecracks on the side. During the question period, one among them raised his hand and, with the full support of his cohort, began his challenge. He said, "Leonard, your book is bullshit! This computerized system of education that you have in your so-called Jefferson School won't work! The computerized system would cost more than the whole school."

Rather than match his confrontational stance with a bigger, tougher attitude of my own, I had the feeling *in my body* of going down, standing next to him, and adopting his point of view. I said, "Well, you know, what you're saying makes sense. And this concern is really worrying me, too—the cost issue."

Instantly, he turned it around and said, "Wait a minute, wait a minute, computers are getting cheaper every year, every month." Right before my eyes, an opponent became an ally and began to argue in favor of my ideas. That was a turning point in my life. A shudder of recognition went through my body as the gestalt of that afternoon embedded the blending concept in my body.

As I toured around the country the rest of the winter and throughout the following spring, the audiences I spoke to were wonderful. Every other week I would go out to give a talk—and blend and blend and blend until my blender was bent. I was blending all over the place. Since that day in Colorado in 1971, I have not had to field a single hostile comment during a platform speech.

Experiences of this type not only shift the context and therefore our experience, they also provide a template for the future. This can be seen at the collective level with, for example, the civil rights movement.

It is very difficult for people of today to understand what American apartheid in the South was like before the Civil Rights movement. I grew up in Georgia; my grandfather was a state representative for Walton County for sixteen years. Between the ages of twelve and fifteen, I spent summers in my grandfather's big white house in Monroe, Georgia, with my cousin Ed Stevenson, who was five years my senior. Ed was fascinated by what was going on in the world—and also by the terrible injustice in this country. My cousin was a born teacher who went on to become a beloved figure at the University of Georgia in Athens. But during those summers, I was his entire student body and he opened a whole new world to me. Together, we did a tremendous amount of reading—Hemingway, Faulkner, James, Wolfe, and many others. He had me read *The Varieties of Religious Experience* when I was only thirteen years old! Those summers represent the high point of intellectual learning in my life. The whole idea of racism

-§-
America is far more divided today than at any other time in the last thirty years.
-§-

was anathema to my cousin, and to me, especially after an incident I witnessed the summer of my thirteenth year.

A black man was brought to the county courthouse in the center of Monroe, Georgia. Everyone knew he was going to receive the death sentence. The boy across the street and I jumped on our bikes and rode the five or six blocks to the county square to see what would happen. When we arrived, I saw the man being led across the square in chains. For one brief, electrifying moment, his eyes met mine. It was a terrifying experience, and pivotal. It led to my becoming completely dedicated not only to desegregation, but integration as well.

As a young journalist, I covered the Civil Rights movement from Little Rock through Selma and Old Miss. Among the greatest moments of my life were Sunday mornings at Ebenezer Baptist Church, listening to Martin Luther King Jr., who I got to know quite well. The Civil Rights movement gave a generation of young activists ideas about how we could change society. I believe that it can serve as a template for the current move toward social change.

America is far more divided today than at any other time in the last thirty years. For the various factions to hear each other, and learn first to tolerate and eventually to embrace each other, we need to learn social aikido. Once we learn to practice blending at a macro level, socially and culturally, everything will be different. But change at the social and cultural level meets with resistance in much the same way as change at the personal level. Therefore, it is important to look at why our resolutions to make positive changes so often fail.

I've written about this at length in both *Mastery* (Plume, 1992) and *The Life We Are Given* (Tarcher, 1995): A characteristic of living systems, *homeostasis* is the tendency to maintain equilibrium by resisting change—whether that change is for the good or the bad. This tendency can be seen in all self-regulating systems, from the smallest single-celled organism to the individual human being; from a nuclear family unit to large organizations—and even entire cultures. The in-built tendency to stay the same within rather narrow limits applies to psychological as well as physical states, and to behavior

-§-
It is important to look at why our resolutions to make positive changes so often fail.
-§-

on both a personal and collective level. Said simply, most of us will do everything to be consistent with who and what we identify with and experience as who we are. We are faced with a special challenge when homeostasis works to keep things the same when things aren't so good. On a personal level, we know this backsliding tendency all too well: two steps forward and three steps back.

Dealing with resistance and homeostatic tendencies requires focused effort, and *awareness* is the first and most important step. Simply knowing and being able to anticipate resistance means that you will be less likely to give up at the first sign of a painful counter-pull. Secondly, it's important to negotiate with your resistance by learning—or inventing—the fine art of playing the edge. A thin line exists between making slow, steady progress—and making a solid push despite resistance. Both require determination, and both are made easier if we make the process fun. Having a support system, and finding companions to share the ups and downs, will help. Following a regular practice, a discipline that you keep for its own sake rather than to reach a goal, lends stability and comfort. That discipline, in turn, becomes a springboard for life-long learning—which involves us in constant change.

-§-

The extent of the resistance is directly proportionate to the importance and power of the change you want to make.

-§-

Often, the extent of the resistance is directly proportionate to the importance and power of the change you want to make. Once you start changing for the better, you may become uneasy. In our experimental classes with LET (Leonard Energy Training) and ITP (Integral Transformative Practice) I teach people the 3-H process: how to bring the *head*, the *heart*, and the *hara* into alignment with the desired change. First, you involve the head, and get the intellect involved, by reading and consulting experts in the field. Once the head has the data and information needed to make a decision, you check with the heart. Imagine the situation you want to change and ask, "How does my heart feel about making this change?" Then, as a final step, you go to the hara—the power center just below the navel where you feel the sense of gut-knowing—and let hara make the final decision. This process has proven useful to many people when homeostasis gets in the way of change.

Society resists change in the same way that individuals do. There are a number of trends in Western culture that reinforce the status quo, and stand in the way of substantial change:

1. The Trivialization of Human Endeavor. It has taken *fourteen billion* years since the Big Bang to create the miracle of life. Humans are the most complex, most highly organized entity in the known universe. There may be others somewhere, but in the known universe, we, above all, have potential. And while the depth of our creative potential lies dormant, waiting to be realized, current cultural trends make human endeavor trivial. Think about this for a moment: What if someone came from another planet and using a high order of intelligence was able to tune into television for just twenty-four hours.

Imagine the picture they would get of humanity. What we watch, what we wear, what we concern ourselves with—all of it so insignificant.

Another indicator of this trend can be seen in the publishing world where it has become more and more difficult to get good work published. Recently, my agent told me that a top editor at one of the big publishing companies said, "If you have a novel, don't send it, because I can assure you it will not be read." *It will not be read.* This generalization shocked me to the core.

2. The Canonization of Celebrity. Hand in hand with the tendency to trivialize our creative endeavors is the canonization of celebrity in the United States and around the world. People watch what celebrities are up to simply because they are famous. And why are these people famous? Are they particularly admirable individuals? Not always, but the mere fact that they are famous means they are watched and discussed. An inordinate amount of attention, press, and airtime, is afforded these people as a simple by-product of fame. This collective fixation on celebrities denies the infinite creative potential of the ordinary individual.

3. Misdirection in Public Education. This I consider to be a most devastating trend. Years ago, in *Education and Ecstasy,* I advanced a model of education that emphasized individuality. One of the most controversial chapters in that book was titled "Testing Versus Your Child," in which I made the case that overtesting would have devastating long- and short-term effects. Today, we have programs like No Child Left Behind that focus entirely on testing. If these programs are successful, we will have *Brave New World,* where everyone will be essentially the same, having lost all contact with their unique essence. The tragic loss of creativity—that human wellspring that really makes things work—and disregard for individual styles of learning is, to my way of thinking, a dreadful negative trend. Very few of the radical changes in education I recommended back in the late 1960s have come about. Perhaps had I better understood the mechanism of homeostasis, I would have been more strategic and less radical in my recommendations.

-§-
Society resists change in the same way that individuals do.
-§-

4. Breakdown of the Separation between Church and State. We are seeing a trend that could lead to the undoing of the separation of church and state that was absolutely essential to the American Revolution. The emerging alliance between religion and governance has gained strength among our leaders; evangelicals and people in high office would like to see religion in the schools. This is truly frightening because once religion is mixed up with governance, tyranny is sure to follow.

5. The Tragic Waste of Human Potential. All of the above trends feed into a larger streaming trend that leaves the incredible capacity of the individual human being and society as a whole largely untapped. We use only a very small portion—some claim less than two percent—of the vast potential available to us. It is possible to experience life in all of its dimensions—physical, emotional, intellectual, spiritual, and social—with far more depth, creativity and meaning than society leads us to expect. Each of us is potentially a genius. Think about that for a moment. There is only one of you in the entire known universe. What a loss if you don't develop fully, if you don't leave a legacy behind, even some tiny achievement. The greatest tragedy on the planet is the failure to realize our potential. And I would like to speculate that a great deal of the neurosis, illness, crime, restlessness, drug abuse, and perhaps even war, is a result of this failure to develop our potential.

-§-
What we watch, what we wear, what we concern ourselves with—all of it so insignificant.
-§-

A friend said to me, as he approached his death, "I realize now that I've wasted my life." Think about that. Would you like that to happen to you? Use your potential; there is nothing more important. Here are a fifteen guidelines to help you access your infinite creative abilities:

1. Assume that your potential exists.

2. Be patient if it does not manifest immediately. We don't access it magically!

3. Follow your hedonic response, your bliss.

4. Run your ideas past good people. Listen openly to what they have to say. But don't let negative responses discourage you if you have strong feelings.

5. Use the principles of play. Make up games whenever possible, which will be far more often than you might think.

6. Prepare, read, and learn the best material relating to your creative idea or direction. Don't let the past stop you.

7. Brainstorm.

8. Practice, practice, practice.

9. Use the 3H decision-making process. Let the body be your teacher.

10. Get expert advice, but don't necessarily follow it.

CHAPTER FOURTEEN

11. Generally trust hara. Your genius may not be in your head.

12. Consistently imagine how you'd like things to be.

13. Know when it's time to give up on a certain approach and go on to something different.

14. Be patient, but remember you don't have unlimited time. You may not get it right, but you can get somewhere.

15. *In potentia,* each of us is a creative genius. Each of us!

Novelist James Agee wrote, "I believe that every human being is potentially capable, within his 'limits,' of fully 'realizing' his potentialities; that this, his being cheated and choked of it is infinitely the ghastliest, commonest, and most inclusive of all the crimes of which the human world can accuse itself…. I know only that murder is being done against nearly every individual on the planet." These words are heart-wrenching, and spark my commitment to realizing the vast potential of humanity.

The crime Agee speaks of affects all of us, not just distant victims of injustice, war, famine, poverty, and natural disasters. I can think of no tragedy so pervasive as the waste of human potential that results from the dogmatic, thought-inhibiting and heart-numbing twists of perception that find humans expecting so little of ourselves. The vision of human evolution and transformation of human societies is growing, however, and we have hope. A collective "peak experience" that changes everything by shifting the context may well be upon us. What form it will take, none of us can yet know. And yet the quest of my lifetime, and that of so many deeply caring people, cannot be denied. The human potential movement, still in its infancy, has touched the lives and hearts of millions of people. As the poet Dante said, "Love is what moves the sun and the stars," and I believe such a movement that fosters love in the human heart and in human interaction is the greatest adventure of all.

-§-

Fixation on celebrities denies the infinite creative potential of the ordinary individual.

-§-

Jean Shinoda Bolen:

Sacred Fire

The heart of the world is fragmented. It is broken into over six billion pieces, the same number as there are people in the world. Every infant comes into the world as a small, vulnerable, inherently lovable being, capable of generating love and expressing love. If all went well, every child would grow into a compassionate and empathic adult; everyone would add another essence of heart to the heart of the world. I heard Maya Angelou speak at a conference once, and under her direction, we all sang "This little light of mine, I'm gonna let it shine, let it shine, let it shine!" The fullness and warmth the song evoked could easily be expressed as: "This little heart of mine, I'm gonna let it glow, let it glow, let it glow." Seven hundred voices—mostly women's—were as one, as we went from belting it out to singing it softly. Our hearts were engaged and connected; we were one in heart as well as in song. Sung with feeling and enthusiasm, the song filled my chest.

Recognized or not, there is a heart center in the middle of the chest, under the sternum between the breasts. The heart center, often referred to as the heart chakra, is not identical to the anatomical four-chambered heart, which mostly lies in the left side of the chest. It is the heart center that emotionally aches, or opens up and trusts; becomes broken or healed; is guarded—or even armored. The heart center is attuned to our feelings about other people, about animals, about the land. I think of the heart center as something both subjective

Jean Shinoda Bolen, M.D., is a psychiatrist, Jungian analyst, clinical professor of psychiatry at the University of California, San Francisco, a Distinguished Life Fellow of the American Psychiatric Association, and the 2002 recipient of "Pioneers in Arts, Sciences, and the Soul of Healing Award" from the Institute for Health and Healing. She is a former board member of the Ms. Foundation for Women, and the author of *The Tao of Psychology* (25th Anniversary Edition, 2004), *Goddesses in Everywoman* (20th Anniversary Edition, 2004), *Crossing to Avalon* (10th Anniversary Edition, 2004), and many other books. Full information at www.jeanbolen.com.

and energetic, it seems to some like a field of color or molecules, or felt as a pressure or vibration. We feel connected to others through it. This heart center, while not the same as the anatomical heart, affects it. A broken heart—or a lonely heart, or becoming disheartened—can increase a person's susceptibility to heart disease. Research attests to this, and also shows that involvement with friends, relatives, and community enhances life and extends it.

There is a collective heart of the world, just Jungian psychology holds that there is a collective unconscious. In theoretical biology this might be an aspect of the human morphic field. In ways that logic cannot explain, but that quantum physics may, human beings are interconnected, linked to each other invisibly across time and space. There is a spiritual dimension to the collective heart of the world.

Heart, Hearth, Hestia, Mother

When I lead a guided meditation or convene a circle with a spiritual center, I often invoke an archetypal image: the sacred fire in the center of a round hearth, often symbolized by a candle in the center of the circle. In classical Greek mythology, Hestia was the Goddess of the Hearth and Temple. She had no persona and was considered to reside in the fire itself. It was her fire that made both home and temple sacred places. Sacred fire goes with the heart meditation that I lead, with the words: "Close your eyes, relax. The more relaxed you are, the more receptive you are, and the more receptive you are, the more vivid this can be. Feel that warm place in the center of your chest, and see or sense a fire glowing in a round hearth. This is an inner source of illumination and warmth. Now imagine this light and warmth spreading through your whole body, which is a temple." The thought that came to mind, when I linked this meditation to the idea of a collective heart of the world: "Let this light and warmth be the love that you have to give. Let it flow from you into the world to wherever it is needed."

-§-
The heart center is attuned to our feelings about other people, about animals, about the land.
-§-

Love is an energy source with unique properties: the more I give away the more I have and the more there is. Almost everything else is a zero sum game; if I give you what I have, I will have less and you will have more.

Love nurtures and sustains life. Whether plants or animals or children, we have the power to support and enhance the growth of that which we love. On the other hand, we also have the ability to stunt growth, especially in the very young. Infants and young children suffer from "failure to thrive," a common diagnosis at hospitals when there is a lack of maternal concern and behavior, often by a mother who is herself overwhelmed and unable to function, sometimes because she is abused and addicted. However, "anaclitic depression" was the reason given for failure to thrive among babies taken from their mothers in wartime London. Kept safe in nurseries in the country, they were kept clean and fed, but were not held, cooed to, and loved. Loving touch, eye contact, and voice—the means through which maternal love is expressed—was lacking. Maternal love is essential for babies and other growing things. Mother is essential for life. Biologically, it is the mother of every species who births life out of her own body, nurses her young, protects them while vulnerable, and teaches them how to fend for and feed themselves. In the animal kingdom, if the mother dies or lacks maternal instinct, her offspring cannot survive.

> -§-
> Let this light and warmth be the love that you have to give. Let it flow from you into the world to wherever it is needed.
> -§-

Missing Mother

In the human world, men survive physically and intellectually who are stunted emotionally and spiritually in the absence of loving and strong mothers. In the patriarchal world, especially under fundamentalist religions, women often cannot protect themselves or their children from men who have contempt rather than compassion for vulnerability. In ancient Greece, women were property. While this is no longer legally so in most countries, in every country, women continue to be treated as such by some men. According to Amnesty International, one out of every three women in the world will be raped or beaten in their lifetime. One million women and children—most of them girls—are trafficked for the sex trade or domestic slavery; they are abducted, abused, used, and then disappear. Such things happen year after year. Compassion is missing; the world is without heart when it comes to these women.

The atomic bomb was created in the mid-twentieth century and dropped on Hiroshima and Nagasaki. It was followed by the nuclear arms race between Soviet Russia and the United States, which resulted in an arsenal that could destroy everything on the planet and leave it radioactive for thousands of years. The power to use these weapons is in the hands of men who sanction war and are caught up in a cycle of conquest, humiliation, retaliation, and revenge. Men who can only feel anger, and not grief, have numbed their hearts.

My book *Urgent Message From Mother: Gather the Women, Save the World* grew out of my concern about this destructive course. *Mother* is the Mother archetype, Mother instinct, Mother Goddess, the Sacred Feminine. "Gather the Women" is a call that will be heard by women with an active mother archetype or sister archetype who—by gathering in circles with a spiritual center and an activist agenda—can bring about changes in the morphic field by becoming a critical mass with a tipping point effect. This is how American women created the women's movement—and changed the world in a little over a decade. This is what will bring the feminine principle of nurturing, sustaining, collaborating, compromising, and connecting through the heart back into the world. The feminine principle and the mother archetype are human patterns that are not active in every woman and can be strong inner qualities in men, especially those in egalitarian families and relationships. By contrast, in patriarchal families and cultures, men learn, as boys, to suppress compassion, expression of their feelings, and empathy.

-§-

One out of every three women in the world will be raped or beaten in their lifetime.

-§-

Overall, the world has very little heart, and the sacred feminine is missing from the world. The two are related. Until the feminine principle is integrated into culture and the feminine voice is heard, there will be no check on patriarchy and the use of power for domination and revenge. Healing the heart of the world results in a shift in consciousness, an awareness that the feelings and needs of others matter. A culture of peace results. The following powerful words are excerpted from "A Women's Creed," written in the Women's Global Strategies Meeting in New York in 1994 by Robin Morgan together with Perdita Huston, Sunetra Puri, Mahnaz Afkhami, Diane Faulkner, Corinne Kumar, Sima Wali, and Paola Melchiori and one hundred forty other women from fifty countries.

Women's Vision for a Culture of Peace

Bread. A clean sky. Active peace.
A woman's voice singing somewhere,
melody drifting like smoke from the cookfires.
The army disbanded, the harvest abundant.
The wound healed, the child wanted, the prisoner freed,
the body's integrity honored, the lover returned.
The magical skill that reads marks into meanings.
The labor equal, fair, and valued.

Delight in the challenge for consensus to solve problems.

No hand raised in any gesture but greeting.

Secure interiors—of heart, home, land—so firm

as to make secure borders irrelevant at last.

And everywhere laughter, care, celebration, dancing, contentment.

A humble, earthly paradise, in the now.

Heart as Organ, Heart as Metaphor

Another song comes to mind; this one is from my years in high school, when I was a delegate to the California Girls' State convention. The song we sang as we marched through Sacramento was "Let There Be Peace On Earth, and Let It Begin With Me." This was hardly what the sponsors of Girls' State convention, the American Legion, would have chosen as a theme song. Yet this is the song that reflected the feelings of sixteen-year-old girls who came together from every high school in the state. It was if we had tapped into an intuitive wisdom that knew that peace is possible if enough humans became peaceful. Without theories such as Malcolm Gladwell's *The Tipping Point*, or Rupert Sheldrake's "morphic fields" to guide us, we linked peace within to peace in the world. We instinctively knew that each of us contributes the heart we have to the heart of the world.

As the center of circulation in the body, the physical heart pumps blood—with its life-giving oxygen, nutrients, and protective cells—to every organ and system in the body. For the heart to pump well, it needs time to open and fill before it can contract and push blood out into the arteries. Inward flow and outward flow, diastole and systole, make up the rhythm of the heart, which when listened to with a stethoscope sounds like *lub-dub, lub-dub*. This heartbeat is echoed by the drumbeat of indigenous dances. A healthy heart fills and empties as it both sends and receives blood to the circulatory system that is literally a tree of life within us.

-§-

Women respond differently to stress; by seeking out friends to share their concerns in conversation; by taking extra care of children; by caring for plants.

-§-

When the heart is out of rhythm, problems arise. Fear and anxiety cause the heart to race. The pulse accelerates, and the heart beats faster and faster. The internal organs needed for digestion, reproduction, and elimination are then deprived of blood flow, which now goes to the muscular-skeletal system. Physiologically, the body gears up to run or do battle, a response that is lifesaving for a man or a woman faced with sudden physical attack. This type of adrenaline activation, enhanced by testosterone, is a typical male response to chronic stress of all kinds. Women

respond differently to stress; by seeking out friends to share their concerns in conversation; by taking extra care of children; by caring for plants; by decluttering the household or office. This is the "tend and befriend" response. As women do this, *oxytocin* – the maternal bonding hormone that is enhanced by estrogen – increases, which calms the psyche and slows the heart rate. Women bond and deepen their friendships through empathic listening, and by sharing ideas.

-§-
Always being busy, always at the beck and call of another person or of circumstance, deprives the soul of nourishment.
-§-

The heart of the world is enhanced by the sum of compassionate understanding, which women accomplish through bonding conversations. The amount of love, connection, and reflection in human consciousness grows when concerns are shared through the "tend and befriend" response. Oxytocin is called the *maternal bonding hormone* because it notably increases when a woman gives birth, nurses, and bonds with her baby. It contributes to the activation of maternal instinct toward her newborn and to the mother archetype, especially if the child is wanted and comes into the peaceful world of a mother who is not fearful or stressed herself.

A healthy psyche behaves like a healthy heart. There is time to be reflective and a time to be active. Time and energy is needed go inward to fill spiritual and psychological needs. The pace of our current life often denies this crucial inward time. As a result, we don't pay enough attention to feelings that could tell us what we really care about, or know, and need to do next. Like the heart that beats too fast to fill fully – and reduces blood flow to internal organs, our internal life gets less and less of our attention. We don't listen to ourselves – to our body's reactions, to the dreams and nightmares that arise – when heart is missing from our personal world and the outer world. Always being busy, always at the beck and call of another person or of circumstance, deprives the soul of nourishment.

Our speeded-up world bombards us continually with messages and images. They come in such quantity and frequency we pay less and less attention. There is no time to truly take in much of what we are exposed to, unless we deliberately take time. Solitude, a walk, meditation, tending a garden, writing, creating – all these require going inward, and shutting out the cacophony that competes for our attention in the outer world. Now that we have digital photography, images come to us over the Internet. We scan them. We might download some after a split-second look. We then go on to other e-mails. The people who take the pictures and send them on may give what they are doing a little more attention, but it is a far cry from the development process that took place in a darkroom lit only by a red light that would not affect film taken out of a camera. In the early days of photography, for masters like Ansel Adams, taking a picture was only the first step in a process of seeing, selecting, and developing.

I think of the heart center as the darkroom of the soul. It is an inward attitude, a receptive emotional intelligence that takes a second look at what we experience, and reflects upon it. It is a feeling response to the important and revealing moments in life, and a means through which the feminine principle develops in us. As a result, the metaphoric heart, and the heart of the world, have reasons which reason does not know. A developed heart can be trusted to know what matters.

Healing Power of the Feminine

The *tend and befriend* feminine principle, which nurtures, sustains and connects, also heals and restores soul and body. The healing power of the feminine was clearly demonstrated in refugee programs that began in Bosnia organized by Zainab Salbi. Since then, the organization she co-founded, Women for Women International, has helped women in refugee camps in Afghanistan, Kosovo, Croatia, Columbia, Iraq, Nigeria, Pakistan, Bangladesh, Rwanda, and the Congo. I first met Zainab on a shuttle bus that was taking us from the airport to the Global Peace Initiative of Women Religious and Spiritual Leaders in Geneva. A year later I met her again in a living room in Mill Valley, California. Listening to her speak, I understood why her organization was highly successful, where most other programs fail. Zainab's program employs the feminine principle—and women who have been refugees themselves as staff.

-§-
A developed heart
can be trusted to
know what matters.
-§-

Women arrive at a refugee camp after physically surviving the devastation of war. They are usually destitute, in shock, and feeling deep shame. Not only have they been through a war zone, lost their homes, and been separated from family and community, they commonly have also been raped. They arrive at the camps exhausted, traumatized, demeaned, and disheartened.

Zainab's healing program begins by simply giving the women money to spend on whatever they need or want. The first thing most women purchase is a supply of menstrual supplies. They are not asked questions, or required to account for how they spend this money. Simply having money to buy a few things they need for body or soul gives them choice and some dignity. Then the women receive vocational training. They learn a skill such as making shoes or baking,

through which they can support themselves and their children. They are taught by women who have themselves been refugees, and have then mastered new information and gained new skills.

The third step uses the feminine principle of compassion and connection for psychological and spiritual healing. This happens after the refugee woman has had some restoration of dignity, learned a new skill, and had the opportunity to work side by side with other women refugees. By this time, she has made some friends, and begun to feel part of a community. Only then do the women enter a circle process, also led by women like themselves. This healing process may take as long as a year, and involves hearing the stories of other women, and feeling the kinship that comes from listening, and through sharing their own stories. This process of witnessing and being valued heals their trauma. The love and empathic understanding generated in these circles of compassion restores their hearts and souls. Women see themselves differently when they are mirrored positively, and realize that they are resilient survivors capable of loving and being loved. Their hearts are restored and added to the heart of the world.

-§-
When we construct a world in which people in the cities cannot see the stars at night, there are fewer opportunities to have the individual heart touched by beauty.
-§-

Love and Beauty

In the mythology of ancient Greece, Aphrodite, the goddess of love, was also the goddess of beauty. Appropriately so, as love and beauty go together. Whoever and whatever is loved, no matter how homely, is beautiful in the eyes of the person who loves. There are, of course, objective standards of beauty, but there is also something subjective and transpersonal about the human experience of perceiving beauty. The classic story of *The Little Prince* by Antoine de Saint Exupéry makes this point. The little prince comes to Earth from an asteroid, on which there is one rosebush with one bloom. The little prince loved his one rose, which for him was the only one in the whole universe. The little Prince took care of it and cherished it, though it was a self-centered rose. Then he came to Earth and saw that there were zillions of rosebushes and even more roses, which initially confused him. Then, he observed that his rose was special because he had loved and taken care of it. Even though some of the other rosebushes might be more perfect, his remained the most beautiful to him. We could say that he saw it with his heart. That which we love is beautiful to us. When we love there is an invisible connection to what we love—an alchemy occurs in which both are affected. In

Goddesses in Everywoman, I called Aphrodite the Alchemical Goddess for this reason.

When we destroy beauty, such as ancient redwood trees, or construct a world in which people in the cities cannot see the stars at night, there are fewer opportunities to have the individual heart touched by beauty. The heart of the world is diminished when this is so. It is through the feminine principle, or heart center, that beauty is felt. Tenderness, as evoked by a sleeping baby, warms the cockles of the heart. Love, beauty, kindness, and tenderness connect us to the Great Mother, the goddess, maternal instinct—all of which are missing from the world.

Healing the Heart of the World

Healing the heart of the world happens cell by cell, and each human being is a cell that contributes to that healing. If maternal instinct, the mother archetype, and the sacred feminine came into consciousness and culture to ensure that, beginning while in the womb, all children, and their mothers, were safe from domestic violence and war, the heart of the world would be healed. Patriarchy, which is based on domination over others, is incompatible with this. Patriarchy and peace are incompatible. People come into the world as infants who seek to be loved; when they are not, they settle for power as adults. When power is exercised by men over other men, there are winners and losers. The losers wait until they become stronger and can exact revenge for the humiliation they have suffered. This tit for tat, do unto others what they did to you (or fear they will do to you if they have a chance) is the patriarchal creed responsible for repetitive cycles of humiliation and revenge, as well as fear-based first strikes. The collateral damage is always the same: women and children suffer.

-§-

Healing the heart of the world happens cell by cell, and each human being is a cell that contributes to that healing.

-§-

A baby comes into the world with billions of neurons. How the world responds to that baby influences how its brain will develop. Recent research has shown that if a mother is terrified and terrorized, the brain of her baby will be affected in the uterus. Further shaping of the brain occurs in infancy and at other crucial times; use it or lose it is the operating principle. Neurons that are used grow dendrites or become myelinated; unused ones die off. Under patriarchy, especially in males, this leads to left-brain dominance. Logic, rather than compassion, rules. Creativity suffers. Love and beauty cease to be primary values.

The cost is staggering—not only in terms of lives lost and psyches damaged, but in terms of who we could be. When we consider the probability that human beings could develop in ways we can only imagine, that loss—of who we could be as a species and how we could serve the planet and all life upon it—is also the cost of patriarchy. Our potential as a species has never been fully developed because we have not had a chance to see what we could become in a peaceful world. There remains a possibility that the heart of the world will emerge as a vital force for transformation if women realize that the power to transform patriarchy lies with them. Through the heart of women, the heart of the world can come into the world. The last verse of "Untapped Source of Peace" from my book *Urgent Message From Mother: Gather the Women, Save the World* fittingly sums it up:

> Untapped source of peace
>
> Women in circles,
>
> Women connecting,
>
> Women together
>
> Bringing the sacred feminine,
>
> Maternal instinct, sister archetype,
>
> Mother power
>
> Into the world.

KIMBERLY WEICHEL:

The Feminine Front Line

Standing with twelve thousand women from every possible cultural, ethnic and religious group at the extraordinary UN Decade for Women conference in Nairobi, Kenya in 1985, was a seminal experience for me. After five days of intense conversations about the common issues facing us as women and facing our world, we stood in an enormous circle on the lawn of the University of Nairobi. As I held hands with my new sisters, Adekeye from Sierra Leone on my left, Rena from Indonesia on my right, surrounded by sisters from a rainbow of cultures and perspectives, I felt viscerally that by harnessing the power of women, we could heal the differences that divide humankind. At a very deep level, I knew that the power to bridge and connect was far stronger than the power to divide, and I knew that women carry the wisdom and responsibility to be the peacebuilders.

This awareness and experience is a recurring theme in my work with women who are on the forefront of change in many societies around the world, leading grassroots efforts, organizing communities, and modeling the kind of feminine power that is so needed today.

In Cape Town, South Africa, I worked for change under apartheid in the late 1970s. The pioneering spirit and courage of many extraordinary women inspires us to find in ourselves the courage to showcase our passion on the world stage. In a twenty thousand-strong squatter community called Crossroads, extraordinary women such as Regina Ntongana worked tirelessly to protect their community from impend-

Kimberly Weichel is a social pioneer, educator, and specialist in global communications, conflict resolution, and cross-cultural projects. She has directed international projects over the past twenty-five years in East and Southern Africa, Europe, the former Soviet Union, United States, and with the United Nations, particularly with women. Kim is co-founder of the Institute for PeaceBuilding, providing courses, training, mentoring, and consulting in peace leadership, including courses for women. She is co-founder of Our Media Voice and producer of Women With Vision TV show. Her passion is to build the foundation for a culture of peace. www.kimweichel.org.

ing demolition by the apartheid government. Regina, and her colleagues in the Crossroads Woman's Movement, were able to keep the peace in the growing squatter camp despite crowded and difficult living conditions. They were the peacebuilders who fearlessly protected their families, speaking out, organizing and providing the leadership to unite against demolition. Because of their efforts, and the efforts of others who supported them, Crossroads remains today.

I traveled many times to the former Soviet Union in the mid-1980s. I watched many women, including my friend Svetlana, hold down two jobs, then go to the store and stand in line to buy food, go home and prepare it, take care of the children, and do the laundry, all without the conveniences to which American women had become accustomed. Svetlana was the one who held her family together, who organized peace vigils in her community, and who made sure that others were taken care of. Her strength and endurance carried her family through tough times. I met many Svetlanas during the Cold War.

The Value of Investing in Women

When I traveled from Nairobi to Mombasa, on the coast of Kenya, I observed the Tototo Home Industries project, comprising forty-five women's groups addressing the needs of low-income women and girls. I was fascinated by one such group, the Bomani Bakery, where women sang together as they baked bread for their community. Tototo expanded over five years to include small-scale loans, a vocational training school, and a women's rural development program. Women reinvested their money to improve the lives of their families and their community, raising the standard of living markedly in their regions.

-§-
"For generations, women have served as peace educators, both in their families and in their societies. They have proved instrumental in building bridges rather than walls."
—Kofi Annan
-§-

Another remarkable model with widespread effectiveness is the Grameen Bank, founded by Mohammed Yunus in Bangladesh.[1] Women are considered to be vitally important in the success of these credit schemes, and the community as a whole benefits as women use loans to build businesses. Experience has shown that women have a high success rate in the repayment of loans, effective loan use, and redistribution of surplus income to the family and community. While conventional banks focus on men, Grameen gives high priority to women; 96% of their borrowers are women. The Bank works to raise the status of poor women in their families by giving them ownership of assets. Today, Grameen serves five million borrowers, with ten thousand families escaping poverty every month. It is a real success story, and disproves the old myth that women and poor people are not reliable.

Women Are Peacebuilders

Why are women well-suited as peacebuilders? One of the leading organizations working with women peacebuilders is called Women Waging Peace, an organization advocating for the full participation of all stakeholders, especially women, in formal and informal peace processes around the world. They have built a network of women peacemakers and have done extensive research about why women are well-suited as peacebuilders. Some of their stories appear below.[2]

-§-
"As a woman my country is the whole world."
—Virginia Woolf
-§-

Women are often at the center of United Nations non-governmental organizations (NGOs), popular protests, electoral referendums, and other citizen-empowering movements whose influence has grown with the global spread of democracy. Because women frequently outnumber men after conflict, they often drive the on-the-ground implementation of any peace agreement.

- As the minister of gender and social affairs in Rwanda, Aloisea Inyumba created programs to bury the dead, find homes for more than 300,000 orphaned children, and resettle refugees after the genocide of 1994. She also served as executive secretary of the National Unity and Reconciliation Commission, which organizes national public debates promoting reconciliation between Hutus and Tutsis, and she has been governor of Kigali-Ngali Province.

Women are adept at bridging ethnic, religious, political, and cultural divides. Social science research indicates that women generally are more collaborative than men and thus more inclined toward consensus and compromise. Women often use their role as mothers to cut across international borders and internal divides. Every effort to bridge divides, even if initially unsuccessful, teaches lessons and establishes connections to be built on later.

- In several instances during the peace talks that led to the Good Friday Agreement in Northern Ireland, male negotiators walked out of sessions, leaving a small number of women, like Monica McWilliams and other members of the Northern Ireland Women's Coalition, at the table. These women focused on mutual concerns and shared vision, enabling the dialogue to continue and trust to be rekindled.

169

Women have their fingers on the pulse of the community. Living and working close to the roots of conflict, they are well-positioned to provide essential information about activities leading up to armed conflict and record events during war, including gathering evidence at scenes of atrocities. Women thus play a critical role in mobilizing their communities to begin the process of reconciliation and rebuilding once hostilities end.

- An obstetrician in Iraq under the rule of Saddam Hussein, Raja Habib Khuzai saw firsthand the violence perpetrated against her country's citizens. In a time when other doctors fled the country or went into hiding, Khuzai expanded her practice. Following Hussein's overthrow, she opened organizations to assist women and children in the community and was named a member of the Iraqi Governing Council, where she continued her important work.

Women have access because they are often viewed as less threatening. Ironically, women's status as second-class citizens in some countries is a source of empowerment, increasing women's ability to find innovative ways to cope with problems. Because women are not ensconced within the mainstream, those in power consider them less threatening, and allow women to work unimpeded and "below the radar screen."

- During the violence of the first Intifada in the Middle East, Israeli and Palestinian women like Naomi Chazan and Sumaya Farhat-Naser created Jerusalem Link, an umbrella group of women's centers on both sides of the conflict, to convey to the public a joint vision for a just peace. In a time when both communities forbade cross-community meetings, Jerusalem Link activities were permitted because "it's just a group of women talking."

Women are highly invested in preventing, stopping, and recovering from conflict. Women are motivated to protect their children and ensure security for their families. They watch as their sons and husbands are taken as combatants or prisoners of war; many do not return, leaving women to care for the remaining children and elders. When rape is used as a tactic of war to humiliate the enemy and terrorize the population, they become targets themselves. Despite—or because of—the harsh experiences of so many who survive violent conflict, women generally refuse to give up the pursuit of peace. My poem below speaks to the special bond mothers share.

Women Unite For Our Children

Mothers all over the world
Are united by the love we have for our children
And we share in our commitment
To ensure that our children are safe

The loss or pain of any child
Diminishes the entire world family
We all mourn when a child dies anywhere
We can deeply feel the pain of the parents

Mothers anguish to see children starving
Or living in poverty or in war
How can we let this happen
When our world has so much?

Children without limbs from stepping on a landmine
Children with big stomachs from malnutrition
Children crying to find scraps of food
These pictures haunt us since we know it shouldn't happen

All children deserve to live in a healthy place
With food, shelter, nurturing and free of war
We must reassure our children
And protect them from violence

Mothers and all women need to unite
To create a world safe for our children
And ensure that they inherit a peaceful world
If women don't do this, who else will?

Women are Critical to Economic Development

Over the past decade, significant research has demonstrated what many of us have known for a long time: women are critical to economic development, active civil society, and good governance, especially in developing countries. As Isabel Coleman says in "The Payoff From Women's Rights",[3] focusing on women is often the best way to reduce birth rates and child mortality; improve health, nutrition, and education; stem the spread of HIV/AIDS; build robust and self-sustaining community organizations; and encourage grassroots democracy.

Coleman argues that backing women's rights in developing countries isn't just good ethics; it's also sound economics, and states that growth and living standards get a dramatic boost when women are given more education, political clout, and economic opportunity. She talks about investing in women as a "high return investment". Achieving gender equality is now deemed so critical to reducing poverty and improving governance that it has become a development objective in its own right. The 2000 UN Millennium Development Goals, the international community's action plan to attack global poverty, lists gender equality as one of its eight targets and considers women's empowerment essential to achieving all of them.

A UNESCO project demonstrated that giving women just a primary school education decreases child mortality by 5% to 10%. According to the United Nations, economies in the developing world grow by 3% for every 10% increase in the number of women who receive secondary schooling. Lawrence Summers, when he was chief economist at the World Bank, concluded that girls' education may be the investment that yields the highest returns in the developing world.

Bringing women to the peace table improves the quality of agreements reached and increases the chance of success. Donald K. Steinberg, Deputy Director, Policy Planning Staff, explains: "Involving women in post-conflict governance reduces the likelihood of returning to war. Reconstruction works best when it involves women as planners, implementers, and beneficiaries."[4]

Women on the Front Lines

Women's groups have arisen around the world to take a stand for peace. The Global Fund for Women, the largest grantmaking foundation in the world that focuses exclusively on international women's rights and empowering women, brings together a worldwide network to support women. Below are a few illustrative examples of women's groups that are on the forefront of peacebuilding and change:[5]

-§-
"After the genocide, women rolled up their sleeves and began making society work again."
—Paul Kagame, President of Rwanda
-§-

Mano River Women's Peace Network, Sierra Leone

MARWOPNET, representing one hundred mostly women's NGOs in Sierra Leone, Liberia and Guinea, was established to ensure that women, the primary victims of war, were central to peace negotiations and strategies to maintain long-term security in the region. MARWOPNET trains women in conflict prevention and resolution and links peace activists across borders. It collaborates on peace initiatives with traditional leaders, heads of state, sub-regional bodies, the African Union and the U.N. Its work aims to prevent the conflicts that place women in vulnerable positions, while insisting that governments allocate resources to displaced women.

Arikal Mahina Foundation, Indonesia

Meaning "woman spirit," Arikal Mahina was founded in October, 2002 in response to the conflict in Ambon in 1999 which devastated the lives of many women and children. The group provides them with both psychological and legal counseling in addition to judicial assistance and support groups. Along with a massive anti-violence campaign, Arikal Mahina hopes to eradicate violations against the Maluku women with skills training leading to economic empowerment.

Women Peacemakers, Cambodia

Founded in 2000, Women Peacemakers (WPM) works in Kampong Cham province to protect women and children's human rights through providing shelter for survivors of abuse, investigating cases of domestic and sexual violence, and training and funding the growth of grassroots responses to women's and children's human rights violations. WPM offers trainings on conflict resolution, criminal law, and legislative procedures for survivors of assault.

-§-
"If we'd had women around the table, there would have been no war; women think long and hard before they send their children out to kill other people's children."
—Haris Silajdzic, former Prime Minister of Bosnia
-§-

These are inspiring and effective examples of what can be done when women organize and bring their own values and perspectives to peacebuilding. They go beyond simply keeping the peace, to building the foundation for a culture of peace in their societies.

A Partnership Model of Society

Women are collaborators for change. We are the primary carriers of the feminine qualities of compassion, nurturing, caring, partnership, and collaboration, qualities that are not separate but an equal and necessary part of the whole. Men possess these as well, but they need to be nurtured.

Women are attuned with the cycles of the body and cycles of nature. We care about and understand renewal and regeneration, developing longer-term perspectives rather than maximizing short-term gain. The feminine is aligned with the Native American core belief of planning for seven generations to come. We know what it means to give life, to preserve life, and sustain life.

The feminine also embodies a deeper awareness and heightened perception, a tracking of what's occurring before it becomes visible. We pay attention to the nuances and are often able to perceive changes in the air before they actually become visible. This awareness helps us to understand what's underneath the tension or conflict, so that it can be truly healed and transformed, not just temporarily resolved while continuing to fester.

-§-
Girls' education may be the investment that yields the highest returns in the developing world.
-§-

What is needed is a true partnership between the feminine and masculine qualities. Riane Eisler in her book the *Chalice and the Blade* describes the historic development of what she calls the Goddess cultures in which the partnership model prevailed, characterized by feminine principles of collaboration, mutual respect, accountability and partnership. She outlines the global shift to patriarchy, and the rise of the dominator model of action in which men and traditional masculine principles rule. This is by and large the society we have today, in which the overplayed masculine qualities of success, power, money, control and achievement, have led us to greed, obsessions, addictions, and disconnection from our true selves.[6] Clearly now is the time for women to step forward and model new types of leadership.

An example of a culture in balance comes from traditional Iroquois society. Its guiding constitution, called the *Great Law of Peace*, was crafted about six hundred years ago by a Native American prophet called the Peace Maker. Clan mothers were a key part of Native society. They were selected from their community. They, in turn, selected the Chief. Clan mothers were responsible for the welfare of the clan and helped to set policy. The Chief carried out the policies. This balance between masculine and feminine made Iroquois society strong. After centuries of tribal wars, the *Great Law* resulted in many years of peace, and was a model for the U.S. Constitution and the United Nations. Sadly our founding fathers left out the important role of Clan mothers as a balance in society.

Overcoming Limiting Myths About Women

So how do we bring the feminine into right balance with the masculine? There are many ways, and the first is to overcome some of the limiting and often dangerous myths about women that have permeated our society. It's not that long ago, really the last generation of women, who became independent economically and were well educated in growing numbers. Many in our mother's generation were homemakers who were dependent on their husbands for survival, often lacking the skills or confidence to make decisions on their own. Here are a few prevalent myths that I see, although in various stages of changing, that still limit women and the feminine from becoming full partners:

Limiting Myth #1 *Women should be the primary caretakers of the home and the raisers of children.*

While some women prefer to stay at home and raise children, we need to move beyond the old belief that women are the primary care-takers while the father does little. There are many Western Svetlanas and they are stretched too thin. Modern men and women should be full partners in raising children and taking care of the home. Government has a role too, in increasing childcare options, women's educational opportunities, their control over resources, and their economic and political participation.

Limiting Myth #2 *Women are passive, subservient, and lack skills for leadership. They are supporters and nurturers, protected by dominant men.*

Because traditionally women have been caretakers at home, they weren't given the opportunities, including the education or training, for traditional leadership. Yet women developed their own style of collaborating, relating and organizing that brought out feminine qualities of leadership—qualities that are deficient in our government and corporate systems. Women's power is a strong inner power that draws on our personal resources, rather than an external power to control. The era of the dominator model cannot serve to build healthy relationships or healthy societies.

Limiting Myth #3 *In order to make it in our current patriarchal system, women need to imitate male roles.*

Women are questioning the toxic myths that pervade our society, like, "There's not enough" and, "More is better," and "That's just the way it is." In order to advance in corporate America today, many women have had to adopt the masculine characteristics of being assertive, of competing, and doing whatever it takes to move forward. When they do so, they are rewarded with career advancement, and enormous salaries. Yet the external rewards don't buy meaning or happiness, and we're seeing tremendous upset and dis-ease amongst millions in corporate America today. Rather than trying to fit into an unbalanced and unhealthy system, we as women need to question the values underneath the practices, speak our truth, and train our colleagues

-§-
"Yesterday is gone. Tomorrow has not yet come. We have only today. Let us begin."
—Mother Teresa
-§-

in the feminine principles of collaboration, partnership, connecting, listening, and supporting others.

Limiting Myth #4 *Adding a few women to the Board of Directors, or advancing a few women into top leadership, creates balance.*

The move toward full equality is much more than slotting a few women into male roles. The feminine offers a different set of skills and qualities that are more sustainable and spiritually fulfilling, and need to become *valued* and *integrated into* business and government life. We challenge each business and organization, each conference, each book to really look beyond the number of women selected to ensuring that the perspectives of women are heard, valued, and included.

Women in World Healing

Women are the peacebuilders. Women are the midwives of a new society based on a balance between the feminine and the masculine. Women are the hospice workers tending to the unraveling of a dysfunctional patriarchal system. Barbara Marx Hubbard, a visionary leader and founder of Foundation for Conscious Evolution, says: "The evolutionary woman that is now appearing is connected through the heart to the whole of life and is awakened from within by a passionate desire to express her unique creativity for the good of the self and the whole human family. Ultimately, it is this evolutionary woman who will guide humanity as this planet transitions toward a new world that works for everyone."[7]

-§-
"We are the
ones we've been
waiting for."
—Hopi Indian Elders
-§-

Women are breaking stereotypes. Their models of effective leadership inspire a renewed sense of purpose and hope for the future. The pioneering spirit and courage of many extraordinary women inspires us to find in ourselves the courage to showcase our passion on the world stage.

My friend and colleague, Karen Wilhelm Buckley, founder of the Wisdom Leadership Initiative, observes: "Women...create a world where the forces of the heart are balanced with the drive for accomplishment. It is a world where we honor the unique gifts and talents of individuals and weave them into coherent collective efforts. It is a world where we hold the Earth's natural cycles in great regard and work toward a peaceful and creative relationship among all peoples, it is a world where we are willing to step out and defend life with a powerful commitment to justice and to truth."[8]

THE FEMININE FRONT LINE

Kimberly Weichel

It's time for the feminine qualities to be valued in our society, and to become integrated into every process and assumption we make. It's time for women to speak up, individually and collectively. It's time for policy makers to be women, and to listen to other women. It's time to bring in the wisdom of the women who have been organizing at the grassroots level, and building bridges across the front lines of the world's conflicts. It's time for women to step decisively into the role of being catalysts for powerful, positive change.

NAOMI JUDD:

The Rhythm of Community

Despite all this evidence that we need one another, people are feeling more isolated and lonely than ever before in history. Things are changing so rapidly that few people have even remained in the same job ten years, let alone lived in the same house or neighborhood. We have larger houses but more broken homes. The electronic media have replaced our hometowns. Sociologists say that you and I need a minimum number of social contacts every week to stay sane. They've found that unless we interact with a minimum of seven people weekly, we're at risk for mental illness. People who feel isolated have a seven to ten times' higher chance of premature death or disease compared to folks who have a sense of connection to their community.

Traveling across America border to border and coast to coast, I've seen firsthand that we're living in a transient, disposable culture. One afternoon Wy and I were enjoying Americana up front on our bus as we noticed a woman pull into her garage. As she hit the garage opener and disappeared from sight, she never looked toward homes on the left or right. That's when Wy and I observed that there were no sidewalks or porches in this neighborhood. It was striking that although we can send a man and woman into outer space, we no longer walk across the street to meet our neighbors. You and I can take back our neighborhoods by paying attention to what's going on.

Naomi Judd is a country music superstar, and one of the most admired women in the entertainment industry. She has sold more than twenty million albums, and won six Grammys and American Music Awards. She is the author of the best selling autobiography *Love Can Build a Bridge* (Fawcett, 1994), *Naomi's Breakthrough Guide* (Simon & Schuster, 2004), and *Naomi's Home Companion* (GT, 1997), a collection of recipes and kitchen table wisdom. Her latest book is *The Transparent Life* (Countryman, 2005). She lives with her husband outside of Nashville, Tennessee, adjoining other members of her family. Photo courtesy of Harry Langdon.

In my childhood neighborhood, I knew everyone. I sold Girl Scout cookies by myself door to door. I trick-or-treated at every house and often went inside. I safely played all over our neighborhood. I walked unescorted to all the schools I attended.

An area of constant concern to me is that real people are underrepresented in the media. My friendly hometown of Ashland, Kentucky, is thankfully still a front-porch town. Some of the dear souls who live there have indoor-outdoor carpeting on their porches, pillows in the glider swings, plants, magazine racks, and sometimes even portable phones. When I visit Mom, I put on my most comfortable walking shoes and strike out in all directions. Walking down Hilton Avenue one summer's eve, I came upon an eighty-year-old couple, the McKenzies, who invited me to join them on their porch for a glass of iced tea. Over the next hour, I experienced the timelessness and hospitality of folks who understand the art of being in the moment.

> -§-
> Just as despair can come to one only from other human beings, hope, too, can be given to one only by other human beings.
> —Elie Wiesel
> -§-

Inner peace begins at home. Larry and I share a peaceful valley with our daughters, son-in-law, and our two grandchildren. We've collectively chosen to live in an underpopulated rural area with a slower beat and rhythm. It nourishes each of us as an individual, as well as our family life. It promotes a strong sense of neighborliness. For example, a week after 9/11, we all worked together to put on a commemorative musical evening and rally to raise money for the Survivors Fund. As I spoke about patriotism and led the prayer from Marty and Bruce Hunt's rambling front porch, I gazed out over hundreds of friendly faces who'd gathered there in unity. Trucks and cars were parked in the field across the road with cattle. Kids and dogs played in the side meadows. The totality of that scene represented everything that's still right about this great nation. My sadness was somewhat assuaged, and I felt hopeful.

Your Turn Now

Take a good look at your support system—individuals, neighbors, and community.

- Who could you call at two in the morning to bail you out of jail?

- When was the last time you had a night out with friends? Have you been so involved in work that you have not been maintaining your friendships?

- Are you facing a specific issue for which you could use a support group's influence?

- Do you and your significant other have couples to hang out with?

- Let your passions lead you to like-minded people and developing a hobby. I had a middle-aged girlfriend who began taking tap dancing lessons. It fulfilled an old dream; she also lost twenty pounds and made new friends.

- Culture vultures live longer. Start going out more to concerts, lectures, museums; join a book discussion group.

- How about forming your own group? I started a monthly book discussion group at our mom-and-pop bookstore in Franklin to discuss holistic healing. It's been going strong four years now. I know a group of wives of Nashville songwriters who call themselves the "La Las" and meet every Thursday for lunch.

-§-
The past is a foreign country. They do things differently there.
—Anonymous
-§-

- Interested in grassroots social activism? Do you even know your neighbors? Create a community group in your neighborhood. For instance, our rural school started a Kids Onstage program to encourage musical talents in shy and underprivileged kids.

- Who do you admire, and why? Take my lead and muster your courage to seek out people in the field of your interest.

- Get rid of energy vampires and hang out with people who replenish, encourage, and inspire you.

- Consider getting a pet, even a fish.

- Read biographies and watch TV and movies about people who've got their act together. You'll be amazed how much you have in common. The company you keep determines the opportunities you meet.

Remember—you and I may not have it all together, but together we can have it all!

Ellen Hayakawa:

Weaving Cultures of Peace

My grandfather, Hideso Shiraishi, was twenty-four years old in 1906. In Japan, the eldest son inherits both the family property and the responsibility of caring for aging parents by tradition. As Hideso was not the eldest son, he was free to seek his fortune elsewhere. He chose Canada, emigrating from our family farm just outside of Hiroshima, Japan to the land of dreams and opportunity in Vancouver, British Columbia.

A spiritual man from a long line of devout Buddhists, Hideso brought with him a small wooden shrine. Every evening before going to sleep, he prayed in front of the shrine. During the season when the salmon were running, he worked as a fisherman in the traditional territorial land and waters of the Owikeeno people. In the tradition of every indigenous tribe who has made their home on the coast of British Columbia since time immemorial, Owikeeno custom held that one should ask permission before entering another's territory to live and work. Unaware of this, Grandfather Shiraishi did not ask the indigenous tribes of Canada for their permission before taking up residence on their land and fishing in their waters. Nonetheless, he lived and worked there for many years, making his living as a fisherman in the natural cycle and rhythm of the seasons.

In Japan, on the side of a mountain above the family farm, our ancestors' ashes are buried beneath the persimmon-laden trees on which the monkeys feast. When it is time to come home to the ances-

Ellen Hayakawa is one of the world's foremost inspirational keynote speak-ers and the author of *The Inspired Organization: Spirituality and Energy at Work* (Trafford, 2003). She coaches CEOs and executives to align their spiritual path with their business. She also coaches the "Children and Youth of Peace." These are children and youth with highly developed spiritual wisdom, psychic, intuitive, and healing abilities. Ellen helps them to discover, apply, and share their gifts in order to heal their own hearts, help others to heal theirs and in so doing heal the heart of the world. For more information, please see www.EllenHayakawa.com.

tral land, our ancestors call to us. In December 1918, still a bachelor, Hideso returned to his home community just outside of Hiroshima. While in his homeland, he married my grandmother, Kiwano Yamasaki, who lived on a neighboring farm. A few months later, they returned to Canada on the long voyage aboard the SS Chicago-Maru. Hideso's younger brother and my grandmother's sister had married and emigrated to the United States a few years earlier. During World War II, through emigration, birth and divine destiny, my family members found themselves the loyal citizens of three nations: Japan, the United States and Canada, and on opposing sides of the war.

-§-
After World War II, Canadians of Japanese ancestry were still considered a possible threat to their own nation even though there was not one documented incident of spying, treason, or subterfuge.
-§-

Grandpa Shiraishi so loved his adopted country of Canada that he named his eldest daughter, "Kanami" after Canada. Imagine his distress when, in the midst of World War II, he and my grandmother, along with their children and twenty-one thousand other Canadians of Japanese ancestry, had virtually all their belongings taken away from them and were wrongfully removed from their homes by authorities in the government including the Royal Canadian Mounted Police. One of the belongings my Grandpa chose to carry along in his 75 lb. luggage quota to the internment camp was his shrine. Interned in isolated, abandoned mining towns amid the snow-capped mountains of British Columbia, my family and all the others were kept under guard. Grandpa continued to pray in front of the shrine for himself and his family, asking for peace in their hearts and for peace amongst their nations.

When Hiroshima was attacked, my grandfather's youngest brother, Minikichi, was within five hundred meters of the hypocenter of the nuclear bomb. Miraculously, he lived to tell his story. On August 6, 1945, Minikichi—his face burned beyond recognition—wandered among the walking dead in the midst of the living hell of Hiroshima. Miraculously, his wife Sumie—carrying their unconscious five-year-old daughter on her back—found him in the city that day. The Japanese term for a survivor of the Hiroshima or Nagasaki bomb is *hibakusha*. As hibakusha, my granduncle and grandaunt were fortunate enough to flee the city to heal in the countryside. After the war, Minikichi and Sumie rose like phoenixes out of the ashes to have more children and create a life full of love and beauty. They, like so many hibakusha, made a commitment to peace on earth. On special occasions such as August 6, the day of the commemoration of the bombing of Hiroshima, I still wear the magnificent silk kimono that Auntie Sumie so lovingly sewed for me when I was nine years old.

When I wear that kimono, I remember the commitment and desire of the hibakusha for peace.

After World War II, Canadians of Japanese ancestry were still considered a possible threat to their own nation even though there was not one documented incident of spying, treason, or subterfuge. They were given the choice by the Canadian government of going to Japan or living away from the West Coast. For my parents, born and raised in Canada and loyal citizens of Canada despite the appalling treatment they had received during and after the war, there was no choice. They decided to move to Ontario in Central Canada, with Grandpa once again taking the little shrine along. Our family has now lived there for four generations. I was born and raised in Ontario, a third generation Canadian of Japanese ancestry.

My family had their hearts and hands in Japan, Canada, and the United States during World War II. What does nationhood and war come to mean to a family when they find themselves on opposing sides fighting each other? And what do they think and feel when one side goes so far as to drop an atomic bomb on the other? My family knows the answer to that. War means terrible devastation, tragedy, loss, and suffering. For too long, we humans have managed to convince ourselves that the side we were or are on is the "right side." The rationale, "The atomic bomb saved lives and ended the war," has been used as a justification for too many years.

Any intention to kill or to wound is wrong. No mother in her right mind would send her child to war to be killed or wounded, or to kill or to wound another mother's child, or to blow another mother's child up with an atomic bomb. Condoning arms and war as a way to resolve conflict comes from an outdated patriarchal model. There is never a right or wrong side in violent conflict or war. No side is a winner. Both sides are losers. War means death, wounding and broken hearts on all sides, no matter who is purported to have "won" the war. Since the dawn of recorded civilization, we have been fighting tribal wars against one another. We have all been victims and we have all been perpetrators. In order to have global peace, we must claim our own wrongdoings and those of our ancestors. Where possible, redress must be offered, and if not offered, then sought.

-§-
War means death, wounding and broken hearts on all sides, no matter who is purported to have "won" the war.
-§-

The importance of apologizing and asking for forgiveness cannot be overlooked. "The sins of the father are visited upon the children" and it is up to us as the children to redress the wrongdoings of our ancestors. This is a powerful healing gesture.

During a traditional pipe ceremony with indigenous elders, I was blessed with the opportunity to redress the wrongful action of my grandfather when he failed to ask for permission to live and work in indigenous tribal land. I apologized for his transgression, as well as my own, for I, too, had lived on the land and benefited from the resources without asking the indigenous people's permission to share in the bounty of spirit. Through the country's government, the people of Canada are recognizing the violation of the traditional territories of the First Nations people with land claim settlements. After years of lobbying by Canadians of Japanese ancestry, the Canadian government also issued an official apology for the violation of my parents' and grandparents' rights, along with monetary redress. They also promised that such a violation of rights would never happen again to any other citizen.

-§-
Any so-called divine guidance that speaks the language of violence and war is suspect.
§-

With apologies, forgiveness and a new way of relating, we can then move forward, embracing each other as members of a global family and citizens of the world. When conflict arises, just as in any family, we commit to using dialogue rather than technological arms, violence, wounding, and killing to work through conflict.

In 1997, in the year that my father passed to the other side, I left the security of my family, friends, and job, and moved to a small West Coast island whose name for the last 160 years has been Bowen Island, but whose Squamish name for at least the ten thousand years before that was *Xwilil'xhwm,* meaning the Fast Drumming Ground. I am the only one of my family to return to the West Coast of our origin; to reconnect to the land of my grandparents' choosing, and to the mountains and the sea. My grandfather's shrine came West with me. Every evening, I pray for peace in my heart, in the hearts of my family, community, and in the hearts of people in all nations in the global family.

Building a Global Community of Peace

A few months after moving to the coast, I delivered a keynote speech at a conference on spirituality in business. On the way home, I received divine guidance to bring together 2,001 leaders in business, politics, science, government, health, education, the arts, and the major spiritual traditions of the world for a global peace summit. The summit would feature the best models of spirituality and sustainability in families, communities, and organizations. More than a summit, it would create a community for global peace.

I had just moved to a small island where I knew no one, not even people in the nearby city of Vancouver. Taken aback by the immensity of the vision of global peace I had received, I asked, "God, how am I supposed to do this?" In reply, I heard the words, "You don't have to know how. I will show you the way." I wondered whether God was really asking me to do this or if I was in the midst of a delusion.

The night of my thirty-fifth birthday, I had a mystical dream that changed my life. Snug in a ski hut deep in the wilderness, I dreamed that I was light. It was a short, yet infinite moment of profound love, peace and beauty, and of feeling totally connected to God and all there is. I knew then that the purpose of my life was to know and love God and myself and to serve all beings with love and compassion.

I made a commitment to God: "I will go wherever you ask me to go. I will do whatever you ask me to do. I will speak whatever you ask me to speak." Although I had always followed my heart and intuition, I began to hear God speak to me in a very distinct voice. I have followed the clear instructions of that inner voice for over a decade. I left my job as a wildlife biologist, and did a 180 degree turn which eventually led to a new career as a highly successful keynote speaker and coach on spirituality at work. I wrote a book called *The Inspired Organization: Spirituality and Energy at Work*. These and other experiences have taught me to trust and obediently follow that voice.

There are also those who say that they have heard the voice of God and that God has instructed them to be violent or to wage war. Any so-called divine guidance that speaks the language of violence and war is suspect. It is connected to the human ego not to divinity. God created all people as equal brothers and sisters in the circle of humanity. All spiritual traditions and nations are also equal in the diversity of the divine fabric of love.

-§-
Thirty-six thousand children die of hunger every day—when there is more than enough food to feed everyone in the world.
-§-

From a scientific viewpoint, a stable mental state and the ability to both clearly receive and act on divine guidance comes when a person can constantly maintain balanced brain wave states that include delta and theta states. We spend most of our waking hours in alpha and beta states. For most people, theta and delta states occur only while sleeping. These are the states of the creative genius and the mystic, characterized by full and profound connection to the divine. Delta is the brain wave state connected to a feeling of peace.

In 1978, scientists at the Medical and Science Research Institute at the University of Texas examined the brain wave pattern of Dadi

Janki, a renowned spiritual teacher and a member of the prestigious United Nations' Wisdom Keepers group. She was described as the most stable mind in the world at the time; she was able to maintain a constant delta state while awake and asleep. Her mental state remained completely undisturbed even while performing complicated mental exercises. She was declared the most peaceful woman in the world.

Dadi Janki says, "When there is understanding of the divine self and a relationship with the Supreme, then no worrisome, fearsome or sorrowful situation can affect us. When the soul experiences the strength that comes from God's love, there is nothing that can distance the soul from its original state of peace and bliss. Nothing can stop it from walking the path of righteousness and truth and inspiring others to do the same."

Even when divine guidance is clear, it is up to the recipient to ensure that it comes from the divine and not from the ego. That requires discernment as well as affirmation, which can come from other human beings. To verify the guidance about the peace summit, I called Robert Muller, former assistant secretary-general of the UN, and left a message asking if he thought this vision could happen. Robert did not know me, and my small human self hoped that he would not call back. The next day he called, emphatically stating that this summit needed to happen.

It took two years to build the summit team—a volunteer effort by hundreds of people—and another two years to organize it. People, physical and financial resources came as needed. We were confident that by consciously co-creating with spirit as a community on a small scale, we would create a self-replicating model of global peace.

Just days after the devastation of the collapse of the World Trade Centre towers in New York City, the global peace summit took place in Vancouver, Canada. Many people were traumatized by the events of September 11 and looked to the summit to provide a positive alternative to violence, death, and destruction. An estimated four thousand people—from every political, religious, and ethnic background—participated in the weeklong event. A Maori elder arrived from New Zealand. Indigenous elders came from many areas of the West Coast. At the final ceremony, attended by nearly two thousand people, participants drummed for global peace in Vancouver's Plaza of Nations. A resounding song of harmonized hearts, minds, spirits, and drums sent an intention and message for global peace into the world.

-§-
If I did nothing but read the facts, I would be more than discouraged. I would be emotionally devastated.
-§-

A Little Child Shall Lead Them

As important as it is to remember and redress the past, we must also look forward to the future. My first career was as wildlife biologist with the federal government of Canada. In that position, I saw scientific documentation of the decline of every major ecosystem on our planet. An entire continent is being ravaged by AIDS. Corruption and civil war are rampant, and thirty-six thousand children die of hunger every day — when there is more than enough food to feed everyone in the world. If I did nothing but read the facts, I would be more than discouraged. I would be emotionally devastated, having devoted my life to environmental and social activism.

But I have also seen evidence of the dawn of a new tomorrow. Many of today's children are being born with remarkable spiritual gifts. Sensitive, wise and insightful, these children have awareness and maturity that far exceeds their chronological age. Many have highly developed psychic abilities: clairaudience, clairvoyance, clairsentience, and healing. Others have artistic, musical, literary, scientific, mathematical, psychological, and spiritual knowledge that can not be accounted for by their life experience. I believe these children foreshadow the physical, psychological, emotional, and spiritual breakthroughs our species must go through if we are to survive.

-§-
Many of today's children are being born with remarkable spiritual gifts.
-§-

When such children are affirmed and acknowledged for their abilities, those abilities expand. Unfortunately, the reverse often occurs. They may be diagnosed with "disorders" such as attention deficit disorder, attention deficit hyperactivity disorder, dyslexia, and autism. Instead of helping children to find and expand their gifts we are often focusing on their so-called disorders. Embedded in every disorder is gift or a different way of perceiving or learning which we would find out about if we patiently asked the children the right questions.

If our generation does not bring about peace, the next generation will carry forth that vision. One of those children, Katie de Sante, wrote the following poem when she was nine years old:

When My Mind Goes Wondering

The wind is blowing, my breath and soul catch the wind currents and I
    fly to eternity.
I do not breathe from my body,

CHAPTER EIGHTEEN

I breathe from the whales that dive deep into the ocean and uncover the
deepest thoughts of the mind and soul.

But the wind has more to show me and it lifts me from the water and
from the creatures I have encountered.

It takes me to a tree that holds a spirit, the spirit of the universe, who sits
high on a branch and holds a pebble of her hope.

She talks to me, she tells me of the sky and fairies that live among the
clouds to the unearthly reaches of the hidden mind.

The wind takes me away from the kind spirit, and takes me to an eagle
that teaches me of the love and kindness of the living human.

But then I fall, falling, falling into the deepest depths of the earth.

I find nothing but blackness in the earth.

Then one star appears then another and another until the blackness is no
longer there.

Instead I am surrounded by stars and light, that light makes me happy
and;

It calls the wind to me and I am no longer frightened for we are rising
from earth to sky and then from blackness to light and from light
to peace.

The wind now takes me to a cave where a wolf is sleeping;

the wolf awakes and guides me to the deepest part of the forest where I
meet earth and the footpath of my heart.

SUSAN SCHACHTERLE:

The Bitch, The Crone, and The Harlot

Yqou were born complete; everything you need to be an extraordinary individual, and to live in an extraordinary way, you carried with you into life. I remember so well the moment at which I first began to grasp this. A man I had loved wildly had suddenly, and in a painful way, left me. Our five-year relationship had been shaped by creativity, humor, elegance, and passion. I grieved deeply for months, mourning the fact that I would never again be creative, humorous, elegant, or passionate. After all, I reasoned, this man had been the source of those things between us, I had simply tagged along, enjoying the fruits of his exceptional essence. I found myself feeling dowdy, boring, and superficial without him to open the door to that way of being I had come to appreciate.

One day, at about the six-month point in my sorrow, and feeling stuck in an overwhelming despair, I raged toward heaven, accusing Spirit of snatching from me the only source of joy I would ever have. "How could you do this to me?" I whined; "How could you give me a glimpse of all those wonderful things and then take them away? You are a cruel and thoughtless God." Suddenly, in a blinding flash, I understood. My lover had not been the source of everything that had made the relationship remarkable; he had been a catalyst, a vehicle to assist me to find those things within myself. He was a unique and outstanding man and I had loved him deeply. However, he had not created the things I had felt with him; those things were already in

Susan Schachterle, director of the Ahimsa Group, has spent twenty years assisting individuals and organizations find and implement their inherent power, wisdom, and joy. Her work is based on the fierce and unwavering belief that just about everything is possible for just about everyone, once they have the tools necessary. In her practice, Susan uses a wide range of cutting-edge tools, most notably neurolinguistic programming (NLP), to ensure that her clients can access their own natural excellence in any situation. This chapter is an excerpt from her upcoming book *The Bitch, The Crone, and The Harlot*. More at www. AhimsaGroup.com. Photo by Susan Goddard.

place within me. He had only helped to bring to the surface qualities and capacities that were part of me but that I hadn't been aware of. This realization changed things almost immediately for me. Although I still missed him, I now understood that I carried in me the ability to experience all the things I had loved about the relationship. That meant that at every moment, even all by myself, I have the opportunity for joy.

This was an important thing for me to remember, especially as I headed into midlife. It was at that point that I found myself faced with a choice: How would I enter this next part of my life? I could regard it as an indication that the end was near; that I no longer had value and should make room for younger women who were more significant than I — or I could recognize the potential inherent in this stage of life, and choose to move more deeply into the power, wisdom, and sensuality that has always been part of me. It was up to me, and the choice I made would have a profound impact on the rest of my life.

-§-
Everything you need to be an extraordinary individual, and to live in an extraordinary way, you carried with you into life.
-§-

In the minds of many, midlife signals the beginning of the end, that final stretch of road leading directly and relentlessly toward death. The result of this perspective is often either a desperate and sometimes embarrassing attempt to cling to youth, or an I'm-powerless-in-the-face-of-aging resignation that has one going through the motions of existing, instead of living large. Because society places such emphasis on youth, beauty, and sexuality, anyone approaching midlife still looking for validation from external sources is heading for a fall.

Women are especially vulnerable; more often than not, as young girls we learn the importance of being cute, just delicate enough to need help occasionally, and as sexy as possible. This is the formula that almost guarantees a secure future. Or so we've been told. It can all begin to crumble, however, when those qualities that characterized us during the first half of life no longer fit; as we metamorphose into beings whose value lies at a deeper place, we must be willing to change the formula.

The archetypes that shape women's early choices become obvious when we are children. They may include the Good Girl, the Bright Student, the Seductress, and later the Good Wife and the Nurturing Mother. Each of these has elements that teach us well, and some elements we will struggle to break free from, like a snake shedding a skin that it has outgrown. But positive archetypes appropriate to midlife are difficult to find. I've seen plenty of negative ones, like the Exhausted and Resentful Old Broad, the Woman Who Gave Up Long Ago, and the Worn Out Old Lady Who Figures She No Longer Matters. None of these brings passion, possibility, or joy.

Rather, I suggest three models for a midlife that is a comprehensive expression of the power, wisdom, and sensuality inherent in the feminine:

The Bitch. The woman who makes things happen without doing damage.

The Crone. The woman who has constant access to a depth of practical wisdom younger women haven't had time to develop.

The Harlot. The woman whose sensuality is not used to manipulate, but rather to express her profound connection to all of life and its source. She has also had the time to develop and refine erotic moves that younger women have yet to learn.

Each of these uncommon beings lives from an aspect of the feminine that is often left either undeveloped, or underdeveloped. As a deeper exploration of each reveals, all are available to every woman.

The Bitch

Several years ago I was leading a discussion about relationships with a group of men ranging in age from twenty-three to eighty-one. In the course of the conversation I asked the group to define "bitch." One of the younger men responded that when he called someone a bitch it meant "a woman who won't do what I want her to do." There were nodding heads and murmurs of agreement among the members of the group.

Then a quiet voice broke through from the back of the room. It was the oldest man in the workshop. "To me," he said softly, "'bitch' means a 'woman who gets in a revolving door behind me, and somehow gets out ahead of me'." There was a stunned silence in the room. This stooped old man, in the midst of a group of self-proclaimed studs, had put a whole new face on a term that had previously been used to belittle and denigrate strong women. The room was quiet for several minutes as the men considered the possibilities in the old man's words. Those words changed the tone of that day.

-§-
At every moment, even all by myself, I have the opportunity for joy.
-§-

The commonly accepted definition of "bitch" has, intentionally or not, tied women's hands by reinforcing the idea that there are two options possible: *bitch,* defined as mean, selfish, harsh, unkind, unat-

195

tractive and unacceptable; or *good girl,* defined as lovable, obedient, eager to please, and acceptable.

With those two options for defining who we are, stepping beyond them is dangerous. This becomes even more frustrating at midlife; if we continue to live as Good Girls, we become invisible, and get rolled over by those who consider us a quiet and well-behaved backdrop to life. If we choose to look for respect by being demanding and inflexible, we are regarded as pissy older women who must be placated but not taken seriously. Neither of those options serves us; a new definition is required.

A positive archetype of a Bitch at midlife is that of a woman who has become so comfortable with who she is that she doesn't hesitate to take appropriate action in any situation. Her actions are no longer so governed by what others think, but rather by what she knows to be true. This is a woman whose intuition is so well-developed that she knows in her gut what to do. Part of her personal mission is to perform actions that are shaped by integrity, insight, and compassion. This woman can make things happen anywhere but, unlike the street-defined bitch, there is no selfishness, no unkindness about her; she takes action and creates results that are the highest and best for everyone involved, within a framework of wisdom and love.

-§-
Anyone approaching midlife still looking for validation from external sources is heading for a fall.
-§-

This may sound too good to be possible and, indeed, it is—if we operate strictly from the limitations of personality and ego. But the divine Bitch has chosen to live from a deeper place; she has chosen, as a result of all she's learned, to be an expression of the Divine in everything she does. She has also learned, through the experiences of the first half of life, to see both the big picture and the small pieces of any situation.

Historically, bitches were women who made things happen. They often did so in a fashion that caused pain and chaos, and their motivations were frequently self-serving. However, we can't ignore their ability to take action and create results. The new model is a woman who is so powerful personally that things and people part before her like the Red Sea, yet is revered for being respectful, compassionate, and loving. Midlife need not offer us the either-or choice of being loved or being effective. We get to be both, but it requires the willingness to remember who we really are, and to transform negative beliefs and emotional barriers we've been carrying, so we can live from the power that remains.

The Bitch, The Crone, and The Harlot   Susan Schachterle

The Bitch has learned to see the big picture — then to break it down into manageable small pieces. This allows her to be both the visionary and the implementer. She can be consistently effective at both because she has come to trust her gut, and because she has learned to put emotion aside once she has determined what needs to be done. That doesn't mean she has no feelings as she uses her power; she has a great capacity to feel. But she knows that unchecked emotion can cloud her judgment, so once she is clear about the goal, her action is based on commitment to that goal. She doesn't waste time and energy wondering if she's made the right decision, or if she's good enough to pull it off, or if someone else could do it better. She knows that second-guessing herself only dissipates her power and insight.

-§-

Midlife need not offer us the either-or choice of being loved or being effective. We get to be both.

-§-

At fifty-eight, Dorothy felt confused, insignificant, and anxious. "I feel old and invisible," she said. "I don't know where I fit or who I'm supposed to be now. I guess it's part of getting older; I'm just not of much value anymore. But why be alive if you have nothing to offer?" It was heartbreaking to hear her pain, and to watch her struggle against tears that had built up over years of neglect, loneliness, and fear. Her grown children, she went on to say, had always treated her like an afterthought, not unkind, but also not aware of her depth. They took her for granted. At work it was simply assumed that she would always be available to do whatever others didn't want to do, and her work went largely unnoticed. "It's OK," she assured me; "I don't need to be in the spotlight. I just wish I could feel like I matter somewhere."

But it wasn't OK. Dorothy had a world of learning she could contribute, a number of opinions she only admitted to behind closed doors, and several things she dreamed of doing but never had, having scared herself out of doing anything that wasn't familiar. "What if I'm too old, too stupid, too weak?" she wondered. "What if there isn't enough money? What if I try something new and fail?" Thoughts like this had become her mantra and her prison.

Dorothy was an excellent example of a woman in need of Bitch energy. She had spent her life in the shadow of numerous other people, serving, nurturing, supporting, and becoming depleted in the process. In many respects, though almost sixty years old, she was still unformed. Although she had opinions and dreams, she had never given herself permission to express them — much less live them. She had set herself up to feel insignificant by her willingness to fade into the background of life and stay there. All this could change, but only

if she was willing to step out of the box her life had become, and begin to live out loud.

As we worked together, Dorothy found options that allowed her to show up differently in her life. She learned to step into a state of calm from which she could access her own courage, power, and focus. She learned that she was much stronger than she had realized; able to set a goal, recognize its meta-outcome, and take action. She developed an internal strategy for finding an unwavering focus, and for saying, "no" when she needed to. As we worked together, the timid, helpless, and uncertain woman who had initially contacted me was replaced by one who spoke with authority, had more energy, and who felt at home in her own skin.

-§-

The Bitch has learned to see the big picture—then to break it down into manageable small pieces.

-§-

Dorothy called me three months after we had completed our work to report that, at a family gathering, she had told one of her kids not to interrupt her, and to treat her with respect from that time on. This was unheard of. After all, it had always been her job to cook, serve, clean up, and not to be heard. She had spoken up at a church council meeting, calling for action on a serious matter before the council, and volunteering to head up a committee to remedy the situation. "They were shocked," she said. "I don't think I had ever spoken a word in those meetings, and here I was taking over and initiating change. I was nervous at first, but I knew it was the right thing to do, and I didn't doubt that I could make it happen." Without raising her voice or behaving in an aggressive way, this tiny, quiet, middle-aged woman had pointed out the path to resolution and rallied the group around her cause. There may have been those present who resented her for requiring accountability and change, but this new Dorothy, this woman to contend with, was no longer shaped by their opinions.

The last time I heard from Dorothy, she had begun taking tango lessons and was planning a trip to Africa, simply because she'd always wanted to see Africa but in the past had found the prospect overwhelming. Not anymore.

The Crone

I recently researched the word "crone" and was surprised to learn that its original meaning was very different from its current definition. The most commonly accepted definition is "withered old woman," a definition based solely, it seems, on the physical. However, in the fourteenth century, the earliest definitions of "crone" meant "cantankerous or mischievous woman." Such an interesting and disempowering journey we've taken, in the minds of those who create such definitions, from cantankerous (which can also mean *feisty*) and mischievous, to withered and old. Consider the impact of this shift in meaning. Who has more power, the woman who is feisty and mischievous or the one who is old and withered? And which one might be found more threatening?

There is an entire world left out of this "withered old woman" designation, and it's a world that, at midlife, we must explore. In a number of ancient fairy tales, reference is made to the "wise old crone," the older woman whose wisdom, insight, and healing power were sought by younger people who had not yet developed their own. In these stories, people in need went to those who had been alive long enough to find the magical divine nature within, and generally those were older women. Young men were sought for their physical prowess, and young women for their ornamental quality and child-bearing ability; but when the need to understand, to intuit, and to heal arose, everyone headed to the wise old crone's place.

At midlife, we have accumulated a body of understanding and insight that allows us to contribute to life very differently than when we were younger. Whether or not we realize it, we have been gathering everything we need to perceive, interpret, and respond at a level deeper than the surface appearance. In the first part of life, knowledge is more valued than wisdom. We get another degree, we develop new skills, and we memorize formulas and philosophies, often with self-serving intentions. But wisdom and knowledge are different, wisdom coming from a deep place within. In the second part of life, with a greater emphasis on the internal, we are able to implement what we have learned in a wiser and more effective way. Our intentions have shifted, our focus is different, and we can see beyond the surface and into the deeper meaning. We can step beyond the limitations of ego, and into a much vaster realm of possibility.

-§-

In the first part of
life, knowledge is
more valued than
wisdom.

-§-

Recently I met a woman who teaches at one of the toughest high schools in a major metropolitan city. She's fifty-three, average-looking, unpretentious, and about as far removed from "cool" as one can be. The school where she teaches has a long history of violence, student to student and student to teacher. The police are frequent visitors, and several teachers have been attacked in the schoolyard, or in their classrooms. For most, it's a scary place. But for Jean, it's a tract of fertile ground. She's greeted warmly by even the toughest kids. Students who have customized their cars, sport new tattoos, or had

their noses pierced seek her out to show off their latest treasures. She has time for everyone and, according to colleagues, is the only staff member who never speaks disparagingly of anyone.

"When I was younger," she told me, "I would have felt scared and defensive in this place. I would have taken all these behaviors personally, and would have probably lashed out to protect myself. But I don't feel that way now. When I look at these kids, it's as if I can see into the core of each one and sense what's possible once they learn to channel their energy in a different direction. I ask myself what might be motivating their actions, and I know it's that they're scared, sad, and lonely. How can I feel afraid or hostile toward anyone in such pain?"

-§-
Sensuality has nothing to do with one's hormone levels; rather it is a product of the choice to live in a very present state.
-§-

Jean chooses consistently to look beyond the behaviors to the soul of each student, to regard each as a spiritual being, and to respond with a love, respect, and acceptance based on who each one is, not what each one does. She comes down hard on unacceptable actions, but no one ever doubts her love and respect. For many of these kids, Jean's classroom is the only place where someone cares about and believes in them. And through her exceptional wisdom, she is magically shaping and saving lives.

The Harlot

Ancient harlots lived by their senses, and their survival depended on their ability to stimulate the senses of others. In many cultures, women expected to provide sexual services were carefully trained in the art of pleasure. While I don't endorse meaningless and indiscriminate sexual behavior, there is something important to learn about sensuality from these women—who were despised in public yet desired in private. Harlots were openly committed to the pleasures of the senses and, in order to do their job well, worked to refine their own sensuality and their artfulness.

Each of us must similarly explore and refine our natural sensuality if we want lives that are filled with beauty, joy, and wonder as well as physical pleasure. Women of all ages are sensuous creatures, and our sensual nature demands our attention.

Rarely do I find the words "sensuous" and "middle-aged" in the same sentence. One of the myths that convinces women to give in and give up at midlife is that sensuality is believed to be the privilege of the young; that after a certain age and particular biological changes, we are no longer sensuous. Yet sensuality has nothing to do with one's hormone levels; rather it is a product of the choice to live in a very present state, very much aware of one's senses. Sensuous women of any age see, hear, feel, taste, and smell their lives in vibrant style.

Sensuous women, through out history, have been considered intriguing and dangerous, in great part because early in life sensuality seems directly connected to the immense power of sex, and behaving sensually is a way to draw attention, attract a mate, and to bask, temporarily, in the illusion that sex and love are the same thing. Later, however, as one moves into midlife, sensuousness reveals itself as something grander and more profound.

Sensuality means living through the senses, a much more expansive arena than simply the act of sex, and women who are sensual live thoroughly aware of all their senses. It is through the senses that we all take in information about the world around us, but those who are truly sensuous not only take in such information but also honor it by responding with energy and grace. They have learned to move in rhythm with the Earth, with the elements, with both the subtle and the riotous beauty in nature, and with the spiritual kinship among all living things.

True sensuousness is the domain of those who choose that awareness. Because of the early focus on sexuality, many subtle sensuous experiences go unnoticed. But at the midpoint of our lives, having been invited to move our attention from the expectations of others to the comfort of our own souls, we can better notice and appreciate what our senses are telling us. Simple things: an intricate flower almost buried in tall grasses; early morning sounds that announce the day; the sensation of a graceful breeze across the skin; the way it feels to move to music, are often passed over by those younger and more concerned with climbing corporate ladders, finding sexual outlets, and establishing themselves as worthwhile members of the community. Having already done those things, those at midlife can shift their awareness to the Mystery around them.

-§-
Sensuality means living through the senses, a much more expansive arena than simply the act of sex.
-§-

This is not to imply that women at midlife can be sensuous but not sexual; the depth of sensuousness we carry can open the door to remarkable sexual experiences. The other evening I went to a dance club where I watched as a middle-aged couple did an impressive salsa routine. As I watched them move together, their eyes locked on each other, it looked like foreplay and I felt like a voyeur. I can only imagine what the rest of their evening involved.

CHAPTER NINETEEN

As I sit writing early in the morning, I notice a window washer on a platform midway up a high-rise building across the street. The rising sun throws shadows of the long ropes holding his platform across the face of the building. As the ropes sway, the huge shadows dance gracefully along the entire height of the building. A simple thing—but as I watch I am captivated by the beauty of the scene. Would I have even noticed this when I was younger? Perhaps, but not with the same degree of awe I have now. Life has brought me to a place from which I notice things I missed earlier. It is only now, with half of life under my belt, that I am equipped to understand the power of the sensuous realm.

So here we are, having been through the joyful wringer that is the first half of life; and having, in the process, gathered everything we need to make things happen, to move through life with unparalleled wisdom, and to find wonder and delight in every sensuous moment. We know more now than we have ever known, and have the possibility of making life a greater adventure than we had ever before imagined. The question now becomes, what will we do with all we have gained? The answer, I believe, lies in a story about the Sufi poet Rumi and his friend, Shams of Tabriz. It is said that Shams took all of Rumi's books and threw them in a fishpond. "Now," he said to the startled Rumi, "you must live what you know." And so it is for each of us.

PART FOUR

Engaging With Nature

CATRIONA MACGREGOR:

Nature as Teacher and Sage

T he rains have come to Northern California. On my morning walk in Deer Park, the sound of a lively stream could be heard in the valley, frothing with the rainwater and newly washed Earth. Many of the streams that run in valleys between the rolling hills are now alive, after a season of dormancy.

In the early afternoon, the mists sat low on the hillsides like mysterious and beautiful silver veils over the redwoods, eucalyptus, live oak, and other trees around our home. Flocks of midnight black crows and ravens called to one another from their tall perches of tree limbs and telephone wires. These are the signs of winter in Marin County, which lies by the Pacific Ocean just an hour north of San Francisco, and is home to Mount Tamalpais, groves of coastal redwood trees, and rolling hillsides of golden grasses.

Two vultures now float masterfully just beyond our living room bay window. Quiet evening visitors, they fly effortlessly toward the northeast with their broad outstretched wings gently lifted by the rising warm currents of air from the valley below. Their flying exhibits the qualities of grace with ease, which beckons a mood of peace and freedom.

Think of the exhilaration you experience watching the powerful and rhythmic flow of the sea. Recall the freedom you sense as a bird soars in flight. Remember the comfort and joy you feel when the first

Catriona MacGregor is a pragmatic visionary and lover of nature. For over twenty years she has led environmental, progressive social change, and human potential initiatives and programs. Catriona is a teacher, writer, and coach who works with the transformative power of nature to help people find their inner voice, live more creatively, and carry out their life's purpose. She is also the founder of Awen Grove (awengrove.org), dedicated to bringing the inspiration, wisdom, and beauty of nature to benefit people's lives and the Earth. Catriona offers workshops, vision quests, nature outings and presentations. Upcoming workshops and events can be found at www.naturalpathfinder.com.

colorful flowers appear in your garden, after a long, hard winter. Simple pleasures, perhaps, and short-lived? Not so. Nature can be a force for the good in our lives; and these simple pleasures can be expanded to transform your life into one of meaning and beauty. This truth is recognized by mystics, naturalists, and healers from around the world and across the centuries. Nature is a portal to unity — unity of spirit, unity of body and unity of knowledge.

Carl Jung said that our earliest memories are what define us, and so it is with my own memories. For as long as I can remember I have been in love with nature, and memorably touched by her. As a child, no matter how uncomfortable or cold it was, or how far I would have to travel, I would get close to nature and animals. I never lost enthusiasm or my curiosity. The sense that something magical and important was right outside my door filled my waking hours.

-§-

"When you walk across the fields with your mind pure and holy, then from all the stones, and all the growing things, and all animals, the sparks of their soul come out and cling to you, and then they purified and become a holy fire in you."
—Ancient Hasidic Prayer

-§-

At the age of four I recall walking home with a nest of baby sparrows accidentally dislodged by our neighbor from her window shutters. At the age of five, my mother and godmother — amazed and alarmed — stood at the bottom of a sixty-foot-tall evergreen tree encouraging me — halfway up — to come down. Little did they seem to understand, I thought at the time, the importance of placing the also overly adventurous downy, fledgling robin back into its nest in the branches above. My earliest experiences in "mothering" wild animals brought great joy and satisfaction — as well as some lessons learned the hard way. I was oblivious to societal norms and expectations, free to dive full-heartedly into the world of nature.

In my teenage years, the complications, drama, pain and sadness of human existence were all too palpable and real; our family suffered one tragedy after another. My mind and being were no longer as easily absorbed by the beauty and interplay of the many living things around me. When my father, a gentle and wise soul, committed to his work as a psychiatrist and the care of his patients, committed suicide when I was twelve, the world completely lost its comprehensibleness.

And then, just when my faith in the very fabric of the world was being most tested, I had a spiritual awakening in the woods near our home. Standing in a tall silent grove of trees, a deep peace filled my soul and a sense of oneness with all living things filled my heart. My cares fell away, becoming small and inconsequential in the presence of an all-knowing, compassionate universe where death and life are but one continuum and a person's spirit is immortal. The trees embraced me with their compassion and knowing. They saved my life.

From that moment on, I did not live in bitterness. I felt a knowing, shared by and through those trees of a truth, that no matter how dark or desperate things may appear, we can reach beyond the illusion to find at the heart of existence faith, companionship, understanding and love around us. This experience, and others like it, have filled me with gratitude and awe for the wisdom, and beauty that awaits just there in nature—in the flight of a red-tailed hawk, or the quiet shy stare of a doe.

Growing Stress and Disconnection From Nature

Walking in nature, playing in nature and even simply viewing nature improve human health and well-being. Exposure to natural scenes reduces stress [Ulrich et al, 1991] and is likely to have long-term physiological health benefits [Parsons, 1991]; views of nature from workplace windows buffer the negative effect of job stress; [Leather, et al, 1998]; views of natural scenes from hospital windows aided patients' recovery from surgery [Ulrich, 1994]; and wilderness therapy can reduce behavioral and emotional symptoms in adolescents [Russell, 2003]. When people live more fully integrated with nature, they suffer less stress and ill health, their culture is richer, their society is well balanced, and their appreciation and caretaking of the Earth is stronger.

Yet perhaps the most significant reason for us to transform our relationship with nature is because we must in order to survive, thrive and ultimately evolve as a species. Nature itself as a key "partner" in inspiring new ways of experiencing and living in the world. The land and animals have greatly influenced human culture and society dating back to our ancient ancestors as exemplified by ancient and wondrous cave paintings. These paintings from 45,000 years ago show that animals represented more than just flesh and bone to our predecessors. According to David Williams and Jean Clottes in *Believing and Seeing: Symbolic Meanings in the Southern San Rock Paintings,* the ability the Cro-Magnons to see the animals around them from a higher perspective both reflected and transformed their consciousness.

-§-
"As we hurtle into the future, the trappings of modern life isolate us from the Earth and leave little room for the inward journey...very few people truly understand what forces have motivated their life or shaped their destiny "
—Denise Linn, *Quest*
-§-

Today, we are in great need of incorporating this higher understanding of nature and animals into our culture to navigate through one of the most perilous times in human history, to come finally to rest on the path of enlightened and beneficial evolution.

Nature As Catalyst

Nature is a catalyst for transformative shifts in energy, understanding, and spiritual access. We often relate to this experience as arising from interactions with other people. An example of this is when you spend time with someone you enjoy, your energy will feel positively boosted, and when you spend time with someone who disliked you, your energy level will feel drained or worse yet—polluted by the ill will or negative feelings that you just encountered.

-§-
"Nature can and does provide a sense of harmony and peace."
—Dora van Gelder Kunz
-§-

Nature can be rejuvenating in two key ways. There are places in nature and specific animals and trees that can enhance a positive energy flow. For example, where there is greater and lesser movement of energy or *chi* on the Earth can be invigorating. Channels of chi on the land can be narrow or broad depending upon landscape features. In the land, obvious influences such as underground water, ocean water, air quality, mountains and other features of the land can create a place where the energy is particularly renewing for people. Just being in these places can be like recharging your battery, leaving fatigue behind and providing greater mental clarity and physical vigor. This is why often a simple walk in the woods can feel so energizing.

There are also places in the land where we can more readily access healing energy while other places are not as beneficial. Polluted and damaged environments can be harmful to human health. We are negatively affected at an energetic and emotional level long before our bodies begin to show symptoms of disease. Nature can also balance your emotional energetic field. Emotions are meant to flow. It is only when they do not flow and are congested within us, that we develop stress, anxieties, unhealthy emotions and ill health. We also become disconnected from others, and ourselves, which leads to poor choices, and unhappy stress-filled lives.

Imagine a pure, clean river flowing vigorously within its banks, encountering debris in its path, and then forming a little tide pool where the water slows and instead of flowing onward, swirls around and around again in the same place, often collecting yet more debris. This is your mind and emotions when they are stuck. Think of a time or times when you have gone over and over and over something in your mind, feeling the anxiety of trapped energy. Perhaps you have even stayed awake at night, letting your mind swirl around, collecting more and more debris as it grows the problem out of proportion.

This is a "normal" condition in a society that tries to replace the work of our emotions with our analytical minds. Newborn babies and toddlers usually always have a healthy flow of emotional energy; they can cry pitifully one moment, and laugh with joy the next. Their emotional reality also proves that having emotional blockages is a socialized condition. There are some things the mind is simply not fit for.

There are simple ways to bring a healthy emotional flow back into your life, mind, and being. When you begin to notice that your mind is going into a swirling and stuck place, acknowledge that whatever it is that your mind is grappling with and appears to be an obstacle in your life, cannot be fixed by your mind in a million years of analytical reasoning alone. Let go, and imagine a new bud allowing the wind to unfold its petals.

The energy in the Earth and nature contains more than fuel for life and vitality; it contains emotion-based awareness. Nature, in its pure, unpolluted state, is totally without emotional conflict. The energetic and spiritual elements that sustain life are always present there. Being in touch with the land, mountains, sea, and forest can enhance our ability to meet our personal storms, even meeting the hostility and violence of others with strength and steadiness. We can then, from this place of poise, calm and contentment, influence the energies of the world around us for the better. We can choose to make a positive contribution to the Earth and other living things by embracing a celebratory attitude toward life.

-§-
Nature, in its pure unpolluted state, is totally without emotional conflict.
-§-

Guiding people to connect with this healing and balancing ocean of energy in nature is one of the key ways that I help people renew themselves and find greater unity and integration in their lives. The energy transference between people and nature can work in a variety of ways depending upon the need, and the interface between the place and the person. The methods I use are simple, and reflect three basic processes used everyday in our bodies and in nature. They are *releasing, filling,* and *radiating.*

Releasing

The energy and emotional awareness that exists as part of our bodies can intermingle with the energy and emotional awareness

around us and in other living things. For example, it is a universal human experience to be lovingly embraced. When we are feeling good, an embrace arising from compassion and warmth and acceptance infuses our own bodies with warmth and loving energy. When we are feeling vulnerable or sad, an embrace can provide the safety, acceptance, and love that we need to release emotions like sorrow, helplessness, and despair and the waves of flowing energy that contain them.

A similar dynamic can take place in the energy between people and between people and nature. This explains why one may start sobbing and releasing pent-up emotional energy containing sadness and grief while being hugged by a person who is filled with compassion. Sometimes we are so overburdened that we cannot possibly experience joy, fulfillment or clarity until we release and clear an unhealthy perceptive-emotional way of being. The Earth and nature offers up their own form of an embrace, which helps us with releasing.

When I first met Sara, her soft-spoken voice tried to convey composure and confidence but she was clearly stressed and her fatigue was palpable. "Can you help me?" were the first words she spoke. Sara was a successful engineer, one of the few women in her field, with a thriving practice. Yet in spite of her outward signs of success and confidence, her life had become unmanageable and her business was beginning to fail.

Sara spoke at length about different unhappy scenarios in her life, primarily related to work, that she believed were making her miserable. Her dialogues were a case study of a clogged river going round and round, trying to do both—explain her specific issues over and over, and solve them in the same breath. We developed a working plan for going through a series of outdoor sessions, phone sessions and homework to help her find a better place in her life, a place of strength and clarity so that she could begin to solve and make sense of her life.

We met a few days later on an early spring morning, the ground was still damp from dew. We walked in silent meditation up the hillside. When Sara entered the site we had chosen, her tightly-drawn shoulders relaxed. She took a full, deep breath. We began to undertake body-mind postures and affirmations to get more in touch with the inner and outer guidance of the place and ourselves. We relied upon the Earth and the elements to assist us. We focused our consciousness on the Earth below us, the sky above us, the ocean just a few miles away, and the radiant awakening sun.

Held in this gentle and safe space, Sara began to integrate her emotional intuitive self with her overall energetic being. I guided Sara to experience the compassionate spirit and nurturing energy of the Earth. She entered into the sacred space that nature offers us. Like layers of an onion peeling off, Sara experienced a healing emotional release. A few tears quietly came to rest on her cheeks — and she had not cried in over a year. The river of her body began to flow, clearing out the "debris" of clogged emotional awareness that had rested there for so long. She discovered that underneath the superficial emotions and problems that plagued her were deeper more heartfelt emotions and truths.

Being in nature renewed Sara's spirit and balanced her energy. It brought her insights and knowledge that she had not been able to find on her own.

Filling

Eden is here now. Opening fully to the beauty and magic that is within nature can make Eden as real as your own backyard. You inquisitively know this and have experienced this already. If you have forgotten it as an adult, the child within you knows it. Do you remember how the world seemed brighter then, the stars more brilliant, the grass a deeper hue of green? You can re-ignite the experience of those childhood days by fully immersing yourself in nature. Who knows what you have the capability of becoming when you are filled with the elixir of nature?

One summer, I was standing on a high ridge overlooking four rounded hills and a small valley below intermingled with open grasslands and trees. The air was filled with a subtle saltiness from the Pacific Ocean just twenty miles West. Suddenly, my eye was caught by a glimmer of silver. Two hundred feet above me was an osprey, carrying a newly-caught fish in its talons. The silver flashes were the reflection of the sun on fish scales; the light struck my eye with gleaming radiance.

The fish was still alive. It swung its tail back and forth in a swimming motion. Its gallant head was held straight forward, its eyes staring into the great innocence of the sky. For an instant, I felt pity for that fish, an apparently unwitting victim in that drama. But the osprey did not carry the fish off in a straight line to its nest (to the tree on the hillside to the West) but instead flew in spiral formations of expanding and higher circles. It gave that fish a majestic ride: over the green and gold hillsides, over a doe and her two spotted fawns silently shy beneath a moss-covered oak, over a long-eared hare standing up on

jumpy hind legs, over an amazed woman (me) and her golden-haired dog. In a moment my perception shifted to encompass the grandeur of that act: I saw that fish like the osprey's holy grail; a sacred vessel, carefully raised.

Just go outside and lie in the grass looking up at the trees and the sky. Take the time to walk beyond the path, over to the flowers, to see if they are fragrant. Look deep inside their petals to see the subtle shadings of color. Do not fool yourself that these acts are not as important, in fact more so, than spending tedious long hours working. You are a different person if you are filled with the warm rays of the sun, the clarity of the blue sky, the freedom of a soaring hawk. Let these things grow inside of you and from this your soul will be richer and fuller than it will ever be from a thousand promotions and titles.

-§-
"Universe is the externalization of your soul."
—Ralph Waldo Emerson
-§-

There can be times when we are just too caught up in our own heads and concerns. We can be in the presence of a beautiful sunset, looking up at a million twinkling stars, or standing before an ocean moving with peaceful and rhythmic waves—and not be able to connect to nature or ourselves at a heartfelt level. It is at times like these that I can guide people to get back in contact, so that they can be open to receive the beauty and positive energy that surrounds them. In many cases, simply letting nature in is all we need do, and the rest occurs naturally in much the same way that a flower opens to the sun.

At times, animals, plants, and even the land can call to us. They can provide new ways of knowing that enable us to see our lives and the world from a different perspective. This new way of knowing arises from feeling perception rather than analytical deduction. It is an integrated way of understanding, taken in through the body at various levels, not just the head and mind. This "whole body" knowing can provide solutions and ways of seeing that we may not reach on our own.

Visioning With Nature

People have gone into nature for thousands of years to gain greater clarity, knowledge and vision through vision quests, walk-abouts, and pilgrimages. Cultures all around the globe have gained from their interactions with nature. A cornerstone of the work that I do is helping people to vision with nature. I often integrate visioning in shorter sessions, and I also have two deeper and longer "focused visioning" processes.

Visioning in and with nature provides us with an ideal environment for peak performance. In a deep state of relaxation or meditation, the electromagnetic field surrounding the human head entrains and attunes to the basic electromagnetic field of the Earth itself. The Earth's harmonic resonance has been measured at approximately eight cycles per second or 8 hertz (Hz). The frequency of the electrical activity of the brain is also around 8 Hz. This is not a coincidence, but one of the many reasons why we feel so rejuvenated in nature. This is an excellent jumping off point for visioning and enhanced creativity.

Rituals can also be helpful in visioning. When we undertake an act of visioning we are consciously calling for a new future, a new way of being, a new way of doing. Rituals can make this transition more real and tangible.

Radiating

A respected Native American elder recently complained that people now are so caught up in their own day-to-day little problems that there is not enough praising, and rituals celebrating life. I believe that if we spent more time actively praising, and celebrating life, we would have fewer day-to-day little problems.

Saint Patrick would certainly agree. His *Confession,* written in the year 450 A.D., praised the world as much as it involved humbling himself. The two belong together in the one breath. We are meant to fill our hearts with gratitude for all that is, and express our gratitude openly, courageously, with fullness of heart. When we do so in the company of nature, the shining energy of the land, the trees and the animals increases. The poet Marie Rainier Rilke had it right when he said that what humankind is meant for is simply to praise the world and sing of its beauty and wonder.

Of all the creatures on this Earth, humans are the only ones capable of emanating sounds that reach all eight of octaves. Our range is superbly vast and well suited for beings meant to bring greater life, joy, and beauty into the world by infusing all life around us with our song. The world, the trees, the animals want to hear you sing. Walk outside of your church or your shower and sing in the open air like your ancestors before you. Sing of your life, the world, and the beauty around you.

-§-
Deep peace
of the running wave to you
Deep peace
of the flowing air to you
Deep peace
of the quiet earth to you
Deep peace
of the shining stars to you
Deep peace
of the spirit of peace to you.
—Scottish Blessing of the
Elements
-§-

Partnering With Nature: Reviving Awe

Nature is our partner on this Earth. We are not meant to be alone as a species—struggling alone for the answers to our problems. Animals and plants are our Earthly companions in the boldest meaning of the term. We came to this Earth "trailing clouds of glory from God who is our home," as Wordsworth put it. Other beings, animate and inanimate, come upon this Earth trailing those same clouds of glory; they just come in different physical forms and with different anatomical attributes. Many indigenous peoples know this. In their traditions, humankind communicates with the Creator through interaction with the animals, birds, and trees in the forest. It is through these messengers of a higher order that humankind connects with sacred and different ways of knowing.

-§-
If you would understand
the Invisible, look carefully
at the Visible.
— *Talmud*
-§-

The Polynesians tell of how their ancestors connected at a higher level with nature and animals (for example by communicating with dolphins and migrating birds) to successfully navigate thousands of miles of ocean. *Beowulf*—one of the oldest written poems in the English language, refers to the seafaring explorers as following "the whale path" to find their way across the vast ocean. When we open our hearts and minds, nature offers us alternative and often more comprehensive ways of knowing and being.

Understanding the importance of nature for the health of humankind leads to us taking better care of the environment, which brings yet greater human health and fulfillment. When people live more fully integrated with nature, they suffer less stress and ill health. Their cultures are richer, their societies are better balanced, and their appreciation and nurturing of the Earth is stronger.

Perhaps the greatest thing that I have learned from nature—the sage—is the simplest: honor and celebrate the world and sing its praises. Specifically, the praises of our brothers and sisters on Earth, the animals that we are so fortunate to live among, the plants that sustain us more than we acknowledge, and this living, breathing planet Earth. As we sing nature's praises, the song is returned tenfold to enrich our hearts.

Nature keeps us in connection with our timeless self. It is no accident that Buddha's enlightenment took place under a Bodhi tree, or that God spoke to Moses through a burning bush. Nature acts as a daily reminder of the enduring bond between animals and humankind, body and spirit, free will and destiny. The ancient Celts frequently relied upon nature and the elements of nature: Earth, fire, water and air for spiritual insight. Like the Native Americans, they looked to nature as a portal to reach and experience the unified divine realm. Geographically separated tribes and clans all practiced an Earth-based religions, and shared many common beliefs and rituals. It was the Earth herself who taught them all. Ultimately, nature brings us face to face with the ultimate creative, compassionate, and intelligent force in the universe.

Nature is in physical — as well as energetic and spiritual — unity. Look at the patterns that we can see all around us in nature such as the five arms of a starfish, the five inner teardrops of an apple core, and the commonality of the five-star-shaped petals of many flowers. Then look as well to your own hand and the five digits that form one of our species' greatest assets. Or observe the many occurrences of spirals in nature, in whirlpools in water, the inner reaches of a seashell, the structure of a tornado, and the spiral fingerprints at the tip of each of your fingers. Like tiny holographic portals, nature mirrors our own innate being and structure. By accessing nature we can more easily step outside of ourselves and experience the world from a perceptive feeling place of many living things — even the elements themselves. We can embrace the wisdom and power of wind, sky, and sea. We can experience beauty multiplied many times over with the combined senses of many.

-§-

To see a World in a Grain of Sand,
And Heaven in a Wild Flower,
Hold Infinity in the Palm of Your Hand,
And Eternity in an Hour.
—William Blake

-§-

Masaru Emoto:

Water as God's Messenger

A heart that is open to possibilities can lead to remarkable new discoveries, and that is how I came to experiment with water. I'd long since been curious about this incredible substance that circulates around the globe and flows in rivers and streams throughout the human body. One day, well over a decade ago now, I happened to open a book and read the words: "No two snow crystals are exactly the same." Like most of us, this peculiar fact had been in my mind since I was a schoolboy, but that day, the words seemed to jump off the page. To think that every snowflake that has fallen to this earth over millions of years has its own unique face baffles the mind, and yet, when I read the words that day, something in my heart heard a compelling message. My next thought, "I could freeze water and look at the crystals," opened the door to a fascinating adventure.

Oddly enough, from the very beginning, I *just knew* that the experiments with water would provide a window into the mystery of the cosmos and the marvel of this life into which we were born. I was certain that my plan to freeze water and take pictures of the crystals would pay off and immediately spoke to a young researcher in my company. It took two months of failed experiments before we got the first photograph of a beautiful hexagonal crystal. Today, our experiments are conducted in a walk-in refrigerator where the temperature is precisely maintained. Looking back at the methods we used to get

Masaru Emoto is a graduate of Yokohama Municipal University and the Open International University. He holds a doctorate in alternative medicine. He has undertaken extensive research on water, and published a series of astonishing photographs of water crystals in *Messages from Water* (Hado, 1999) and *The Hidden Messages in Water* (Sunmark, 2001), which have sold almost a half-million copies. He is married to Kazuko Emoto, who shares his passion and is head of Kyoikusha, the publishing arm of his company, IHM Corporation, in Tokyo, Japan. They have three children. You can find him on the web at www. masaru-emoto.net.

that first photograph in light of what we now know, that first photo was a miracle.

In the years since, we have performed many, many experiments with water and the photographs have gone out around the world. The message in the water starkly reveals that, as it says in the Bible: "In the beginning there was the Word." Said another way, everything comes into existence from vibration. The crystal photographs we have taken demonstrate this with remarkable eloquence.

In one series of experiments, we typed words on pieces of paper and then wrapped the paper around bottles of water. We put the wrapped bottles in a freezer that was –5 degrees Centigrade (23 degrees Fahrenheit). Once they were frozen, we looked at the water specimens under special microscopes and were quite surprised by what we found. The bottles of water that had been wrapped in words like "Beauty," "You're cute," "Thank you," and "Wisdom," created beautiful crystals in the water. But the ones wrapped with words like "You fool!" and "You make me sick," or "I will kill you!" had produced

> -§-
> Everything comes into existence from vibration.
> -§-

Water Crystal from Fujiwara Dam Before Offering a Prayer.

218

incomplete crystals or no crystals at all. A valuable lesson about the power of words can be gleaned from this experiment.

In our experiments, we used both Japanese and English. Regardless of the language used, we found that the words affected the formation of the crystals. Water produces formations based on circumstances, not because of a specific language. If a circumstance is positive and the words used express goodness, the water will make a formation that reflects beauty. If a circumstance is negative and the words used express a mean-spirited quality, the water will create a formation that is ugly and evil looking.

-§-
If we send out thoughts and feelings that are filled with fear, anger, or negativity, we are contributing to the destruction of the universe.
-§-

The results were equally revealing when we exposed water to music. Beautiful crystals with delicate detail resulted when we exposed the water to classical music. But water that was exposed to heavy metal music either did not form a crystal at all, or formed an ugly, malformed image.

In one experiment, we wrote the words *Love* and *Gratitude,* wrapped them around various bottles of water, and placed them near mobile phones, computers, televisions, and microwave ovens. What we found is that when water is put in a microwave, it produces an ugly ring that looks similar to the structure we found when water was

Water Crystal from Fujiwara Dam After Offering a Prayer.

exposed to the word "Satan." The water placed next to the computers and televisions produced an insignificant-looking, blurry-edged ring. The water placed near the mobile phones wouldn't produce a crystal at all.

Substances in nature, like water, respond to our human thoughts. They can accept our thoughts to change their condition and quality. Our thoughts have an effect on the world around us. If we send out thoughts and feelings that are filled with fear, anger, or negativity, we are contributing to the destruction of the universe. If we emit thoughts of love, kindness, and beauty, we are contributing to the creation of a beautiful world. This is what water crystals reveal.

Another demonstration of the power of thought to influence the natural world occurred at Lake Biwa in a part of Japan called Shiga. The waters of Lake Biwa had become quite polluted. Every summer, the surface of the lake would be covered with a species of aquatic plant called Kokanada Algae. When the algae would putrefy, it created a very bad odor. For twenty years in a row, the local government had a large-scale operation in place to remove all the algae. Then, one summer, the aquatic plant hardly emerged at all. Nobody could explain why the Kokanada had not returned.

What they didn't know until later was that I had led a group of 350 people to that lake to pray. As the rising sun came up, we assembled by the shore and faced the surface of the lake. Praying together, we spoke the following chant out loud ten times: "The eternal power of the universe has gathered itself to create a world with true and grand harmony."

A powerful statement infused with the eternal energy of the universe, this chant spreads the energy to our surroundings and penetrates them with healing intent. By requesting harmony in our thoughts, we transformed the surface of the lake into a clean state. Our thoughts and prayers not only curbed the very bad smelling aquatic plant and changed the quality of the water; the quality of the grasses surrounding the lake also changed. Vocalizing this declaration, we influenced the natural world, resulting in greater happiness, peace, and the fulfillment of many wishes. I believe that vocalizing our intent in this way can also help us to actualize world peace.

-§-
When people are pure-minded—their prayers create crystals that are beautiful and clear.
-§-

What we have seen in our experiments again and again is that praying produces a beautiful pattern in water. The effect, which is almost immediate, does not depend on whether one is a high-ranking monk or a preacher. When people are pure-minded — when they have what I call "a very good mind" — their prayers create crystals that are beautiful and clear. In general, we see the most beautiful crystals appear in response to the prayers of little children. The crystals that form as a result of prayers spoken by children are much more beautiful than that of the adults.

In our experiments, the water changed according to the words it was exposed to. When it was given negative words, it did not form crystals. When it was given positive words, it changed and beautiful crystals formed. The words "Love" and "Thanks" produced the most beautiful results. Love and gratitude are in relationship to one another with love being active and gratitude passive. I think of these two existing in a one-to-two ratio where "love" is one and "gratitude" is two, much like water with its one part oxygen and two parts hydrogen. In this case, we have one part love to two parts gratitude. I believe the response of water to these two words gives us a very important message.

-§-

The world is made more beautiful when we infuse it with our love and gratitude.

-§-

To get the message of water out to a worldwide audience, I recently joined the United Nations. I have also started a "World Day of Love and Thanks to Water" which is July 25. We all have an important mission: to make water clean again, and to create a world that is healthy to live in. In order to accomplish our mission, we must first make sure that our hearts are clear and unpolluted. Water is showing us that the world is made more beautiful when we infuse it with our love and gratitude.

CONNIE GRAUDS:

The Indigenous Heart

Allopathic medicine defines the human heart as an organ consisting of four chambers: the right and left atria, and the right and left ventricles. The shaman would also define the heart as having four chambers—but of a spiritual rather than physical nature.

I'm a pharmacist who has worked in the world of conventional Western medicine for nearly thirty years, and I'm also a shamana who has apprenticed in the world of the spirit for over a decade. I stand with my feet firmly planted in these two very different worlds. It is from both these perspectives that I consider healing the heart of the world.

We know that the physical heart is responsible for pumping blood around the body, thus keeping good nutrients and oxygen flowing in, and pulling waste and toxins out. Our organic heart essentially keeps everything flowing and connected throughout the human body. The spiritual heart, on the other hand, keeps us in an energy flow and a spiritual connection much greater than only our body. Our own spiritual heart connects us to the spirit and the heart of the world.

Four Chambers of the Spiritual Heart

In the many days, weeks, months, and years in a decade of apprenticeship to spirit deep in the jungles of the Amazon in the arms of the green mother, I have come to know there are four chambers of

Constance Grauds, R.Ph., is President of the Association of Natural Medicine Pharmacists (www.anmp.org), and Assistant Professor of Clinical Pharmacy at the University of California, San Francisco. Grauds is also author of the books *The Energy Prescription* (Bantam, 2005) which gives prescriptives for the age-old complaint of fatigue; and *Jungle Medicine* (CSM, 2004), which recounts spirited tales of her apprenticeship in Amazonian jungle shamanism. Grauds is Director of the Center for Spirited Medicine (www.spiritedmedicine.com), where she lives her passion and life's work of integrating the spiritual and scientific healing aspects of plants as medicine into today's modern medicine.

the human spiritual heart. They are: the romantic heart, the religious heart, the indigenous heart, and the heart within. How I have come to know this has been the process of coming to know the depths of my own heart.

The Romantic Heart

Who doesn't know the power of the romantic heart?! After all, love makes the world go around, as we say. The romantic heart is the love of *another*, the love of that special person in our life. It is about extending the deep feelings of care and connectedness to someone other than ourselves.

Romantic love is the act of loving another, of opening our hearts to include another person. We all know that special feeling of opening up to another with whom we share romantic love. It is a deep feeling inside yourself that is now expanding out to two people, a circle of energy that is now larger than one.

In that expansive state, we feel bliss, connectedness, love, care, and a willingness to share what we have with someone else—to offer up part of our life for the sake of the other. We have opened beyond the self-centeredness of our own survival and into the realms of spirit.

-§-
"We don't set out to save the world; we just set out to wonder how other people are doing and to reflect on how our actions affect other people's hearts."
—Pema Chödrön
-§-

The biblical passage puts it this way, "When two or more are gathered I am there." The spirit of love arrives when we open to another.

It is spirit of love that heals; heals us, and heals the other. To be in the spirit of love is what we all desire by our very nature. In order to be in the spirit of love, we must be in our hearts.

My maestro, shaman don Antonio, recently taught this to me in the following way. I had just stepped off the plane and onto the hot tarmac in Iquitos, Peru, when don Antonio came rushing up to greet me with a broad warm smile. He took me by my two white hands in his two brown hands, and stepped back to give me the shamanic "once over" look that he always does upon meeting me. While it looked like he was sizing me up physically, he was actually looking at me energetically. He nodded his head in approval and told me that I had good energy. Later that afternoon, over a glass of *agua mineral con gas*, I mentioned to him that I had a new love in my life. He answered, "Yes, I know. I saw it in your heart as you stepped off the plane." I inquired, "How so?" He replied, "I can see from the spirit of love that radiates out from your heart and your entire body." "Soon, when we go into the jungle and do our work together," he added, "you will learn that this craving you have in your heart for the new beau in your life is actually your desire to connect with Great Spirit." As don Antonio and I started down the jungle path, walking through the emerald doors into deep primal nature, he continued, "In our seeking the love of another physically, we are really seeking a deeper connection to nature and life itself. This love is larger than just you two. If you let it, this heart that is growing within you will connect you ultimately to the heart of the world."

The Religious Heart

While the romantic heart is the desire to connect with someone across from you—hearts and love connecting person to person—the religious heart is the desire to connect upwards to the heavens above us. In the religious heart, we connect with the invisible.

The religious heart is the heart of our desire to connect to a power greater than ourselves. That power greater than ourselves we may choose to call God, Spirit, Brahman, Atman, Christ, The Supreme Being, to mention a few of the many names of the Great One. While we call it the religious heart, it is not of one particular religion or dogma. It is larger than any one set of ideas or principles. It is the devotional heart, and we are the devotee. We pray or connect to that greater power each in our own way. The practice of prayer is universal. That act of connecting to the divine within our religious heart is our spiritual practice in its many forms.

> -§-
> There is no need for us
> to be joined at the head.
> We are joined by our
> human hearts.
> —Margaret Wheatley,
> *Turning to One Another*
> -§-

Stephen Levine says, "Spiritual traditions yearn for the direct experience of the thing called 'the Beloved.' Spiritual traditions... whose mystical and devotional aspects...seek this hidden mystery. The beloved is neither a person nor a place. It is an experience of deeper and deeper levels of being and eventually of beingness itself." As we go deeper in our spiritual practice, Stephen goes on to say, "...the boundrylessness of your own great nature is expressed in rapture and the absolute vastness by the word 'love'."

I have never been so deeply touched as I was during my apprenticeship to spirit in the jungles of Peru. At times I weep when I speak of this place deep within myself, this place of profound connection with spirit. In these moments, I cannot discern the difference between me and the absolute. We are one; there is no difference.

Our connection to spirit is true for all of us all of the time, whether we are in that peak experience state or not. The sense of our connec-

tion to spirit varies; sometimes more, sometimes less. We humans long to do spiritual practices, set up rituals, come together in spiritual communities, to do all the things that evoke more of this special state. We create these special events and places that connect us up more deeply with spirit, the divine, the Beloved, ecstatic rapture, great love. It's part of who we are.

One such event of a deep connection with the divine happened to me with the unwitting help of don Antonio. Several years ago, don Antonio had the opportunity to visit my home in the San Francisco Bay Area. He had never been out of the jungles of the Amazon before, quite an experience of new realms for the shaman. As his stay here unfolded, we had the opportunity to go into the city of San Francisco itself for a short visit. We had the opportunity to ride the famous cable cars from the Embarcadero wharf waterfront to the stop high up on top of a hill at Grace Cathedral.

This was to be our turning point. The plan was to go down the hills of San Francisco, through Chinatown, and back to the wharf again. Once at the top, don Antonio wanted to pay a visit to Grace Cathedral Church, saying he wanted to learn about how we pray to the gods in our country. We stepped inside. I stayed in the church vestibule, while don Antonio walked the perimeter of the church. He looked closely at the sacred scenes of saints, Jesus, lambs and lilies, Mary, and the apostles depicted in the stained glass windows.

-§-
The religious heart is the desire to connect upwards; connecting to the heavens above us.
-§-

Stopping at the votive candles, he watched a man giving his offering and prayers there. Don Antonio then came to me to ask for some money to put into the offering in order to light a prayer candle there. Giving him the money, I chose to stay in the waiting area, some 200 feet away, while he made his offering and prayer.

Don Antonio put his money into the tin box, lit a candle, and began to pray. In that moment, mostly oblivious to what don Antonio was doing, I was overcome and thought I was going to faint. My heart blew wide open. In that moment I was one with something that could lift mountains and stop wars. And that something was Love, big love. The humble and earnest prayers of an indigenous shaman, in a country foreign to him, within this Catholic church, taught me about the power of the religious heart.

The Indigenous Heart

While none of these four spiritual chambers of the heart is really different from the other, and function together just as our own physical heart does, we can point to a special place within our heart that we will call the indigenous heart.

The indigenous heart is the heart of the Earth and its inhabitants. The term "indigenous" may originate from many sources. I'd like to tell one such story of origin, true or not, that helps us grasp a deeper meaning of the word. I was told that the term "indigenous" may have originated from the time of Christopher Columbus. When Columbus came to the New World and met up with the native peoples of this part of the globe, he was most taken with their way of life. He noted how these peoples lived close to the land, in rhythm with the rising and setting sun, in harmony with all of nature. Writing a report back to the Old World of his observations, Columbus was to have said, "I have found a people who live 'in dios'...or 'in god'." Columbus's term "in dios" eventually became the word "indigenous."

-§-
Our connection to spirit is true for all of us all of the time, whether we are in that peak experience state or not.
-§-

This story, fact or fiction, makes a point. The indigenous way of life is one of harmony with nature. The indigenous heart is the chamber of our spiritual heart that connects with the Earth, its people, and all its inhabitants. It is the heart of agape love, a heart of global love. Sir John Templeton says that, "Agape love is unlimited, pure, and unconditional. It is altruistic love, given for its own sake without expecting anything in return. Judaism, Christianity, Islam, Hinduism, Buddhism, Taoism, Confucianism, and Native American spirituality share common values. These qualities include goodwill, kindness, and compassion to others—also known as agape."

This is the "do unto others" Golden Rule state of being in the heart. Spiritual leaders and perennial philosophers down through the ages have mused as to what the world would be like if we all came from this place in our hearts. It is almost incomprehensible, as humanity falters when it comes from a lesser place in the heart.

Coming from the place of the indigenous heart lifts humanity to a higher state of being. Don Antonio says that this indigenous heart state of being is "the way it should be." Early one morning, to demonstrate the point, don Antonio lead me down a moist jungle path to a small clearing surrounded by trees. In that clearing was a small wooden table, upon which two lit candles were nestled amongst assorted objects surrounded with tree boughs. This table was don Antonio's sacred *mesa,* or altar. The assorted objects on the mesa consisted of a picture of the Virgin of Guadalupe, a balsa carving of a tapir, a blood wood carving of a dolphin, and a large ceramic statue of what don Antonio called "the spirit of the jungle."

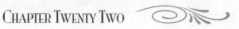
The ceramic statue was an elaborate composition of humans, animals, and spirits, all huddled within the hollows of a huge ceramic tree. It reminded me of the manger scene, jungle style. What a treat. I had never seen don Antonio set up such detailed holy mesa before. He said that the combination had come to him in a dream.

> -§-
> "We heal in relationships. We are not separate. To quote shaman don Antonio, 'There is only one disease...the disease of disconnection.'"
> —Constance Grauds
> *The Energy Prescription*
> -§-

Don Antonio proceeded to explain, "This is the spirit of the jungle and of its people. You see a father and mother, holding their infant baby. This represents the love of the family unit. The jaguar here at their feet is there to protect them. High above the family, notice the angel, their spiritual guardian. And standing in the background behind the family, you see an indigenous person dressed in native garb, there to remind them of their indigenous heart. And they are all together within this jungle tree to represent the spirit of the jungle." I inquired, "And what *is* the spirit of the jungle and its people, don Antonio?" He threw both arms open wide to the heavens, and exclaimed, "It is love for all!"

The Heart Within

The fourth chamber of the spiritual heart is the heart within. In this chamber, we are in the heart of love for ourselves. This is the heart of self-love and self-acceptance. On the surface of things, this seems to be a given. But when we go deep within ourselves, many of us would admit some amount of low self-esteem and unworthiness, the symptoms of lack of self-love and self-acceptance. There are those of us who suffer from self-loathing, and even the extreme of self-hatred.

How can we profess the love of another (from our romantic heart), the love of the divine (from our spiritual heart), the love of other people and the Earth (from our indigenous heart) if we don't first have love of self? It is the heart within where we must look first if we are to be connected to a greater love and a greater good outside ourselves.

Troubles with self-love seem are endemic in our modern societies. To what do we owe this problem? Where do we get the idea that we are not lovable? How did this all begin?

One afternoon, in a jungle village on the Yarapa River in northern Peru, shaman don Antonio and I were sharing some idle chatter and jungle gossip. Lingering together under two shade trees, hoping to catch the hint of a late afternoon breeze, we were approached by a young indigenous mother and her new baby. As the mother presented her precious baby girl to don Antonio as a way of introduction, his eyes lit up. Don Antonio immediately put his right forefinger under the baby's chin and began stroking it to evoke a smile from the child. In a soft heartfelt voice, don Antonio said, "Love in the night," as he smiled knowingly. That was the beginning of a night filled with teachings from don Antonio. He poured forth his love and passion for children, "the lifeblood of our culture." Stirring the fire with the thick end of a palm branch, don Antonio told me that every child born in the jungle is given a ritual with special prayers at the time of birth. Midwives perform this spiritual ritual while assisting with the mechanics of delivering the baby. Each baby is welcomed not only physically but spiritually. Every precious child is born with love and into the field of love. That newborn is immediately connected to the spirit and the love of the new world into which it is born. What starts out as "love in the night" becomes "love of life itself." Don Antonio concluded his story with the announcement that, "every child born in the jungle knows love at its core."

> -§-
>
> "In medicine we are in an economic crisis, but one that goes far beyond the problem of not being able to pay for medical care. Fundamentally, these are side effects of a greater crisis, and that is our failure to respect men, women, and children, a failure to honor humanity, to honor life, and a failure to ask with each thought, 'Is this life-giving' Is this life sustaining? Or is this destructive?"
> —Jeanne Achterberg, Ph.D., *Relationships Are the Best Medicine*
> -§-

The storytelling continued, and the burning fire took me deep inside myself as I listened with an even more open heart. Don Antonio went on to say, "The other side of 'love' is 'not love.' Our indigenous people don't have such a concept as 'self-hated. We don't even know what that means. It's not part of our experience." The fire flared brighter in that moment to reveal more of don Antonio's somber face, "To have no love is to have no spirit in the heart. To have no love for yourself means that you are not connected to the spirit and the heart of who you are. This is a very serious thing. Where there is no spirit, there is no life. If you cannot love the life within yourself, you cannot love the life around you."

When we open our heart to ourselves, we are in good relationship with ourselves. It is then that we can also open our hearts and have good relationships with others and the world around us.

Healing in Relationship

Good relationships with ourselves and those around us are vital to our health and well-being. In June of 1946, at the International

Health Conference in New York, the Preamble to the Constitution of the World Health Organization (WHO) defined health as "a state of complete physical, mental and social well-being and not merely the absence of disease or infirmity." We heal within our bodies and also within our communities.

To be in relationship means to be open; open to ourselves and others, to our Earth and its inhabitants, to the spirit of our gods, and to life itself. To heal in relationship means to open our hearts to the aspects and elements of these relationships. To be in good relationship of any kind is all about heart and love.

Our environment is everything surrounding us—all of the animal, vegetable, and mineral kingdoms. It is all of the Earth and its inhabitants. To the degree that we feel separate from the environment is the degree to which we do not have a relationship with it, and have not opened our hearts to it.

Environmental medicine is the study of how the quality of the air, water, land, animals, and plants around us affects our health. Medicine now knows that there is a correlation between bad water, bad air, bad soil, and bad health. The science of environmental medicine is now proving through research what we intuitively know to be true.

Our cancer epidemic is but one example of the effects of our increasingly toxic environment and our relationship to it. There is overwhelming evidence that the increase in cancer rates is a direct result of exposure to carcinogens in the air, water, and soil. As Dr. Samuel Epstein has noted, "...cancer is the only major adverse impact for which we can clearly relate a direct causal relationship between avoidable carcinogenic exposures and escalating trends. Cancer is thus a quantifiable manifestation of runaway industrial technologies that affect all of us."

> -§-
> "The coming ecological disaster we worry about has already occurred, and goes on occurring. It takes place in the accounts of ourselves that separate ourselves from the world."
> —James Hillman
> *The Soul's Code*
> -§-

Don Antonio says, "We are suffering from a cancer of our hearts, a black rot that is eating away at the goodness within our hearts." Over the years of study with this man of nature, I have marveled at the power of the simplicity of his words. Never having gone to school a day in his life, don Antonio speaks from the purity of The Truth itself. Knowing no other way, he speaks from the heart about what is reality. "The medicine we all need is love," he reminds us.

While our environment is everything around us — the animals, birds, water, land, sun, moon, and stars — ecology is the dynamic interplay between these things. The environment is the "things" — the nouns. Ecology is the "relationship" — the verb.

Ecology is the dynamic interplay, or *homeodynamics,* of the relationships of all nature's systems. There is the ecology within our own bodies, the ecology of our surroundings, and the ecology of the dynamic interplay between the two. Ecological medicine, then, is the medicine of right relationship with every aspect of life.

As we look at the origins of modern medicine and where it is going, we get a story of expansion and perspective. Allopathic medicine, the basis of modern Western medicine, is based on a system of looking at body parts as separate from each other. If a patient is suffering from bronchitis, it is the lungs that are the problem. If a patient has a headache, it is a function of the head.

-§-

"Simply stated, improving human health is inextricably linked to restoring ecological well-being. The interconnectedness of all life is a fundamental biological truth."
— Kenny Ausubel, *Ecological Medicine*

-§-

Within the last decade or two, medicine has begun to realize that the mind and the body are connected. The terms "mind/body medicine" and "holistic medicine" were coined, recognizing that our body and mind are not separate systems. We are a whole, integrated system. Medicine, faced with new knowledge, realized that it must fully recognize and treat the whole person.

Now medicine is taking the next step, expanding the concept of medicine even beyond the mind-body. New thinkers in modern medicine today are talking about "ecological medicine" — healing in relationships outside of ourselves. Medicine is now realizing the wisdom in the WHO's earlier definition of health. Good relationships with family, community, and our surroundings — society and nature — are as important to our overall health as the wonders of modern pharmaceuticals and surgery. This is not to say that body parts and mind-body concepts are no longer important, but that there is a larger picture of health emerging.

As we love and care for ourselves and those around us, let us not forget to include care and love of the Earth itself, our environment. The health of the Earth itself is inextricably bound to our own health and well-being. It is imperative that we continue to heal ourselves *and* heal the world.

CHAPTER TWENTY TWO

From Healing to Creation

In *Being Green: On the Relationships Between People and Plants,* Larry Dossey, M.D., writes: "In the dream I saw a gorgeous vine sprout and expand to about a foot in diameter. Its emerald leaves were perfect, without flaw of blemish. The vine rapidly began to grow laterally and it beckoned me to follow its growing tip. It led me into every area of the planet, from the smallest villages to the greatest cities. The vine was a green thread uniting all the peoples of the Earth. Then, having completed a journey over the entire planet, the vine turned upward and began to grow vertically. I hung on. The next stop was the Divine."

-§-

"Love is much more demanding than law."
—Archbishop Desmond Tutu

-§-

The shaman's way of healing ourselves and healing the world is done ultimately by creating the Garden of Eden. By creating a Garden of Eden in our lives, we create a positive world, a life-affirming world. We move into the light. This is a very different way of approach than fighting against what's wrong with the world, though that sometimes needs doing, too. In the life-affirming creation of a Garden of Eden for ourselves, we create a heaven, a place where we are whole and all is healed. In the Garden of Eden, the rivers are clean, the air is pure, the hungry are fed, broken bones are mended, and the spirits of the downtrodden are restored. In this heavenly world of the shaman, all are healthy and have a sense of well-being. There is harmony and peace.

When I asked don Antonio how this might be accomplished, he retorted with his usual answer, "The jungle itself will tell you." He then took me on a long walk through verdant jungle trails, knowing that the walkabout experience itself would take me deep into the experience of what he was about to teach me. The answers began unfolding just like the uncurling tendrils of fuzzy green ferns at our feet.

Don Antonio first instructed me to walk in silence, to experience the jungle without the noise of our human voices. The jungle began to envelope me in an intense, sensurround experience; the squawks of the colorful macaws, the deep calls of the elusive howler monkeys, the green-against-blue shade of the tops of the tall *cecropia* trees reaching the sky. The perfumes of the jungle orchids mingled with the spicy smells of the rotting leaves underneath my feet.

After some twenty minutes of silent walking, don Antonio whispered to me, "Tell me what you are experiencing right now." I answered in a hushed voice, "I'm completely open. I cannot tell if I am breathing, or if I'm being breathed. I am one with everything around me. It is a very heady experience, as if the sense of myself is disappearing. My spirit feels expanded. My heart is so immense that it could fill the universe at this moment. I'm filled with a deep love of myself and everything around me."

Don Antonio responded knowingly, "Welcome to the garden of heaven. The medicine of love is in the sights. The medicine of love is in the sounds. The medicine of love is in the smells. Here, there is nothing but the ultimate medicine of love. From this state of being, all will be healed. You will be healed. From this state of being you will offer to do great things for the benefit of others and the world. I tell you this, for love is the master and you are the servant. Bless you and all the others who have opened your hearts and stepped onto the path of love, for you will now all help to create heaven on earth."

FRITJOF CAPRA:

Landscapes of Learning

Experiencing ecological relationships and community is the key to ecoliteracy.

The concept of ecological sustainability was introduced more than twenty years ago by Lester Brown, who defined a sustainable society as one that is able to satisfy its needs without diminishing the chances of future generations. This classic definition of sustainability is an important moral exhortation, but it does not tell us anything about how to actually build a sustainable society. This is why the whole concept of sustainability is still confusing to many. What we need is an operational definition of ecological sustainability. The key to such a definition is the realization that we do not need to invent sustainable human communities from zero, but can model them after nature's ecosystems, which are sustainable communities of plants, animals and micro-organisms. Since the outstanding characteristic of the biosphere is its inherent ability to sustain life, a sustainable human community must be designed in such a manner that its ways of life, businesses, economy, physical structures and technologies do not interfere with nature's inherent ability to sustain life.

This definition of sustainability implies that, in our endeavor to build sustainable communities, we must understand the principles of organization that ecosystems have developed to sustain the web of life. This understanding is what we call "ecological literacy." In the

Fritjof Capra, Ph.D., is the author of four international bestsellers, *The Tao of Physics* (Shambala, 1979), *The Turning Point* (Bantam, 1984), *Uncommon Wisdom* (Bantam, 1989) and *The Web of Life* (Anchor, 1997). His most recent book is *The Hidden Connections*, (Anchor, 2004). Dr. Capra also co-wrote the screenplay for *Mindwalk*. Dr. Capra has a Ph.D. in theoretical physics, does research in particle physics, and is one of the co-founders for The Center for Ecoliteracy in Berkeley, California. This chapter appeared first in *Resurgence* magazine, a journal of ecology, spirituality and the arts, www.resurgence.org. Photo by Kate Mount.

coming decades, the survival of humanity will depend on our ability to understand the basic principles of ecology and to live accordingly.

We need to teach our children—and our political and corporate leaders!—the fundamental facts of life: for example, that matter cycles continually through the web of life; that the energy driving the ecological cycles flows from the sun; that diversity assures resilience; that one species' waste is another species' food; that life, from its beginning more than three billion years ago, did not take over the planet by combat but by networking. Teaching this ecological knowledge, which is also ancient wisdom, will be the most important role of education in the twenty-first century.

The complete understanding of the principles of ecology requires a new way of seeing the world and a new way of thinking in terms of relationships, connectedness, and context. Ecology is first and foremost a science of relationships among the members of ecosystem communities. To fully understand the principles of ecology, therefore, we need to think in terms of relationships and context. Such "contextual" or "systemic" thinking involves several shifts of perception that go against the grain of traditional Western science and education.

-§-

Instead of seeing the universe as a machine composed of elementary building blocks, scientists have discovered that the material world, ultimately, is a network of inseparable patterns of relationships.

-§-

This new way of thinking is also emerging at the forefront of science, where a new systemic conception of life is being developed. Instead of seeing the universe as a machine composed of elementary building blocks, scientists have discovered that the material world, ultimately, is a network of inseparable patterns of relationships; that the planet as a whole is a living, self-regulating system. The view of the human body as a machine and of the mind as a separate entity is being replaced by one that sees not only the brain, but also the immune system, the bodily tissues, and even each cell, as living, cognitive systems. This view no longer sees evolution as a competitive struggle for existence, but rather as a cooperative dance in which creativity and the constant emergence of novelty are the driving forces.

Consequently, teaching ecology requires a conceptual framework that is quite different from that of conventional academic disciplines. Teachers notice this at all levels of teaching, from very small children to university students. Moreover, ecology is inherently multidisciplinary, because ecosystems connect the living and non-living worlds. Ecology, therefore, is grounded not only in biology, but also in geology, atmospheric chemistry, thermodynamics, and other branches of science. And when it comes to human ecology we have to add a whole range of other fields, including agriculture, economics, industrial design, and politics. Education for sustainability means teaching ecology in this systemic and multidisciplinary way.

When we study the basic principles of ecology in depth, we find that they are all closely interrelated. They are just different aspects of a single fundamental pattern of organization that has enabled nature to sustain life for billions of years. In a nutshell: *nature sustains life by creating and nurturing communities.* No individual organism can exist in isolation. Animals depend on the photosynthesis of plants for their energy needs; plants depend on the carbon dioxide produced by animals, as well as on the nitrogen fixed by bacteria at their roots; and together plants, animals and micro-organisms regulate the entire biosphere and maintain the conditions conducive to life. Sustainability, therefore, is not an individual property but a property of an entire web of relationships. It always involves a whole community.

This is the profound lesson we need to learn from nature. The way to sustain life is to build and nurture community.

When we teach this in our schools, it is important to us that the children not only understand ecology, but also experience it in nature—in a school garden, on a beach, or in a riverbed—and that they also experience community while they become ecologically literate. Otherwise, they could leave school and be first-rate theoretical ecologists but care very little about nature, or about the Earth. In our ecoliteracy schools, we want to create experiences that lead to an emotional relationship with the natural world. Over the past ten years, my colleagues and I at the Center for Ecoliteracy have developed a special pedagogy called "Education for Sustainable Patterns of Living," which offers an experiential, participatory and multidisciplinary approach to teaching ecoliteracy. We are sometimes asked: "Why all these complexities? Why don't you just teach ecology?" The complexities and subtleties of our approach are inherent in any true understanding of ecology and sustainability.

-§-

The way to sustain life is to build and nurture community.

-§-

Experiencing and understanding the principles of ecology in a school garden or a creek restoration project are examples of what educators nowadays call "project-based learning." It consists in facilitating learning experiences that engage students in complex real-world projects, reminiscent of the age-old tradition of apprenticeship. Project-based learning not only provides students with important experiences—cooperation, mentorship, integration of various intelligences—but also makes for better learning. There have been some very interesting studies on how much we retain when we are taught something. Researchers have found that after two weeks we remem-

ber only 10% of what we read, but 20% of what we hear, 50% of what we discuss, and ninety per cent of what we experience. To us, this is one of the most persuasive arguments for experiential, project-based learning.

Community is essential for understanding sustainability, and it is also essential for teaching ecology in the multidisciplinary way it requires. In schools, various disciplines need to be integrated to create an ecologically oriented curriculum. Obviously this is only possible if teachers from the different disciplines collaborate, and if the school administration makes such collaboration possible. In other words, the conceptual relationships among the various disciplines can be made explicit only if there are corresponding human relationships among the teachers and administrators.

Ten years of work has convinced us that education for sustainable living can be practiced best if the whole school is transformed into a learning community. In such a learning community, teachers, students, administrators and parents are all interlinked in a network of relationships, working together to facilitate learning. The teaching does not flow from the top down, but there is a cyclical exchange of knowledge. The focus is on learning, and everyone in the system is both a teacher and a learner.

-§-
Creating a sustainable world for our children and for future generations is our common task.
-§-

In the conventional view of education, students are seen as passive learners, and the curriculum is a set of predetermined, decontextualized information. Our pedagogy of education for sustainable living breaks completely with this convention. We engage students in the learning process with the help of real-life projects. This generates a strong motivation and engages the students emotionally. Instead of presenting predetermined, decontextualized information, we encourage critical thinking, questioning, and experimentation, recognizing that learning involves the construction of meaning according to the student's personal history and cultural background.

Education for sustainable living is an enterprise that transcends all our differences of race, culture, or class. The Earth is our common home, and creating a sustainable world for our children and for future generations is our common task.

AMY RACINA:

Angels in the Wilderness

August 4, 2003: "So this is how it ends." The thought resounds through my shaken body. I have not blacked out: I remember the seconds of the free-fall with brutal clarity. I took a single step, just one more step in hundreds of thousands of steady paces along the trail. Suddenly, without warning, I was falling. I saw the harsh slab of rock rushing up toward me from sixty feet below. There was no way to stop my descent, nothing to grab onto, no time to shift position, no action that could alter my fate as I plummeted through the air.

This was it. I was going to die. No gentle, easy passing into some brighter place. No life flashing gloriously before my eyes. No beckoning tunnel of light. Just this abrupt, thoughtless termination of life. I felt bitter disappointment at all that was lost to me. My mind screamed out in frustration against my own impotence, and my world went gray around me. I did not even have time to pray.

Months later it would come back to me, the sickening feeling of my own bones shattering as my body crashed like a rag doll upon the rock. But at the moment of impact, I felt nothing. Now I lie on my back on a slab of shale, legs crushed under me at an awkward angle, and look up at the wall of the ravine towering above me.

I had been hiking solo, with my backpack for company, for twelve days already, having covered 136 miles of a glorious loop through

Amy Racina was introduced to backpacking at the age of sixteen, and began soloing in her early twenties. She has trekked hundreds of miles through the high country of the Sierra Nevada Mountain Range, has traveled alone all over the world, and has led groups in wilderness adventures. She lives and works in Healdsburg, California, and has received numerous awards for her graphic design work, including a Clio nomination. She is the author of a moving chronicle of a near-fatal fall while hiking, and her subsequent recovery, also entitled *Angels in the Wilderness* (Elite, 2005)—which is winning rave reviews. More at www.AngelsInTheWilderness.com.

California's Kings Canyon National Park. I was descending a rugged, unmaintained trail into the Tehipite valley, feeling strong in body and illuminated in spirit as I hiked along, looking forward to experiencing the legendary beauty of the remote valley. Having temporarily lost my trail, I had been threading my way cautiously around the circumference of a steep hillside. Holding on with my hands, and carefully reaching out my right foot, I allowed my weight to sink gradually onto it. With that one step, everything changed. The ground gave way, and I plummeted downward.

Seconds later, here I am, lying smashed on the rock at the bottom of the ravine. I'm alive. I had not expected it to be so.

Reeling with shock, I struggle to sit up. I begin to assess the damage. There is blood on the rock around me. A front tooth has snapped off. My nose is smashed. One wrist resists bending, and several fingers stick out at odd angles. A ten-inch long, oozing scrape slashes across my right thigh. Multiple bruises and cuts cover my face and the rest of my body. My right ankle bends inward at an unnatural angle. My left hip brings excruciating pain when I attempt to shift it. A bone protrudes through the skin below my right knee, with muscle and sinew exposed to the air, and flesh shredded around it. Worst of all, both legs are useless, limp as last night's ramen. I cannot move either one so much as an inch.

-§-
I lie on my back on a slab of shale, legs crushed under me at an awkward angle, and look up at the wall of the ravine towering above me.
-§-

I appraise my situation. I am seriously injured. I cannot walk, crawl, or even stand up. I am in the most remote area of Kings Canyon National Park, deep in the backcountry of the Sierra Nevada. I am at least twenty-five grueling miles from the nearest trailhead. I have not seen a soul for two days.

Only a handful of people hike this valley each season, the rangers had told me. I had lost the overgrown path shortly before I fell, so I am off-trail. Even if hikers do pass by, they will not see me. My friends and family do not expect me back for five or six more days, so they will not yet post a search. I am utterly alone in an untraveled portion of the backcountry. My chances for survival are grim.

But I am alive.

§   §   §

Usually, I love being alone in the wilderness. In solitude, I find the feeling of connection that eludes me in the presence of others. Connection is a primal craving that impels us to band together, to seek out other people, to yearn for spiritual definition. The promise of connection is that we will be understood, be known, be accepted, be appreciated, and ultimately be loved for who we truly are. It means being oneself, and yet being a part of something bigger than one single self. Alone in the wilderness, I feel connected to spirit, to God and Goddess, to nature, to the Earth, and to me. My longing is satisfied. I feel the connection that I crave.

The land itself is my friend. A legacy of experience passed down from generations of mountain-hiking ancestors has provided me with an assurance that often evades me in more urban environments. Nature speaks to me in a way that humankind does not. My spirit exults in the wild, responding to the gentle voice of my beloved wilderness, bringing my body and soul into perfect focus. My heart expands. The clear air touches the pure high note that sings forth the harmony of my own being. There are no other voices to interrupt the ecstatic union of self with nature. I feel I have a personal relationship with the natural world, and I love the intimacy of being alone in the wild. I am alone, but rarely lonely.

My relationship with humanity is less certain than my association with nature. Frequently ill at ease among groups of people, I often need to withdraw from the swirling angst of troubled emotions and unidentified energies that seems to define much of the human experience. I grow weary of chattering voices and the perils of human interaction, and head out into the backcountry, where I find the peace that I crave. My connection to the human race rarely provides me with the same degree of solace.

Now, badly injured and stranded in this ravine, I wonder how much people will miss me if I do not return. Not much, I think. I've lived alone, except for my child, for close to ten years now. At the age of sixteen, my son is almost grown. I have no partner, no enduring intimate relationships. My parents are long dead. I have a brother in Olympia, Washington, and a sister whom I seldom see. I have many friends and acquaintances, but they come and go in my life, and all are accustomed to my solitary ways. I disappear often, going off by myself on some jaunt, tromping about Asia for a month here, wandering through Scotland for a few weeks, then heading up into the wilderness of the ancient Sierra mountains of California. It will take a while for anyone to notice that I've disappeared. They'll shake their heads a bit, then forget about me and move on with their lives. My passing will have little impact on the world. Pulling myself away from these thoughts, I turn my focus to my present situation.

-§-

The promise of connection is that we will be understood, be known, be accepted, be appreciated, and ultimately be loved for who we truly are.

-§-

Mercifully, my pack has fallen near me in the ravine. I strain to pull it toward me, and grope inside for my first aid kit. Shaking with shock, I do what little I can for my injuries. With every movement an effort, I heat up some instant chicken soup, and then lower myself awkwardly back onto the cold rock. Clutching my sleeping bag over the top of my shivering body, I pass into blessed oblivion.

After a restless night, drifting in and out of sleep, I struggle again into consciousness. The morning light shines its harsh illumination on the desperation of my situation.

Alone in my ravine, with nobody but myself to rely upon, I consider my chances. It is unlikely that I will be found if I stay where I am. I have fallen next to a small gurgling stream, flowing gently away down the sloping rock. Somewhere below where I now lie, this stream flows into the Middle Fork Kings River. Beside the river is a trail. If I can somehow drag myself to that trail, there is at least a chance that I will be found. By moving, I may increase the extent of my injuries, but to stay here will surely be signing my own death warrant. My decision is made.

-§-
Frequently ill at ease among groups of people, I often need to withdraw from the swirling angst of troubled emotions and unidentified energies that seems to define much of the human experience.
-§-

I organize my battered body for the journey. Collecting up my scattered gear, I stash it carefully, and tie my pack to my waist with a rope. I ease myself, sitting on my butt, into the small brook. Pushing hard with trembling arms, shoving my limp legs in front of me, I find I can scoot myself along downhill, aided by the flow of the streamlet. All that long day, inch by painful inch, I scootch myself down the obstacle course that is my ravine, terrified that I will get a limb stuck in some crevice, slide out of control down a steep slope, or pass out from pain while navigating a tricky pool. Finally, my small store of energy is exhausted. I drape myself over a rock, slipping again into the sleep of total depletion. I have covered about thirty yards.

The next morning I make a cup of instant coffee and continue on, praying for help and for strength, fighting down the pain from my broken limbs, focusing on my goal, and dragging myself onward. Both legs are by now grotesquely swollen. Saturated with stream water and my own urine, I am filthy, bloody, and exhausted. But I will not give up. I want to be rescued. I want to live. Randomly, I call out into the forest. The only response is the wind whispering through the trees, and the relentlessly cheerful gurgle of my little brook.

By the end of the third day, I have come to an impasse. My path is blocked by a pool of water, a small tangle of rocks and sticks, and a grassy embankment. Try as I might, I cannot get past these obstacles. I can go no further. My strength is fading. Infection and shock are catching up with me. Will this, then, be my final resting place?

Ghostly voices from other realms are drawing closer. I see angelic hosts, spirit beings in human form, gathered in quiet commemoration. They are there for me, I know. On one side, there are those who have passed on. I pick out faces: my Mom, my Dad, my first husband—gone for over twenty years. I see others who have been special to me, and many that I don't remember, hundreds of souls assembled in an etheric army, their numbers stretching out in ranks behind them, on into infinity; quietly, gravely waiting. On the other side, I see the souls

-§-

I walk now that narrow path between the living and the dead.

-§-

of those who are still alive, my friends and family and loved ones. They too are a silent presence, biding their time patiently to see what will come to pass. Their ranks as well stretch out behind them as far as my eyes can see. So many souls, so many people. I perceive my connection to all of them, and I feel a sense of sacred celebration. There is no pressure, no pleading, no attachment, no fear or sadness. They are here in solemn ceremony, to honor me, and to venerate this moment. I feel a vast peaceful acceptance from the congregation, and also from within myself. I walk now that narrow path between the living and the dead. Whichever way I turn, my passing will be consecrated. I feel honored to be thus acknowledged. I feel myself to be one of these spirit beings, a part of this vast shimmering host. How had I thought myself to be so alone? So many people, here for me, touched by my life, by my presence. The silent company of this gentle multitude comforts me.

I have, by now, little hope of being found before I pass over into the spirit world. But I call out once again into the wilderness, lifting my voice to join that of the twinkling waters, echoing across the rock walls of my ravine. This place is exquisitely beautiful and strangely welcoming even in my time of despair.

And then I hear it. Two faint toots of a whistle, so soft that at first I think them some illusion of my fevered brain. I hear it again. "Tooot. Tooot." Someone is out there.

Frantic with renewed hope, I call out wildly, straining my lungs for maximum volume. Has someone really heard me? Will they be able to find me? Have they given up, and gone away? After what seems like hours of fear and uncertainty, I peek through the trees and catch my first glimpse of the person who has responded to my calls. He has scrambled down the treacherous slope, and is now standing on firm ground. I cannot begin to say what that first sight of a human

being means to me, after the solitary desperation of those long days and nights. For the first time since the fall, I begin to cry.

"I'm Jake." Says my rescuer.

"I'm Amy."

"I'm not going to leave you." Somehow Jake knows just what to say. I cry still harder, smiling through my tears. I am not alone anymore.

"Can I put my arm around you?" asks Jake, sensing that human touch is what I need most at this moment, but not knowing how badly injured I might be. All he knows is that something horrible has happened. I nod my consent, and he puts his arm around me, gently and without hesitation.

§ § §

Jake, hiking by with his wife and a friend and miraculously hearing my distant calls, is the first of many human angels who will come to my rescue. Twenty-four hours later, one of the other hikers has run ten miles to find help, and—with the help of a group of vacationing firefighters—I have been located. I am airlifted out of the ravine in a liter, swinging fearfully from two straps, dangling beneath a helicopter high above the valley where I had fallen. Expertly transported by teams of skilled rescue rangers, helicopter pilots, and medics, I arrive at UMC hospital in Fresno, and begin the long process that will restore my body to health.

It will take many surgeries, weeks of hospital care, months of convalescence, and many more months of physical therapy before I am whole again, and able to walk, to work and to care for myself.

Before the fall, I had always felt healthy and capable. Certainly I had friends, but I assumed that people liked me for my independence, for my strength and competence, and for what I could do for them. This was how I defined my own worth, and I was certain that if I lost these qualities, I would no longer be considered worthy by the people in my life.

-§-

In the aftermath of the accident, I had lost all of the attributes that I thought gave me value in the world.

-§-

In the aftermath of the accident, I had lost all of the attributes that I thought gave me value in the world. Unable to walk, or even stand, I was physically incapable and totally unable to care for myself. I would not be able to work for months. Since I was self-employed, I had no income. With massive amounts of hospital bills and no health insurance, I was financially destitute. Desperately ill from infection and the after-effects of many surgeries, I could not act on my own behalf. I could not think clearly, and could hardly even ask for the many things that I needed so desperately. With my often solitary life and lack of ease with human connection, I did not expect to receive any help.

I was wrong.

The morning after I was flown to the emergency room, I was lying on a gurney in the hospital corridor. The nurses told me that I should call someone. I was going into major surgery, and I might die. "Who should I call ?" I wondered. I called my girlfriend Carla. Hers was the only number that my drugged brain could recall. I don't remember much of the conversation, but I did tell her where I was.

That one call ignited the support of my communities. Carla sent out a quick message on the Internet, made a couple of phone calls, and speeded off to find me in the hospital, two hundred fifty miles distant, scooping up her son and mine on the way. The word spread like wildfire.

Messages poured in. Carla was swamped with letters, cards, emails, donations, and offers of assistance. Everyone wanted to help. Several friends took turns being with me, during the long weeks in the hospital, so that I wouldn't be alone. Others cared for my son, cleaned my home, watered my plants, fed my cats, and rescued my businesses. They retrieved my car from the trailhead. They advocated for me with the hospital staff, with doctors and financial assistants, and the workers from social services. My brother and sister-in-law flew in to help. Other friends brought me food, flowers, clothing, teddy bears, pillows, emails, writing paper, books, and magazines. They collected medical information, and opened a bank account for donations. They paid my bills and organized fundraisers. They set up a Yahoo group, and a website so that friends could be informed of my progress. I was engulfed in care and concern.

In later weeks, when I could finally be moved, Carla created a convalescent room in her tiny home, and other friends donated hospital equipment and wheelchairs, walkers, and crutches. They changed my IVs, took away my bedpans, provided transportation, physical therapy, healings, and wonderful meals.

Most importantly of all, they shared their love, and their joy that I was alive, and would be with them still. My friends, people from many different social circles and many walks of life, were united in their caring, and in their desire to help. Their cumulative delight in my resurrection was unguarded and very real.

This tangible evidence that I was loved by the people of my world touched me deeply. More moved than I ever was during my lonely

ordeal, the terrifying rescue, the many surgeries, and the uncertainties of recovery, I could do nothing but retreat into my own weakness as I let all the activity flow around me, tears of raw emotion trickling constantly down my cheeks. How was it that I deserved so much? Yet there was now no doubt in my mind of the size and unity of the love that inspired this saving of a life and of a soul.

I began to see myself differently. I, who had thought that my life, and my passing, would provide only the slightest of ripples; I, who had felt myself to be so alone and unconnected that no one would miss me when I was gone, was surrounded by people who cherished me. In my time of greatest need, I found that I was not abandoned, but held close. I discovered that many people loved me, lifted me up in their collective arms, and restored me to life and to living.

I could not defend myself against this overwhelming demonstration of love. Too frail and ill to do anything but cry often and take it all in, I had no choice but to believe in the miracle of these diverse people who gave so generously of their time and energy.

I remembered the ghostly assembly from my vision in the ravine, infinite numbers of people, touched by my one insignificant life. I began to see myself as one of this host, an integral part of all humanity, always connected, and never truly alone at all.

For the first time in my recollection, I felt that I belonged here, on this planet. I felt welcomed by the people upon the Earth. Certain now of the essential goodness of humankind, I began to believe also in the benevolence of our environment. Surely a place that would provide help to a person such as me is an amicable place in which to live? Just as definitely, the people who surround me are ones that I want to share this world with.

-§-

There was now no doubt in my mind of the size and unity of the love that inspired this saving of a life and of a soul.

-§-

In a greater sense, I feel my story is universal, symbolic of all of the grace that exists in our world. I now believe this world is a place in which despair can be replaced by hope, in which humankind can triumph over disaster; a world in which the warmth of human kindness can thaw the desolate chill of isolation.

My gratitude for my salvation is both intensely personal and infinitely universal. When I think of how grateful I am to the many who contributed to my experience, I think first of the individual people. I see their faces in my mind's eye, and I smile. I remember the three hikers who found me, the firefighters, the CHP medics, the Park Rangers. Without them I would not be alive today. I think next of the many generous people who helped during my long recovery.

I think of ways that I might be able to show my appreciation, to return their help. Of course I am grateful to my friends. Of course I will help them in whatever ways I can. Gratitude inspires reciprocity.

I consider also that these people are a microcosm that represents the rest of humanity. My personal gratitude expands to include others. With my new understanding of the miracles of human interaction, I owe allegience to the pool of benevolence that nurtures us all. Appreciation for my own restoration inclines me to want to bless other beings in similar ways. With my new awareness of connection, no person whose need touches my life can be disconnected from my gratitude. I reach out a hand, smile at a lonely face, give a dollar to a person on the street. I show someone else, in whatever way I can, what I have learned. That people are good. That help is out there. That we are all connected.

-§-

I now believe this world is a place in which despair can be replaced by hope, in which humankind can triumph over disaster; a world in which the warmth of human kindness can thaw the desolate chill of isolation.

§

To live in awareness of the benedictions that have come to me is to acknowledge an existence in which miracles are available to all, and to enlist myself in the perpetuation of a world that offers up those blessings. If the world is a compassionate place, and I am a part of that reality, then my nature must reflect the same generosity. I know now that this is a world worth living in. Such a world is worth participating in as well.

My gratitude includes spiritual dimensions. I give heartfelt thanks for whatever divine intervention guided the choices of the people who saved me. I thank whichever angels and ghosts and spirit guides and Gods and Godesses may have watched over me in that ravine, and during my rescue and recovery. I give thanks for the many miracles that have comprised my life since.

My consideration broadens to include the bounty of the universe. I think of how grateful I am, and my heart swells, engorged with a sweet rush of tingling emotion. I imagine the boundaries of my body expanding beyond their current definition, moving outward, swirling through the vastness of the cosmos, until I know no limits of space and time, no isolation or separation from myself or from the others. I am grateful for love, for life, for feeling, and for spirit. I am thankful to all existence.

Restored now to physical health, I still like to go by myself to wild places. I cherish the solitude and the welcoming beauty of the natural world. But I've learned that, even when I solo, I am not alone. I carry with me my gratitude, my thoughts of the many wonderful people in

my life, the assurance of my connection to all of them, the awareness that I would be missed if I didn't return, and the certain knowledge of how much I am loved.

-§-

If the world is a compassionate place, and I am a part of that reality, then my nature must reflect the same generosity.

-§-

How glad I am to be able to live my life, to share it with the people whose paths cross my own. The world has proved itself to be a better place than I had ever suspected it to be, and I am honored to be inhabiting it with people like those who helped. How is it that I thought my life had meant nothing? How could I have believed that nobody would notice if I quietly slipped away? How very wrong I was, and how happy I am to be alive to learn this lesson.

PART FIVE

Empowered Outer Action

Anne Wilson Schaef:

The Whispered Culture of the Soul

Communities exist whether we participate in them or not. The reality is that they're there. Most of us have several communities of which we are a member that are often overlapping. We have our living communities, our social communities, our work-organizational communities, and our spiritual communities. Some may have the same memberships and some may be made up of persons not active in any other aspect of our lives. They are still communities. For example:

Benjamin told me about when he worked at a major metropolitan newspaper as an editorial assistant. He had the task of working in the sports department editing box scores and answering phone calls. He said he had no concept personally and wasn't aware of anybody else having the concept that they were a community — that they had any responsibility or connection to anything other than their particular job function and task at hand.

The employees came to work, did their specific job, but never questioned the overall function or community of the newspaper. Benjamin said they were unaware that they were part of anything bigger than their specific job. He said he never considered taking responsibility for the opinions of the newspaper, or for the fact that they were using so many trees

Anne Wilson Schaef has a Ph.D. in clinical psychology and an honorary doctorate in Human Letters from Kenyon College in Kenyon, Ohio. She left the field of psychology and psychotherapy in 1984. She has since conducted intensives and training sessions in the U.S. and throughout the world in an approach to healing that she has developed called Living in Process. Living in Process is an alternative approach to healing which comes out of ancient teachings. Dr. Schaef is internationally known as a speaker, consultant, and seminar leader. She has published thirteen books and numerous articles. Photo by Third Eye Photography.

to produce the newspaper, or for the overall well-being of the workers.

He believed that such questions were "not his responsibility." All of the employees he was aware of accepted the illusion that they were not part of the bigger community. They did their work and when it came to issues larger than their specific job or their specific department, they took no responsibility whatsoever. He was a member of the community of the newspaper staff but never saw himself participating in anything other than his own compartmentalized job.

Modern societies have experienced an alarming breakdown in communities. As I mentioned earlier, when colonizers have invaded a country, in addition to killing off the native people through disease and violence, they have always focused on breaking down community. The most effective way to destroy a culture is to destroy the language, the spirituality, and the community, all supported by the introduction of alcohol and drugs. This pattern of destruction has been used and is continually used throughout the world.

One of the major breakdowns that we are experiencing in modern society is that there is no mediating process between the nuclear family and the society. If we accept the fact that the nuclear family cannot possibly meet the needs of its members, we can then more clearly see the importance of community and nurturing healthy communities. If the nuclear family is dysfunctional, which is statistically true, this means that we are using a dysfunctional building block with no functional intervening processes or structures to create a society. Given this reality, we can see why we have not produced a very functional society. We need to take the issue of community seriously.

-§-
Communities are not built, they emerge.
-§-

In the last few years, I have noticed a growing interest in and deepening awareness that we need to build functional communities. Unfortunately, many of the attempts have been exactly that, to structure and build communities. This approach is based upon the same assumptions that the mechanical method employed to "fix" people. In this approach we see the old assumption of "form as a fix" being applied to the "problem." We diagnose the problem assuming that a mechanistic adjustment will solve it. Just like in individuals, relationships, and families, the solution is not mechanical. The solution is a process. What happens when we take our new paradigm, our path of living, our path of the soul into our communities?

We truly cannot change anyone or anything other than ourselves. So, as we change ourselves, those changes reverberate through all of the spheres of our existence. When we practice honesty with ourselves and with our family and in our relationships, that honesty will begin to show up in our communities. As we get more in touch with ourselves and our spirituality we begin to know deep in our beings that we are part of larger and larger wholes. We begin to see that we must practice the same basic truths on a community level that we practice on an individual level.

-§-
"In the Western world, we have learned to live with the unimportant and to leave the important behind."
—Anonymous
-§-

Some of us make a distinction between our work and our vocation, believing that work is the way we earn a living and our vocation is our life's work. When one Lives in Process, splitting ourselves into segments makes little or no sense. A process is a process. Processes cannot be divided into pieces. When we are Living in Process, we do the work that unfolds before us as our life progresses, and we get what we need to live a life of spiritual abundance. Material wealth or any specific goals or agendas are irrelevant. Living in Process means that we live a life of faith and trust that we will get what we need. And, we need to take responsibility for our material welfare and not be ruled by it.

Trusting our process doesn't mean that we sit around and wait for something to happen. No, quite the contrary. When we Live in Process, we often work very hard. We must do our footwork and participate in our life. Since Living in Process is a life of participation, we welcome the opportunity to participate in and live our life, and this means that we do our personal work and we contribute.

A friend of mine who is an Indian medicine man put it very well. "When I was drinking, everything I did was for myself and that didn't work too well. After I sobered up, I realized who my boss is. My boss is the big guy upstairs. And since I realized that, I just do what He wants and things go real good."

Many of us with inner knowing about the nature of our work have possessed this wisdom from the time we were very small. In fact, some of us knew what our work was even before we had language to describe it.

Unfortunately, most of us do not receive the kind of education that teaches us the language of the internal, or the language of the Creator. It's sad when our training at home and at school has taught us to stifle, shut off, and tune out the whisperings of our soul. Our intuitions, knowings, sensings are all very necessary in finding our

work. Each of us has a unique work; we just need to find it. It is very difficult to listen to that which we cannot hear!

I have often said that I never really trust someone who doesn't know how to work. There is something about a person who knows how to pitch in and get her hands dirty that can be trusted. I've known people who believe that their goal in life is to make enough money so they never have to do anything for themselves. I don't trust them. It is as if their inability to deal with their material world leaves them groundless, floating out of touch with their spirituality.

Good work is a prayer. When people work well together, they feel bonded and grounded. Westerners seem to be able to use routine work as a meditation when it is approached in a prayerful way.

When we are doing "right" work in tune with our spirituality and ourselves, we are one with all things. Our right work will find us if we risk Living in Process and do our deep-process work. When we live our process, our work is integrated into our life. We don't go to work and have a life. We don't have a worklife and fall exhausted in a heap. We have a life that includes work. Our work contributes to our life and our life contributes to our work.

-§-
People who work together
pray together.
-§-

Earlier I imagined what it would be like if every home was designed with a deep-process room. I have carried the image further and imagined each corporate office with a similar room, complete with mats, near the boardroom. When board members felt angry, confused, or uncomfortable (of course, they would have to be aware of these feelings), or when the board reached an impasse or sensed something was wrong, they would hit the mats. Imagine, if you can, board members stretched out and doing their deep-process work until they felt clear and were ready to make decisions congruent with their spirituality.

Along with boardrooms, we could make deep-processing rooms available to all workers. What a different society we would have if we had a room open to anyone wishing to do their deep-process work or supporting that of others.

Yet, being spiritual beings, we all have spiritual needs and many of us look longingly to organized religion to meet these needs. We sense something is there, yet sometimes whatever it is, it is difficult to find.

Perhaps the biggest mistake we and organized religion make is in attempting to separate spirituality from the rest of our lives and to place it in the hands of religious institutions. Historically, it was the Christian Church that at the time fostered this split with the rise of mechanistic science and materialism. The Church supported the secular belief in and adherence to mechanistic science while maintaining the realm of the spiritual for itself. This split gave the organized church tremendous power in Western culture. For most of us personally, it has been devastating to separate our spirituality from ourselves. When we relegate our spirituality to a time and a place, we lose our awareness that we are a spiritual process. Our spirituality can't be divided from our daily life. Everything we do is spiritual. Whether we know it or like it, it is.

When we splinter off our spirituality from the rest of our being, we fragment our process, become disempowered, and disconnected from the oneness with the Great Mystery. We do not need intermediaries to connect with our God. We are connected. That connection is our birthright.

A very wise American Indian elder once said to me, "We don't care *how* a person prays. What we care about is that he *does* pray. The Great Mystery can hear all kinds of prayers. Whenever a person prays I can stand beside her/him."

Societies and nations are created by individuals. Sometimes we give our power away to others and let them assume the responsibility of building and molding the society. When we do this, we *feel* disempowered on a larger scale. We cannot control the society. We can participate in it. All too often we give our power away to people who are not clear, who have compartmentalized their spirituality and do not have the best interests of all the members of that society at heart.

-§-
It is possible for a society to be organized around the spiritual needs of the individuals and the culture and not around money and economics.
-§-

In Samoan society, when people become ill, and they go to a healer, the healer does not just focus on the individual. The healer assumes that the normal state for the human being is health and that if the person is ill, there must be something in the internal or external environment that is causing the illness. The healer looks at the person, his family, his village, and the larger society to see where the problem is and how balance can be restored.

The society in which we live is an illusionary society. It has been built by isolating our spiritual reality and using disembodied mental concepts. Our thinking has become our reality and often is not grounded in our experience of reality. Frequently, we live out of our disembodied, nonexperienced interpretations of our world. We casually accept "experts" who pass along disembodied information that

fabricates causality—"This is because of this," and "This means that." We never stop to check out for ourselves what is real for us and if what the experts are saying rings true. Often such interpretations are logical and rational. They just don't make any sense. When we come to realizations in our deep process, they are on a soul level and free us from the virtual reality around us.

-§-
We need visionary
leaders who are
spiritually functional.
-§-

We have created a society based upon the illusion of control, imagined dualisms, the illusion of perfection, dishonesty, and distorted thinking ungrounded in our true oneness and connectedness with the All. Is it any wonder that economics and money (both abstractions) have become our Gods?

The beauty of living in process and doing our deep-process work is that we do not have to confront everything at once. We do not even have to deal with issues on a timetable that has been artificially constructed. When we Live in Process, we only have to put one step in front of the other and do the next "right" thing for our process. Life, with its opportunities, obstacles, and possibilities will unfold only as we are able and ready to deal with them. As more of us are one with the Creator, new options will emerge.

Joan Borysenko:

Putting the Soul Back in Medicine

O nce upon a time, when the rays of the morning sun rose over peoples who were still hunters and gatherers, the clock of the bodymind was regulated by the magnetic forces of nature. By sun and moon, by cycles and seasons, by feasting and fasting.

The wise ones, known as healers or shamans, believed that illness was a result of being out of tune with the natural cycles. The disharmony, and the dis-ease which resulted from it, had different types of cures. There were powerful herbs which could rebalance the flow of energy which, in turn, determined physical function. Some cultures developed a large pharmacopia of active agents. Others, such as some of the Native American cultures, employed only a few plants. The shaman or medicine person dreamed which herb to use and invoked the specific healing quality required through prayer and ritual.

But the shamans were much more than intuitive pharmacologists. They were also intuitive psychologists. The patient was questioned about their life, their role in the tribe, their relationships and their dreams. Turbulent emotions could cause turbulence in the bodymind. The cure in this case was to correct the source of the emotional disbalance. In cases where the patient had been traumatized by grief, accident, heartbreak or abuse, it was not the energy body or the emotional body that required healing, but the soul.

Joan Borysenko, Ph.D., has a powerfully clear personal vision—to bring science, medicine, psychology and spirituality together in the service of healing. Her brilliance as a scientist, clinician and teacher have placed her on the leading edge of the mind–body revolution, and she has become a world-renowned spokesperson for this new approach to health, sharing her pioneering work with a gentle graciousness, enthusiasm and humility. She is the author of the best-seller *Minding the Body, Mending the Mind* (Bantam, 1987) and a series of other books, the most recent of which are *Saying Yes to Change* (Hay House, 2005), and the forthcoming *Spiritual Guidance* (Hay House, 2007).

Soul retrieval was a common medical treatment in which the shaman entered a state of non-ordinary reality similar to what people describe during near-death experiences and mystical visions. In this state, the shaman tracked parts of the patient's soul that had been split off and lost as a result of trauma. The retrieved soul parts were then blown back into the patient's body through the heart and the top of the head and oftentimes a physical and emotional cure was achieved. Our modern psychology and psychiatry, in contrast, has a much poorer track record with post-traumatic stress disorder and the cure of dissociative disorders resulting from childhood physical abuse, sexual abuse or unusual trauma.

The soul of medicine itself has become fragmented. We have retained the pharmacology and refined the technical aspects of pathophysiology, diagnosis and treatment, but we have lost the emotional and spiritual components that can make healing a sacred art as well as a more effective science. Nearly two millenia ago, coincident with the spread of the Catholic Church to Europe, tremendous sociological and religious upheavals occurred which resulted in the stamping out of shamanic cultures. This in turn had a far-reaching effect on the development of medicine. Illness was viewed as evidence

-§-
We have lost the emotional and spiritual components that can make healing a sacred art.
-§-

of sin, an idea that is poignantly considered in the old testament Book of Job. After all, if illness and misfortune are the result of offending God, then all you have to do is to be is very, very good and then you'll be safe. Or if you are beyond reproach, then all you have to do is get rid of the bad guys who are offending God. Enter the Crusades and the Inquisition.

During the middle ages the Black Death killed one third of the population of Europe. A search for the sinners who must surely have caused it gave rise to a bloody chapter in the history of religious persecution. Entire villages of Jews were murdered and several million women were condemned as witches in the hope of defeating the plague. But when the plague continued to spread, religion ultimately lost its authority over illness and the age of science began. For an excellent review I heartily recommend *Sacred Eyes,* by psychologist and minister Robert Keck.

By the sixteenth century, modern science was being birthed by the famous triad of scientific reductionists—Francis Bacon, Renee Descartes and Isaac Newton—who succeeded in reducing nature to a machine devoid of soul or guiding intelligence. To their credit, they exorcised the toxic notion of disease as punishment by a peevish deity. But they also threw the baby out with the bathwater. Bacon's stated purpose was to subjugate nature altogether by desouling it. To take her by force and to "torture and vex" her into revealing her secrets so that mankind would have dominion over the earth—over life and death itself.

This is the thinking that underlies the rape and plunder of natural resources, the dehumanization of third world cultures, and the de-souling of modern medicine. It presumes a lack of organizing intel-ligence in the universe and since life is therefore not sacred, resources become expendable in the name of progress. Soul loss ultimately leads to amoral behavior- acts performed with oblivion to their eventual consequences. Were we, like our native predecessors, conditioned to assess the consequences of our health-care sys-tem seven generations into the future we would have to ask some very penetrating questions. Is it appropriate that the majority of monies spent on the medical care of any one individual are spent in the last few months of their life? Would they be better spent in prevention programs, or in early childhood education programs, or in parenting programs that would aid emotional wellbeing and therefore cut down on illness and suffering?

-§-
Soul loss ultimately leads to amoral behavior—acts per-formed with oblivion to their eventual consequences.
-§-

And what is a soul approach to an individual patient? Once again, it has to do with a macroscopic view that investigates the ill-ness as part of a life, rather than as an isolated symptom. The physi-cian who practices fragmented medicine and cures a symptom may actually compound the patient's problems. For example, a diuretic may decrease Mrs. Jones blood pressure, but if it is high because of an alcoholic husband, poor self-esteem and ruinous health habits has her physician healed her with a prescription or has he colluded to help her maintain a sick status quo? To be a healer, a physician needs to have a larger vision of the human being than is taught in most medical schools which pander to molecules while denigrating the emotional and spiritual aspects of life.

Part of the problem in medicine's loss of soul is that death is seen as unnatural, as the enemy, so that disproportionate resources are put into discouraging death as opposed to encouraging life. Let me tell you a story. My mother died in a Boston teaching hospital about five years ago, and overall, she had a wonderful quality of care. But on the last day of her life, as her heart and lungs and kidneys failed, she developed internal bleeding and was whisked off to nuclear medicine so that the source of the bleed could be determined. Why? Was it going to make a clinical difference? Four hours passed, and the fami-ly, which was gathered around her empty bed to say goodbye, started to get impatient and scared. Since I had worked in that hospital for a decade, they dispatched me to rescue her. I knew it wouldn't be easy. When I got down to nuclear medicine, she was still waiting on the gurney that had brought her down four hours before. I demanded her immediate release and the doctor was equally adamant about getting a diagnosis. My mother broke the stalemate by virtually resurrecting from near-death to give the doctor a dose of common sense, "A diagnosis. Is that all you need? I'm dying. That's your diagnosis." And with that, the doctor gave in.

Fortunately, we had time to say goodbye back in her room before she slipped into a last morphine-assisted sleep. My son Justin, who was twenty at the time, and I were at her bedside at about three in the morning. I was meditating when I had a vivid vision that seemed far more real than waking life. In the vision I was a pregnant mother giving birth and I was also the baby being born. As the baby, I was being propelled down a long, dark tunnel. And then I came out into the presence of the ineffable light that so many of my patients who have had near-death experiences describe. The light is omniscient, incomprehensibly loving, infinitely wise and perfectly forgiving. It feels like home. In the presence of the light, my relationship with my mother, which had been a difficult one, seemed perfect. I saw the lessons we had learned from one another and felt immense gratitude toward her. She had birthed me into this world, and I felt as though I had birthed her soul back out again.

> -§-
> Part of the problem in medicine's loss of soul is that death is seen as unnatural, as the enemy.
> -§-

When I opened my eyes, Justin had a look of total awe on his face. He asked me if I could see the light in the room. When I said that I could, for indeed the whole room was glowing, Justin said, "Grandma is holding open the door to eternity to give us a glimpse." Justin felt that he had received a priceless gift, because he knew with certainty that we are not our bodies. We inhabit our bodies, but our souls are immortal. He wept as he told me that he would never be afraid of death again. The only type of death that is really worth fearing, after all, is a living death in which we fail to become ourselves because we get stuck in some one else's definition of who we should be.

Albert Camus wrote, "There is but one freedom, to put oneself right with death. After that everything is possible." When people visit their doctor, they might not be thinking in terms of their immortal souls, but most are looking for emotional and spirtual healing. They want to know they are worthy and lovable. They want to confess, to complain, to be forgiven, to make meaning of their lives. Clearly, this can't always be done in an eight-minute office visit. But compassion can be communicated, and when appropriate the patient can be referred to a therapist or clergyperson who can help them with the big questions that illness puts to us. "Who am I?", "What is the purpose of my life?" and "How can I profit from this illness as an opportunity to find greater freedom and happiness?"

Consumers are patently dissatisfied with a mechanistic medicine that denies its own soul and theirs. It's time we heed the symptoms indicating that our medical system is dangerously out of balance. Modern technology is marvelous and lifesaving, and if we can integrate it with the deep wisdom of the past then we can birth a medicine that exalts and nurtures life rather than one than is predicated on the fear of death.

MICHAEL PETER LANGEVIN:

The Shaman in the Office

In 1974 I journeyed to the magic country of Peru for my first time. While traveling there for six weeks, I experienced a mystical initiation—and life-altering transformation. I have spent the majority of my life since then studying spiritual secrets and lost knowledge. I have come to believe that the European conquest of the majority of our planet in the fourteen and fifteen hundreds, the spread of Western culture, and the globalization of culture and commerce in the twentieth and twenty-first centuries, have all served to obscure the wild and life-freeing knowledge and magic known and lived by most pre-Columbian peoples.

Reconnecting with these secrets, and utilizing them to live a meaningful life, to maintain a loving healthy family, and to own and operate an inspirational revolutionary business, has been my life's work over the subsequent decades.

Why use shamanism in an office—or at all, for that matter?

I know without a doubt that most humans alive today chose to be born into their lives right now, in order to learn, experience, and achieve certain things that could only be achieved on this Earth at this unique moment in history. Ancient pre-Columbian cultures knew that every plant, stream and rock that exists has a spirit. They knew that human potential and destiny was to evolve into Gods and Goddesses. They understood that the most important aspects of our universe can-

Michael Peter Langevin is the CEO and founder of MB Media, publisher of the magazines *Magical Blend, Natural Beauty & Health,* and *Transitions.* He has authored three books: *Spiritual Business* (Hampton Roads, 2004), *Secrets of the Amazon Shamans* (New Page, 2006), and *Secrets of the Ancient Incas* (New Page, 2002). He hosted a Magical Blend TV show in San Francisco, and speaks regularly at conferences, as well as doing radio and TV interviews. He travels often to Peru and other countries. He lives with his family in Chico, California. He offers wilderness magic classes, spiritual advice, and private consultations at www.michaelpeterlangevin.com.

not be seen—nor even be sensed with our five senses. These beliefs and tools for achieving humanity's and Earth's fullest potential are now being rediscovered, and will continue to be reintroduced into our society. This is the essence of shamanism and magic. This is why many souls chose to be born at this time.

In pre-Christian, and pre-organized-religion cultures, people viewed the world, and moved through reality, very differently than we do today. They were aware that all things that exist have spirits and can be recruited as allies. They knew that the universe of influences that affects our lives is far greater than what we usually perceive— yet far more real and important than any material world achievement or reward. They knew the power of words and stories, and used them to alter and enhance their lives. Many had experiences where they were one with the divine. They could think and experience beyond the human mind's ability to define. This gave these people a belief that human power and potential was limitless.

-§-
Ancient pre-Columbian cultures knew that every plant, stream and rock that exists has a spirit.
-§-

In Greek myth we have Hercules, a half-human son of Zeus, who spends his life breaking out of his human limitations and becoming his true, limitless God-self. In Peruvian history, we have the Sapa Inca Pachacuteq. He was a younger son, not destined to become the supreme king, or Sapa Inca. Yet he stood bravely against overwhelming odds. Pachacuteq not only saved the Inca Empire; he achieved near-miracles for his people. Similar entities existed in most ancient cultures, pantheons and myths.

How does one use English words—or any words—to describe concepts, and ways of being and acting, in expanded realities far beyond our society's accepted limitations? This is a challenge I have accepted personally, and one of the roles of my publishing business, MB Media.

For over twenty-five years, I have experimented with using shamanism and magic to grow what began as a single magazine in my living room in San Francisco in 1980. I started with a volunteer staff, none of whom had any experience. I had no financial backing, and many anti-establishment and anti-capitalist beliefs and issues. In recent years, MB Media publishes three international magazines, with print runs of over 120,000 each. I supervise and pay a twenty-five-person staff, and manage a cash flow of over a million dollars annually.

While in the early stages of birth, the first magazine was referred to as "Spirituality and Creativity can Sell and make a Profit." Pragmatically, the name was shortened to *Magical Blend*.

I often compare the shamanic experiment of MB Media—and my life—to a compost heap. It is often messy and chaotic. It breaks most rules. It even gets smelly from time to time. But it usually produces the richest loam. That loam grows the most beautiful flowers, and produces the sweetest and healthiest fruits and vegetables.

All growing businesses move in spirals. They have growth cycles. They have ebbs and flows, expansions and contractions. MB Media has had wild growth periods where money flowed in torrents and we couldn't make mistakes. These are usually followed by times when the cash flow slows to a trickle and we can't seem to do anything right. The business has almost ceased to exist countless times. Massive staff layoffs and financial near-ruin have occurred all too often. We have reinvented our magazines' editorial style, layout and design more times than a teenager changes his moods.

As I write this, MB Media has never been better positioned for major financial growth. Yet because risk and near blind faith are essential ingredients of shamanistic existence, everything is on the line. I feel once again like the cartoon character Charlie Brown. If we catch this fly ball, we will be heroes and win this game. If we miss, we will be failures. We will have to go back to the drawing board and reinvent what we do. Persistence and unwavering intent are two main ingredients of shamanic magic.

In shamanism, as in Buddhism, loss of attachment to outcome is an essential ingredient. A shamanic magic worker needs to take right actions that she feels passionately are guided by spirit and her highest vision. Taking the action is its own reward. Actions, in a shamanic universe, seldom bring the desired results in the desired fashion. However, right actions, taken with clear intent, accumulate to create fruitful, rewarding results, and accelerated self-evolution. I love creating, operating and publishing magazines that enrich peoples'

-§-

In shamanism, as in Buddhism, loss of attachment to outcome is an essential ingredient.

-§-

lives. However, I must attempt to always remain unattached, and if MB Media stopped producing magazines, I believe that I would be guided to where spirit wants me most, in order to spread the spiritual insights I have been given and allowed to play with.

The reason that shamanism, magic, and the like have been replaced by the world views of religion and science in the Western world is that science claims to offer an exact, nonbiased, reproducible, provable and dependable approach to life. On the other hand, shamanism—like nature and the rest of life—is chaotic, unpredictable and even relatively undependable. Why should we consider embracing it?

I had a boyhood hero whose name was Spider Rand. He was ten years older than me and he was cool—ultra-cool. Like James Dean cool and James Brown cool and Bob Marley cool. Spider had a thousand schemes to achieve a thousand ends. Anyone who spent any time with Spider dedicated much of that time to hearing about his plans. Nine out of ten never succeeded.

Yet the schemes that Spider pulled off were legendary. He lived a more magic- and miracle-filled existence than most people ever dreamed of. Everyone who spent time with Spider hoped his average would improve with time, but were joyous about those plans that succeeded. He supervised a landscaping company that employed witches and astrologers. He managed a hip restaurant in a happening neighborhood where the artistic Who's Who hung out. He played bass guitar on stage and on CD with Bonnie Raitt. His acted as agent for his live-in lover, and helped her open in a comedy play on Broadway. He was featured coast to coast on TV. Spider is my older brother one of five amazingly wonderful siblings with whom I have been blessed.

-§-
Every major league baseball player misses many more balls than he hits.
-§-

We each individually possess the abilities—and can develop the skills and tools—to create the lives and worlds we desire. We are each born with a mission and a pre-life tentative plan. We have the power to transform our lives and bring about miracles.

Yet we also bring with us past life karma. Add these to the wills and desires of the people we interact with, and overlay the whole mix with society's variables, and you can see how we might fail, might make mistakes, might create results that are often less than we intended. Just as every major league baseball player misses many more balls than he hits, Spider Rand often fell in the mud. Yet he was a successful modern day magician. Shamanism works that way.

There have been some recent shamanic miracles at MB Media's office. For its first twenty years, MB Media printed only *Magical Blend* magazine. Then, in 2000, reader requests for ever-more editorial about truly natural health and beauty tools, ideas and lifestyles, threatened to take over the magazine. So we took a risk and launched *Natural Beauty and Health* magazine to fill this need, while still allowing us to keep *Magical Blend* dedicated to a wider array of self-improvement and spiritual ideas and tools. Then, in 2003, our loyal readers—many of them baby boomers—began demanding more articles on aging and how to deal with entering your fifties, sixties, and beyond, with wisdom and enjoyment. They wanted MB Media's magazines to become everything that the AARP wasn't. They requested this so strongly that we put a planned launch of a magazine for younger readers called

Fresh Blend on hold, and began work on *Transitions* magazine, aimed at people fifty and better.

The earlier launch of *Natural Beauty and Health* was amazingly easy and profitable. The attempt to launch a third magazine has stretched our abilities, skills and resources. It has caused heated debate among the entire staff, the departure of many long-term employees. We've had to reinvent every aspect of what MB Media has done for the last twenty-five years. The unplanned loss of long-term staff—and resulting mishaps—have resulted in many major challenges for both the business and myself. Yet the difficulties fed my personal spiritual evolution, even as they brought MB Media into a cutting-edge role as an information-providing company.

One Friday afternoon I was leaving work after a long-term friend and loyal staff member had resigned, after accusing me of all manner of manipulations, and multitudes of character flaws. My usual rock-solid self-confidence, and trust in my guiding spirits, was faltering. I was questioning all aspects of the business and myself. I was think-ing that maybe that staff member was correct. Maybe I am a terrible, Machiavellian supervisor, and a dishonest, incompetent businessman. The faces of all the staff members who had left angry over the course of the previous twenty-five years paraded before my eyes. I began to think that all my past employees hated MB Media and me. I stopped my car as I pulled out of the parking lot, and prayed for clear vision, self-honesty, and a clear sign of what was real.

A passing van beeped franticly and the people in it flagged me down. It was Allen Payne, one of MB Media's best-ever advertising sales executives, and former music editor. He had worked for MB Media for four years, then moved to North Dakota with his wonder-ful wife Candie and four teenage kids to pursue his dreams.

Allen had left MB Media feeling very frustrated, angry and criti-cal. We had been close friends and his leaving had left a sad memory. I stopped my car, and received hugs and love from all six of the Payne family. I listened to the tale of their adventures for the last four years. They remembered MB Media fondly, and had received strong spiri-tual guidance that it was time to come back. Allen is now MB Media's new advertising sales manager and Candie is the office coordinator and distribution administrator. Their eighteen-year-old daughter Amanda works in the office too. Their return is a shamanic miracle.

Recently we filed some papers wrong with the State of California, and got caught in its bureaucratic tangles. By the end of that day, I sat alone in the office, fighting for perspective in the nightmare that threatened to engulf me.

Unexpectedly, in walked Freddy and Madeline, two spiritual facilitators of whom I had heard. After recounting their adventures in India, they asked me to relax, close my eyes, and imagine I was on a mountain listening to the music of the wind. Madeline laid her hands on my head, followed by Freddy. First their hands felt warm and tingly. Then the feeling became intensely pleasurable. Finally it felt like a powerful hallucinogenic. I felt giddy and fantastic — still me, but much, much more.

I went home to my family and had a lovely evening. I hardly slept. The next three weeks were full of major challenges, yet I felt more connected to God, and to the divine creative force of the universe, than at any previous time in my life! The experience allowed me to solve many problems and make many inspired and effective decisions.

A business can begin in many ways. Some start with lots of knowledge, experience, and investment money. I have seen countless magazines and businesses of all sorts come and go during these last twenty-five years. Yet the ones that have survived and prospered didn't start with much more than a vision, a dream, enthusiasm, and the will to do whatever it takes to make things work. That's *Magical Blend.* Money is a great reward, however in and of itself it doesn't usually create success nor maintain it. *Magical Blend* has survived, evolved, and prospered because it gives people the inspiration to improve their lives. That has been the dream and the vision from the beginning. Most people spend so much time worrying and concentrating on what's wrong in their lives. Our thoughts are far more powerful than most people realize. *Magical Blend* reminds people to focus on what they want to happen. We advise people to concentrate on what is working and what feels right about their situations. When an employee is not performing well, I will often sit in their chair after hours and radiate images of their best successes.

-§-

Most people spend so much time worrying and concentrating on what's wrong in their lives. Our thoughts are far more powerful than most people realize.

-§-

When the staff energy or morale is slipping I often come in to the office when no one is there and do a small success ritual, cleansing out the old energies with sage, and bringing in new, successful, inspired teamwork energies. I occasionally invite open-minded staff members to share such a focused ritual in which we all are responsible for five to ten minutes of the ritual or affirmations.

When I am most overwhelmed, disappointed or confused, I make time to walk in nature and blank my mind. I walk in an open, quiet, meditative state for an hour or so. Many great inspirations and new approaches appear to me at these times.

One spell for success is to assemble a room full of people who are open to magic being real and who want your business to succeed. Agree on three to five important goals for the next six months. Then light a candle and some incense. Call on the spiritual essences of your business. Call on whatever other spiritual powers will listen. Tell them your goals. Pray for their assistance. Chant together. Affirm one goal at a time. Speak as many details as you can imagine. Picture what your lives will look like when this goal is achieved. End by extinguishing the candle and reciting "So must it be."

Every enlightened master, spiritual writer, speaker, teacher, movie star, athlete, or diva I have met has feet of clay, inner demons, weaknesses, failures, shortcomings, and blind spots. Most fart and burp and have huge egos or inferiority complexes. Everyone's feet smell when they've worn their shoes too long on a hot day. No matter how far a person evolves spiritually, no matter how wealthy or famous she becomes, she never stops being tempted by forces that could destroy all she has achieved or corrupt her very soul. Our lives progress in spirals, and we all have down times, failures, mistakes, and setbacks, no matter who we are.

-§-

Every enlightened master, spiritual writer, speaker, teacher, movie star, athlete, or diva I have met has feet of clay.

-§-

Many advanced spiritual teachers I have held in the highest regard one year have lost their high, pure spiritual vibration a year or two later. Some wear out, burn out, or get lazy; others fall for the lure of easy sex or money and material possessions. Others trip out on power and become insensitive, egotistical dictators; still others fall prey to addictive substances. Perfect lives and even dependable shamanic magic seldom exist on our planet. However, that does not make them any less attractive as life goals.

Meanwhile, back in the office, using shamanic ideas in your day-to-day management of cash flow is challenging. If you spend money wisely, you increase your investment. Every penny you don't spend is two you don't have to earn. When I get into financial trouble or dangerous situations, my wife calls me a Pollyanna Ostrich. That's her extreme interpretation of my one of my basic beliefs: that you must be positive and trusting; keep your eyes, mind, and heart on the desired outcome; and remain detached.

Following this prescription can mean on the one hand, for instance, risking too much cash on an impressive, expanded issue that doesn't sell because it is too unorthodox; or on the other hand, creating a blockbuster: a sold-out issue, a great increase in subscriptions, and a reputation for being on the cutting edge of magazine evolution.

I have made many decisions, all of which at the time seemed likely to succeed. Some have led to major setbacks, others to major leaps forward. Once we did a special issue of the magazine dedicated to innovations in education. Our usual readers were uninterested because the topic strayed too far from our normal themes, and education-oriented people didn't buy it because it was too edgy. However, after our first eighteen years, we made some changes that had great results. We changed our logo design and shortened the articles and interviews (with expanded versions available on our website). We changed the emphasis from philosophy and in-depth metaphysics to everyday, practical spiritual tools and ideas. Focusing on tracking the magic and mystical in the mundane brought us a much wider audience — our mainstream circulation soared.

There will be ups and downs, and you can't know ahead of time how things will turn out. But follow the prescription — be positive and trusting; keep your eyes, mind, and heart on the desired outcome; and remain detached. You won't always have outward success, but it will be a good ride.

What about supervising from the shamanic approach? In the Inca Empire there were no locks on doors, no jails, no stealing, and little crime. All citizens knew their roles and duties, and the vast majority enjoyed life. Lawbreakers received one warning without consequences. For the second offense, they might be pushed off an Andean cliff; cruel, but efficient.

Every citizen had to dedicate about fifteen hours, one third of the work week, to the empire. They worked in the fields, tended the empire's herds, worked on the highways, or held jobs in building and maintenance.

The Sapa Inca and political and religious leaders held great wealth. They were responsible for care of the elderly and of any citizens with disabilities who were unable to work. In times of natural disaster the leaders gave freely of their food and wealth to restore normal life for victims in the devastated areas.

These Inca ways guide me in how I supervise my ever-evolving staff. I work with heart, set high standards, give abundant support and encouragement, and weed out ruthlessly. When the principles work, we build a team that creates and achieves miracles daily. When they don't work, the quality of our products suffers, and so does cash floWhen I interview potential new employees, I look for people with passion, enthusiasm, clear goals, and dedication to self-improvement. Often I have to settle for hiring people who have great potential that is yet unrealized or for some reason lost.

Once I hire new people, I give them an overview of the business and a description of their job, and we discuss how their role fits into the big picture. I offer varying amounts of training, and soon I set high goals for achievement. If people do not achieve the goals, I let them go fast. Or, if I see hope or have a feeling for why they fell short, I work more closely with them on another high goal. Half the time the people pull it together and join the team. The other half have short-lived employment with MB Media.

When an employee is with the company and has a track record of great achievement, I tend to indulge them and let them choose their own work style and hours. My employees often feel a sense of ownership in the company and our mission, and they consistently perform far beyond what would be expected of average employees.

My favorite employees have generally been productive staff members for four to twelve years. However, advertising sales, distribution, the creative process, constant deadlines, and all the stresses of a creative, experimental business often wear people down in one to three years. Some people learn what they need, build up their resume, contribute greatly to MB Media, and then follow their professional evolution to a position with a larger company. Some can't flow with the magic spiral and also can t leave gracefully when their season of productivity has ended. They either explode with resentment over having worked so hard, or I have to let them go because they have devolved into bad influences. Being a shamanic supervisor can be painful. You live and lead from your heart and constantly attempt to help each employee achieve the highest potential, while at the same time meeting the company's needs—the bottom line of paying all bills and, in good years, turning a profit. Yet an open heart is a key ingredient in shamanic magic, and combining heart with the requisite ruthlessness is an art.

Some people see the last two thousand years as an experiment in how much ignorance, suffering, victimhood, and limitation we humans could endure—and in how our divine essence would cope, endure, adapt, and on occasion shine through. Many descendants of the Inca see the last five hundred years as a time of refining—as in the refining process of gold ore when all the impurities are burned out. The hotter the fire, the more impurities are burned. At last, now, humanity has almost become the purest of refined gold.

In the past two thousand years religions have been one effective coping mechanism. They have many faults and have often been outright suppressors of free thought and any spiritual teachings that threatened their power. Yet for individuals with burning desires, they have provided tools to transcend materialism and live at one with higher vibrational spirit. The religions have been candles in the darkness. In the future they will continue to exist to provide community and spiritual answers for those who desire what they offer.

Humanity has entered a new crossroads where true spirit, oneness with the divine, and the secrets of becoming creative gods are becoming readily available. When I teach workshops, many people ask me what they should do now that they have begun to realize their potential.

I tell them to take baby steps. Do not quit your job. Your present job or position offers you the spiritual lessons you need right now. Start planning how to transform your work and how you affect everyone you interact with. Do not leave your lover unless you are in an unhealthy or abusive relationship. Most of the weaknesses and shortcomings of our lovers are mirrors that urge us to heal our souls. Turn off your television more often and eventually, completely. Limit your exposure to all electronics (yes, even computer and email) and mainstream news. Then take this time that is freed up and begin to use it to explore your creative expression. Find or expand creative outlets that bring you joy. Creative expression can be writing, art, music, cooking, gardening—the form matters not. If you feel like you are making something original, and your effort makes you happy, the creative process connects you to the gods.

-§-

Some people see the last two thousand years as an experiment in how much ignorance, suffering, victimhood, and limitation we humans could endure.

-§-

Creativity brings us oneness with God. Our society makes most of us feel uncreative and tempts us to consume or observe rather than explore our creativity. Creative expression is a sacred ritual, even when done badly—and even if your work is never seen by another person. I have kept journals since my junior year in high school. I am often tempted to burn them, for they were written for me only. Yet I haven't. They are my way to practice, refine, and explore my writing—to explore its limits, to let off steam, to do self therapy, and to get stupid or inspired thoughts out of my head onto paper so I can laugh at them or expand and share them. I have a friend who teaches T'ai Chi and rides a bicycle. Another friend builds homes. My wife expresses her creativity through healing, gardening, and cooking. Any activity can be transformed into a way to explore and express your creative inner self. Creative expression can often be a better catalyst to spiritual growth than prayer or meditation.

If each of us could make a commitment to believe we can create, and then set aside one night or morning a week to do it faithfully, the world would be transformed.

The gods are thrilled by the creative process, as well as by love and joy. So find ways to give more love and to live more in joy. Spend more time praying, meditating, and setting goals for self-improvement and world improvement. Visualize achieving your goals and creating your idealized future. Some of the shamanic goals most important to me are cultivating love, joy, and unselfish giving; forgiveness of myself and others; giving thanks daily; maintaining and expanding an open heart and mind; and becoming solid in my calm, self-confident center. We are all holograms of the entire universe, and when awakened, we have access to all knowledge and all answers. Tune in, and begin checking to determine when the answers that come into your mind are your inner voice, wishful thinking, or old, early programming.

Will the shaman in the office transform the world? It will be an important catalyst when enough people realize that the ancients knew reality in a more magical, real, and empowering way than we do. When the energies of planet Earth reach the critical point sometime in the next eight to twenty-five years, the shadows will fall from people's minds, and we will realize the future is ours to co-create as gloriously as we can imagine. We all, consciously or unconsciously, agreed to work to reach this awakening in these decades. We are destined to create a new golden age. How difficult the getting from here to there will be depends on each of us and our willingness to trust, risk, and stretch.

-§-

Most of the weaknesses and shortcomings of our lovers are mirrors that urge us to heal our souls.

-§-

Shamanism and ancient cultures had many tools and techniques that are now lost and forgotten. Today we have inner and outer ways to get back to these nearly lost spiritual treasures. We were born to fully use this unique opportunity.

When the number of people who are exposed to this information and begin using it reaches critical mass, we will evolve into almost unimaginable magical beings. There is a God experiment going on in the next eight to twenty-five years that has never been conducted before in the universe. Humans have, by fate, errors, and a roll of the cosmic dice, been given a chance to evolve in a way that will expand God's existence and transform all reality. And each of us has a choice with our every thought, word, and deed to take risks, believe, and transform—or to succumb to the forces that want humans to fail and to live victimized, limited lives. Shamanism in the office and in our lives may sound far-out or unachievable, yet if we embrace it, it offers us an opportunity to alter our whole reality. Let's do it!

DAVID LEWIS & MICHAEL McNEIL:

Heartstreaming:
The Mind of God at Work

At the age of five, Joseph Patrick Kelly's father left his wife and four children. Right then and there, Joseph went from little boy to man of the house. After his mother reaffirmed his new state, Joseph started having to make big decisions for both himself and his family.

Fifty years later, Joseph is the founder and CEO of e3 Energy, a company that provides alternatives to the polluting, expensive fossil fuels that we use today—and solves the worst of our waste management problems as well. He and the e3 team have created solutions that turn virtually all waste streams into sources of renewable energy—pollution-free.

Joseph turned to *heartstreaming* at an early age in order to solve his problems. He was searching for a way to allow divine inspiration to guide him, as an alternative to the chaos he saw in his family. He describes "getting" his solution to transform waste streams into a source of green energy in a series of inspirations that occurred over a period of fifteen years. The goal for him was to just be open to the process and allow the knowledge to flow through him. Here is how he did it:

David Lewis is a co-founder and president of The Hearts Center (www.heartscenter.org), an organization devoted to both personal enlightenment, and to bringing the wisdom of spirit into global affairs. From the age of twelve, he has dedicated his life to helping others achieve enlightenment; he began conducting a mystical study group at the age of fifteen. He travels widely, conducting spiritual and healing retreats, group mission tours, and heartstreaming seminars.

Michael McNeil is executive director and a co-founder of The Hearts Center. He has a background in management and business administration. He received an M.A. in Theology from Trinity Theological Seminary, where he is currently a candidate in the Doctor of Religious Studies program. He reluctantly confesses to being a New Age Christian Buddhist with a disposition toward Sufism and a love for Hinduism.

First, he awoke daily before the sunrise and reflected on the mind of Christ, with respect to the issues at hand. He asked for guidance for himself and all of the people involved in the situation and he tuned into the hearts of all involved.

Then, he waited for inspiration. After he received the inspiration, he would write a plan, and then immediately act to implement it. On the seventh day, he would evaluate the outcome. And then he would start again.

The key was in building the proper team of people that shared the vision and values, allowing them to be magnetized by this process, so that each person became a part of a tapestry that gradually unfolded.

-§-
Invite divine intelligence to co-create with us solutions that leap the bounds of human logic and awareness.
-§-

For Joseph, this wasn't just a practice; it became a way of life. Today he heartstreams with people all over the world, and continues to magnetize the best and the brightest to his mission. He calls the heart a *sacred fire magnet.* He tunes into the resonance of the heart with everyone he meets in order to discern if they are part of his life's-mission.

Most of us who've worked in corporate settings have used techniques such as visualization and brainstorming. They're useful, whether we're upsizing, rightsizing, downsizing or supersizing. Yet our best ideas are often still inadequate to the challenges we face. Heartstreaming shifts us into a new realm of consciousness, in which we invite divine intelligence to co-create with us solutions that leap the bounds of human logic and awareness. We perfect our rhythm by dancing to the heartbeat of the invisible maestro.

Heartstreaming is a shift into consciousness that moves us from seeking the best mental models and ideas of think tanks and corporate brainpower to evolving or even *magnetizing* inspired solutions that simply await our discovery and application.

The process of heartstreaming is and has now proved successful in producing creative solutions to many types of knotty problems by engaging the spiritual light of the heart, to work through the etheric, mental, emotional, and physical causes behind the effects we see.

Heartstreaming works with groups as well as individuals, both young and old. Though the term *heartstreaming* may be a new term in our lexicon, examples of its use in the past are evident in the literature of the great spiritual movements, born by revelation received through a heightened communion with the divine architect. Who can deny that many of the greatest inventions, epic stories, and artistic renderings were born from flashes of illumination in visions, dreams and altered, mystical states of consciousness? Time and space are only real to those who live in their grip.

For example, can you picture Hiawatha heartstreaming to gain co-equal rights for warring Indian tribes? He is sitting in a circle with the warring tribes, smoking a peace pipe and communing with the Great Chief of the sky spirits, chanting, "Peace, power and righteousness be our guide"? Or imagine Einstein saying, "We cannot solve problems with the same thinking we used when we created them." He also said, "Imagination is more important than knowledge." He went first to the realm of gnosis, after which he could help solve the pressing problems of his day. The heart of heaven may flash in waves through the stream of synapses of a nuclear physicist solving a complex problem, while unconsciously dialed into other worlds. The heart of the Earth may sing in the ideations of the mystic poet translating the metered rhythm inspired within.

Children do this all of the time. They gaze at objects for long periods of time, absorbing their fullness to a degree that busy adults cannot fathom. The stars on a clear night in a campsite can provide hours of reflection. They may ask, "Are we alone?" as they witness the higher geometry in the patterns of the Milky Way. They may sense that they are part of this starry body, forgetting the gravitational pull of the Earth beneath them. At that moment, they know that they are not alone. When we are attuned to a higher frequency, creativity flows in a childlike state of joy; simple acceptance of divine harmony flows through our spiritual and physical centers. The heart of the Earth beams in a smile in the rush of joy of a new discovery made by a young child as it gazes on the patterns of a sunflower, whose seeds reflect the inner pattern of divinity.

-§-
Improve your rhythm. Dance to the heartbeat of the invisible maestro.
-§-

Many of us believe that solving our most serious global problems — like environmental pollution, lack of reverence for life, lack of spirituality in leadership, religious fundamentalism, and political extremism — is often beyond the ken and reach of our brightest thinkers. Yet by using this new approach, we can utilize our hearts in unison, generating the immense energy required to heal the heart of the world.

There are five keys to initiating a successful heartstreaming session, moving a group from a place of reasoning with their minds, to finding the magic that springs from a shared heart. The five keys are these:

281

Goodwill: First, approach each other with a sincere, heartfelt presumption of goodwill, which lays the foundation for mutual respect and trust. Mutual respect implies an approach that is without preconceived notions of who will produce the best ideas, without assigning greater weight to mental prowess or hierarchical position within the group. Rather than presuming ill will in others, or being self-concerned, or believing that good intentions will solve our problems, heartstreaming assumes that ideas fraught with love and wisdom are often born as shared expressions.

Surrender: Second, surrender all prejudices. Even a favorable disposition toward people involved in an issue may be destructive to the ultimate outcome, because prejudice, positive or negative, is primarily a quality of the mind, not of the heart.

-§-

Make "aha" experiences *ahabit.*

-§-

Be aware of the tendency to justify a few prejudices in the name of reason, which is the favorite hiding place of static mindsets. The infinite has an uncanny ability to shake us when our salt has become too crystallized. Grow your will as a bamboo plant—and your love as a redwood.

Harmony: Third, always strive to maintain a state of group harmony. When deviation occurs, stop and breathe. Say a brief prayer, meditate for a few minutes, or use another technique for quieting the mind. Groups vary in what techniques bring them back to a heart-centered state. Use any technique that works for your group, and use it whenever you sense that you've departed from a sense of harmony.

Faith: Fourth, have faith in the process and expect positive results. Approach it without driving expectations. You don't need to engineer results. Have faith in knowing that, when the creative fires of the heart are engaged, productive change occurs, that every serious personal and planetary need of healing has a divine solution. We have simply to quiet our minds and hearts, and tune into the field of all possibilities, in order to discover it. Make "Aha!" experiences *ahabit.*

Heart-Centered Practice: Fifth, conscious communion with the heart is strengthened through practice. If you work out on the weight machines at the gym each day, you will build big muscles. Prayer, mantras, meditation, contemplation, and similar techniques develop the heart. When the heart's fires are regularly engaged, we easily hear its voice. Heartstreaming comes naturally when there has been a cultivation of the heart, an ongoing spiritualization of the heart. The heart is our bridge to the subtle world of spirit.

Heartstreaming is approached not simply with the presumption of goodwill and absence of prejudice, but with a sense of expectation that results are inevitable and that pure genius may come from any and all members of the group. Sometimes the perfect idea springs, crystal clear and complete, from one member of the team. Other times, the group may come up with a seed thought that requires refining. Heartstreaming may also be done with only one of the parties fully aware of the process, as David relates in this experience of one-person heartstreaming:

"I had a conflict with an out-of-state client in my Montana art business wherein a promised timeline to deliver a signed and numbered, unframed lithograph as an anniversary gift was not going to be met because of a slip-up on the part of a third party gallery in Texas who had the rare print. Just before I picked up the phone to relate the bad news to my client I felt an impulse to heartstream.

"I entered into a deep state of relaxation and meditation and asked permission for all three parties involved to meet in their finer bodies to heartstream for a solution to our dilemma. I decided then and there to have complete faith in the process and trust that something could be done to resolve the issue. I visualized light streaming forth from the hearts of all of us and then released all sense of urgency or attachment to the situation, ending the session with a great sense of peace that all would be well, and then I returned to my other business at hand.

"Within twenty minutes I received a call from the Texas gallery. They located the same rare print through a wholesaler in a city within a half hour's drive of my client, and in order to make up for the faux pas they were covering the cost of having a courier hand-deliver the print to my client that day, thus meeting the timeline! I was floored at the instantaneous response and the outcome."

We don't know what method the great field of cosmic intelligence is using to produce such remarkable outcomes, but we know that, examples of miracles have been described by human beings from the earliest recorded scriptures. Whether we attribute them to angels, to a superconscious, to the "mind of Christ" that may be "also in me" as St. Paul did, to nature spirits,

-§-
Time and space are
only real to those
who live in their grip.
-§-

to angels, to great sages and saints of East or West, we know that they remind us that "We are not human beings on a spiritual path, but spiritual beings on a human path." Infinite possibilities are just that.

Heartstreaming allows us to tap into this infinite storehouse of universal wisdom—by whatever name we call it. In 1935, author Helena Roerich wrote, "Space is filled with all sorts of mental mes-

sages, and we receive exactly what is in correspondence with our own mental receiver." Include in your plans a word from The Word.

Early one spring, David was giving a presentation at the Bodhi Tree Bookstore in West Hollywood on developing personal and group spirituality and decided to elicit the energies of the thirty or so people in the room to work on the problem of air pollution in the greater Los Angeles area. They first listened to soothing music and quieted themselves in a meditative state. David led them in a guided meditation, visualizing violet light radiating across the sky, cleansing the toxic hydrocarbons and pollutants and dissolving them on contact. After this meditation they gave a simple mantra together for a few minutes, again visualizing violet light cleaning up the air.

As they finished the mantra the area was drenched with a short, powerful downpour, though no rain was forecast for the area. The next day when David took his morning jog he noticed a clean, azure sky, when the day before a smoggy haze had hung over Los Angeles County.

As we cultivate a sense of harmony within ourselves as individuals, and in our groups, and bring ourselves back into harmony when we've strayed, we place ourselves in a position to heartstream the most harmonious solutions to be found in the universal mind.

-§-
The infinite has an uncanny ability to shake us when our salt has become too crystallized.
-§-

We are a bridge to the future and how we address now will be the building blocks of the next cycle. As we review the past, we discover that even the early Christians and the apostles described a similar dilemma and applied a similar process. The disciples of the risen Christ came together "in one place of one accord," and in that place, "the power of the Holy Spirit came upon them."

The tragic events of our times are a teacher, compelling us to look deep within ourselves to find our highest sense of service. Being of one accord doesn't mean achieving consensus, taking a vote, finding win-win solutions, weighing the options, or negotiating mutually agreeable terms. These all reflect an emphasis on the mind, on reason, rather than invoking the magic that flows from the cosmic intelligence through the heart. They produce limited and quantitative solutions, rather than the great leaps in consciousness required to solve the immense problems with which humankind finds itself confronted today.

Where attunement is sought with the reality of the All, there we find the heart of beauty and grace. It is through the fires of the heart,

invoking divine will, wisdom, and compassion, that positive healing can occur—even such as dire problems as civil war, racial strife,
economic disparity, and environmental pollution. Reason alone only
takes us so far. Just as heartfelt prayer can induce
miraculous physical cures, heartstreaming has
the potential to induce miraculous environmental cures, such as the plasma reduction of toxic
wastes described by Joseph Kelly, or the reduc-
tion of pollution in a lake described by Japanese scientist Masaru
Emoto. As geologist Gregg Braden observes, the heart is the nexus,
the meeting point, for the integration of thought and the power of
emotion. That nexus is a matrix of perfection, a symmetry of gnosis
that is everywhere present yet nowhere more profoundly abundant
except in the core of reality in the heart of the Earth. Heartstreaming
integrates all of these into a point of equilibrium that is the seed
source of all creation; the core of consciousness, the spark of divinity
radiating a frequency or pattern that harmonizes all things.

-§-

Include in your plans
a word from The
Word.

-§-

EDWARD MILLS:

The Evolutionary Warrior

My daughter, Ella, is learning to feed herself. It's an often-entertaining, sometimes frustrating, and always messy process. She is a study in concentration and joy as she throws peas on the floor, or uses yogurt as finger paint, or smears almond butter into her hair. I gently encourage her to keep her food on her plate, in her mouth, or at the very least, somewhere on her body, resisting the powerful urge to impose my desire for orderliness onto her. If I did, how would she learn? How would she discover her world and herself? How would she evolve?

If you've ever witnessed the miracle of birth, you know that we enter life in a very messy way. There is nothing neat and clean about it, no matter how sterile the hospital. But from that messy moment on, we're taught to keep the messiness out of our lives. We're taught to clean up our rooms and put away our toys when we're done. We're taught to keep our mashed potatoes off of our peas. Those early lessons infuse and inform the rest of our life and shape the way we move through the world.

The natural joy of discovery that we bring with us into this world is dampened by those lessons. That joy is crucial, for it serves to balance the frustration that is an equally vital aspect of learning. Without the joy, what motivation do we have for entering into the learning process? Practicing scales on the piano because of the not-so-gentle urging of our parents is far less effective than exploring exciting new

Edward Mills is the creator of the *Personal Evolution Toolbox* audio series, and the *Life Black Belt* virtual dojo for Evolutionary Warriors. Through private and group coaching, workshops, writing, and audio programs, he facilitates and inspires the process of personal and planetary evolution. He teaches *From Purpose to Path,* a popular life-visioning course at New College of California and is on the faculty of the Academy of Intuition Medicine. Edward is a husband and the father of an amazing two-year-old master. He holds a second degree black belt in Okinawan Goju-Ryu karate. You can find him online at www.edwardmills.com.

sounds and harmonies because of the urging of our inner curiosity and joy.

When joy fuels our journey into the messiness and chaos of discovery the possibilities are limitless. When obligation, responsibility, or need fuel that journey, we limit our potential for discovery and transformation before we even begin.

On some deep level, we know the messiness we have been taught to avoid is a natural and, indeed, vital part of the learning process. Messiness, chaos and frustration, all inherent in learning, generate the energy and motivation needed to break through the barrier of our current level of skill or awareness to a new, more advanced level. Whether we are learning to feed ourselves, play the piano, or incorporate a new belief system into our life, messiness, chaos, and frustration are positive signs, reminding us that we are growing.

-§-
If you want to awaken all of humanity, then awaken all of yourself. If you want to eliminate the suffering in the world, then eliminate all that is dark and negative in yourself. Truly, the greatest gift you have to give is that of your own transformation.
—Lao Tzu
-§-

Unfortunately, when the going gets messy, most of us get going...with the broom and mop, doing our best to clean up. But no matter how hard we try to push the messiness of life away, it has an irritating ability to find us. And the more we resist the messy parts of our life, the messier they become. The "out of sight, out of mind" philosophy just doesn't cut it when it comes to life and our evolutionary process.

Most of us understand that ignoring or resisting the force of gravity would create a big mess. Taking a jump off a tall building will probably lead us to the doctor or the undertaker. Many early attempts at flight were based on the belief that we could ignore or overpower the force of gravity. And many of those attempts resulted in a big mess.

On the other hand, as we have discovered ways of working in harmony with gravity we have been able to create seemingly miraculous results. By learning to cooperate with the force of gravity we have literally taken flight. I still find myself in awe when I am pushed back against the seat of an accelerating jet and watch the Earth drop away. I don't care what physicists say: There is magic in that experience.

Just as the ever-present force of gravity pulls our bodies toward the center of the Earth, the force of evolution pulls us always toward the center of our Source. Resisting evolution's powerful pull can be just as messy as resisting the force of gravity. However, as our understanding of the evolutionary force grows and we learn to work in harmony with it, the miracles we can create are literally beyond our ability to conceive. The goal of the evolutionary warrior is to penetrate ever deeper into the evolutionary force and discover its secrets.

But like anything that holds great power, powerful guardians protect the evolutionary force. These guardians are not somewhere out there; these guardians live within us and their sole purpose is to keep us out of the evolutionary force. They do not want us to discover its hidden secrets. They do not want us performing the miracles that are possible when we work in harmony with the force of evolution.

The Forbidden Room

These guardians are masters of deception. Imagine walking up to a closed door. As you approach, you hear vicious dogs barking and see signs that say, "Warning! Off Limits! Extreme Danger: Do Not Enter." Most of us would quickly turn around and head off in search of a more inviting door.

Now, imagine that deep inside you, beneath the chatter of your mind, you hear, or perhaps feel, a gentle suggestion to wait for just a moment longer. Despite the frantic urging of your fear, you trust that inner sense and wait. In that moment of trust, a pair of glasses falls from above the door. You put them on and discover they are x-ray glasses, allowing you to see through the door. Within the room you see a vast treasure, heaps of gold and silver and jewels of every imaginable color, shape, and size. You notice also that there are no dogs, only an old tape recorder. With this new information, what would you do? Would you still turn around? Would you still search for a safer, more inviting door to enter? Or would you enter that room?

The guardians of the evolutionary force stand before many doors, disguising them, hiding them, making them appear forbidding and dangerous. And while financial rewards do await the explorer willing to seek out and enter those rooms, the evolutionary warrior seeks treasure far more valuable. She knows that within those hidden and well-protected rooms wait clues that will lead her to her Source. Indeed, she knows that many of those rooms hold missing and lost parts of her very Essence. Each room that she discovers within the uncharted territory of her inner landscape leads her one step closer to wholeness.

-§-
Messiness, chaos and frustration are positive signs, reminding us that we are growing.
-§-

Why do we have these inner adversaries? Why must we spend our lives struggling to overcome fears, doubts, and beliefs that hold us back and create turmoil? If we assume that the Creator of this

Universe is a perfect being, why would She place these adversaries within us? For that matter why would She include conflict and violence and death in Her creation? Why not create a utopian, peace-filled Universe?

The answer is simple: Without these outer conflicts and inner adversaries we would not evolve. At our present level of individual and collective consciousness we require these inner adversaries to fuel our evolutionary process. The ultimate evolutionary warrior—God, Creator, Mystery, Source—understands that the evolutionary process requires friction. Just as muscle will not grow without resistance, evolution needs something to push against. Our inner adversaries provide the resistance needed to push through to continuously new levels of evolutionary awareness.

-§-
Would you like to save the world from the degradation and destruction it seems to be destined for? Then step away from the shallow mass movements and quietly go to work on your self-awareness.
—Lao Tzu
-§-

Evolutionary warriors understand the importance of these sources of friction. And understanding this, they are able to offer gratitude to the people and circumstances that create friction in their life. But the evolutionary warrior also understands that the true source of the friction and the true adversary is always within.

When the Inner Adversary Strikes

Before stepping onto the path of the evolutionary warrior, the temptation to focus on the external irritant is overpowering. The guardians of the evolutionary force are masters of distraction and diversion. They know that keeping us focused on the outside world splits our forces, stretches our resources thin, diminishing our ability to effectively engage in our inner battle. Because they live within our minds, our inner adversaries have access to our deepest thoughts, thoughts that we are often not consciously aware of. And they put these hidden thoughts to good use in their attempt to keep us focused on the external world.

Evolution is inevitable. And so too are the battles that catalyze our forward movement on the evolutionary journey. When we avoid our evolutionary battles for too long, our inner adversaries gain power, and eventually they will launch an attack that takes us by surprise. When that happens, it is very likely that we will lose that battle.

These sneak attacks can come at any time and may take the form of an accident, serious illness, divorce, or layoff. When these unexpected events shake our life, they are signs that we have not been watching our inner landscape.

A friend of mine was left with a substantial amount of money when her father passed away more than a year ago. Since then she has faced a constant struggle between her desire to put this money to good use and the old beliefs she learned from her father: "You have to work hard to make money." "Money is earned." "You have to save for a rainy day."

One area where this struggle was particularly acute was her car, an old Ford with ripped upholstery, mechanical problems and a big dent on the front from an earlier accident. She continued to milk the car along, putting more and more money into it to keep it running. She wanted a new car, she knew it made sense to get one, and yet she was unwilling to confront the inner voices that kept telling her it would be irresponsible and a waste of her father's money.

And then one day, her inner opponent launched a surprise attack. This inner adversary had grown powerful while my friend waited. And on that day, my friend was in a car accident. Fortunately, she was physically unharmed but her car was totaled. She was forced into battle, into a place where she had to face her inner opponent and face the old beliefs she held around money and responsibility.

Burying your head in the sand will not keep evolution away from you. All it will do is make the force of its impact more traumatic. The evolutionary warrior knows that turning her back on her inner adversaries will not make them go away. It will only give them more strength and the opportunity to surprise her, to attack when she is unprepared and weak.

-§-
Our inner adversaries provide the resistance needed to push through to continuously new levels of evolutionary awareness.
-§-

The evolutionary warrior acknowledges the inevitability, and indeed, the importance, of battle but also the need for balance. A warrior knows there is time for battle. But there is also time for resting, time for celebrating the victories, time for mourning the loss of allies. And time for training in the ways and weaponry of the evolutionary warrior.

The Evolutionary Warrior's Weapons

Just as there are many weapons of physical warfare, the arsenal of evolutionary weapons is vast. Some of these weapons can only be wielded by the evolutionary warrior himself. His inner adversary cannot touch them, cannot turn them against him. These weapons include playfulness, love, compassion, gratitude, and joy. The evolutionary warrior knows that when he calls forth these weapons, when

he wields them with skill and consciousness, he is likely to vanquish his inner adversary.

There are other evolutionary weapons that can only be wielded by the inner adversary. Hatred, rage, and judgment are just a few. When the evolutionary warrior feels these weapons slashing him from the inside or feels himself lashing out with these weapons on the outside, he knows that his inner adversary has successfully broken through his defenses and called him onto the evolutionary battlefield. He knows too, that if he cannot extricate himself from these weapons that his inner adversary will be victorious.

-§-

Joy is crucial, for it serves to balance the frustration that is an equally vital aspect of learning.

-§-

There are also weapons that cut both ways, weapons that can be used by both the evolutionary warrior and his inner adversary. Some of these include anger, grief, power, and humility. When channeled and focused in a conscious, intentional manner, these weapons can be transformative tools. The evolutionary warrior chooses to be the master of these weapons. She knows that if used unconsciously and indiscriminately these weapons can grow out of control and become her master.

Every day we witness and experience the acts of people who have become the servants of hatred, anger, judgment, and power. Nor does it take much exploring to reveal times in our own life when we have acted as the servant of one or more of these destructive weapons.

When the evolutionary warrior perceives the need to use one of these weapons, she does so with the utmost caution and consciousness. She knows that, regardless of her level of training, as an evolutionary warrior, she is inherently more powerful than others who have not yet stepped onto the path. Because of that, she recognizes the importance of remaining in control of these weapons. And she knows that in every battle with her inner adversary she faces the possibility of losing that control and becoming the servant of one of her weapons.

Victory Without a Fight

We face external battles every day. We argue with our partner, get passed over for a promotion, watch the clock tick as we sit in traffic. Every irritating external situation is a sure sign that your inner adversary is probing your defenses, checking your level of preparedness, and watching for an opening to launch a full-scale attack.

Recently, I faced a battle with an inner adversary. On a clear, quiet morning, my daughter and I went to the window to watch the sun rise. Instead of seeing the sun, my attention was immediately drawn to the big truck blocking our driveway. Recognizing it as the work truck of a gruff neighbor, I instantly entered a place of frustration and irritation.

I caught myself going into that place and recognized the work of my inner adversary. I felt him trying to draw me into an external battle. I knew my neighbor and his truck were tools, decoys to draw my attention away from my inner landscape. If I refocused my awareness inward, I would discover my true adversary.

Evolutionary warriors know that the true opponent is always within. The battles we face every day, whether in the boardroom, the bedroom or on the streets of Baghdad, are reflections of our inner battles. These external confrontations, large or small, provide opportunities to face the adversary within. No matter how frustrating, irritating, violent, oppressive, or chaotic the outer world becomes, the evolutionary warrior knows that she is facing a much more important battle in her inner world.

-§-

The battles we face every day, whether in the boardroom, the bedroom or on the streets of Baghdad, are reflections of our inner battles.

-§-

I tried to meditate but found it impossible. My mind was obsessed with conflict. I saw myself knocking on his door, asking him to move the truck, only to have him yell at me and slam the door in my face, or push me aside, or laugh. I imagined calling the police to have them tow the truck away. My mind was endlessly creative in the confrontational outcomes it could dream up.

Clearly these scenes were my inner adversary's attempts to keep me focused on the external situation. While frustrated at my inability to turn off these images, I was grateful that I was aware of the inner battle. And, so far, I had not fallen deeper into the trap my inner opponent had set for me.

There was no rush; neither my wife nor I needed to use the car anytime soon. I could continue the exploration of my inner world. I could let my inner adversary make the first move and allow the inner battle to unfold before addressing the external circumstances that had triggered it.

Meditation continued to be ineffective. So knowing that playfulness is a powerful tool in the evolutionary warrior's arsenal, I decided to settle in for a lesson with my daughter. Sitting with her on the floor, she showed me how to play one of her favorite games: dumping all the crayons out of the box and then gathering them up and putting

them back in, only to dump them out once again. After mastering the basics of the game, I added the "hide the crayon in Ella's pants leg" element, increasing our mutual enjoyment of the game, especially when she began attempting to shove handfuls of crayons up the legs of my sweatpants.

As I allowed myself to settle deeper into this moment with my daughter, I noticed the irritation I felt toward my neighbor decreasing. The shift in my attention and attitude freed much of my energy and awareness that had previously been tied up in the prospect of battle. Gathering these newly freed resources, I directed them onto my inner adversary. And with that, the tide of the battle shifted. I felt him retreating, knowing he would not win this battle. And, as if on cue, I heard a truck start. Walking to the window I saw my neighbor — barefoot and still in his pajamas! — moving his truck from in front of our house to a space in front of theirs.

-§-
It is possible to live a life of joy, abundance, ease, meaning, and success while walking steadfastly upon the path of the evolutionary warrior.
-§-

In *The Art of War*, Sun Tzu says, "To fight and conquer in one hundred battles is not the highest skill. To subdue the enemy with no fight at all, that is the highest skill."

The evolutionary warrior knows that by focusing on his inner adversaries he will often subdue the external enemy with no fight at all. He also knows that, on occasion, it may be necessary to accept defeat in the external battle in order to vanquish the true opponent, his inner adversary.

The ultimate goal of the evolutionary warrior is to reach a level of mastery in which he subdues his *inner* adversaries without a fight. When the evolutionary warrior reaches that level, there is no longer a need for the external sources of friction that fuel the inner adversary. The conflict, violence, aggression, and fear that fill our external world become unnecessary to the evolutionary warrior who has learned to willingly and actively confront his inner adversaries. In this way, as more people step onto the path of the evolutionary warrior, we will create a world of peace.

Becoming An Evolutionary Warrior

How do you become an evolutionary warrior? It is not necessary to be accepted by any school. You need not be taken under the tutelage of any master. There are no special techniques for you to learn. All that is required is the desire. By saying "I am an evolutionary warrior," you become one. The moment you make that affirming statement, you step onto the path of the evolutionary warrior.

A new generation of evolutionary warriors is awakening. These new warriors do not go off and meditate and fast for forty days. They do not sit in caves contemplating their navels. These new evolutionary warriors are actively engaged in life. They strive to bring their full presence to the daily events and situations of life: to relationships, to work and play, to financial matters and matters of the heart.

The new evolutionary warrior is not learning to consciously slow his heartbeat; he is learning to more fully bring an open heart into his relationships. She is not learning to generate enough heat to melt ten feet of snow; she is learning to use her inner heat to burn away the fog shrouding her essential nature.

Through their active engagement in the world, these new evolutionary warriors teach us about abundance and joy and peace. We need more evolutionary warriors like Oprah Winfrey, whose battles with her inner adversaries expand our understanding of abundance and generosity. We need more evolutionary warriors like Ray Anderson, whose battles with his inner adversaries expand our awareness of sustainable business practices. We need more evolutionary warriors like Dennis Kucinich, whose battles with his inner adversaries expand our understanding of compassion and peace.

The path of the new evolutionary warrior does not require us to give up the comforts of life. In fact, quite the opposite. It is time for the world to see that it is possible to live a life of joy, abundance, ease, meaning, and success while walking steadfastly upon the path of the evolutionary warrior.

-§-

Masters carry peace with them wherever they go, even into the most violent battles.

-§-

Wherever they stand, masterful warriors project peacefulness into the world around them. These advanced evolutionary warriors understand that their purpose is not to create peace in the outer world but to create an inner peace deep and strong enough to withstand any external circumstance. These masters do not get drawn into external battles against their will. And when they choose to enter a battle in the outer world, they do so with consciousness and consideration. These masters carry peace with them wherever they go, even into the most violent battles. In so doing, these warriors bring peace into the world.

No longer is it enough for a few evolutionary warriors to lead the way for the rest of us. It is time to create an army of evolutionary warriors. We are building toward the critical mass of evolutionary

warriors that will tip the balance and allow us to create a world of peace.

Are you ready? Are you prepared to become an evolutionary warrior? In order to transform our world we must transform ourselves. You can step onto the path of the evolutionary warrior at any time. No matter where you stand on your external path, no matter where you are on your inner journey, you can become an evolutionary warrior. All it takes is the desire.

The time is now. Speak the evolutionary warrior's oath and become the evolutionary warrior you were born to be.

I am an evolutionary warrior.

My purpose is evolution.

My goal is inner peace.

My true adversary is within.

My most powerful weapons are gratitude, compassion, and joy.

I serve others by transforming myself.

RANDY PEYSER:

Miracle Thinking

I was driving down a long stretch of road one day, when I asked myself a question: If I had a million dollars and could only spend it on myself, what would I want? The answer came quickly. "I'd like to take some fun and inspiring workshops."

The next day, a friend called. Her husband couldn't attend a seminar for which she had purchased tickets. She gifted me the $85 ticket.

Two days later, an email arrived from someone else. "Randy, I heard a guy on the radio. He was offering free tickets to his $350 workshop this weekend. I called in and won them, so I signed you and me up. Want to go?" Of course, I wanted to go.

A month later I said to myself, "I'd still like to attend more workshops." That week, I received an email from an organization asking for volunteers to help with their upcoming $3,500, five-day workshop in Southern California. I'd wanted to attend this workshop for quite some time. Although hundreds of people offered to volunteer, only 30 were selected. I was one of them.

Three months later, I was offered the opportunity to attend a $10,000 year-long training program in trade for my writing services. I accepted.

What allowed all of these wonderful opportunities to effortlessly flow my way, as if from out of the blue? And why did these oppor-

Randy Peyser is the author of *Crappy to Happy* (Red Wheel, 2002), the forth-coming book *Miracle Thinking,* and is featured in *Visionary Women Inspiring the World* (Inspiration Place, 2004). A dynamic "Miracle Thinking" speaker and workshop trainer, she is also the creator of a one-woman show called "Comic Intervention for Closet Visionaries and Almost-Manifesters," where she teaches audience members how to "practice random acts of chutzpah." In addition, she edits books, helps authors find agents, creates feature articles, bios and press materials for entrepreneurs, and writes on assignment for national magazines. www.miraclethinking.com.

tunities come to me so easily, while at other times when things or circumstances have been desired, they haven't occurred so readily?

For the past two years, I've been in search of the formula or recipe that people, either knowingly or unknowingly, have used to create miraculous results in their lives. In the process, I've interviewed people who have experienced all kinds of miracles, large and small. For example, Steven Walters was given twenty-four hours to live. Eleven years later, he still shows no signs of leukemia. In another startling example, a fire that consumed 500,000 acres swept across Ronnie Chittim's property in Southern Oregon. While the fire took everything in its wake, Ronnie's two cabins remained untouched. Or take the case of Dawna Markova, who was being wheeled down to the morgue, having been pronounced dead on a hospital gurney. Just imagine how the attendant felt when she suddenly awakened.

These people have quite different stories, yet they all had one thing in common: each experienced a highly desired miracle. In my interviews, I was determined to find out what actions each of these people took, if any, and the kinds of beliefs and attitudes each of them held that might have contributed to their miracles having occurred.

What I learned from people like Steven, Ronnie, and Dawna is that there are a number of principles that contribute to what might be called a *miracle thinking mindset*. Once these principles are incorporated into our inner fabric, energy automatically flows forward, and miracles can, and will, occur for us.

Let's examine the case of Dawna Markova.

During her first long hospital stay, Dawna, then in her early thirties, was facing a medical procedure for cancer, which terrified her. Late one night, she heard a swishing sound coming from the hospital hallway. The sound came closer until it stopped in front of her door. Looking up, she saw a rather large woman pushing a mop. The woman entered her room, and plopped herself into the chair by her bedside in a way that one does when they're in the company of an old friend.

-§-
You're more than
your pain.
-§-

Without saying a word, the woman reached over and put her hand on Dawna's ankle and began to breathe in unison with her. As Dawna closed her eyes, she imagined the woman's breath sounded like ocean waves washing back and forth against the shore. A while later, the woman stood up and grabbed her broom. Before she left, she turned and said in her thick Jamaican accent, "You're more than your pain." Then she was gone.

All day long, Dawna questioned herself, "How could I be more than my pain? In processing this question, she thought about how her pain didn't cover her entire body. Truthfully, only 20% of her body was in pain. Logically, didn't that mean that 80% of her body wasn't in pain? She decided to just take notice of that fact, instead of putting all of her attention on the source of her discomfort.

The next night, Dawna heard the familiar swishing sound of the mop coming down the hallway. Once again, the woman reappeared and proceeded to collapse into the chair as she reached for Dawna's foot. The comfort Dawna received from the woman's loving presence felt palpable. Then the woman said, "You're more than the sickness in that body."

-§-
What's unfinished for you to give?
-§-

Every night, her "Jamaican angel" would appear, collapse in the chair beside her, and place her hand on her foot as Dawna lay silently in the bed. Dawna stopped taking her bedtime morphine just to make sure she wasn't hallucinating. The night of her last visit, the woman said, "You're not the fear in that body. You're more than that fear. Float on it. Float above it." Then she left.

"What does it mean to be more than one's fear?" Dawna asked herself. Eventually, she arrived at an answer. Of course! Her capacity for joy was so much greater than her fear. Instead of focusing her attention on anything that made her feel fearful, Dawna decided to focus only on those things that brought her joy.

Dawna never saw her "Jamaican angel" again. Was she really an angel, or just the nighttime cleaning lady? To Dawna, it never really mattered. This kind being provided a deep and abiding sense of loving comfort to a woman who was in great fear and pain, and by doing so, had inspired Dawna to focus her attention in a new way that changed her perspective.

Still dealing with the cancer a few years later, Dawna had another experience in which she was pronounced dead on an operating table. While being wheeled to the morgue, she felt as though she was "falling upward."

"During this time which felt timeless, all the questions I'd ever asked and all the experiences I'd ever had came together," she says. "I had the comprehension that I was light, that I was love, and that love can't be destroyed, whether or not you're in a body."

As she watched from above, the doctor came out of the operating room and delivered the news to her eight-year-old son, David.

"In my experience, there was a one-way wall, and the wall was only on David's side," says Dawna. "This wall was made up of his anger, his fear, and his belief that I was dead. But I wasn't! My love and my consciousness were right there. I knew everything that was happening to him."

"I also comprehended how incomplete my loving had been to him," she continued. "There were many lessons I hadn't yet learned at that point. I understood that David would suffer as a result. All I wanted was to get through to David so that I could help him not suffer from my incomplete lessons. But I couldn't get through because of that wall of his belief."

Next, a voice began to engage her in conversation. It asked, "Have you had enough joy?"

She responded, "Well, no. I'm only thirty years old."

"What are you waiting for?" said the voice.

Then the voice asked, "What's unfinished for you to give?"

"What do you mean? I want a Ferrari, and I want my own house…"

The question was repeated over and over again, "What's unfinished for you to give?"

Upon her return, four and a half minutes after being pronounced dead, Dawna's understanding of the meaning of her life deepened dramatically. Most importantly, her focus shifted from the desire to get, to a desire to give.

Dawna began writing books and developed a prolific career as an author. Remembering the question, "What's unfinished for you to give?" at one point, she approached her publisher, Conari Press, and originated the idea for the wildly successful *Random Acts of Kindness* book. One book became a series, propelled thousands of people across the planet to give of themselves to others, and spawned an International Random Acts of Kindness Foundation. In keeping with her desire to give, all profits from the sale of the book were donated to the AIDS Foundation and the Kids' AIDS Foundation.

-§-
The bigger your joy,
the smaller your fear
will be.
-§-

Here are some of the Miracle Thinking tips that Dawna offers, based on her experiences described above:

- "Fear can either be an ending to one's growth and dreams or a beginning." Being aware of my passion, for example, gave fear a companion, someone to hold it as if the Madonna were holding an infant. Do not ignore fear; rather notice it as sensation in the body. By caring about it, and then by shifting your focus to what is more than your fear, the energy is released to move forward."

- "When you're going through an experience of fear or anxiety, you can also ask yourself, 'What is it that brings me joy?' and begin to focus on your joy. The bigger your joy, the smaller your fear will be. It's not that the fear will go away. It's just that it will become less and less relevant. The joy will carry you forward."

- As a Miracle Thinker, it's important to understand the following distinction that Dawna makes: "Don't confuse joy with pleasure. Joy is about the connection that comes when you've given of yourself. For example, when you deeply connect with yourself, another, or nature, you experience joy. Pleasure, on the other hand, is about receiving, not about giving. For example, a therapeutic massage can bring pleasure, but I've found that my fear is not bigger than that. If I think in terms of pleasure, it's never bigger than my fear. When I see my infant granddaughter's eyes light up at her first taste of ice cream—that's joy."

Over the past year, Dawna decided to start another global movement. This time, she has begun a venture called SmartWired, in which she is creating programs that offer educators around the world a new way of teaching children. The movement is based on the idea that every child has special gifts and talents, as well as their own ways of accessing their gifts and talents, through their own particular learning style. Rather than label children as learning disabled, ADHD, or any of the other labels that children receive, her approach is to teach educators how to become aware of each child's unique learning style and use their individualized learning styles to develop those natural gifts and talents.

-§-

In order for a miracle to occur, we must ask very clearly for what it is we want.

-§-

What I've learned from Dawna and the many Miracle Thinkers I've interviewed is that each of us holds a piece of the Miracle Thinking puzzle, as there are many different attitudes, thoughts, and beliefs that can contribute to the creation of miracles. However, if I had to condense them, I'd say that some of the top Miracle Thinking principles are as follows:

1. *The universe likes a good target.* In order for a miracle to occur, we must ask very clearly for what it is we want. In the original example above, I gave the Universe a good target, namely the desire to take fun and inspiring workshops.

2. *The universe will never give you a "yes...but."* This is one of the most important, and often trickiest, of principles to understand. Many of us have gotten quite good at declaring our target, whether it be a new job, a healthy relationship, x number of dollars, or healing the world in some way. However, we often unknowingly cancel our intention in the same breath.

For example, we might say or think, "I want a relationship," then we'll mumble to ourselves, "but I don't want to get my heart skewered again like I did in that last relationship." Or, "I want a new job…but I never want to work for someone like that boss ever again."

-§-
Allowing yourself to live in God's "bigger dream" for you will help open new doors that you couldn't even possibly imagine.
-§-

A "but" that is voiced at a conscious level, or hidden in the subconscious, will keep the energy flow of a miracle from coming our way. In the original example, if I had said, "I'd like to take some fun and inspiring workshops, but I can't afford them," the doors for that stream of miracles to occur would have swung shut.

If you are claiming that you want something to occur in your life, look for any "buts" that might be lurking under the surface.

3. *The universe has a bigger plan for you than you have for yourself.* Accepting an award on a televised awards show, Oprah said, "I always believed that God had a bigger dream for me than I could dream for myself, so I always ask, 'What is Your dream for me, and will You allow me to live in that dream?'" If you want to heal the heart of the world, or create any number of miracles in your life, allowing yourself to live in God's "bigger dream" for you will help open new doors that you couldn't even possibly imagine might open for you.

4. *It's not about knowing the right answer; it's about asking the right question.* You don't have to have everything about how to accomplish your goals all figured out yourself. Asking open-ended questions, such as the very powerful question Oprah asked above, allows the universe to fill in the blanks of your life for you.

Recently, one of Dawna's juicy questions may have even helped save the planet in some significant way. One of her clients, a corporate CEO who manages one of the twenty largest companies in the world, had to give a speech to five thousand individuals from around the globe who represent a major industry. According to Dr. Markova, these people were "part of destroying the world right now."

The morning of his speech, she asked the CEO this question: "What are you going to tell your daughters at the end of the day about what you talked about?"

At first, he questioned her. "What do you mean?"

304

She replied, "What if you told them, 'Tonight I gave a speech to five thousand people, and what I said in this speech was for you to...' What would you say?" The CEO didn't answer.

That evening, in the middle of reading his speech, he stopped and looked up. Then he said, "A friend of mine asked me what I'm going to tell my daughters at the end of this speech. I think all of us need to think about what we're doing and how we would describe it to our daughters. If we can't describe it to our daughters, then maybe we ought to rethink what we're doing."

"This man has more money than he could ever spend in his and his children's entire life, but he's so poor," says Dr. Markova. "His heart is poor; his life doesn't nourish him. He doesn't nourish life. While his speech would have fostered more of the Earth being destroyed, one simple question opened the door to a new possibility."

5.   *The universe can only give you as much as you are able to receive.*

Many people who desire to heal the world are comfortable in the role of giver, but feel entirely uncomfortable when it comes to receiving. If you say "No," or feel any sense of resistance or discomfort when you are offered a gift of any kind, you have set principle number two into motion: *The universe will never give you a "yes...but."* The more you say, "No," to the little gifts that come your way, the more you close down the opportunity for bigger gifts to reach you.

-§-
Do whatever it takes to let go of the victim stance, no matter what the situation.
-§-

On the other hand, if you keep saying, "Yes," to the little gifts that are offered, and put up no resistance, just look at the stories above to see how far your "Yes" might take you. In my case, I went from an $85 ticket to a $10,000 training.

6.   *Reach for joy.* Every time we lighten up, good things happen. The universe will never reward whining, moaning, or negativity from anyone. If you want to see a miracle occur in your life, do whatever it takes to let go of the victim stance, no matter what the situation. Step into a place of empowerment in the midst of any difficult circumstances and watch for miraculous outcomes.

When Suzanne Baker heard the news that she had cancer in her bottom eyelid, at first, she felt tremendous apprehension and disbelief. The news that her doctor would not be

able to perform surgery for three more months left her feeling even more upset. However, as a Miracle Thinker, Suzanne decided that staying in fear and being upset would not help her. Instead, she chose to focus on the outcome she wanted, which was to have the surgery within the week, before her new teaching job started up. A few days later, the doctor's office called. They could fit her into surgery that week.

A few days before the surgery, as her fear was mounting, Suzanne realized she needed to reframe the whole situation if she wanted a miraculous outcome to occur. She decided to think of the experience as if she was going to a party. When the doctor's office called three different times to change the time for the surgery, each time, Suzanne got excited that they were making plans for her party. The night before she went to surgery, she also had a chakra-balancing energy session with a woman who could help her prepare even more for her party.

-§-

Divine right timing always trumps our own sense of what we think the timing of circumstances in our lives should be.

-§-

The morning of the surgery, instead of feeling fearful, Suzanne awakened in peace. When the doctor's office called to confirm that she was on her way, she told them, "I wouldn't miss my party!"

Arriving at the surgical unit, she wore a "party hat": a straw voters' hat with a red, white, and blue ribbon around it, which was significant to her because her birthday was on July fourth. Red, white, and blue were colors that she always wore for her party on her birthday.

"This is my party hat," she told everybody. "Let's go to the party." Of course, all of the surgeons and medical personnel appearing in their scrubs were all wearing their own versions of party hats.

Although Suzanne didn't know one person in the town where she was being operated upon, the nurse who prepped her for the operation turned out to be a friend of a friend who participated in a miracles group that was an hour away from that town. The serendipity of the moment contributed to Suzanne's special party atmosphere. The nurse asked her if she wanted a tranquilizer. Still feeling completely at ease, she declined.

Suzanne's attitude was contagious. A young man who was being prepped for his surgery behind an adjoining curtain overheard Suzanne's party talk. As he was being wheeled into his surgery, Suzanne overheard him say, "Let the party begin!"

Next the anesthesiologist arrived. His party hat featured an assortment of colorful canines. Suzanne and the doctor began to banter as though they were old friends sharing a laugh. Continuously, she felt no fear about what was about to happen, even though the doctor warned her about the stinging that might occur as the anesthesia was administered and the nausea that might happen afterwards.

When she was in the surgery room, the medical team made a big production over her hat. One said, "What is this here for?" Another replied, "That's her party hat." The anesthesiologist said, "Let her keep it if it makes her happy." Laughing, a nurse replied, "Well, this is a first." They all laughed about it and it lightened up the feeling in the room.

The surgery was entirely successful. The cancer was isolated in a very tiny area. Suzanne felt no stinging from the anesthesia or nausea afterwards. She remained happy to have had such a fun party.

During what might be considered a very stressful experience, it seems that the more she reached for joy, the more it kept unfolding.

7. *Just do it!* Miracle Thinkers take action. They don't just sit around waiting for miracles to happen. When you are clear on which way to go...step forward. Every time you come up with a great reason as to why you didn't accomplish what you said you intended to accomplish, say to yourself, "The dog ate my homework." It's all just an excuse. You will see that what is stopping you is some sense of underlying resistance. Since the universe will never give you a "Yes...but," if you find yourself saying "The dog ate my homework" frequently, you'll know you've chosen a direction that is not in alignment with your core at this time, at which point, you can choose again.

More often than not, Miracle Thinkers:

*   Make choices and take actions that continually lead to the cultivation of a miracle mindset.

*   Express themselves without censoring themselves due to a fear of being judged.

*   Step into and live their truth.

CHAPTER THIRTY

- Choose to never withhold anything from anyone for any length of time.
- Take action that supports their growth.
- Make phone calls and do follow-ups.
- Let go of the victim stance.
- Step away from that which is not for their highest good.
- Say "Yes" to life more often than they say "No."
- Go with the flow.

As you develop your ability as a Miracle Thinker, you might notice results beginning to occur immediately. On the other hand, if it feels like it's taking forever to create your desired outcome, one of three things is possible: 1) either you are not clearly aligned with your perceived goal and a part of you still fears the achievement of it; 2) the goal you've chosen is not for your highest good and the highest good of all; or 3) you might be going through "W-A-I-T Training," in which case a) there are more things for you to learn before you can have what it is that you want, or b) there is a timing issue involved in which there are certain people you need to meet, or resources you need to have, that aren't in place yet. Divine right timing always trumps our own sense of what we think the timing of circumstances in our lives should be.

You also can't manipulate the universe into giving anything to you. When no doors seem to be opening, think of this time as the "ripening time." Even if you are already a very deep person, it's guaranteed that you are being deepened even more by the divine source that created you.

Miracle Thinking is strengthened by faith. If your faith is strong, does this mean that your desired miracle will happen every time? It won't if the result you've chosen is not in your highest and best interest, and for the highest and best interest for all. However, cultivating a Miracle Mindset will move you closer to receiving the highest good that is intended for you, which may or may not bring you the specific outcome you desire. The trick is to maintain your Miracle Mindset and stay the course, regardless.

We've got this little space called "life"...and it happens between birth and death. It's just this little space with our name on it, for however long we have it, so make the best of it. Apply some of these Miracle Thinking tips and come up with more of your own. The more you develop your Miracle Thinking mindset, the more miracles will flow to you to heal yourself and the heart of the world.

PART SIX

The Emerging Scientific Revolution

DEAN ORNISH:

Love As Though Your Very Survival Depended On It

I am not aware of any other factor in medicine—not diet, smoking, exercise, stress, genetics, drugs or surgery—that has a greater impact on our quality of life, incidence of illness, or possibility of premature death than love and intimacy. Scientific studies show that people who feel lonely, depressed, and isolated are five times more likely to get sick and to die prematurely compared to those who have a sense of love, connection and community. The need for love and intimacy is a basic human need that's as fundamental as eating, drinking, and sleeping. And we ignore it at our own peril.

For example, one study at Duke University found that five years after an angiogram, half of those who were unmarried and had no confidant had died, compared to only 20% of those who either were married, or were unmarried but had a confidant. If they were married, but not particularly happily married, they still lived longer than people who weren't married. Again, I think it comes down to feeling known. Even in an unhappy marriage, at least the person knows you.

An extended family, a long-term neighborhood, or a church or synagogue used to provide a place where you were seen—and not just the parts of you that were the most likable, but also your darker parts. Those people were there for you, regardless.

Part of the value of a group is the re-creation of that lost sense of community where people feel safe enough to talk about their experiences without fear of abandonment or rejection. At a feeling level, we

Dean Ornish, M.D., is one of America's best-known medical authorities. His ground-breaking experiments led to the development of diet- and exercise-based therapies that reversed heart disease without drugs or surgery, and earned him international renown, including the covers of news magazines and appearances on many national television shows. He is the author of *Eat More, Weigh Less* (HarperCollins, 1997), *Love and Survival* (HarperCollins, 1998), and several other books. He is the founder and president of the Preventive Medicine Research Institute in Sausalito, (www.pmri.org) and Clinical Professor of Medicine at the University of California, San Francisco.

all want to be happy. We all want to avoid suffering. We struggle with similar life issues. When we talk about our issues it gives other people the courage to open up as well.

Healing is linked to how you react to suffering—be it betrayal, loss or any other aspect of being human. It's not that we should be without emotional defenses—they serve a function to protect us from pain. But if you have nowhere that feels safe enough to let down those defenses, and you have no one that you trust enough to open up to, then in effect, your walls are always up. If you've been hurt or betrayed, there's a natural fear of opening your heart. Ironically, the same defenses that we think protect us are actually killing us, or making us more likely to get sick and die prematurely. Hopefully, knowing this will give people the courage to begin the process of opening their hearts again.

-§-
The same defenses that we think protect us are actually killing us.
-§-

The heart is a pump that needs to be addressed on a physical level, but our hearts are more than just pumps. A true physician is more than just a plumber, technician, or mechanic. We also have an emotional heart, a psychological heart, and a spiritual heart. Our language reflects that understanding. We yearn for our sweethearts, not our sweetpumps. Poets and musicians and artists and writers and mystics throughout the ages have described those who have an open heart or a closed heart, a warm heart or a closed heart, a compassionate heart or an uncaring heart. Love heals. These are metaphors, a reflection of our deeper wisdom, not just figures of speech.

The real epidemic in our culture is not only physical heart disease, but also what I call emotional and spiritual heart disease—that is, the profound feelings of loneliness, isolation, alienation, and depression that are so prevalent in our culture with the breakdown of the social structures that used to provide us with a sense of connection and community. It is, to me, a root of the illness, cynicism, and violence in our society.

The healing power of love and relationships has been documented in an increasing number of well-designed scientific studies involving hundreds of thousands of people throughout the world. When you feel loved, nurtured, cared for, supported, and intimate, you are much more likely to be happier and healthier. You have much lower risk of getting sick and, if you do, a much greater chance of surviving.

You can only be intimate to the degree that you're willing to open your heart and make yourself emotionally vulnerable to someone else. In my own case, I am in a committed, monogamous relationship with my wife. Our commitment to each other creates a sacred space— sacred meaning the "most special," a place where we feel increasing trust and safety with each other. We have that intentionality, that commitment to open our hearts wider and wider as we begin to trust each other more and more. As we do, the level of joy and intimacy and ecstasy is like nothing we ever could have dreamed.

Love promotes survival. Both nurturing and being nurtured are life-affirming. Anything that takes you outside of yourself promotes healing—in profound ways that can be measured—independent of other factors such as diet and exercise. There is a strong scientific basis documenting that these ideas matter—across all ages from infants to the most elderly, in all parts of the world, in all strata of life.

-§-

Love promotes survival. Both nurturing and being nurtured are life-affirming.

-§-

I've had patients say to me, "Having a heart attack was the best thing that ever happened to me." I would say, "That sounds crazy. What do you mean?" They'd respond, "Because that's what it took to get my attention—to begin making these changes I probably never would have done otherwise—that have made my life so much more rich, peaceful, joyful and meaningful."

Part of the value of science is to help raise the level of awareness for people so that they don't have to suffer as much to gain insight. Awareness is the first step in healing. They don't have to wait until they get a heart attack to begin taking these ideas seriously and making them part of their lives.

Intimacy is anything that takes you out of the experience of feeling separate and only separate. It can come in many forms. Most people think in terms of romantic intimacy, but intimacy can be between friends or family members, or even with pets. In fact, in one study, people with heart disease who had a dog had four times less sudden cardiac death than those who didn't have one. Intimacy can also be on a spiritual level, where prayer, meditation, or other spiritual practices can give us the direct experience of feeling like we're part of something larger that connects us all. In that timeless moment, wherever we go, we find only our own kith and kin in a thousand and one disguises; the Sufi poet Rumi wrote:

> There is a community of the spirit.
> Join it, and feel the delight
> of walking in the noisy street...
> Why do you stay in prison
> when the door is so wide open?
> Move outside the tangle of fear-thinking...
> Flow down and down in always
> widening rings of being.

BRUCE LIPTON:

The Biology of Inspiration

While I hold a vision of a wholesome future, we are currently confronted with a crisis of global proportions. Scientists have determined that Earth's biosphere is in the throes of experiencing its sixth mass extinction. Five previous mass extinctions, each of which almost wiped out life on the planet, are attributed to extraterrestrial forces such as comets or asteroids hitting the Earth. The current extinction is driven by forces much closer to home, for it is recognized that human civilization is the primary cause behind the current crisis.

This is not the first time, nor will it be the last, that civilization will come face to face with its own mortality. Historian Arnold Toynbee described society as a living "organism" that grows with momentum, reaches equilibrium—and then goes into "overbalance," which produces new environmental *challenges*. Social cycles are driven by patterns of *challenge-and-response*. *Challenges* from the environment provoke a *response* in society.

According to Toynbee, the cultural mainstream inevitably clings to fixed ideas and rigid patterns in the face of imposing challenges. From among their ranks arise *creative minorities* that resolve the threatening *challenges* with more viable *responses*. Creative minorities are active agents that transform old, outdated philosophical elements into new, life-sustaining cultural beliefs.

Bruce Lipton, Ph.D., is an internationally recognized authority in bridging science and spirit. A cell biologist by training, he taught anatomy at the University of Virginia, and later performed pioneering studies at Stanford University's School of Medicine. He has been a guest speaker on dozens of TV and radio shows, as well as keynote presenter for national conferences. His breakthrough studies on the cell membrane presaged the new science of Epigenetics, and made him a leading voice of the new biology. His new book *The Biology of Belief* (Elite, 2005) quickly became a best seller, and you can find him on the web at www.brucelipton.com.

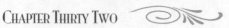

For over four hundred years, Western civilization has chosen Science as its source of truths and wisdom about the mysteries of life. Allegorically, we may picture the wisdom of the universe as resembling a large mountain. We scale the mountain as we acquire knowledge. Our drive to reach the top of that mountain is fueled by the notion that with knowledge, we may become "masters" of our universe. Conjure the image of the all-knowing guru seated atop the mountain.

Scientists are professional seekers, forging the path up the Mountain of Knowledge. Their search takes them into the uncharted unknowns of the universe. Through each scientific discovery, humanity gains a better foothold in scaling the mountain. Ascension is paved one scientific discovery at a time. Along its path, Science occasionally encounters a fork in the road. Do we take the left turn or the right? When confronted with this dilemma, the direction chosen by Science is determined by the consensus of scientists interpreting the acquired facts, as they are understood at the time.

Occasionally, scientists have embarked in a direction that ultimately leads to an apparent dead end. When that situation arises we are faced with two choices, continue to plod forward with the hope that science will eventually discover a way around the impediment, *or*, return back to the fork and reconsider the alternate path. Unfortunately, the more Science invests in a particular path, the more difficult it is for Science to let go of beliefs that keep them on that path. As Toynbee suggests, the cultural— and scientific—mainstream inevitably clings to fixed ideas, beliefs that no longer serve us on our mission. Even when confronting a dead end, the scientific discoveries acquired on that path are important contributions to our collective knowledge.

-§-
Scientists have determined that Earth's biosphere is in the throes of experiencing its sixth mass extinction.
-§-

The path that Science is currently navigating has inadvertently brought us to our current moment of global crisis. Since the Modern Scientific Revolution, starting with the publication of Copernicus's observation that the Earth orbits the sun in 1543, Science has perceived of the universe as a physical machine that operated on the mechanical principles later defined by Newtonian physics. In the Newtonian worldview, the Universe is defined by its material reality and its operation could be understood through *reductionism*, the process of taking matter apart and studying its bits and pieces. Knowledge of the universe's parts and how they interact would enable science to predict and control nature. This notion of control is contained within *determinism,* the belief that with knowledge of something's parts, we can predict its behavior.

The reductionist approach to understanding the nature of the universe has provided valuable knowledge that has enabled us to fly to the moon, transplant artificial hearts and read the genetic code. However, applying this science to world problems has hastened our demise. It is a simple fact that society cannot sustain itself by continuing to adhere to its current worldview. To extricate ourselves from the problems we face, we must appeal to a "new" science, one that offers the *new thinking* needed to generate intelligent responses to our global challenges.

Leading edge research is currently questioning fundamental assumptions long held as dogma by conventional science. New science curricula must be developed to accommodate challenges to the following three conventional tenets of biomedical research:

1. Life operates according to Newtonian mechanics;

2. Life is controlled by genes, and,

3. Life arose through neo-Darwinian evolution.

In contrast to conventional reductionism, a new science curriculum would be based upon holism, the belief that an understanding of Nature and the human experience requires that we transcend the parts to see the whole. Though materialism has engendered the idea that we are disconnected from and above nature, the new vision emphasizes that life represents an integration and coordination with both a physical and an immaterial universe. The resolution of our global crisis will be solved through an integration of both reductionist and holistic principles.

The accumulated knowledge of scientists has been assembled into a hierarchical construction resembling a multi-tiered building. Each level of the building is built upon the scientific foundation provided in the supporting lower levels. Each floor of the building is classified as a scientific subspecialty.

The foundation of the "Science" building is Math. Upon math, we assemble the building's second level, Physics. Built upon physics is the building's third level, Chemistry. Chemistry serves as the platform of the next tier, Biology. Built upon biology is the building's current top floor, Psychology.

Curriculum renovations would not only strengthen Science's foundation, they also provide for Noetic Science, a new scientific tier. Hopefully, as one ascends through the curriculum, the integration of the evolving sciences, from tier to tier, will provide them with the mastery to enable humans to thrive on this planet.

Fundamental to a new scientific curriculum is the foundation offered by Math. Mathematical laws are absolute, certain and indisputable, while those of other sciences are to some extent debatable and in constant danger of being revised by newly discovered facts. As Einstein once remarked, "…there is another reason for the high repute of mathematics: it is mathematics that offers the exact natural sciences a certain measure of security which, without mathematics, they could not attain." Before Newton could derive his principles of physics he first had to create its mathematics: differential calculus.

The emphasis of the new math program is on Fractal Geometry and Chaos Theory. Geometry is the science of structure in space, the way the different parts of something fit together in relation to each other. For centuries our math has been used to isolate and divide the

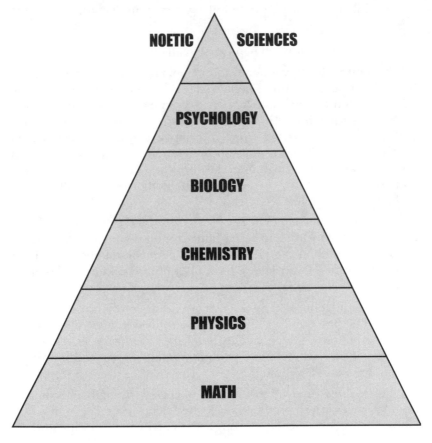

The Structure of Science

universe into separate measurable components that allowed us to focus on the nature of the individual parts.

Formerly we emphasized Euclidian geometry, the math involved with cones, cubes and parabolas whose points and shapes we mapped on graph paper. While we use Euclidian geometry to construct our material world, it is a math that does not readily relate to nature. A mountain is not really an inverted cone. When we were children, we drew "Euclidian" trees that were composed of cylindrical trunks crowned with spheres. Though representative of a tree, it is not the shape of a natural tree.

Fractals are a modern version of geometry, officially defined in 1983 by IBM scientist Benoit Mandelbrot. It is actually a simple mathematics based upon an equation involving addition and multiplication, in which the result is entered back into the original equation and solved again. Repetition of the equation inherently provides for a geometry expressing self-similar objects that appear at higher or lower levels of the equation's magnitude. The organization at any level of nature, like nested Russian dolls, reflects a self-similar pattern to organizations found at higher or lower levels of reality. For example, the structure and behavior of a human cell is self-similar to the structure and behavior of a human, which in turn is self-similar to the structure and behavior of humanity. This math substantiates the ancient wisdom implied in the axiom, "As above, so below."

Fractal geometry provides for structures resembling those of the natural world, such as mountains, clouds, plants, and animals. The dynamics of fractal structures are directly influenced by Chaos Theory, a math that is concerned with the nature by which small changes may cause unexpected final effects. Chaos theory concerns the processes by which the flap of a butterfly's wing in Asia may influence the formation of a tornado in Oklahoma. When chaos theory is combined with fractal formulae, the math further defines the behavioral dynamics observed in our physical reality—from weather patterns to human physiology; from social patterns to market prices on the stock exchange.

This new math offers profound insights into the operation of the universe. Information acquired by studying a process at any particular level of nature can be applied toward an understanding of knowledge of self-similar events at other levels of nature. A study of cells enables us to understand the behavior of a human. The behavior of cells within a human can provide us with the behavioral patterns needed by humans to learn to survive as a coherent civilization. Fractal geometry emphasizes that the observable physical universe is derived from the integration and interconnectivity of all of its parts.

Fractal geometry and chaos mathematics are fundamental to constructing modern physics, science's "first floor." A century ago, a creative minority launched a radical new view of how the universe works. Albert Einstein, Max Planck and Werner Heisenberg, among others, formulated new theories concerning the underlying mechanics of the universe. Their work on Quantum Mechanics revealed that the universe is derived from a holistic entanglement of immaterial energy waves—and not from an assembly of physical parts as suggested by Newtonian physics. Quantum mechanics shockingly reveals that there is no true "physicality" in the universe; atoms are made of focused vortices of energy, miniature tornados that are constantly popping into and out of existence.

Atoms are not made of physical matter as we have perceived it; consequently, neither are the molecules, cells or humans made from them.

> -§-
> Quantum Mechanics revealed that the universe is derived from a holistic entanglement of immaterial energy waves—and not from an assembly of physical parts.
> -§-

Newtonian physics emphasizes *separatism*, while quantum physics stresses *holism*. Atoms as energy fields interact with the full spectrum of invisible energy fields that comprise the universe; atoms are intimately entangled with each other and the field in which they are immersed.

A fundamental conclusion of the new physics acknowledges that the "observer creates the reality." As observers, we are personally involved with the creation of our own reality! Physicists are being forced to admit that the universe is a "mental" construction. Pioneering physicist Sir James Jeans wrote, "the stream of knowledge is heading towards a non-mechanical reality; the universe begins to look more like a great thought than like a great machine. Mind no longer appears to be an accidental intruder into the realm of matter... we ought rather hail it as the creator and governor of the realm of matter."

Quantum mechanics was acknowledged as the best scientific description of the mechanisms creating our universe eighty years ago. However, some branches of science rigidly cling to the prevailing Newtonian, matter-oriented, worldview, simply because it "seems" to make better sense out our existence. This is probably the first time in history that scientists have refused to believe what their reigning theory says about the world. To grapple with the contradictions, most physicists have chosen an easy way out: they restrict quantum theory's validity to the subatomic world. Renowned theoretical physicist David Deutsch wrote, "Despite the unrivalled empirical success of quantum theory, the very suggestion that it may be literally true as a description of nature is still greeted with cynicism, incomprehension, and even anger." (Folger, 2001) However, quantum laws *must* hold at every level of reality. We can no longer afford to ignore that fact. We must learn that *our beliefs, perceptions and attitudes about the world create the world.*

Quantum physics advances have provided a new foundation for Chemistry, the building's second floor. While conventional chemistry has focused upon the atomic elements as miniature Newtonian solar systems composed of solid electrons, protons and neutrons, our new chemistry is Vibrational Chemistry, based upon quantum mechanics, and it emphasizes that atoms are made of spinning immaterial energy vortices such as quarks.

Traditionally, we emphasize the particulate character of atoms, resembling the ball and stick models built in chemistry lab courses. However, the assembly and interaction of molecules cannot be predicted by matter-based principles of Newtonian physics. Chemical mechanics and behaviors are derived from constructive and destructive interference patterns of entangled energy waves. The new chemistry is concerned with the role of vibration in creating molecular bonds and driving molecular interactions. Energy fields, such as those derived from cell phones or from thoughts, entangle with and influence chemical reactions. Vibrational Chemistry defines the mechanisms that mediate mind-body connections.

-§-
Atoms are not made of physical matter as we have perceived it; consequently, neither are the molecules, cells or humans made from them.
-§-

Science's third floor, Biology, is built upon a foundation of Physics and Chemistry. Biology, like chemistry, has been investigated using a reductionist philosophy; organisms are dissected into cells, and cells into molecular parts, to gain understanding as to how they work. The new biology perceives of cells and organisms as integrated communities that are physically and energetically entangled within the environment.

The new holism endorses James Lovelock's hypothesis that the Earth and the biosphere represent a single living and breathing entity known as Gaia. Our careless disregard for Nature's holism and our insistence that we are here to "dominate and control Nature" has unwittingly led us to injure and damage the very environment that gives us life. Gaian Physiology would represent a course designed to reacquaint us with our connection to the planet and to our ancient role as the Garden's caretakers.

Central to the new biology is the emerging science of Epigenetics. Epigenetics, which literally translates as "control above *(epi-)* the

genes," provides for a second genetic code that controls the activity and programming of an organism's DNA. This new hereditary mechanism describes how behavior and gene activity are controlled by an organism's perception of its environment.

The fundamental difference between the old view of DNA as containing the entire genetic code, and epigenetics, is that former notion endorses *genetic determinism,* the belief that genes predetermine and control our physiologic and behavioral traits. In contrast, epigenetics reveals that our perceptions of the environment, including our consciousness, actively control our genes. Through epigenetic mechanisms, applied consciousness can be used to shape our biology and make us "masters" of our own lives.

Rather than endorsing a Darwinian evolution based upon random mutations and a struggle for survival, a new sense of Fractal Evolution defines the biosphere as a cooperative communal venture among all living organisms. Rather than invoking competition as a means of survival, the new view of evolution is one driven by cooperation among species and with their physical environment. A change in our perception, from a life based upon competition to one of cooperation is vital to our survival.

-§-
Our beliefs, perceptions and attitudes about the world create the world.
-§-

The fractal character of evolution reveals that the patterns of life are reiterated throughout nature. Applying the principles of biopolitics used among the cells of our trillion-celled bodies to human civilization would readily support a healthy thriving world of seven billion people, allowing us to live in harmony. As Toynbee suggested, humanity is an evolving living organism in which every human is a constituent "cell." We must own that every human being counts, for each is a member of a single organism. When we war, we are warring against ourselves.

Holistic revisions in the supporting sciences of physics, chemistry and biology provide for a radically remodeled fifth tier, Psychology. For centuries, our materialistic perspective dismissed the immaterial mind and consciousness as an epiphenomenon of the mechanical body. We believed that the action of genes and neurochemicals, the hardware of the central nervous system, were responsible for our behaviors and our dysfunctions.

The foundation of quantum mechanics, vibrational chemistry and epigenetic control mechanisms provide for a profoundly new understanding of psychology. It is now recognized that the environment, in conjunction with the perceptions of the mind, controls the behavior and genetics of biology. Our life experiences are recorded as the programmed perceptions constituting the mind. Rather than being "programmed" by our genes, our lives are controlled by our perceptions of life experiences.

The switch from Newtonian to quantum mechanics changes the focus of psychology from physiochemical mechanisms to the role of energy fields. The new psychology is an Energy Psychology. Energy psychology deals with the software of programming consciousness rather than focusing on the physiochemical hardware that mechanistically expresses behavior. Energy psychology directly impacts subconscious programming rather than trying to manipulate genetics, physiology and behavior.

An informative and important course on Conscious Parenting would emphasize the vital role that parents play in programming their child's genes and behaviors. Understanding this new science will enable parents to provide developmental experiences that will enhance the health, intelligence and happiness of their children. Fundamental perceptions have the power to program the subconscious mind. Primal life-shaping experiences are primarily downloaded between fetal development and the first six years of a child's life. Dysfunctional-programmed perceptions, like computer files, can be edited and rewritten using non-invasive energy psychology healing modalities.

This new pyramid only strengthens the conventional sciences; it forms the foundation for a new tier, an all-encompassing field of Noetic Science. Investigations of the cell's brain, its membrane, reveal that the community of cells comprising each human is distinguished by unique clusters of protein markers on the cell surfaces. No two humans are the same and no two humans display the same sets of membrane surface proteins. The membrane protein receptors on the cell's surface are literally antennas that receive and respond to a precisely defined spectrum of environmental "energy waves." Consequently, the individuality of each human is defined by the unique spectrum of extracellular environmental signals received by their "self-receptors." Simply put, our identities are environmental vibrations that play through our cells; we are not in our bodies.

-§-
Epigenetics reveals that our perceptions of the environment, including our consciousness, actively control our genes.
-§-

These environmental signals precede and transcend our earthly life. Life experiences perceived by the body are incorporated into our personal information fields. Our lives are connected to an energy information pattern comprising our environmental field. The information spectrum represents an invisible moving force, which many refer

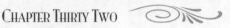

to as a soul or spirit, that is in harmonic resonance with our physical bodies. This spiritual realm is the creative force behind our conscious minds. Noetic Science recognizes that there is a larger, more encompassing Noetic Consciousness from which the spirit is derived.

By integrating and balancing the awareness of our Noetic Consciousness into our physical consciousness, we will be empowered to become true creators of our life experiences. When such an understanding reigns, we and the Earth will once again have the opportunity to create the Garden of Eden.

The first half of Modern Science was preoccupied with reducing our world to separate bits and pieces. These efforts have provided information that has enabled humans to look out into the deepest regions of the universe and peer into the inner workings of a single atom. While the technology derived from reductionist science is miraculous in its nature, our use of it is destroying our civilization.

-§-
Fractal Evolution defines the biosphere as a cooperative communal venture among all living organisms.
-§-

New science recognizes that life is more than the study of its individual parts. The revised curriculum balances our historic reductionist perspective with the evolving concepts of holism. By focusing on the power of interactive, autopoetic communities, whether they are comprised of energy waves, chemicals, cells or humans, we will be able to realize the peace inherent in our oneness.

As human beings engaged in the great work of re-creating our selves, our species and our planet, our mission is to seek creative responses to the challenges before us. Traditionally, reductionist science has sought resolutions by delving deeper into the material fabric of nature. In contrast, new science directs our attention to the heretofore-invisible matrix of entangled immaterial forces that shape and energize our world. Our holistic pursuit compels us to pull back from studying the trees, and own the scope and magnitude of the forest. From that perspective, we are obliged to recognize the power Noetic Consciousness plays in shaping our lives, our world and our challenges. This new life-sustaining awareness echoes the words of physicist R.C. Henry in his recent essay in *Nature*, "The Universe is immaterial—mental and spiritual. Live and enjoy." (Henry, 2005)

Joseph Patrick Kelly with Cryslea Russell:

Unpollution

Imagine driving along a country road in a convertible sports car on a gorgeous spring day. Enchanted by the scent of wild flowers in the air, you say a prayer of praise and appreciation, taking pleasure in the warmth of the sun on your face. As you wind around a slow banking curve, the sight of a mother deer and her two spotted fawns grazing on a bright green ridge takes your breath away. Coming out of the curve, you accelerate to take the next ridge and spot a hawk circling high in the sky.

At the crest of the hill, you see a lush valley spread out before you with a small industrial plant nestled against rolling hills to the west. There is a flurry of activity around the plant. *A factory?* You wonder. *Out here?* It strikes you as quite odd that a factory would be built in this lovely natural setting.

Once you get closer, you can see that a string of green refuse trucks is pulling into the plant from a neatly paved side road. You notice that the trucks bear the logo of the local garbage company. An occasional white truck with red crosses painted on the side comes down the road. You recognize them as medical waste trucks from the local hospital. You wonder, *why here?* You are aware that hospitals wards are a major source of hazardous and toxic waste. The next thing you see really gets your curiosity pumping—giant brown dump trucks you know are part of a fleet that serves the most serious industrial polluters in the region: the paper mill, a fertilizer factory,

Joseph Patrick Kelly is the president and CEO of e3 Energy Company (www. e3energyco.com). He played a critical role in a wide variety of global energy projects, valued at several billion dollars, with Westinghouse, General Electric, and Exxon. He holds a B.S. in Thermo-mechanical and Energy Conversion Engineering from the University of Illinois, and an MBA from Fordham. He directed the commercial activities of a $500 million clean coal project as the Vice President of Commercial Operations for the U.S. Department of Energy, and chaired the Regulatory Affairs Committee of the Gulf Coast Cogeneration Association. His executive assistant Cryslea Russell co-authored this chapter.

a computer chip manufacturer, several industrial chemical plants, a steel mill, and the largest oil refinery in the state.

You pull into the factory's parking lot and get out of your car to investigate. Over the next hour you learn that this is no ordinary factory. From the far side of the plant, pipes that produce hydrogen rich *syngas* run into the ground. The first pipe contains hydrogen. It feeds all the hydrogen-fuel stations in the neighboring cities. Everyone you know has switched to a fuel-cell vehicle. The new streamlined cars have almost completely replaced the dirty petrol-burning cars of old since hydrogen became cheap and plentiful.

> -§-
> Visionary entrepreneurs will construct hundreds more clean and green plants across the globe over the course of the next decade.
> -§-

A second pipe running out of the plant carries ethanol. Pumped into tanker trucks, the ethanol is delivered to gas stations and sold to those who still drive vehicles with an internal combustion engine.

The third pipe contains shimmering, iridescent glass bricks. These bricks—much prized for both their decorative beauty and their durability—are loaded onto flatbed trucks and sold to contractors in the construction and landscaping trades.

You learn that this is one of the plants you vaguely remember hearing about that generates clean electric power and produces fuel cells. It is obvious from the look of the thriving landscape all around that the plant emits no pollution. No smokestacks, no belching fumes, no thrumming transformers or high-voltage lines bringing in power. The entire plant is self-contained; it generates its own electricity, and is completely pollution-free.

This scene may sound like futuristic fantasy or science fiction, but in actuality, it is not all that far off. A plant very much like the one described above is demonstrating this technology today in Bristol, Connecticut. Visionary entrepreneurs will construct hundreds more clean and green plants across the globe over the course of the next decade. That's the vision and mission of my company, e3 Energy Company. In partnership with Startech Corporation, we are changing the face of this world—or, better yet, bringing an all-natural face-lift to the world.

How the Miracle is Worked

Plasma conversion technology takes hazardous organic waste material and breaks the molecular bonds, transforming it into basic gaseous elemental forms. Our computer-controlled Plasma Converter™

consists of a feed system, a plasma vessel, a power supply, and a gas polisher. No matter what material is fed into the converter—solid, liquid, or gas, organic or inorganic—the Plasma Converter accepts the material and renders its content harmless. Other than radioactive material, the converter accepts all forms of hazardous or non-hazardous, toxic or nontoxic waste. It operates safely and quietly at normal atmospheric pressure.

The converter uses plasma—which is basically a form of ionized gas that many scientists call the fourth state of matter. Plasma is by far the most common material in the universe. Plasma—which has been used for decades in many ways by business and industry, as well as in the space program, transportation, energy, education, and national security—is a highly effective electrical conductor. Within the vessel of the Converter, it is made to produce a lightning-like arc of electricity. The arc in the plasma plume within the vessel exceeds 30,000° Fahrenheit—three times hotter than the surface of the sun. When subjected to such an intense energy transfer within the vessel, the molecular bonds found in most waste materials are excited past the point of rupture and broken into their elemental atomic components. Said simply, the powerful radiant energy of the plasma arc rips apart the molecular bonds in waste.

The extremely high temperatures created in the oxygen-starved vessel within the converter result in the complete and irreversible destruction of virtually any type of input waste material. This is a far more effective method of waste management than the pollution-producing practices of incineration, or digging more and more landfills. The plasma recycling process always yields elemental atoms, or very small molecules in the form of a combustible gas or an inert glass-like material.

-§-

Plasma conversion changes waste substances into simplified, highly useful, and environmentally-friendly forms.

-§-

Inorganic material contained in the waste—such as metals, salts, and rocks—either retain their atomic structure or get broken into individual atomic components as well. Either way, they are sealed in a non leachable glass-like matrix.

The plasma process is one of no-loss elemental recycling. Plasma conversion changes waste substances into simplified, highly useful, and environmentally-friendly forms. Elemental recycling recovers the inherent energy found in all organic materials, dealing with all such substances equally. Every waste material—no matter how toxic or troublesome in its original form—is simultaneously rendered harmless—and made useful and valuable.

The Hydrogen Economy

Our domestic and worldwide energy needs are rapidly changing. The excessively high price of oil early in this new millennium is compelling us to take concrete steps toward alternatives to traditional fossil fuels — including adopting new sources of renewable energy. One such solution is the use of hydrogen as a day-to-day primary energy source. Termed the hydrogen economy, this solution puts hydrogen — in either liquid or gas form — to use as the principal source of chemical energy, replacing natural gas, heating oil, gasoline, and other petroleum products.

There are many benefits to using hydrogen as a fuel source. Hydrogen is the most abundant element in the universe. It is colorless, odorless, tasteless, and nonpoisonous. It typically exists as a molecule of two atoms of hydrogen, thus the common expression "H2." Hydrogen is attractive as a fuel source for a number of reasons. It is the most pristine of all the fuels, and readily combines with oxygen to form water and give off heat to produce power. Pound for pound, hydrogen contains more energy than any of the traditional fuels — nearly three times that of gasoline. Simply put, hydrogen used as a fuel is an ideal source of green energy.

Hydrogen is viewed so favorably not only because it eliminates tailpipe emissions when used in an internal combustion engine, but because it can reduce our dependence on foreign oil and the dwindling reserves of fossil fuels. Hydrogen is already being used in many applications, including electrical generation, industrial process heating, residential heating, transportation fuel, and much more. It is also a starting material used in numerous industrial processes to make many of the products we use in our daily lives. It can be made in very small plants, unlike the massive electric generation plants that characterize today's grid. This allows it to be made close to end-users, rather than having to be carried hundreds of miles over power lines. This exciting vision of a pollution-free "distributed power generation" industry is a radically simple yet effective model.

-§-
Pound for pound, hydrogen contains more energy than any of the traditional fuels — nearly three times that of gasoline.
-§-

The sun and stars are composed largely of hydrogen. It is found everywhere in the universe, yet is surprisingly inaccessible here on Earth. Essentially all the hydrogen produced today is made from fossil fuels, including natural gas, as their hydrocarbon molecules are dense with hydrogen atoms. The products of this "hydrogen reformation" are hydrogen and simple carbon gases. U.S. industry produces a modest fifty-five million tons of hydrogen each year.

One of the key obstacles standing in the way of a viable hydrogen economy has been the problem of finding an inexpensive source of hydrogen. Plasma Conversion is opening the door to a steadily growing supply of lower-priced hydrogen.

In fact, hydrogen obtained in this manner—from a virtually inexhaustible supply of waste—becomes a renewable energy resource, achieving an essential stepping stone in the transition to a hydrogen economy. Most common wastes and hazardous materials are excellent feed-stock for extracting hydrogen. The ever-present and constantly increasing nuisance of waste now has the potential to become a valuable, renewable resource.

-§-

The ever-present and constantly increasing nuisance of waste now has the potential to become a valuable, renewable resource.

-§-

The hydrogen produced directly from a plasma converter processing waste is perfectly suited to today's internal combustion engines. In fact, one can literally throw banana peels and apple cores in one end of a converter unit and get hydrogen out the other. Nearly all our industrial, medical, electronic, and household wastes are rich in carbon and hydrogen. Even full, inactive landfills can be valuable, as they are mined to unlock another source of inexpensive hydrogen from recovered trash.

Internal combustion engines running on hydrogen will also serve as a bridge toward developing the infrastructure needed for more advanced technologies like fuel cells, which are promising, but still have technological challenges to overcome before they become commercially viable.

Looking to support the advancement of a less expensive, significantly less polluting and more secure energy supply, the U.S. Government is on the verge of providing new incentives to promote the investment and development of a hydrogen infrastructure.

A New Business Culture

Taking care of nature, and living sustainably on the Earth, has been a passion of mine from the earliest ages. As a child, I was an explorer with a great sense of wonder, always excited to discover new things. At eight A.M. on days there was no school, I would leave the house and start running or riding my bike out into nature. The hunger to explore and discover new things stirred deeply within me. I thrived in natural surroundings—the woods enchanted me and the river

beckoned me to sail. I'd spend hours and hours in a dinghy sailing down the river, listening while treetops called me to a high adventure. Often, I climbed so high up in a tree the neighbors were frightned for my safety. Confidence and agility were always my strong suit. Being in nature always brought great joy to my soul.

After graduating as an engineer from the University of Illinois in Chicago, and getting an MBA from Fordham University, I became a consultant to Exxon and General Electric, handling worldwide energy projects running into the hundreds of millions of dollars a year. I left the U.S. to build a joint venture in Mexico City for an international consortium. I got married, and had two children. I was on track to become a corporate director. By my early thirties, every goal I had set for myself had been accomplished.

Yet despite my success in my outer world, I did not feel inner peace. My inner world was full of voids. I began a process of extensive soul searching. I began to pray deeply. I developed a more intimate relationship with God through Jesus Christ. I refocused my attention on spiritual values. I left my job, and ultimately became a consultant. My self-worth had previously been connected to my business and athletic achievements. After this transition I felt my perception of self-worth became a direct function of my relationship with God. I now knew that I had perceived life improperly through the veil of my inner wounds. I began to disconnect from the erroneous thinking of an old paradigm. This awareness began to fill the inner voids that nothing in the outer world of money, success, and power had ever been able to do. I knew I had to seek a healing process that would grow with me as I began to walk upon the path of self-discovery. I studied many spiritual philosophies. Their

-§-
Landfills can be valuable, as they are mined to unlock another source of inexpensive hydrogen from recovered trash.
-§-

insights altered my consciousness—and heart—in profound ways. The mysteries of the cosmos began to click into place in sync with my daily life. I found myself on an emotional path of healing, peace, and joy. All these experiences led me to set up e3 Energy Company as a reflection of my inner values.

While the technology described above is essential, for any solution to be effective, it must integrate the best technological solutions with cultural innovation and spiritual renewal. When our springs of spiritual inspiration meet our vocational passions, the kinds of transformational magic we witness at e3 Energy Company can result. At e3 Energy Company, we accomplish this through our core values. The acronym we use to remind ourselves of them is: CEHI 8 VBAE.

CEHI 8 VBAE is more than our favorite acronym, and is even more than the standard operating protocol for e3 Energy Company. It is our stand about the way we live our daily lives. As a business protocol, it fosters the highest quality product and working relationships. As a set of core values, it drives motivation and allows us to function at the highest level. We apply these values on a daily basis with enthusiasm and discipline.

CEHI stands for Charity, Excellence, Honor, and Integrity.

1. **Charity.** To be generous and helpful to others in our intentions and actions. The attitude of charity opens the door for growth and grace in all areas of life. The working relationship can flow for greater creativity and productivity.

-§-

My perception of self-worth became a direct function of my relationship with God.

-§-

2. **Excellence** does not mean that we have perfection. Excellence is to produce the very best quality with the resources available while ever seeking that, which is greater.

3. **Honor** relationships with respect and dignity for the contribution each person offers. Communications and transactions are entered into with honorable straightforward values.

4. **Integrity.** We expect that one's word and actions are of a high ethical order with:

   a. A strong moral code in all activities;

   b. To perform and follow through with those things we have committed to do; and

   c. To offer consideration for others to be kept aware of all pertinent aspects to maintain a high level of credibility.

The "8" in CEHI 8 VBAE represents the "as above-so below" concept. Rotated on its side the 8 becomes the symbol for infinity. Inspiration, vision, and creativity are sought to manifest the 8 principals of CEHI and VBAE.

Any value is only as good as the disciplines under which we apply it. This discipline is expressed as Vision, Blueprint, Action, and Evaluation—the VBAE.

1. **Vision.** I seek inspiration and guidance, from which vision flows.

2. **Blueprint.** I write down my blueprint every morning, after meditation and contemplation, to show me the highest good for the day ahead.

3. **Action.** When the blueprint is written and clarified I act on it.

4. **Evaluation.** This is a constant process for every aspect of the manifesting vision through the blueprint and actions taken. Did I get the vision right? Did I implement it properly? We consider what adjustments may be necessary. After a period of time we may find circumstances have changed, objectives may shift and we may need to make the appropriate changes. Flexibility is key.

A Bright Future

It is clear that the demand for hydrogen will continue to grow dramatically. e3 Energy Company Plasmatizers™ are in line to play a key role, serving as a powerful commercial force in the transition to a low-cost, renewable and pollution-free source of hydrogen.

The beauty of elemental recycling lies in the production of harmless, yet valuable by-products. Most of the world's waste products — including nearly all hazardous materials and complex molecules rich in carbon and hydrogen — are transformed into their basic elements, typically ready for use in other applications. The practical application of this technology allows e3 to turn undesirable waste streams into a continuous, recurring, and growing profitable venture.

There is significant value in the materials produced, with more uses being explored every day. Hydrogen-rich syngas (synthetic gas) can be used to make electricity, heat and cool buildings, produce fresh water and power vehicles, as well as serve as a starting material to produce useful chemicals and plastics. The inert, glass-like melt material has already filled ongoing needs in construction, insulation, road building, abrasives, and the metals industry, while new applications are constantly being developed.

-§-
Plasma conversion technology can help us capture the power of the stars to clean up the Earth!
-§-

A company called Startech, e3 Energy Company's partner in building plasma converters, is currently constructing several plants in Poland, in addition to the demonstration plant in Bristol, Connecticut, which processes five tons per day. Facilities to process from fifty to five hundreds tons per day in Poland, Germany, and Italy are on their way to completion. e3 Energy Company is also designing small mobile units that can be driven to factories, and used on site. These would take in hazardous waste from the factory and generate electricity to power the factory. These mobile units can be driven to landfills, where they are fed by hazardous wastes, and emit hydrogen syngas to fuel boilers or produce heating and cooling.

During the personal and work crisis that I experienced in the midst of my corporate career, I went on a vision quest. It was one of the most powerful experiences of spiritual renewal I have ever experienced. There is something very powerful about being alone in the wilderness, fasting and praying for inner revelation and vision. This initiation, so lacking in our society, leads to deepened understanding of ourselves, society, the natural environment, as well as the meaning and care of the soul. In the Native American tradition, the vision quest is a time to pray for a spirit name. After completing the ordeal, I received the medicine name, "Loving White Eagle."

-§-

There is something very powerful about being alone in the wilderness, fasting and praying for inner revelation and vision.

-§-

On my way home, while driving over a mountain pass in the Inyo mountains of California, a huge eagle landed on the road. It was so large, and so magnificent, that all cars stopped in both directions. The drivers stared. This was the first time in ten years that such a huge eagle had been seen in that area of the Last Chance mountain range. Members of the caravan got out of their vehicles, awestruck at the sight. I spoke to some of the drivers near me, and shared my story of receiving the spirit name I had been given.

Training as an engineer led me to look for patterns in my search for solutions. It has become clear to me that the basic equations of nature apply to all of life. Fractal patterns relate the smallest of the cosmic particles, molecular and atomic, to the same equations that govern the whole of the galactic systems.

This recycling of the basic elements found in literally all hazardous waste into safe and useful commodities offers a refreshing new way of looking at waste disposal and promises a tremendous long-term benefit to the environment and to human beings. In essence, plasma conversion technology can help us capture the power of the stars to clean up the Earth!

e3 Energy Company takes one of society's biggest problems and turns it into one of society's biggest opportunities. This kind of radical paradigm shift is possible in many other areas of our common endeavor, such as government, education, transportation, and health. Before the end of the next decade, processes and technologies will be commonplace that have not been dreamed of today. Taking our biggest problems and finding opportunities for innovation, growth, and inspiration in them requires that we think of ourselves and our world in entirely new ways. While e3 Energy Company is commit-

ted to this vision in the fields we serve, our current global crises are forcing visionaries everywhere to create solutions within their fields of endeavor — and outside of them; think of the Austrian patent clerk who conceived of the Theory of Relativity a century ago, turning physics on its head. Our planetary challenges are calling forth a generation of Einsteins; their theories and breakthroughs will ensure that the planet our children live on will be light-years more humane, clean, productive, and peaceful that the best that our generation has been able to achieve.

Jeff Schweitzer With Giuseppe Notarbartolo di Sciara:

Evolutionary Ethics

Perseverance is an admirable quality. Only with persistent and tenacious commitment can we face and overcome obstacles standing in the way of our life goals. But like any attribute, perseverance can be taken to a frustrating extreme. At some point, all of us have been in the back seat of the minivan as Dad heads down yet another dirt road, clearly lost, refusing to admit the obvious, and stubbornly refusing to ask for directions. The more noise the kids make and the more Mom rolls her eyes, the more determined Dad becomes as he obstinately plows on through back roads that have never been graced with even an honorable mention on a map.

While this example of determination gone bad has little consequence, other than getting to the hotel a few hours late and a few quarts low, the result of extreme perseverance is not always so benign. For two thousand years, humanity has obstinately pursued a path of exploitation and aggression that may well lead to our extinction. Despite numerous signs over two millennia directing us toward a more sustainable future, we drive on, pursuing with deep conviction the very course that will lead us to an evolutionary dead end. The human species is now sitting in the back of our collective minivan

Jeff Schweitzer, Ph.D., (www.jeffschweitzer.com) spent much of his youth underwater pursuing his lifelong fascination with marine life. He obtained his doctorate from Scripps Institution of Oceanography through his neurobehavioral studies of sharks and rays. He has published in an eclectic range of fields, including neurobiology, marine science, international development, environmental protection and aviation. Jeff and his wife live in central Texas since Jeff retired from the White House as Assistant Director for International Science and Technology.

Giuseppe Notarbartolo di Sciara, Ph.D., (www.disciara.net) is an evolutionary biologist with a doctorate from the University of California. He serves as a marine policy advisor to various national and international bodies, and has recently represented Italy in multilateral environmental negotiations. Through appearances on television and radio, and the publication of articles and books, he strives to increase public awareness of marine conservation. Giuseppe lives with his family in Northern Italy.

as our religious and political leaders take us down the wrong road, refusing to see the obvious, refusing to change course as we drive toward the precipice of our demise.

Going headfirst lemming-like over the edge of existence is not the only possible outcome. With the right roadmap, we can steer toward brighter times in which humans grow and prosper indefinitely in a healthy environment. The journey there requires some adjustments on our part. First we must embrace our heritage as natural members of the animal kingdom, with no special privileges on Earth and no special mandate from above. Standing at ground level, off our pedestal, we see more clearly that humanity is having a global impact on our sustaining resources through behavior and norms conditioned by a moral code inadequate to accommodate the demands of the day. With that fresh perspective, we can do something uniquely human, something that no species in the history of life has done before: we can change our ways. We can adopt a new moral code firmly rooted in a modest view of our evolutionary history, one that encourages sound environmental stewardship, promotes a general respect for life, and strengthens humankind's better side. Let's now see how to cross over to that Promised Land.

-§-
"There are only two ways to live your life. One is as though nothing is a miracle. The other is as though everything is a miracle."
—Albert Einstein
-§-

In fairness to current leadership, the cliff's edge forcing a change in direction has only recently come into view over the horizon. From the time of early civilizations up to the nineteenth century, societies across the world could be enlightened or destructive, oppressed or free, but whatever a particular group of people did, the impact tended to be constrained geographically. Rapid advances in technology over the past two hundred years have altered that landscape. The incredible benefits of our technological prowess are undeniable, but we have not always managed all of our advances responsibly, nor applied them equitably. As a consequence, the critical need to change course is now clear, evidenced by the state of our planet and the sorry plight of the vast majority of human beings.

One billion people live on less than one dollar per day. About 1.2 billion people have no access to safe fresh drinking water. Worldwide about eight hundred fifty million people live with chronic hunger and nearly nine million people die of hunger-related causes each year. In the last century, estimates are that one hundred eighty-five million people have died as a direct consequence of the carnage of war. While hard to fathom when riding in a monster SUV en route to the mall, munching on a Big Mac and fries, the common human condition is one of poverty, hunger, disease, and suffering.

But our destructive nature is not sated by exploiting each other, so we also turn our attention to the planet. We pollute the air we breathe and the water we drink; we pump billions of tons of carbon dioxide into the atmosphere, enough to change the global climate; we destroy critical habitat leading to loss of biological diversity through accelerated species extinction; we deplete fish stocks beyond the point of recovery and just move on to the next, with fewer and fewer choices each year. Orange Roughy, a fish obscure to most but sold commonly under other names, is the most recent victim of such overexploitation. The fish first became popular in the early 1990s when other commercial species were in decline; within ten years the global stock had been virtually depleted. Orange Roughy on the menu in a good fish restaurant is now as rare as fresh air in Beijing.

The Orange Roughy story is not terribly intriguing unless you like fish. But the rapid decline of an abundant fish, once widely available throughout the world's oceans, tells us a story that is potentially more interesting. Our reliance on technology to exploit resources for our growth and survival has had global effects over a short time period. All species exploit the environment to the maximum extent possible, until competition, predation, resource depletion, disease, or other constraints limit growth and expansion. Social animals, from insects to mammals, find equilibrium between cooperation and competition among existing and potential enemies. Human survival strategies are little different from those pursued by other species, except that we have a huge technological advantage.

-§-

One billion people live on less than one dollar per day.

-§-

In struggling to survive, as is our right, we have with our technology successfully co-opted a significant percentage of the planet's available resources, and waged war in shifting alliances at ever-greater cost. As a result, our efforts to survive and prosper with all available means may have the paradoxical consequence of causing our premature extinction, either directly through the use of weapons of mass destruction, or through the degradation of the resources on which we depend.

The sad state of the planet and the lamentable condition of the human occupants along for the ride are not inevitable. We could have taken a different road, but did not. Instead, the extreme impact of our global stewardship has been exacerbated by a flawed worldview dominated by a deeply-embedded but false morality that reinforces our natural tendencies to destruction. In the Western world, morality is derived directly from religion, and has been for two thousand years. As Mark Twain observed, "Man is a Religious Animal. He is the only Religious Animal. He is the only animal that has the True Religion—several of them. He is the only animal that loves his neighbor as himself and cuts his throat if his theology isn't straight." Religion, each of the True ones mentioned by Twain, has had ample time to prove itself worthy as a guiding moral force. Yet the result of that two thousand-year experiment is a world in which humanity consumes itself and the planet at an accelerating pace.

Can two thousand years of moral thought be wrong? Yes. What was appropriate in the ancient world works no longer. A moral vacuum has developed, creating a society with deeply-rooted destructive behavioral maladaptations. War, overpopulation, unrelenting poverty, indifference to the needs and rights of other life forms, and intolerance of our fellow humans all result, to an important extent, from an obsolete moral code that is unable to check our behavior in modern times. We can ill afford to wait another two thousand years to figure out that our existing worldview is not sustainable. We can and must do better.

-§-
Can two thousand years of moral thought be wrong?
-§-

The first step on the road to survival for our species is to change our perspective of self, with a more humble understanding of our evolutionary history and current place in the biosphere. Golda Meir once said to a visiting diplomat, "Don't be so humble—you are not that great." That admonition can be applied more broadly to the entire human race. We as a species pretend a false humility, but we are simply not as great as we would like to believe. Since our early ancestors first organized into clans, nearly all cultures have taught that humans are special in the eyes of their god or gods, and that the world is made for their benefit and use. Most myths concerning the origin of life, and of human life in particular, hold a special place for human beings across the globe and across time. Genesis 1:1 sets the tone:

God said, "Let us make man in our image, in our likeness, and let them rule over the fish of the sea and the birds of the air, over the livestock, over all the earth, over all the creatures that move along the ground." So God created man in his own image, in the image of god he created him; male and female he created them.

Christian origin myth though is by no means unique in placing humankind in an exalted position. With a few notable exceptions, Greek gods came in the form of human beings, apparently all of whom went to the gym regularly. The female gods all appear to have flat tummies and pert breasts, sometimes with one exposed, while their male counterparts boast the ultimate hard bodies, even before being rendered in stone.

Many of our problems originate in this hubris of imagining ourselves at the center of the universe, separate from and better than other animals. But human beings are neither special nor inevitable. As a minor branch on a vast evolutionary bush, modern humans have been roaming the earth for no more than a few hundred thousand years of the earth's 4.5 billion year history. If the earth's lifespan were one year, humans would come on the scene only during the last 50 minutes of the year. Ours has been a truly brief presence, barely a cameo on the stage of life, with too little time to demonstrate if the evolution of large brains is a successful strategy for long-term survival of the species.

As are all creatures, humans are a genetic experiment resulting from selective pressure, random mutations, and pure chance that our ancestors avoided extinction from catastrophic events, such as meteorite impacts. Humans are certainly unique, with their combined abilities to reason, to communicate with complex language, and to modify their environment on a global scale. But cheetahs are unique too in their ability to run over one hundred km per hour (sixty mph). Sperm whales alone can dive to two thousand meters (nearly sixty one hundred feet) on a single breath. Hummingbirds are the only aviators that can hover in mid-air, shift sideways and fly backwards by flapping their wings up to two hundred times per second while precisely controlling the wing's angle of attack. Specialized bacteria live in deep sea volcanic thermal springs in temperatures up to 113°C (235°F), where no other creatures on Earth could survive.

-§-

Since our early ancestors first organized into clans, nearly all cultures have taught that humans are special in the eyes of their god or gods.

-§-

Each species, including humans, occupies a special place on the evolutionary bush according to its unique characteristics. As humans we happen to possess a well-developed central nervous system as one of our defining traits; this evolutionary development has provided us with the ability to contemplate ourselves and our future. But large complex brains are simply another extreme in the development of animal traits, just as speed and strength are found in extremes in other animals. It is the height of folly to claim that evolution was driven toward humans as the pinnacle of achievement. One could claim with equal validity that evolution advances toward a pinnacle of speed, or that bacteria are the perfect creation because only they can occupy extreme conditions of temperature, salinity, pressure, and acidity.

In fact, if evolution had a pinnacle, bacteria would rest on top. A small digression into their microscopic world will help illustrate that the evolution of large brains confers no exalted status on the human race. While our sensitivities may be offended, we are living not in the Age of Man, but in the Age of Ancient Bacteria, an idea first promoted by the late Stephen J. Gould. These single-celled prokaryotes are the most successful of all life forms, and have been dividing away for more than three billion years, compared to our paltry few minutes on Earth. Regardless of the fate of humanity, bacteria will survive and prosper. Bacteria can easily live without us, but we would die quickly without them. If we were able to kill every bacterium in our body, we would be dead within a month. Rapid asexual reproduction is one key to microbial success. Some bacteria populations can double every twenty minutes. One bacterium becomes two, then two become four in forty minutes, then four become eight in the first hour. Not too impressive, really, considering that eight bacteria would hardly catch your eye. But at that rate, left unabated, a single bacterium would produce in just twenty-four hours more than one million billion billion (10^{24}) offspring. In forty-eight hours the progeny of just one bacterium would weigh four hundred times the weight of the planet. Of course food scarcity, waste buildup and other constraints prevent such ridiculous proliferation.

-§-
Many of our problems originate in this hubris of imagining ourselves at the center of the universe.
-§-

One might question this odd fascination with bacteria, but they indeed teach us a vital lesson. We must be humble in the face of their biological dominance and impressive longevity. We are nothing special, and bacteria are the proof.

Our ancestors made it far enough to yield us, but the prospects for our future survival, unlike bacteria, are not particularly bright. In the history of life, 99.9% of all species that have ever lived are now extinct. The *rate* of extinction, currently nearly one thousand times the rate seen historically before humans entered the scene, is what causes present concern with loss of biological diversity, not the fact of extinction itself. Extinction is the norm; our brief cameo is by no means preordained to become a leading role comparable to that played by unicellular organisms. The notion that "we didn't lose the game; we just ran out of time" might work for football coach Vince Lombardi, but applies poorly to our survival strategy.

If *Homo sapiens* are to have a continued presence on Earth, we must change our game plan. Task number one is to re-evaluate our sense of place in the world and modify our strong species-centric stewardship of the planet. If our extinction is not something we wish to accelerate, we must adopt a new moral code based on that modified perspective of place, a new *natural ethic* to help put us on a more sustainable course. After two thousand years the clock is ticking with no timeouts remaining. Fortunately, the large brains that gave us hubris, technology and war also give us the potential to see the error of our ways, perhaps just in time.

The central tenants of a natural ethic are founded on a humble view of human existence, derived from three fundamental principles: First, life on Earth began as a natural event based on standard laws of physics and chemistry. Yes, we are all just aged stock from a primordial soup of inorganic ingredients. Second, life is not the result of some magic spark, but instead is a broadly defined phenomenon in which the living and nonliving share a wide region of overlap. Frankenstein hunched madly over the inert body of his creation on a dark and stormy night, hoping with clenched fists to have that last bolt of lightning strike his overheating transformers and yield a compelling image, but not one in which to base the theory of life. Third, evolution is a random process with no direction, drive, or purpose, to paraphrase Richard Dawkins. Fortunately, in the face of this randomness we have a natural ethic to guide us through the void, with a foundation far more fundamental to our nature than a bunch of commandments carved in stone by withered old men.

The new ethic can be fully embraced only through the radical but liberating concept that life has no goal or guiding force. We have no father above waiting to send us to our room if we misbehave. We are all responsible for our own actions. We cannot seek guidance from, blame or credit a nonexistent god for our own decisions and behaviors. True human morality is developed from within, not handed down from above. A natural ethic is a code embedded in each of us, one that guides our behavior toward a general good, pursued for its own sake, and not for hope of personal gain or fear of punishment. We have

-§-

In the history of life, 99.9% of all species that have ever lived are now extinct.

-§-

to rediscover this natural phenomenon that has been suppressed by two thousand years of displacing responsibility for our actions onto a deity, one who apparently takes sides in our sporting events if all of that praying by athletes is any guide.

An immediate objection to this thesis could be raised: if we possess such a natural talent for good, why or how has it been suppressed for two millennia? The answer lies in the fact that fear of the unknown and fear of death are powerful masters that have overwhelmed rational thought. In seeking solace from the unknown, and in hopes of allaying fears of mortality, people look to leaders who provide answers to life's mysteries and promise a happy afterlife. Fairy tales can be comforting. But those same leaders dictate the rules of entering paradise; morality becomes an issue of power and politics. Morality becomes a means of controlling followers, threatening those who violate rules with something less pleasant than paradise, for eternity. The very idea of morality, therefore, is corrupted as a political tool used to suppress those uncomfortable with uncertainty by providing a false sense of security with mythical answers to everything unknown.

But uncertainty can be embraced rather than feared. Our inner life, our own thoughts, our acts of kindness, and our responsibility and honesty are immune to the random events in the world around us, blind to the inherent purposelessness of the universe. The world can be seen with amazing clarity upon realizing that life is not manipulated by some unseen force, but instead is guided by an individual's power to make decisions and a personal choice to be moral. There is tremendous joy in understanding that the purpose and meaning of life are self-derived. These precious commodities are not gifts from above that can be taken away by a wrathful deity working in mysterious ways. Being alive is an amazing roll of the dice. We have tremendous power to create our own path. We are masters of our own thoughts. Our free will is not a gift from god; it is ours alone. We are responsible for our lives and can guide our own destiny.

-§-
After two thousand years the clock is ticking with no timeouts remaining.
-§-

Since the choice to be moral is ours alone, and is guided by no higher purpose, is morality relative to each person's personal worldview? Is moral relativism necessarily implied when adopting a natural ethic? The answer is, "no" to both questions: absolutely not. A natural ethic does not lead to a moral free-for-all in which anything goes according to personal whim. Certainly, culture influences moral practices. Differences among societies can exist that fall more into the category of tradition than ethics, where societies can agree to disagree without any moral quandary. For example, Jane lives in a society in which eating dog meat is considered immoral, whereas Tom's society encourages the consumption of canine flesh as a means of eliminating hunger and culling orphan dogs from society. An impartial observer from neither society would be hard-pressed to render judgment that one approach is moral and the other immoral. In some limited cases, morality relative to society is indeed plausible when moral variance remains within reasonable bounds. But recognizing cultural imposition of differences in moral codes does not, however, imply any support for moral relativism, either at the level of the individual or society.

Relativism fails because elements of morality are essential to humanity across time and across cultures. Each of us is constrained within certain limits of behavior bound by fundamental notions of good and evil. While these concepts are difficult to define precisely, and gray areas make for some uncomfortable uncertainties, all of us have a basic intuitive sense of what is good and what is not. In 1964, Justice Potter Stewart famously said, "I know it when I see it" in reference to obscene material, which he found difficult to define but easy to recognize. The same standard can be applied to the notion of what is morally acceptable and what falls outside that boundary. That approach to understanding good and evil is not entirely clean, and even a bit unsatisfying, but that is a reflection of the ambiguous nature of the problem. Morality is not a black and white issue.

By evaluating moral issues facing society today from the perspective of a natural ethic, we can bring a fresh approach to some of humanity's most vexing problems, many of which are exacerbated by rapid advances in technology. Current political and religious institutions are inadequately armed to address the moral consequences ensuing from scientific achievements. In any society dominated by a non-secular moral code, technology often proceeds at a pace greater than society's ability to address the associated moral dilemmas. The solution is not to make some futile attempt to retard technologic advances, from which people benefit greatly, but to adopt a moral code capable of addressing these challenges.

Complicating the issue is the fact that society is still largely scientifically illiterate. Although understanding the basics of science is critical to everyday life in a technology-driven society, the subject is given only cursory treatment in most public schools. As a result, people are often poorly equipped to understand the complexities of an issue before forming an opinion about the costs and benefits of adopting or restricting a particular technology. The issue of therapeutic cloning offers a prime example. Religious bias and scientific illiteracy combine powerfully to restrict a technology with extraordinary potential for good, with little associated risk. The upside of therapeutic cloning could be cures for diabetes, Alzheimer's, Parkinson's, multiple sclerosis, and a host of other devastating diseases, while the downside is… well, there is no downside. Education will always be fundamentally important to the success of a natural ethic.

-§-
True human morality is developed from within, not handed down from above.
-§-

Only through education will society understand that a natural ethic requires, *as a moral imperative,* prudent stewardship of the environment and sound resource management. To succeed, a natural ethic must be widely adopted so that society is positioned to pass and enforce laws that promote improvement in quality of life while indefinitely preserving a healthy environment. The two goals are not incompatible and can be mutually reinforcing when wisely pursued in the context of a new natural ethic.

Our future is at risk, though, because of mankind's noted inability, at least to date, to reconcile its needs with environmental conservation. Admittedly, no other animal in life's history has assumed that responsibility, so the burden is not to be taken lightly. But human beings have an option to choose a path different than all others that have come before. In spite of decades of polarized debate, improving the human condition and protecting the environment are one and the same challenge. Earth is the extraordinary product of billions of years of transformations and balanced interactions between the physical world and biological evolution. The future trajectory of this amazing past will be affected to an important degree by how well we respond to the unprecedented risks and opportunities we face today.

-§-
Uncertainty can be embraced rather than feared.
-§-

The challenge of sustainability can be met successfully only with a change in attitude from current norms. If we are to survive, an alternative approach to defining our place in the biosphere must be found. If we fail to seize this opportunity, we will be no more than pond slime with library cards. Changing the perspective of humanity is difficult, perhaps impossible, but with a natural ethic we have hope. A natural ethic provides us with a means of rising above the common fate of extinction suffered by most species, but with no claim to privilege. We should choose a natural ethic because we can. With that choice we define our humanity and help secure our future.

Peter Russell:

From Science to God

The worldviews of science and spirit have not always been as far apart as they are today. Five hundred years ago, there was little difference between them. What science there was existed within the established worldview of the Christian church. Following Copernicus, Descartes and Newton, Western science broke away from the doctrines of monotheistic religion, establishing its own atheistic worldview, which today is now very different indeed from that of traditional religion. But the two can, and I believe eventually will, be reunited. And their meeting point is consciousness. When science sees consciousness to be a fundamental quality of reality, and when religion takes God to be the light of consciousness shining within us all, the two worldviews start to converge.

Nothing is lost in this convergence. Mathematics remains the same; so do physics, biology, and chemistry. The shift may throw new light on some of the paradoxes of relativity and quantum theory, but the theories themselves do not change. This is a common pattern in paradigm shifts; the new model of reality includes the old as a special case. Einstein's paradigm shift makes no difference to observers traveling at everyday speeds; as far as we are concerned Newton's laws of motion still apply. In a parallel way, making consciousness fundamental does not change our understanding of the physical world. It does, however, bring a deeper appreciation of ourselves.

Peter Russell studies the deeper spiritual significance of the times we are going through, and as one of the world's foremost futurists he is has lectured at many international conferences he is a fellow of the Institute of Noetic Sciences, the World Business Academy, and the Findhorn Foundation. He studied theoretical physics, experimental psychology, and computer science, before assuming the first-ever research position on the philosophy of meditation. His first best-seller was *The Global Brain* (Tarcher, 1983), and his most recent book is *From Science to God,* (New World Library, 2004). His multi-image shows and videos have won praise—and prizes—from around the world.

The same applies on the spiritual side. Much of the wisdom accumulated over the ages remains unchanged. Forgiveness, kindness, and love are as important as they ever were. Many of the qualities traditionally ascribed to God remain, they being equally applicable to the faculty of consciousness. The difference is that spiritual teachings and scientific knowledge now share a common ground. This too often happens in paradigm shifts. Newton brought terrestrial and celestial mechanics under the same laws. Maxwell integrated electricity, magnetism and light in a single set of equations. With the shift to a consciousness metaparadigm — the paradigm behind the paradigms — the integration goes much further. It is the two halves of humanity's search for truth that are now brought under the same roof.

> -§-
> "The only devils in this world are those running around inside our own hearts, and that is where all our battles should be fought."
> —Mahatma Ghandi
> -§-

This meeting of science and spirit is crucial, not just for a more comprehensive understanding of the cosmos, but also for the future of our species. Today, more than ever, we need a worldview that validates spiritual inquiry, for it is the spiritual aridity of our current times that lies behind so many of our crises.

The Great Awakening

The more I explored the nature of consciousness, the more I came to appreciate the critical role that inner awakening has to play in the modern world — a world which, despite all its technological prowess, seems to be getting deeper and deeper into trouble.

Almost every problem I considered — from personal problems, to social, economic and environmental problems — involved human decisions. These decisions were based on human thinking, human feelings and human values, which in turn were influenced by our need be in control of things, and our need to bolster an ever-vulnerable sense of self. It was clear that inner issues such as these that lay at the root of our problems as much as any external factors. Our continuing social, environmental and economic crises were symptoms of a deeper inner crisis — a crisis of consciousness.

This crisis has been a long time coming. Its seeds were sown thousands of years ago when human evolution made the leap to self-awareness. Consciousness had become conscious of itself.

Our early self-awareness probably involved a sense of identity with one's tribe and kin, but not a strong personal self. Gradually this inner awareness evolved, becoming more focused, until today it has reached the point at which we have a clear sense of being a unique self, distinct from others and the natural environment.

But this is not the whole story. Dotted through history, have been those who have discovered there is much more to consciousness than most of us realize. This individual self, they tell us, is not our true identity. Moreover, it has shortcomings. If this is all we know ourselves to be, our actions are misguided, and we bring much unnecessary suffering upon ourselves. To free ourselves from this handicap, we must complete the second half of our inner journey and discover the true nature of consciousness.

In the past, becoming more self-aware was essential for one's personal salvation. Today it has become an imperative for our collective survival.

Our knowledge of the external world has grown far faster than our knowledge of ourselves, bringing with it an unprecedented ability to control and manipulate our surroundings. The technologies we now have at our disposal have amplified this potential so much that we can now create almost anything we dream of. Unfortunately, however, technology has also amplified the shortcomings of our half-developed sense of self. Driven by the dictates of a limited identity, and by our belief that inner well-being depends upon external circumstances, we have misused our newfound powers, plundering and poisoning the planet so much that our collective future is now at stake.

-§-
"If men and women have come up from the beasts, then they will likely end up with the gods."
—Ken Wilber
-§-

We have reached what Buckminster Fuller called our "final evolutionary exam." The questions before us are simple: Can we move beyond this limited mode of consciousness? Can we let go our illusions, discover who we really are, and find the wisdom we so desperately need?

These questions face us everywhere we look. Our degradation of the environment is forcing us to examine our priorities and values. Our disillusionment with materialism calls us to ask what it is we really want. The ever-accelerating pace of change demands we become less attached to how we think things should be. Our personal relationships are challenging us to move beyond fear and judgment, to love without conditions. Social problems often reflect the meaninglessness inherent in a materialist worldview, while various political and economic crises reveal the short-comings of our self-centered thinking. From all directions, the message is "wake up!"

PART SEVEN

Passionate Spirituality

DAVID SPANGLER:

The Great Work of Blessing

W hy learn to bless? If I'm a kind and generous person, if I remember to say "Bless you!" when someone sneezes, and cultivate a sense of gratitude in my life by counting my blessings instead of sheep, isn't that enough? Aren't blessings the purview of the sacred anyway? Surely, it's God who blesses, and my role is to pray for those blessings to be abundantly manifested in our world.

The answer for me is neither that God—or the sacred by whatever name we choose—does not bless, nor that we should fail to invite those blessings through prayer or invocation. My answer is that through a spiritual act like blessing, we learn to discover ourselves in a deeper way, and we become a human source of enrichment for our world. The art of blessing becomes a mode of service, a spiritual practice, and a participation in what the Western mystical alchemical tradition termed the Great Work.

When I first moved to Seattle fifteen years ago, it took me all of five minutes to drive to the grocery store. Now with many more cars on the road that same trip can take me as much as half an hour if traffic is particularly heavy. And I'm lucky. I live in one of the less congested areas of town.

There's a lot of congestion in our modern lives. Far from living in an unobstructed world, some days it seems like everyone and

David Spangler was a codirector of the Findhorn community in Scotland in the 1970s, and in his travels touched thousands of people worldwide with his humor, insight and wisdom. Today, through the Lorian Association, he lectures and writes on his favorite theme of "Incarnational Spirituality." Among his books are the bestseller *Everyday Miracles* (Bantam, 1995), *The Call* (Riverhead, 1998), *Revelation* (Lorian, 1979), *Emergence* (Delta, 1989), and *Blessing* (Riverhead, 2001), from which this chapter is excerpted. He lives in Washington, and a schedule of his lectures and online classes can be seen at www.lorian.org. Photo courtesy of *Alternatives* magazine.

everything gets in our face, blocking us mentally and emotionally as well as physically. Synchronicities or moments of grace, harmony, and flow stand out like oases in a desert of wasted efforts, stymied energies, and stress. To lead a spacious life seems more and more difficult. Speaking as a father in a household of four children from six to eighteen years of age (and a pack rat myself), what will get us all in the end will be clutter!

Looking at humanity as a whole, I'd say that much of our psychological and spiritual energy is stuck. It's blocked by old habits and by images of conflict, separation, and violence. Our fears limit our imaginations. They cripple our will to change, to embody new visions of a more humane and ecologically harmonious world. This image of "stuck energies" isn't simply a metaphor; at a psychic level of perception, it's a very real condition of obstructedness, whatever terms I may choose to describe it.

-§-
Synchronicities or moments of grace, harmony, and flow stand out like oases in a desert of wasted efforts, stymied energies, and stress.
-§-

This obstructedness is not due to the physical nature of our world, as some philosophical teachings might lead us to believe. The idea that we dwell in a dense world that's intrinsically resistant to spirit or the flow of energy, or that somehow our souls are weighted down by the materiality of the earth, is flat out wrong. It comes from a failure to fully experience the zest and power of life, a failure to perceive that every particle of our world radiates with a soulfire drawn from the hearth of the infinite.

No, the experience—and the reality—of obstructedness doesn't inherently come from the Earth, but from our own incomplete and still-maturing state of being. It comes from our own thoughts and feelings, our own imaginations and fears. It comes from our own failures to connect. If anything, we obstruct ourselves because we resist being fully present in our world, for each other, and within our own incarnations with all their pains, risks, limits—and challenges as well as their joys, their creative potentials, and their opportunities.

Unobstructedness is not the same as having no limits. A limit is something that defines us and channels our efforts, giving us focus, but it's not an obstruction. An obstruction blocks; it disperses our focus. It adds nothing to our lives and can even threaten them. A road has limits that indicate where I can drive and where I cannot; if I cross the center dividing line, I become an obstruction—and most likely a deadly one—to anyone driving in the opposite direction.

None of us like limits. We revel in myths of unbounded, unimpeded power and activity, forgetting that in such a state we can become like the floodwaters in my earlier metaphor. A flood is obviously powerful but it's also dispersed; floods don't drive turbines and create electricity. Only rivers do that. Limits concentrate power in order to create freedom in a different way.

The unobstructed state is not one of license to do whatever we wish; it's a state of relatedness based on mutual empowerment and respect that enables energy, life, ideas, and power to flow freely between us. Unobstructedness is a shared state, not one I can enjoy irrespective of others. Indeed, what is really unobstructed isn't our actions but our capacity to relate. Think of a relay race in which a baton is passed from runner to runner. The success of the race depends not only on the swiftness of the individual runners but also on the ease and grace with which they can pass the baton from one to another. And in the end, it's not a single runner who wins but the whole team.

In the unobstructed world, we all win or no one wins; there's no partial victory for just a special few. This perspective is beautifully and powerfully embodied in the Buddhist doctrine of the Bodhisattva. This is a person who has achieved enlightenment and, being free from any need for rebirth, could pass on into the mystery of nirvana. But instead, he or she remains in the world to serve others

-§-

Our fears limit our imaginations.

-§-

and empower their quests for enlightenment, for he or she knows that until all are free, no one is. Until all are enlightened and unobstructed, no one is.

The effort to bring into our human experience the liberation and creative power of the unobstructed spirit is what has been called the Great Work: the enlightenment of humanity and the upliftment of the world. Sometimes, within a Christian perspective, this Great Work is described as the work of redeeming ourselves and the world. But I like to think of it as a work of reclamation.

Amidst all the tragedies in our world — the pain, loss, and sorrow that parade in an unending march of tears across our nightly TV news — there is one tragedy that seems to sum up the anguish of our obstructed world. This is the tragedy of waste.

The fact that through violence and neglect we waste lives and resources is obvious. But we waste other things that are not so obvious. We waste dreams, efforts, hope, and all the potential of relatedness. We waste opportunities to serve, support, and connect with each other. We waste the creative energy that could be there between us. We waste possibilities for joy and ecstasy. We waste possibilities to

know the sacred not as something distant but as a presence at the core of our being, infusing our every action with holiness.

We waste our humanity. It's so visible in our endless conflicts and wars; in the distrusts and suspicions that thwart our relationships; in the arrogance that leads one group to put its race, its religion, its customs and beliefs, above those of any other; in the fear that makes us hide our faces from each other and build walls between us. We waste who we might be. We waste what could be humanly and spiritually possible if we learned how to create unobstructedness with each other, if we learned how to pass batons of love, wisdom, creativity, and energy between us with grace and skill.

-§-

Every particle of our world radiates with a soulfire drawn from the hearth of the infinite.

-§-

And beyond a doubt we waste our world: its breathable air, its drinkable water, its fertile soil, its regenerative forests and oceans. We waste the lives of all the creatures that not only share this planet with us but share our beingness and potential as well. For they hold keys to the unobstructed world that we don't. They're part of the music we dance to. If they disappear, there will be only silence where there once was melody, and we will find ourselves trying to dance to memory and not to the full rhythm of unbroken life.

The essence of the Great Work is the reclaiming of this waste. It's the work of replacing the obstructedness that promotes such waste with a spirit of unobstructedness that allows all of us to experience ourselves and each other in full measure. And it's in this context that the art of blessing is important to me. For when we bless, we extend this spirit of the unobstructed world into our lives and the lives of others. We become participants in the Great Work.

The term Great Work does sound imposing, even intimidating. But in fact, the Great Work is really made up of a multitude of individual Little Works. Just as the towering cathedrals of medieval Europe were built one stone at a time, the transformation of the obstructed into the unobstructed takes place one act at a time, one choice at a time, one blessing at a time.

It's a transformation that takes place through an interior alchemy, through our own personal version of the Great Work. That's why the art of blessing may be seen as a spiritual path. For to bring the unobstructed spirit into our world we must ourselves experience that spirit and make it part of who we are, part of our blood and breath. We ourselves must become unobstructing.

This obstructedness is more than just traffic jams on the way to the grocery store or bad weather that forces the cancellation of a sporting event. It's the obstructedness of our attitudes, feelings, images, and habits, whether directed inward towards ourselves or outward towards others. It's these subjective obstructions that can scatter and block our energy.

For example, fear of failure may keep me from accepting a major new assignment at work, thus wasting the potential for a liberating advancement in my career. Envy and resentment may cause me to lash out at someone who might have been a friend, wasting the potential of that relationship. A poor self-image may lead me to denigrate or even hate people who are different from me racially or religiously, wasting the opportunity for gaining new insights that may enrich my own perspective.

All of these attitudes become impediments to living my life in its fullness, and to reaching my potential. But they also lead me to choose obstruction over liberation and a creative relatedness; they lead me to project my own obstructedness onto others. I become a curse, rather than a blessing.

So the personal Great Work, the individual art of blessing, lies in discovering how to gather these inner obstructions together and bring them into the unobstructed world. It's the work of freeing our internal energies that are stuck in habits and divisive perspectives. It's the work of personal reflection and honesty. It's the work of seeking out and learning from the examples of unobstructedness and flow, creativity and spirit, joy and spaciousness in our world. And it's the work of giving unobstructed-ness and the spirit of blessing room to grow in our lives.

-§-
We all win or no one wins; there's no partial victory for just a special few.
-§-

There are probably as many ways to do this as there are people. But one way is through our relationships with others. Although it sounds tautological, the way to discover blessing is to bless. For then we are stepping into the flow of a loving, spiritual presence that moves through the world. And when we do, it circulates through us as well, unblocking what is blocked, unsticking what is stuck, regenerating what has become stagnant.

To bless is a holy act. And learning the art of blessing is akin to learning to manifest holiness in our lives. As I said earlier, we must remember that holiness is not a state. It's not a crown that we wear but a spirit that emerges from an act of engagement. It radiates from any act in which we dissolve any barrier between us and another, any barrier between us and the sacred.

When, because of any action we take, another person feels his way has become less impeded, and the potentials of his soul more capable

of being realized, then we've brought the spirit of the unobstructed world into his life. And we've brought it into our own life as well. It may not seem like a transcendent power zapping us from heaven, but it's a moment of grace, offered from one person to another. It's a blessing—a moment of holiness—that two people can create together.

The more mindful we are of this process, the more we add our blood and breath, the more our acts resonate with the power of blessing. And while a kindness may satisfy the heart and mind and create what might be thought of as a localized unobstructedness, a blessing—because we reach into our own souls to do it—touches the soul of another. There the effects can be long-lasting and far-reaching in ways we may not realize or imagine. For the Great Work is more than an effort to change the outer conditions of humanity: It's also the work of inner transformation—an effort to change a quality of energy that, like a pollutant in the ocean, affects all of us who share this world. I might call this energy a habit of erecting obstructions, or a will to impede based on feelings of fear, hatred, and separation.

> -§-
> The Great Work is really made up of a multitude of individual Little Works.
> -§-

Anyone who works consistently with the non-physical dimensions of the world can recognize the existence of this habit and the energy or motivations it generates. It's like one discordant voice in the midst of a choir, throwing everyone off-key. The purpose of the Great Work is to restore that voice to harmony by sounding over and over again the proper notes it should be singing. These are notes of love, of compassion and caring, of an intelligent and wise relatedness that empowers and unobstructs. These are the notes of blessing.

When we bless, we connect ourselves, the sacred, and others in a spirit of spaciousness and unity, love, and unobstructedness. When we bless we sound those notes. We release what we can certainly imagine as an energy into the world. And since the world of spirit doesn't operate with the same laws of scale as our physical world does, the impact of this energy can far outweigh the size of the event that generated it. For each blessing that we perform, great or small, private or public, the obstructing tendencies of the world are diminished and the melody of the Source can resound with greater clarity than before. With each blessing, the unobstructed world becomes more of a reality.

This is the promise of the art of blessing. In discovering how to bless, we add ourselves to the Great Work, which is, after all, simply the work of Life in pursuit of unfoldment, harmony, and the potentials of infinity.

Prince Charles:

A Sense of the Sacred in the Modern World

37

During the last three centuries the Western world has seen the growth of a damaging division in the way in which we see and understand the world around us. Science has tried to assume a monopoly—or rather a tyranny—over our understanding of the world around us. Religion and science have become separated, and science has attempted to separate the natural world from God, with the result that it has fragmented the cosmos and placed the sacred into a separate, and secondary, compartment of our understanding, divorced from the practical day-to-day world of man.

We are only now beginning to understand the disastrous results of this outlook. The Western world has lost a sense of the wholeness of our environment, and of our inalienable responsibility for the whole of creation. This has led to an increasing failure to appreciate or understand tradition and the wisdom of our forebears, accumulated over the centuries.

But what is it about tradition and traditional values that, at the mere mention of these words, normally intelligent people go into paroxysms of rage and indignation—even vilification? Is it because they feel threatened? It is as if tradition represented the enemy of humankind's lofty ambition; the "primitive" force which acts as an unwelcome reminder—deep in our subconscious—of the ultimate folly of believing that the purpose and meaning of life on this Earth lies in creating a material form of Utopia—a world in which technol-

His Royal Highness, Prince Charles is heir to the British throne. His wide range of interests are reflected in 'The Prince's Charities' a group of not-for-profit organizations of which the Prince of Wales is president. The organizations are active across a broad range of areas including opportunity and enterprise, education, health, the built environment, responsible business, the natural environment and the arts. He served as a pilot and commander in the Royal Navy from 1971 to 1976. He has two sons, William and Henry. He and his wife Camilla travel widely, and are actively involved in Britain's evolving social dialog. Photo courtesy of the Associated Press.

ogy becomes a "virtual reality" God; the arbiter of virtual reality ethics—and thus the eventual murderer of the Soul of humankind. To my mind, tradition is not a man-made element in our lives—it is a God-given awareness of the natural rhythms and of the fundamental harmony engendered by a union of the paradoxical opposites in every aspect of nature. Tradition reflects the timeless order, and yet disorder, of the cosmos and anchors us into a harmonious relationship with the great mysteries of the Universe.

Likewise, I believe that humans are much more than just a biological phenomenon resting on the "bottom line" of the great balance sheet of life, where art and culture are increasingly in danger of becoming optional extras in life—so contrary to the Muslim craftsman or artist's traditional outlook, which was never concerned with display for its own sake, nor with progressing ever forward in his own ingenuity, but was content to submit his craft to God. While appreciating that this essential innocence has been destroyed, I do believe that the survival of civilized values, as we have inherited them from our ancestors, depends on the corresponding survival in our hearts of that profound sense of the sacred.

-§-
Tradition anchors us into a harmonious relationship with the great mysteries of the Universe.
-§-

Let me give you three examples. Whatever the scientists may say, the disjunction between religion and science, between the material world and a sense of the sacred, has important practical consequences for our everyday lives.

In **medicine** it has led to a one-sided and largely materialist approach to health care, and a failure to understand the wholeness of the healing process. Hospitals need to be designed, for instance, to reflect the wholeness of healing if they are to help the process of recovery in a more complete way. And modern medicine is too often a one-dimensional approach to illness which, however sophisticated, can still benefit from the help of more traditional approaches.

Our **environment** has suffered beyond our worst nightmares, in part because of a one-sided approach to economic development which, until recently, failed to take account of the inter-relatedness of creation, and the importance of finding a sustainable balance working within the grain of nature and understanding the necessity of limits. This, for example, is why protection of our environment is such a relatively recent concern; and why organic and sustainable farming are so important if we are to use the land in a way that will safeguard its ability to nourish future generations.

A third area in which this separation of the material and spiritual has had dramatic consequences is architecture. I believe this separation lies at the heart of the failure of so much modern **architecture** to understand the essential spiritual quality and the traditions from which they want to live. Titus Buckhardt wrote: "It is the nature of art to rejoice the soul, but not every art possesses a spiritual dimension." We see this so clearly in the intricate geometric and arabesque patterns of Islamic art and architecture which are all ultimately a manifestation of Divine Unity—the central message of the *Qur'an*. After all, the Prophet himself said, "God is beautiful and He loves beauty."

-§-
The survival of civilized values depends on the corresponding survival in our hearts of that profound sense of the sacred.
-§-

Look at urban planning. Ibn Khaldun, a great Islamic historian, understood that the intimate relationship between city life and tranquility was an essential basis for civilized and spiritual life. Can we ever again return to such harmony? Ibn Khaldun wrote that, as civilizations decay, so do the crafts.

I believe all these principles come down in the end to a battle for preserving civilized values. It is a battle to restore an understanding of the spiritual integrity of our lives, and for reintegrating what the modern world has fragmented. A world in which science and religion form an integrated part of a common understanding of our world will be better balanced, wiser, and more civilized.

NEALE DONALD WALSCH:

What God Wants

All that has happened since the attack on the World Trade Center on September 11, 2001, points to a very dangerous phase for humanity. The sociology of our world seems bent on self-destruction. We have created, in effect, not a sociology but a pathology. If we want to change the pathology of humanity, we have to change the sociology of humanity. What we have now is a sociology of separation based on a theology of disunity. All of the force and energy of my being is now focused on this matter of human theology, and on how we can cause a New Spirituality to emerge upon the Earth.

By "new spirituality," I mean a form of spiritual expression that allows humanity to experience its natural impulse toward the divine in a way that does not cause conflict and does not involve making each other wrong for the manner in which each of us is doing that, while producing the highest ultimate outcome and experience for all of humanity: peace and harmony, joy and love.

I believe it is possible to create a New Spirituality that meets those objectives. Those were the objectives of the "old spirituality," but those objectives have not been met, except in a few specific cases. In the main, those objectives have not been met, largely because our understandings of what is theologically true have been limited and incomplete.

Most people do not believe that they can experience communion, or a conversation, or a friendship with God. Most people do not

Neale Donald Walsch's life was transformed in 1992, when, in frustration he fired off an angry letter to God, asking the questions burning in his heart. To his great surprise, he received an answer, in the form of a book that became *Conversations With God* (Hampton Roads, 1996). This divine dialogue has continued, and has now expanded into five volumes of wisdom and insight, the latest of which is *What God Wants* (Simon & Schuster, 2005). He recently created Humanity's Team (www.humanitysteam.com), a worldwide grassroots movement to catalyze the emergence of a new form of spirituality on earth.

believe that they are worthy, or, if they are worthy, that the process of life itself even allows for such a possibility. In fact, millions of the world's people would suggest that what I have claimed to experience in my *Conversations With God* books is really a blasphemy. The very

-§-
Most people do not believe that they can experience communion, or a conversation, or a friendship with God.
-§-

idea that we are so separate from God that we can't even talk or hear back from Him in a direct and personal way is the thought which creates the sense of separation that we experience with each other. We go about interacting with each other as if we were separate beings having nothing to do with each other, when, in fact, there is only one of us here, in a multiplicity of individuations.

If we understood that, and interacted with each other from that highest truth, it would eliminate all wars and all conflict between us overnight. As it is, we behave as if we were one being—biting our nose to spite our face.

My books are successful because people everywhere have been willing to take a new look at a very old subject. This marks a new beginning for these people in their understanding of their right relationship with God, and their divine right relationship with each other.

My intention in *Conversations With God* was to be authentically in touch with my own personal understanding of God. I was not attempting to write a best-selling book, much less several of them. I was having a private process and a very private conversation within the deepest reaches of my own mind. I kept a record of that conversation for my own personal purposes that had nothing to do with publishing a book. People who read the material once it was published were privy to the innocence and purity of that private conversation simply by opening the page. When the material was published, it became instantly successful.

People who deeply understand the process by which life is experienced and created know intuitively that outcomes are chosen and selected. It is important to realize that all possible outcomes have already occurred. Time is an illusion that has nothing to do with ultimate reality. In ultimate reality, every conceivable outcome to every conceivable circumstance and situation has already occurred and merely lies in wait for us to select from those outcomes, so that we might move into the experience of them.

It's like taking a CD-Rom and putting it into one's computer and playing an electronic game with the computer itself. Every outcome of the game is on the CD-Rom. Virtually every conceivable outcome—billions and billions of choices—have already been previewed and pre-selected by the computer. It knows, therefore, exactly how to respond, move-by-move, to the choices we are making on a move-by-move basis. Ultimately, our move creates its response, which creates our move, which creates its response, which produces some kind of outcome in the end. We either win the game or we lose the game.

The computer doesn't care one way or the other. The computer just says, "Congratulations, you've won. Want to play again?" or it says, "I'm sorry, you lose. Want to play again?" It doesn't chortle. It is not pleased with itself, nor is it sad if you win and it loses. It has no preference in the matter. It simply is the container that holds every conceivable outcome, and it gives us the opportunity to make—on a choice-by-choice and move-by-move basis—the decisions that will produce an outcome that already exists.

-§-

There is only one of us here, in a multiplicity of individuations.

-§-

To choose is to make an active decision out of a place of willfulness. It's a willful decision and a willful choice. To want something, on the other hand, is an announcement of lack. It suggests that there is something we do not now have that we want. At the subtlest levels of the language there is an enormous difference. The difference is so great, in fact, that God says, "You may not have anything you want, but you may have anything that you choose."

The reason you may not have anything you want is that your very declaration of wantingness produces that result—the experience of wanting. Whereas, if you choose something, the result is that you will experience your choosing of it and you will, therefore, have it. I know that is a very subtle difference in the mind of some people, but as subtle as it is, it is extremely important.

Through the creation of Humanity's Team—a worldwide movement of over 10,000 people in villages, towns, and cities across the globe—we are working to create a space of possibility for the new spirituality to emerge. This grassroots movement offers educational programs, audio and video materials and workshops. They are also busy producing classes and groups for "get out the vote" campaigns, campaigns to support women's rights, minority rights, and civil rights of every kind.

Humanity's Team describes itself as a "Civil Rights Movement for the Soul." This volunteer effort is the last great civil rights movement taking us now to the final frontier, the frontier of the soul of humanity. This is the place where the soul at last meets both the mental and the physical expression of what it means to be human in a synergistic way for the first time. This undertaking is under way all over the world

and is one way that we hope to alter our collective reality. The effort is to awaken the human family to the possibility that there is something we do not fully understand about God, about life, and about each other, the understanding of which would change everything. We could choose to decide and define who we really are as a human species—in relationship to each other, in relationship to the experience called life, and in relationship to that aspect of life experience that we call God, Allah, Brahmin, Yahweh, Jehovah, or whatever name we've chosen to identify and to define the transcendent experience of the essence of life.

-§-
Every conceivable outcome to every conceivable circumstance and situation has already occurred and merely lies in wait for us to select from those outcomes.
-§-

Collectively, we have never achieved the kind of unified expression of what it means to be human that certain individuals such as the Christed One, the Buddha, Mohammed, and others have achieved. We now seek to create a collective expression of that experience; that is the endeavor of Humanity's Team.

Our intrinsic nature is unification. Simply put, we are all one. When I say, "We are all one," I don't mean that we are merely one with each other, as in "I am my brother's keeper," nor that we are all one as in a member of the family human. I mean that we are all one in a much larger universal sense: We are one with everything. Nothing is separate from anything at all. When I say we are all one, I say that I am one with you and you are one with me. We are one with the grass, the trees, the rocks, the fish and the birds, and with everything that is, which includes God itself. We are all one with God.

Given that this is so, the highest vision for humanity would find us experiencing and expressing ourselves through the paradigm of oneness or unity, rather than through the error of separation. This would be a planet in which what I call "Separation Theology" would disappear forever, as would all of the pitfalls that such a theology has put into place.

Enormous injustices are done on the planet in the name of Separation Theology. Separation Theology produces separation sociology. Separation sociology produces a separation pathology and pathological behaviors. The type of behavior we see in the headlines every day could only be produced by an idea that we are not intrinsically connected, but rather separate from each other, and, therefore, dependent on ourselves alone for our survival.

In this world, for example, 225 people hold more collective wealth than 3 billion of the world's poor. What is regrettable about this is not even so much that this is true, but that when you tell people this, many say, "Uh-huh. So what's the problem?" as if there is nothing wrong. We have created a sociology out of our theology that has produced a pathology in which we fail to see the self-destructive aspects of such a paradigm.

Here is another example: last year, the world's wealthiest nations — in an act of sharing — spent roughly 60 billion dollars on programs to assist the world's poorest nations to address problems of poverty, illness, disease, and lack of appropriate education and hygiene. In the same year, the same wealthy countries spent 900 billion dollars on defense. This lead the president of the World Bank to wryly suggest that if the world flipped its priorities, it would not have to spend even 60 billion dollars on defense.

The reason we have to spend 900 billion dollars annually on defense in today's world is to defend ourselves against the onslaught of those people who we are spending 60 billion dollars a year on just to make sure they have a piece of dry bread or a little brown rice in a bowl once a day.

-§-
God says, "You may not have anything you want, but you may have anything that you choose."
-§-

If we thought we were all one, or if we imagined for one year — 365 blessed days of our existence — that all of us were a single being, expressing as individuations of itself, we would never allow 400 children an hour to die of starvation, or 50,000 to be murdered in Darfur. We would not allow ourselves to remain impotent in the face of genocide. We would rise up in the first hour that it occurred and say, "No. We cannot allow ourselves to do this to ourselves."

Only a separation pathology, produced by a separation sociology, produced in turn by a Separation Theology, could sponsor such abysmal behavior and lack of response to it. The idea that "I'm over here and you're over there, and I have nothing to do with you except when it impinges upon my own personal experience and threatens my own personal survival" is what is destroying humanity at its roots.

In my perfect idea, I envision a world in which we all deeply understand and functionally practice the truth of our oneness. Such a shift would produce an experience of peace and joy and harmony among the human family. At last, the plaintive cry we have declared on holiday greeting cards for centuries would become reality. We would no longer plead with each other year after year, decade after decade, century after century, and beg God to bring peace on Earth and good will to humans everywhere. We would be the *source* of that peace on Earth, rather than supplicants *asking* for peace on Earth.

ANDREW HARVEY:

Mystical Activism

While in South India making a program for the BBC many years ago, I made the most momentous connection of my whole life. I had the great grace to meet Father Bede Griffith, a man who gave his life to live out the birthing of the new divine humanity. At that time Father Griffith was eighty-five years old, and that birthing was radiating from him in divine beauty, in divine clarity, in divine intensity, and in divine compassion. We spent ten days together talking about his life and the experience of his mystical evolution. Toward the end of those early conversations, he graced me with a terrible and beautiful clue to the time we are living in. Everything I have lived through—and the world has lived through—in the last ten years has proven to me that this conversation came from the heart and mind of God to play a part in the transformation of the world. The time for that transformation is now and there is no time to lose. I wrote the essence of that conversation in my book *A Walk with Four Guides:*

"The whole human race has come to the moment when everything is at stake, when a vast shift of consciousness will have to take place on a massive scale in all societies and religions for the world to survive. Unless human life becomes centered on the awareness of a transcendent reality that embraces all humanity and the whole universe and at the same time always transcends whatever level of consciousness we are in, there is little hope for us."

Andrew Harvey was born in South India in 1952 and lived there until he was nine years old, a period he credits with shaping his vision of the inner unity of all religions. At the age of twenty-one, at Oxford University, he became the youngest person ever to be awarded a Fellowship at All Souls College, England's highest academic honor. He then abandoned academic life to embark on a spiritual search, and was the subject of a 1993 BBC documentary *The Making of a Mystic.* His books include *The Direct Path* (Broadway, 2001), and *The Sun at Midnight* (Tarcher, 2002). Find him on the web at www.andrewharvey.net. His passionate spirituality has inspired thousands worldwide.

We are, as a race, going into the eye of an apocalyptic hurricane that will decide the future of the race and the planet. This storm of destruction will demand everything of all serious seekers who long to see the future transfigured. As the hurricane deepens and darkens, it is critical to know in the deepest part of ourselves that what will look and feel like destruction is actually the necessary stripping away of illusions we do not need anymore, the smashing of fantasies we have outgrown, and the necessary, unavoidable waking up to our true divine power.

The core knowledge and secret that helps us get through this apocalypse and give birth to a new divine humanity is one the great mystical traditions have always known. Enshrined in the depths of all the traditions is the essential secret wisdom that total destruction, absolute stripping, horrible pain, apocalyptic annihilation and death are the birth canal of a wholly new reality. I call it the wisdom of the dark night. It is the wisdom that all the great mystics—like Rumi and Ramakrishna and Teresa of Avila—who have come into the splendor of divine love—have known. Jellaludin Rumi said it this way: "The King never thrashes you without offering you a throne." The secret of the dark night is this: the crucifixion and the resurrection come together.

-§-
Enshrined in the depths of all the traditions is the essential secret wisdom that total destruction, absolute stripping, horrible pain, apocalyptic annihilation and death are the birth canal of a wholly new reality.
-§-

A vast apocalypse is going on. A vast birth is also going on, in and through this apocalypse. Both are manifesting at the same time because both are interdependent. The apocalypse is the birth canal. The sooner we grasp that, the sooner we resonate with all of our being with that, the sooner we can become what we must become—mystical activists and warriors for the new transformation.

The angel of human destiny is standing before every single human being. She is standing uncomfortably close to every being, much closer than the prescribed thirteen inches of personal space. In her hand, she holds a magical mirror, a terrible and beautiful mirror. When she turns the magic mirror to the left, it turns black—revealing a seven-headed snarling beast. This appalling beast of total destruction is menacing all of life on this planet. It is essential that we look into that dark mirror and see each one of these seven heads very, very clearly and stare directly into their eyes.

The first head is a massive, unstoppable explosion of population. By the year 2050, there will be nine billion people on the earth if population continues to expand at the current rate. That is three billion more than the most conservative ecologists believe are supportable. An absolute nightmare which the religions of the world have wholly failed to address, this problem makes nearly all of our agendas pathetic.

The second head is that the environment is already in the midst of Armageddon. It is being massacred. A hundred and twenty species are vanishing into extinction every single day. Nothing real has been done, nothing real has been risked by society, to avert this catastrophe. Every serious person must face this heartbreak.

The third head of this seven-headed monster is the growth of fundamentalism. At the very moment at which it is essential that all of the religions of the world pull together, overcome their differences, relinquish their claims of exclusivity, and cry out with one voice to the divine for transformation, all instead have factions that are retreating into a terrifyingly separatist fundamentalism.

The fourth head of this monster makes this separatism even scarier. We are now seeing—on a massive and seemingly unstoppable scale—is the spread of the selling of weapons of mass destruction. There is not necessarily a growth of evil. There is a growth of the absolutely lethal powers that evil now has in its control.

The fifth head is something we are all very well aware of. The technological worldview has created a great cement garden here on the planet. At the very moment when we need to be connected to nature at every level, the closest most people get to nature is a salad. People are perishing from inner meaninglessness and despair at a moment when finding meaning is the source of all hope.

-§-
The closest most people get to nature is a salad.
-§-

The sixth head of this apocalyptic monster is the media. If the media had any sense of responsibility, any sense of crisis, it would be pouring out the truth about what is happening to the environment, to the poor, and to the defenseless. Instead, media moguls create reality shows. Those voices that are radical, and really empowering—that could teach the mystical truth that could liberate and transform the world—are kept out of mainstream media.

The seventh head keeps people in a state of terrifying anxiety, desperation and fear. In our culture, we have become so hideously busy, so unspeakably hectic, that it is extremely difficult to have any peace of mind, any calm in which to taste the depths of the divine identity which could empower us to transform ourselves and the planet.

This dreadful machine of destruction—an exploding population, combined with an environmental holocaust, the growth of fundamentalism, the proliferation of weapons of mass destruction, technology that alienates on every level, a mass media addicted to triviality, and a human race in a state of perpetual, despairing motion—is a confluence of devastating forces that is supremely intelligent in a black way. This is what the mystics of the Christian tradition call the anti-Christ.

But this is not the only thing that is going on.

For when the angel of human destiny turns the same mirror the other way, it turns into a golden mirror. And in that golden mirror, seven pulsing, interconnected stars appear—the seven stars announcing the birth of divine humanity. This is not something that will happen in ten years, or twenty years. This is happening in me. It is happening in you. It is happening in movements all over the world in astonishing ways.

-§-
This crisis is so horrific that it will shake us to our depths and awaken the great slumbering divine secrets that lie at our core.
-§-

The first star represents the very extent of the crisis we now face. This crisis is so horrific that it will shake us to our depths and awaken the great slumbering divine secrets that lie at our core. This crisis is a supreme opportunity.

The second star is that the very technology that has created the cement garden is now developing astonishing new advances across the board. It is revolutionizing medicine, shaking loose the potential of quantum physics, and opening up all kinds of new fuel sources. These advances could, if we have the political will, transform everything that we are and do on Earth. One example is the hydrogen economy, which could free us from our dependence on fossil fuel at little cost to the environment—if we have the courage to embrace it.

The third star is the media itself. In the last few years the Internet has opened an unprecedented opportunity for the grassroots conveyance of radical information—under the radar of governments and corporations. This opens up the possibility of mobilizing tremendous forces all over the planet.

And the fourth star radiating right at this moment is the great mystical texts of the world's traditions. They have been translated into English and all the other major languages in the last thirty years. Mystical technologies and practices of meditation and inner transformation, kept sacred and secret for very long periods of time, are now open to anyone. This has never happened before. It's no coincidence that right as the apocalypse is shaping, an enormous array of divine power, awareness and knowledge is being given to humanity, to wake us up, to give us courage, to give us joy, and to give us the means to change. This is a huge gift.

The fifth star is one I have devoted my whole waking life to radiating more completely and helping to birth: the return of the divine feminine. For 2,500 years, the bride, the mother aspect of God, has been kept in a dark cellar with her hands and her feet bound. And now, at a time when we need the wisdom of the sacred marriage between heaven and earth, transcendence and immanence, human and divine, body and soul, politics and action, the bride is being brought back in all her wildness and glory, her splendor and fury, and in all her majestic tenderness.

The sixth star in the astounding firmament of birth is the lives of the servants of God's love we witness in action in the world. In the last century we had two World Wars, we had Nagasaki and Hiroshima, we had the horrific exterminations in Nazi Germany, China, Russia and Cambodia. But we were also given in the lives of Gandhi, Martin Luther King, the Dalai Lama, and Nelson Mandela. These lives are examples of how non-violence, when lived with total sincerity and total truth, can transform insuperable difficulties by sheer, holy, God-given power. Gandhi secured the release of India by just standing in place, a semi-naked fakir, radiating the holy knowledge of divine truth and love. Martin Luther King ensured the triumph of a humiliated minority, and ensured the safety of a white population in the middle of a cauldron of hatred on both sides, by preaching and living the truth of Christ. The Dalai Lama, faced with the holocaust of his whole world, has never for one moment lost his unshakeable belief in the transfiguring power of compassion. And in South Africa, we saw a situation that could have degenerated into a total bloodbath transformed by the work of Nelson Mandela and F. W. De Klerk, working together in a spirit of non-violence.

> For 2,500 years, the bride, the mother aspect of God, has been kept in a dark cellar with her hands and her feet bound.

The lives of these people clearly suggest that God is on the side of those who are brave enough to go into the storm with their divine truth and their divine beauty and their divine power radiating from a full heart, mind and body, giving themselves up to be the perfect servants of love that all of us are meant to be.

The seventh star is one that has blown my mind and my heart and my body and my soul wide open. Rather than a detached spectator watching the play—as the patriarchal traditions tend to think of God—God is also a mother. In the mother aspect, God has an agenda. That agenda is the saving of the human race, the transfiguring of the human race, the co-creation with the human race of a new world. God as mother is protecting us, and pushing us deeper and deeper into divine mischief. Knowing that, we will stop at nothing because we know that the angels and the archangels and the bodhisattvas and all the ascended masters and mistresses are crying out for the transfiguration of the human race and pouring down on the earth blessing and power and protection and knowledge.

Having now seen what is in the black mirror and what is in the golden mirror, we must look at what it takes to align ourselves wholly with those seven stars in the golden mirror. All of these stars are interconnected, part of an enormous mercy being given us. What it takes to galvanize their power and magic is to become a mystical activist.

The future of the planet hinges not on mysticism alone, not on activism alone, but on the inspired marriage of these two potent forces. Mystics, vibrating and bathing the whole cosmos in light, are absolutely adorable. But in a crisis like this, they are so heavenly as to not be of much earthly use. Private pursuit of spiritual experience is absolutely not enough when the world is burning to death. It is absolutely incumbent on every single human being—including the ones who see the light dancing in the trees—to do something real about the real problems in the real world. It is not spiritual to hide from them in a cloud of bliss. The detached, transcendent spiritual ideal which reveals the world as an illusion is not true, because the world is not an illusion. That is bad mysticism. No government and no corporation fears people with Sanskrit names wandering about burning incense, saying, "All is One and we should love everybody."

-§-

God is on the side of those who are brave enough to go into the storm with their divine truth and their divine beauty and their divine power radiating from a full heart, mind and body.

-§-

My first real mystical awakening happened when I was about twenty-one years old. It was winter, and I was a Fellow of All Souls College at Oxford University. I had just been left by someone I was very much in love with and was in a state of extreme suffering and distress. The suffering had gone on for about three weeks of sleeplessness. One particular and devastating night, I woke up after only two hours' sleep, to see the entire world softly coated with fresh snow. Gazing out of the window in the early morning, I experienced the purest and most complete peace and rapture I had ever experienced, far greater than I had imagined possible.

Although I didn't know what was happening at the time, I later realized that at that moment I had touched my own inmost divine being. It was a tremendous experience that opened up all kinds of hungers in me. And it was largely because I had that experience that I found the courage to return to India when I was twenty-five, and start giving up academic life in favor of a larger, mystical life. For once I returned to India, all kinds of mystical experiences started to bombard me and open me. That hour of calm, healed ecstasy gazing at the snow gave me the courage to transform my life later.

To the New Age, and to teachers who purvey the transcendental claptrap that people feed off like heroine addicts to stay in a bliss state while the world burns, I say it is time to realize that there are two initiations on the real path: the initiation into the light which is enormously important and which changes everything, and the initiation into the dark. I am not speaking of something I have not lived. When the dark spears your heart open, the horror and the heartbreak and the pain turns you into a helpless babbler before the awe and majesty and terror of God. Witnessing that real agony of the real world, everything in you cries out to be of use. When those two initiations are combined, a real mystic is born—one whose divine illumination transforms him or her into a fearless love-warrior and love-servant.

Neither can activists change what is happening, for the simple reason that they are fed only by human sources of energy. Their hearts get broken, their wills become exhausted, and their bodies get tired when faced with the prevailing situation on the planet. They give up. Neither mysticism nor activism alone can give us the passion, wisdom, clarity, peace and strength we need. But if we marry a totally lucid, adoring connection with the transcendent in direct relationship with a wild, passionate outraged commitment to correcting the imminent injustice; if we marry the divine energies that are given through a connection to God with a focused plan to unnerve the powerful and the cruel and the destructive on every level—what we will give birth to is a new kind of human being. This birth is what this apocalypse is helping to bring about. The illusions of progress of the activists and the illusions of progress of the mystics must both be shattered. Fusing the two in a massive heartbroken realism can give birth to the power of God in action on Earth.

-§-

We will stop at nothing because we know that the angels and the archangels and the bodhisattvas and all the ascended masters and mistresses are crying out for the transfiguration of the human race.

-§-

This great fusion is the equivalent, in human terms, of the leap from Newton's to Einstein's physics. This fusion asks for nothing less than the abandonment of all the illusions of the past and a seizing of the divine identity at the very core of us. A fusion of that core with a cry for justice for animals and women and gay people and poor

people is a revolutionary power that none of the powers of the world can stop. The reign of the dark and of the ignorant, the reign of the demonic, will be over.

Becoming a mystical activist demands blood, sweat, tears, and real hard prayer. It is not a game. It is not something to do after the third vision of the light, it is something to do in total response to a crisis that could destroy everything we hold sacred. Mystical activism is a fusion of the forces of light. It fundamentally threatens all the dark forces that have kept the human race ignorant. In that act of threatening all the dark forces, all the dark forces are aroused against it. That includes all the occult, demonic forces, which means that all of us must get over our naiveté about evil. After the twenty-first century—after Dachau, Hitler, Hiroshima, the desolation of the environment, and all the other atrocities of the last hundred and fifty years—we can no longer paint ourselves into a corner with a koan that says "evil does not exist." Evil is real and terribly powerful in this dimension. It is not so within in the absolute realm, but it is horrifyingly real in its human, its demonic, and its occult forms here and now. At a certain very important stage on the mystical path, we must meet it head on. This is what Rumi did in his dark night, this is what Jesus did in the crucifixion, and this is what is happening on the planet in its dark night. It is very important to become lucid about this and to prepare for this. Otherwise, we will be like lambs going to slaughter.

-§-
Private pursuit of spiritual experience is absolutely not enough when the world is burning to death.
-§-

These are the seven laws of mystical activism:

First, to be mystical activists, we must get real about sacred practice. We don't have a hope in the real world, dealing with real problems, and real people with destructive agendas, unless we are rooted in sacred practice. Develop a profound practice which grounds you and irrigates you with holy intensity every single moment. We need to combine two kinds of practice: cool practices to chill out in the storms of neurotic karma, and warm practices that keep the heart open in hell, because we will all suffer from compassion fatigue. It is almost impossible, in a world of nightmare, to keep on hoping, and to find the energy to go on loving, without the warm heart practices. Like a bird that can fly on two wings, we need the cool practices for times when we become hysterical and need to taste the truth of divine being, and we need the warm practices when we need energy. By marrying these sacred practices of peace and passion at the deepest depths, the masculine-feminine sacred androgyne is born.

The second law feathers into the first. In a time as devastating as ours, I have found that only one thing works at all moments, and that is to keep steady awareness of our divine and deathless identity. All of us have to go on a very profound journey, not simply to read about our divine identity, nor to taste it in the occasional moment of bliss, but to steadily be in touch with that indestructible soul that is our immortal reality. Knowing that the core of what we are cannot die makes us fearless in all situations.

The third law, I cannot emphasize strongly enough: Know that evil is real. The demonic is here, and it will avail itself of your shadow side, acting through what I call the anti-Christ energies. Evil is not a poetic metaphor. I have met it, and I have been wounded by it. Love and evil are in a profound cosmic war, a mystery of antagonism that has a divine meaning we can only learn by becoming discriminating, by being realistic about our own addictions, and by understanding the amazing power of this darkness. Jesus said, "Be wise as serpents and innocent as doves." Becoming a mystical activist will arouse tremendous antagonism from that darkness. Terrible things will manifest to try and unnerve you. If you don't know this, you will be defeated. But if you know that this is an occult war and the most deadly game imaginable — and that you have to stay steady in your calling, and deeply at peace within your divine identity — then you will be strong.

-§-
When the dark spears your heart open, the horror and the heartbreak and the pain turns you into a helpless babbler before the awe and majesty and terror of God.
-§-

The fourth law is a very subtle one. It has involved and tormented all of us at different moments. This law is a response to the question, "What do we do with anger?" The patriarchal religions have an interest in us not getting angry. They have told us that anger is an absolute obscenity and that we must get rid of it. That, of course, keeps us obedient slaves.

If unleashed, anger can blind us and lead us into hatred. Yet where are we without the power of outrage? In this world at this moment, millions of us ought to be absolutely speechless with outrage at what is being done in our name. But if we are so outraged that we are blinded by hatred, then the power that outrage can give us, rather than being a transfiguring energy, becomes a dirty, corrupt, damaging energy. So the fourth law is that you must awaken your outrage, face your outrage, and master your outrage by purifying your heart. You must constantly ensure, through deep sacred practice, that your outrage doesn't get sidetracked into hatred of others. To do that, we enact our outrage before God, offer our outrage to God, and beg the divine force to take that outrage and transform it into the living sacred fire of sacred passion. Outrage transfigured is the gold that is alchemized from the black, swirling, boiling power of anger. That sacred passion, when mobilized in the service of activism, makes you tireless, undaunted, extravagantly wild and unstoppable.

The fifth law is absolutely central to the great Christian, Hindu and Buddhist teachings on action. Very simply, it is this: You must learn to give up the fruits of action to the divine. You do not act with a private agenda, followed by despair when your agenda is not enacted. You act from a love of God, for God, giving yourself selflessly up to God, and offering your actions to God as a sacrifice of divine love. If you can do that, what you do and what you say will have miraculous effects because it is not you who are doing it anymore. You are like a feather floating on the breath of God, a pen held in the hand of God. You have died to yourself; the God that loves the world is using you for God's inscrutable and mysterious purposes. If you are still acting from the ego you can be defeated. But if you're standing in the Self nothing can defeat you, not even endless defeat.

The sixth law has to do with ferocity. When somebody has the guts to stand in front of us, and rage like the lion on behalf of the lion in each of us, they are not assassinating us; they are trying to raise us from the dead. That ferocity is the fiercest and most gorgeous kind of love. We recognize it when it's in the room. I recognize it in the living Christ. I recognized it one incredible evening when the Dalai Lama finally lost his smile because he was so overcome with grief. He stood before his audience and said, "When will you wake up to what is happening to my people?" He didn't do it to hurt or humiliate people, he did it to appeal to their hearts, to wake them up. So the sixth law is this: As a mystical activist, act with deep love and compassion, with a total commitment to non-violence. It may not always be possible, but we need to steep our whole being in *satyagraha* and soul force, to act from that deepest place so the truth of the divine can constantly flame out and inspire.

-§-

Evil is not a poetic metaphor. I have met it, and I have been wounded by it. Love and evil are in a profound cosmic war.

-§-

I cannot emphasize the seventh law enough. It is this: None of us can do it alone. I cannot do my work without my husband and my great spiritual helper and warrior Ellia who is an incredible mystic and healer and wild woman. I cannot do my work without the help of Rumi, Jesus, without the help of all the beings on whose lives I imperfectly model my life. None of us can do it alone. We have to reach out to all of the people who share our concern. We have to pool our resources, become brothers and sisters, give up our egos, give up our private organizations, open our hearts, and work together.

When all is chaotic and burning and terrible, there are three main ways that I reconnect with the source of divine love. The first, and simplest, is this: When I breathe, I imagine breathing in the living golden light of the mother's alchemical radiance. That golden light goes to the ends of my toes, to the top of my head, and into every cell of my entire body until I imagine myself glowing like a molten ingot. I then hold the breath until I can feel that gold light in every pore of my body. I then release the breath, and with it, all my fatigue, all my sadness, all my rage, all my desolation. Do this several times, for five or six minutes, and you will be recharged by peace and power.

-§-

Evil is not a poetic metaphor. I have met it, and I have been wounded by it. Love and evil are in a profound cosmic war.

-§-

The second way I retune with the source of love is by saying the Hail Mary very slowly and calmly while focusing my mind on an image of the Virgin that I love and hold dear. If you do not have a relationship with the Virgin, then choose another divine figure and see her very clearly in her most radiant and divine aspect. Saturate your every cell with devotion. The power will come, and the peace will come.

Another wonderful exercise is to lie on the floor and imagine a black, powerful magnet, about seven inches below the ground. Imagine that black magnet literally pulling out of your body, heart, mind and soul, all the stress and pain you are feeling. Imagine all the different worries and doubts and sufferings looking like little black needles. They're dragged out of you and into that black magnet. I conceive of that black magnet as the secret Kali, birthing us into generosity. Then imagine a light figure of the divine mother in exactly the same shape as your own body, about two feet above you, radiating your whole body with golden light. You are being worked on in this exercise both by the immanent mother, the black magnet below the ground, and by the transcendent mother saturating your whole body with deep healing power. It helps to say your preferred name for the divine mother in your heart, opening your whole being up for healing.

Staying attuned to love in these ways is absolutely essential to being a mystical activist. Simple, powerful practices constantly re-attune you to the source. The simpler the practices are, the more they can be done in the hurly-burly of everyday life. Keep re-aligning yourself in these ways, and fuse your deepest mysticism with the most radical and brave action you are capable of. In this way you will help birth the new humanity that is appearing in blood and pus and shattered fragments of buildings and unutterable torment through the birth canal of the end of a world.

Thich Nhat Hanh:

The Birth of Love

Why do you have to love your enemy? How can you love your enemy?

In the Buddhist teaching, this is very clear. Buddhism teaches that understanding is the ground of love. When you are mindful, you realize that the other person suffers. You see her suffering and suddenly you don't want her to suffer any more. You know that there are things you can refrain from doing to make her stop suffering, and there are things you can do to bring her relief.

When you begin to see the suffering in the other person, compassion is born, and you no longer consider that person as your enemy. You can love your enemy. The moment you realize that your so-called enemy suffers and you want him to stop suffering, he ceases to be your enemy.

When we hate someone, we are angry at him because we do not understand him or his environment. By practicing deep looking, we realize that if we grew up like him, in his set of circumstances and having lived in his environment, we would be just like him.

That kind of understanding removes your anger, removes your discrimination, and suddenly that person is no longer your enemy. Then you can love him. As long as he or she remains an enemy, love is impossible. Loving your enemy is only possible when you don't see him as an enemy anymore, and the only way to do this is by practic-

Thich Nhat Hanh has been a Buddhist monk and a peace activist since the age of sixteen. He is the master of one of the most prominent temples in Vietnam, and his lineage is traceable directly to the Buddha himself. He has survived three wars, persecution, and more than thirty years of exile. He has written more than one hundred books of poetry, fiction, and philosophy, including *No Death, No Fear* (Riverhead, 2002) and *Going Home: Jesus and Buddha As Brothers* (Riverhead, 1999). He was nominated for the Nobel Peace Prize by Martin Luther King Jr. He makes his home in France and in America in the state as Vermont. Photo by Plum Village Practice Center, France.

ing deep looking. That person has made you suffer quite a lot in the past. The practice is to ask why.

When you are unhappy, your unhappiness spills all around you. If you have learned the art of understanding and tolerance, then you will suffer much less. Looking at living beings with compassionate eyes makes you feel wonderful. You do not change anything. You only practice seeing with the eyes of compassion, and suddenly you suffer much less. What are the eyes of compassion? The eyes are to look and to understand. The heart is to love. "The eyes of compassion" means the eyes that look and understand. If there is understanding, compassion will arise in a very natural way. "The eyes of compassion" means the eyes of deep looking, the eyes of understanding.

In Buddhism we learn that understanding is the very foundation of love. If understanding is not there, no matter how hard you try, you cannot love. If you say, "I have to try to love him," this is nonsense. You have to understand him and by doing so you will love him. One of the things I have learned from the teaching of the Buddha is that without understanding, love is not possible. If a husband and wife do not understand each other, they cannot love each other. If a father and son do not understand each other, they will make each other suffer. So understanding is the key that unlocks the door to love.

Understanding is the process of looking deeply. Meditation means to look deeply at things, to touch things deeply. A wave has to realize that there are other waves around her. Each wave has her own suffering. You are not the only person who suffers. Your sisters and your brothers also suffer. The moment you see the suffering in them, you stop blaming them, and you stop the suffering in you. If you suffer and if you believe that your suffering is created by the people around you, you have to look again. Most of your suffering comes from the lack of understanding of yourself and others.

-§-
Looking at living beings with compassionate eyes makes you feel wonderful.
-§-

In Buddhism, I don't think that compassion and loving-kindness are practiced for the sake of our individual salvation. The truth taught by the Buddha is that suffering exists. If you touch suffering deeply in yourself and in the other person, understanding will arise. When understanding arises, love and acceptance will also arise, and they will bring the suffering to an end.

You may believe that your suffering is greater than anyone else's, or that you are the only person who suffers. But this is not true. When you recognize the suffering around you it will help you to suffer less. Get out of yourself and look. Christmas is an opportunity for us to do this. Suffering is in me, of course, but it is also in you. Suffering is in the world.

There was a person who was born nearly two thousand years ago. He was aware that suffering was going on in him and in his society, and he did not hide himself from the suffering. Instead, he came out to investigate deeply the nature of suffering, the causes of suffering. Because he had the courage to speak out, he became the teacher of many generations. The best way to celebrate Christmas may be to practice mindful walking, mindful sitting, and looking deeply into things, to discover that suffering is still there in every one of us and in the world. Just by recognizing suffering we relieve our hearts of the suffering that has been weighing on us for so many days and months. According to the Buddhist teaching, when you touch suffering deeply, you will understand the nature of suffering and then the way to happiness will reveal itself.

-§-
When understanding arises, love and acceptance will also arise, and they will bring the suffering to an end.
-§-

In Buddhism, nirvana is described as peace, stability, and freedom. The practice is to realize that peace, stability, and freedom are available to us right here and now, twenty-four hours a day. We only need to know how to touch them, and we have to have the intention, the determination, to do so. It's like the water that is always available to the wave. It is only a matter of the wave touching the water and realizing that it is there.

NOTES & SOURCES

NOTES

CH. 13. THE NEXT RITE OF PASSAGE FOR HUMANITY

1. For more on chakras and developmental stages of childhood, see *Eastern Body, Western Mind: Psychology and the Chakra System as a Path to the Self.* Anodea, Judith. Celestial Arts, 1997.

2. Jantsch, Erich. *Design for Evolution: Self-Organization and Planning in the Life of Human Systems.* NY: George Braziller, 1975.

CH. 16. THE FEMININE FRONT LINE

1. Grameen Bank, http://www.grameenfoundation.org.

2. Women Waging Peace, http://womenwagingpeace.net.

3. Coleman, Isobel. "The Payoff From Women's Rights," *Foreign Affairs,* May/June 2004. http://www.foreignaffairs.org/20040501faessay83308/isobel-coleman/the-payoff-from-women-s-rights.html.

4. From a talk entitled "The Role of Women in Peace Building and Reconstruction: More Than Victims" by Donald K. Steinberg, Deputy Director, Policy Planning Staff. Remarks to the Council on Foreign Relations, New York City, March 6, 2003.

5. Global Fund for Women, http://www.globalfundforwomen.org.

6. Eisler, Riane. Center for Partnership Studies, http://www.partnershipway.org.

7. Marx Hubbard, Barbara. Foundation for Conscious Evolution, http://www.evolve.org/pub/doc/index2.html.

8. Buckley, Karen Wilhelm. Wisdom Leadership Initiative, http://www.wisdomleadership.org.

CH. 18. WEAVING CULTURES OF PEACE

1. Hayakawa, Ellen. *The Inspired Organization: Spirituality and Energy at Work.* 2003. Spirit Unlimited Publishing/Trafford Publishing. Victoria, BC.

2. *The Holy Bible.* 1962. The World Publishing Company, Cleveland, Ohio.

SOURCES

Many of the chapters in this book are based on interviews with the authors. Occasionally the interviews were, with the author's permission, woven together with comments they made during public speeches. The interviews were then transcribed, rewritten, and approved or polished, either by the authors, or their agents, prior to publication. John Gray was interviewed in his office on September 14, 2004, by Dawson Church, and his comments interspersed with those he made at International Forgiveness Day 2004. Gay Hendricks was interviewed in his home on May 19, 2004, by Dawson Church. Caroline Myss was interviewed at the Institute of Noetic Sciences on September 29, 2004, by Dawson Church. Fred Luskin was interviewed in his home by Dawson Church on April 29, 2005. Vasant Lad was interviewed at his mother's home in India by Mary Kay Walstrom, Ph.D., on September 10, 2005. Gabriel Cousens was interviewed in his office by Mary Kay Walstrom on May 6, 2005. George Leonard was interviewed by Dawson Church on September 7, 2005. Prince Charles's chapter was adapted from a speech he made on July 10, 1995, and is reprinted with kind permission of Clarence House. Andrew Harvey was interviewed by Geralyn Gendreau on August 18, 2004 in his home, and his comments interspersed with those he made at the Prophet's Conference, 2004. Neale Donald Walsch, Masaru Emoto, and Dean Ornish were interviewed by phone by Randy Peyser in 2004 and 2005. Jean Shinoda Bolen was interviewed in her office by Geralyn Gendreau September 14, 2005.